INTERROGATING THE REAL

Also available from Continuum:

Interrogating the Real

Slavoj Žižek

Edited by Rex Butler and Scott Stephens

continuum
LONDON • NEW YORK

CONTINUUM
The Tower Building, 11 York Road, London SE1 7NX
15 East 26th Street, New York, NY 10010

British Library Cataloguing-in-Publication Data
A catalogue record for this book is available from the British Library.

ISBN: 0–8264–7110–2

Library of Congress Cataloging-in-Publication Data
A catalog record for this book is available from the Library of Congress.

Typeset by Aarontype Limited, Easton, Bristol.
Printed and bound in Great Britain by MPG Books Ltd, Bodmin, Cornwall

Contents

Acknowledgments

The editors would like to thank Sarah Douglas and Hywel Evans for their consistent enthusiasm and patience throughout the preparation of this volume, and Tristan Palmer for first commissioning it.

In particular, Scott Stephens would like to acknowledge the support of the Australian Research Theological Foundation, whose generosity at the early stages of this project was vital for its completion. He is also grateful to Stephen Morton for his assistance in locating and acquiring certain hard-to-find references.

Editors' Introduction

'THE THING ITSELF' APPEARS: SLAVOJ ŽIŽEK'S EXEMPLARY THOUGHT

While it is by now something of a cliché to point this out, it is nevertheless true that the work of Slavoj Žižek begins with the philosophical concept of the 'beginning'. One thinks immediately of the well-known discussion of this topic in Žižek's book on Schelling, *The Indivisible Remainder*, in which he returns to the classic Idealist problem of freedom and the origin of the world. But there are also a number of other instances where Žižek takes up this concept: for example, the moment of the emergence of human civilization from the undifferentiated domain of animals, the origin of Presocratic philosophy in economic exchange, the birth of capitalism against the background of medieval theology, and indeed the beginning of the very idea of Europe in the 'primitive' Balkans.

Of course, this philosophical quest for first principles runs counter to the usual perception of Žižek as a pop cultural iconoclast, whose trademark gesture is to collapse genres, level the distinction between high and low cultures and use inappropriate examples to illustrate and ultimately ironize serious philosophical issues. And we would not even argue that this reading is strictly speaking incorrect, only that it does not go far enough. It is, after all, easy and even conventional now to illustrate philosophical or psychoanalytic concepts by means of popular culture. It is further a feature of our contemporary situation that the distinction between high and low cultures has been abolished, making everything equal in value and import. But, in fact, Žižek's real question is: What allows this confusion to take place? What is the secret distinction, the exception that permits the universalizing of economic and aesthetic value? (Marx was already posing the same question in terms of his generalized conception of the commodity form.)

In his familiar method of reading Lacan through Stephen King, Žižek is not suggesting that King holds the key to Lacan or that Lacan is 'reduced' to King's level as just another item in contemporary culture. He is not simply making them equal, or seeing one as providing the truth of the other. Rather, each can be compared to the other precisely because each breaks with any context or framework in which they can be understood. That is, what Žižek seeks to bring out through holding them together is what is 'in them more than themselves', something beyond the biographies of their authors, the circumstances of their composition, or even their histories of reception and interpretation.

We may thus observe the following paradox in Žižek: on the one hand, he operates by a series of analogies or comparisons (we can only understand Lacan through King, or Lacan can only be read in a world in which he exists on the same level as King); on the other hand, he is trying to bring out, by means of this comparison, something that exceeds this context or reading, a sort of innate kernel or formula that at once is repeated throughout his work and occurs each time singularly in the Real of the encounter with a particular author or concept. How to put this another way? In the texts selected here, and throughout his work as a whole, one can find Žižek reversing his position many times. He writes, as has been noted, prolifically and seemingly with little concern for consistency. It is as though the activity of writing itself is Žižek's chief motivation, the reason why he writes at all. This is reflected in the very form of his texts, where there is inevitably an unnecessary final chapter, consisting of *faits divers* or 'related matters' added on, after the main theoretical work of the book has been completed. In fact, strangely enough, what Žižek actually wants us to see is this very nothingness, this 'nothing-to-say' or 'empty speech' that underlies his texts. Let us call it his theoretical *drive*, or in more technical language a kind of *enunciation without enunciated*.

On the other hand, as one reads through these texts – and, again, as has been noted – we observe a tremendous consistency of approach in Žižek. He is, in his own words, a 'dogmatic philosopher', who has remained strictly faithful to his first great loves, Lacan and Hegel, from whom he has never wavered. More than this, we get the uncanny impression that, no matter what Žižek writes about, however far-fetched or extravagant his examples, he always ends up saying the same thing. It is almost as though his is a predetermined system that follows its own course, despite obstacles or contingencies, personal events in his life or world-historical upheavals. And this finds expression in Žižek's own work: when he speaks of the analyst's discourse as 'oracular', as beyond interpretation; the meaningless Real of the human genome, which reproduces itself without interruption; and those immortal works of literature like *The Iliad*, which seem to go beyond any single author. Here, in contrast to that empty speech before, we have a kind of 'full speech', or to use more technical language an *enunciated without enunciation*.

Undoubtedly, Žižek's work exhibits both of these qualities. It appears entirely context-bound, responsive to contemporary political events, affected by his own private pathology etc. But, as Žižek himself says, it is also a kind of impersonal 'machine', a form of objective, externalized knowledge embodied in a neutral medium that repeats itself endlessly. How to bring these two together? How to reconcile these opposites? What is it of 'Žižek' that is transmitted in every text, despite its mistakes, retractions, distortions? The answer is perhaps to be found in the unique procedure of the Lacanian clinic. For Lacan, analysis comes to an end – that is, the analysand becomes an analyst – at the moment of the so-called *passe*. This would be when the analysand attempts to transmit to the analyst via a neutral third party what they have learned in analysis. Of course, insofar as they are still involved in analysis, they get things wrong, distort the message, are moved by unconscious impulses. The message is thus lost, not passed on. But – bearing in mind the Lacanian dictum that the letter always arrives – it is in just this way that the analysand demonstrates their knowledge of the unconscious. It is in these distortions and exaggerations, in the contingencies and inadequacies of expression, that the truth is to be found and relayed. In a sense, these distortions *are* the truth.

And it is this very truth that is repeated throughout Žižek. His work both demonstrates and speaks at every level of the truth of this contingency or distortion. This is why both the cultural studies and the straightforwardly philosophical understandings of Žižek are incorrect. The former because it does not understand the Truth contained in

Žižek's method; the latter because it does not understand that this Truth may only be attained through the detour of this method. Žižek goes further than simply finding examples for philosophical concepts, or even reducing those concepts to the level of examples. For what persists in both of these cases is the assumption of some external Truth of which these would be the examples. In fact, Žižek's real point is that *no* philosophical Truth can ever exist apart from its exemplification, that is, its enunciation. In a kind of abyssal self-reflection – and here we return to the origins of philosophy – Žižek's work constitutes an endless enquiry into its own discursive conditions. It takes up and makes something of the 'imbecilic' medium that comprises its readers, the cultural context, and even Žižek himself. It is in this way, finally, that his work is not to be divided into its concepts and examples. The crucial point is not simply that concepts can only be grasped through their examples, but that the only proper philosophical concepts are those that take into account their own conditions of transmissibility, the always transferential relations in which thought finds itself.

These are the specific contours of Žižek's work that we have sought to demonstrate in this selection and arrangement of texts. The book is divided into three sections corresponding to a progressive 'concretiza-tion' and specification of the material. In Section I, *Lacanian Orienta-tions*, we look at the origins of Žižek's thought, both in terms of his institutional location and those inaugural philosophical encounters with Lacan and Hegel (including his extremely radical, but perhaps by now comprehensible, gesture of equating them, bringing out the excess of both). We also see in this section Žižek engaging most extensively with the methodological questions raised by thinking Lacan and Hegel in other contexts – those of the biological sciences and popular culture. Žižek's polemical proposal, however, is that it is not a matter of *applying* Lacanian psychoanalysis or Hegelian idealism to these fields from a position of conceptual superiority. Rather, genetics and popular culture are themselves already Lacanian and Hegelian, and vice versa.

In Section II, *Philosophy Traversed by Psychoanalysis*, we have selected five 'works-in-progress' that follow the chronology of Žižek's major books: 'The Limits of the Semiotic Approach to Psychoanalysis' consists of material from *For They Know Not What They Do: Enjoyment as a Political Factor* (1991); 'A Hair of the Dog that Bit

You' from *Tarrying with the Negative: Kant, Hegel, and the Critique of Ideology* (1993); 'Hegel, Lacan, Deleuze: Three Strange Bedfellows' from *Metastases of Enjoyment: Six Essays on Woman and Causality* (1994); 'The Eclipse of Meaning: On Lacan and Deconstruction' from *The Indivisible Remainder: An Essay on Schelling and Related Matters* (1996); and 'The Parallax View' from *Organs Without Bodies: On Deleuze and Consequences* (2003). However, our point here is that these are not lesser or merely provisional forms of the canonical texts. On the contrary, what is revealed through a consideration of these essays is that even those final versions came about only through an arbitrary decision, a momentary quilting or *capitonnage* of their arguments. The alternate organization of the material that we see in these texts causes their arguments and examples to take on different meanings and nuances than in those later canonical versions. These drafts are thus 'empty', mere effects of how they were performed at the time; and yet each of them is utterly faithful to and consistent with their 'final' form and with Žižek's work as a whole.

In Section III, *The Fantasy of Ideology*, we take up one 'privileged' example of Žižek's method in action: the analysis of ideology. In a sense, this is Žižek's key contribution to contemporary theory – the bringing together of Marx and Lacan in an attempt to understand how ideology still functions today in a seemingly post-ideological world – and yet everything Žižek says here is to be found everywhere else in his work: in the relation between masculine and feminine, in the social as antagonism, in the question of anti-Semitism, and even in the operas of Richard Wagner. In other words, the analysis of ideology is not a central concept in Žižek, but merely another example. But it is the very way that concepts (or what he calls master-signifiers) can only be grasped as examples, and examples attempt to usurp or hegemonize other examples and thus become concepts, that constitutes the fundamental operation of ideology. It is for this reason that an ideological 'example', like Wagner, can also function as a critique of ideology, that is, can allow us to speak of it from somewhere outside of it (on this point, see the essay 'Why is Wagner Worth Saving?'). Wagner is never simply 'Wagner': there is always something 'in him more than himself', which we might even think of as his 'concept', or let us even say his symptom. This highlights the irreducible difference between

Žižek and any vulgar historicism. In striking contrast to the cultural studies imperative always to contextualize, or even the Jamesonian 'Always historicize!', Žižek's fundamental gesture is always *to decontextualize*. But this does not mean an escape from History or the pressures of context, but precisely the attempt to bring out the non-historical or noncontextualizable within context itself. That is to say, to bring out what it means to say that history and context are themselves incomplete, 'not-all'.

As we have argued throughout, Žižek challenges that economy within which everything is reduced to the level of an example (either as a mere pathological effect of its objective life-circumstances, or a contingent element within an *ad hoc* bricolage of texts as in poststructuralism). Such a reduction, we have suggested, implicitly conceals a Truth against which everything is judged and that remains structurally external to it. Against this economy – as will become clear in the third section of this book, where he discusses the relation between 'masculine' and 'feminine' logics – the concept of Truth in Žižek's work does not constitute any kind of exception or Truth external to the order of things, but rather renders totality itself as not-all. To put it another way, there is nothing outside the reign of Truth in Žižek (literally everything can be theorized), but this Truth can never be stated apart from its distortions and examples. It is, to use the language to which Žižek will increasingly have recourse (see, for instance, 'The Real of Sexual Difference'), partisan, one-sided, interested, but for precisely this reason universal, all-encompassing, that to which everything (including its own position of enunciation) is subject.

This is the point that Žižek's commentators do not grasp when they either approve of or criticize him as a philosopher or pop-cultural iconoclast. For they necessarily miss the way that Žižek brings these categories together in thinking of what frames thought itself (an undertaking that in fact characterizes philosophy from the very beginning, not merely as any kind of interdisciplinary undertaking but as the attempt to articulate that empty place from which all disciplines come, including its own). In other words, the many ways that Žižek has so far been read are, to evoke Hegel, just so many 'evasions of the Thing itself'. But let us be clear here: this 'Thing itself' is not some noumenal or teleological end point secretly dictating our actions and toward which all of our words are aimed, but rather the very movement toward this end point; it comes about only through the reflection of this end into practice itself. What this book above all tries to demonstrate is the *practice* of Žižek's work: the constant reworking of concepts, examples and even actual passages of prose testifies as much as anything to the repeated attempts to seize the Thing itself. As the Marxist cultural critic Fredric Jameson says, with reference to Bertolt Brecht – important touchstone for Žižek – the true Hegelian moment lies not in some mystical Absolute Knowledge, but in a practice that becomes substantial and worth doing in its own right, as an end in itself:

> So [Brechtian] activity itself is one of the features of knowledge and art as those flow back into the useful: the 'means' inherent in turning the useful slowly around into an end in its own right – yet not an empty formalist end, not the end-pretext, the 'any-old' purpose that we invoke in order to be able to keep ourselves busy: but, rather, a substantive and Hegelian coming together of means and ends in such a way that activity becomes worth doing in its own right; that immanence and transcendence become indistinguishable (or their opposition transcended, if you prefer); or, in other words, that 'the thing itself' appears. 'Die Sache selbst' . . .
>
> (Fredric Jameson, *Brecht and Method*, London and New York, Verso, 1998, pp. 3–4)

Author's Preface

THE INHUMAN

Slavoj Žižek

In the first half of 2003, I came across two remarkable stories that were reported in the media. A Spanish art historian has uncovered the first use of modern art as a deliberate form of torture. Kandinsky and Klee, as well as Buñuel and Dalí, were the inspiration behind a series of secret cells and torture chambers built in Barcelona in 1938; these so-called 'coloured cells' were the work of French anarchist Alphonse Laurenčič (a *Slovene* family name!), whose 'psychotechnic' torture was his contribution to the fight against Franco's forces.[1] The cells were as inspired by ideas of geometric abstraction and surrealism as they were by avant-garde art theories on the psychological properties of colours. Beds were placed at a 20-degree angle, making them near impossible to sleep on, and the floors of the 6ft-by-3ft cells were scattered with bricks and other geometric blocks to prevent prisoners from walking backwards and forwards. The only option left to prisoners was staring at the walls, which were curved and covered with mind-altering patterns of cubes, squares, straight lines and spirals, which utilized tricks of colour, perspective and scale to cause mental confusion and distress. Lighting effects even gave the impression that the dizzying patterns on the wall were moving. Laurenčič preferred to use the colour green because, according to his theory of the psychological effects of various colours, it produced melancholy and sadness in prisoners.

According to the second story, Walter Benjamin did not kill himself in a village on the Spanish border in 1940 out of fear that he would be returned to France and thus to Nazi agents – instead, he was killed there by Stalinist agents.[2] A few months before he died, Benjamin wrote his 'Theses on the Philosophy of History', a short but devastating analysis of the failure of Marxism; at this time many former

Soviet loyalists were becoming disillusioned with Moscow because of the Hitler–Stalin pact. Consequently he was assassinated by one of the 'killerati', Stalinist agents recruited from socialist intellectuals. The ultimate cause of his murder was probably the contents of the brief-case that Benjamin clutched to his chest as he fled through the Pyrenees toward Spain: the masterwork he had been working on in the *Bibliothèque Nationale* in Paris, the elaboration of his 'Theses'. The manuscript was then entrusted to a fellow refugee who conveniently lost it on a train from Barcelona to Madrid ...

What these two stories have in common is not just the surprising link between high culture (top art and theory) and the lowest level of brutal politics (murder, torture). In one respect, this link is even not as unexpected as it may appear: is not one of the most vulgar common-sense opinions that viewing abstract art (like listening to atonal music) *is* torture (one can easily imagine, along the same lines, a prison in which the detainees are exposed constantly to atonal music)? On the other hand, the 'deeper' judgment is that Schoenberg, in his music, already rendered the horrors of Holocaust and mass bombings before they effectively occurred ... But the true connection between these stories is far more radical and disturbing: what they establish is an *impossible short-circuit* of levels which, for structural reasons, cannot ever meet. (It is simply not possible, say, for what 'Stalin' stands for to operate at the same level as 'Benjamin', i.e., to grasp the true dimensions of Benjamin's 'Theses' from the Stalinist perspective ...) The illusion on which both these stories rely – that of putting two incompatible phenomena on the same level – is strictly homologous to what Kant called a 'transcendental illusion', the fallacy of being able to use the same language for phenomena that are mutually untrans-latable and can only be grasped by a kind of parallax view, constantly shifting perspective between two points between which no synthesis or mediation is possible. There is thus no rapport between the two levels, no shared space – although connected, they are as it were on opposite sides of a Möbius strip. The encounter between Leninist politics and modernist art (exemplified in the fantasy of Lenin meeting Dadaists in a Zurich café) structurally cannot take place; more radically, revolu-tionary politics and revolutionary art move in different temporal-ities – although they are linked, they are *two sides* of the same phenomenon which, precisely as two sides, can never meet.[3] It is more than a historical accident that, in matters of art, Leninists admired great classic art, while many modernists were political conservatives, proto-Fascists even. Is this not already the lesson of the link between the French Revolution and German Idealism: although they are two sides of the same historical moment, they could never directly meet, i.e. German Idealism could only emerge in the 'backward' German conditions where no political revolution had occurred.

In short, what both of these anecdotes share is the occurrence of an insurmountable parallactic gap[4] – and my entire work circulates around this gap that separates the One from itself, for which the Lacanian designation is the Real.[5] There is a whole series of modalities of this gap in the different domains of contemporary theory: the parallax of *neurobiology* (the realization that, when one looks behind the face into the skull, one discovers nothing, there is 'nobody home', just stacks of brain-meat – it is almost impossible to tarry within this gap between meaning and the pure Real); the parallax of *ontological difference*, of the discord between ontic and transcendental-ontological (one cannot reduce the ontological horizon to its ontic 'roots', but one also cannot deduce the ontic domain from the ontological horizon, i.e. transcendental constitution is not creation); the parallax of the *Real* (the Lacanian Real has no positive-substantial consistency, it is just the gap between the multitude of perspectives on it); the parallactic nature of the gap between *desire* and *drive* (let us imagine an individual trying to perform some simple manual task – say, grabbing an object that repeatedly eludes him: the moment he changes his attitude, starts to find pleasure in just repeating the failed task [squeezing the object, which again and again eludes him], he shifts from desire to drive)[6]; the parallax of the *unconscious* (the lack of a common measure between the two aspects of Freud's theoretical edifice, his interpretations of the formations of the unconscious [*The Interpretation of Dreams*, *The Psychopathology of Everyday Life*, *The Joke and its Relation to the Unconscious*] and theories of drives [*Three Essays on Sexuality*, etc.]); up to – why not – the parallax of the *vagina* (the shift from the ultimate object of sexual penetration, the embodiment of the mystery of sexuality, to the very organ of maternity [birth]).

And last but not least, one should assert the parallax status of philosophy as such. From its very beginning (the Ionian Presocratics), philosophy emerged in the interstices of substantial social communities, as the thought of those who were caught in a 'parallax' position, unable fully to identify with any of the positive social identities. This is what is missing in Heidegger's account: the way, from his beloved Presocratics onward, philosophizing involved an 'impossible' position displaced with regard to any communal identity, be it 'economy' as the household organization or *polis*. Like the process of exchange, according to Marx, philosophy emerges in the interstices *between* different communities, in the fragile space between exchange and circulation, a space which lacks any positive identity. Is this not especially clear in the case of Descartes? The grounding experience of his position of universal doubt is precisely a 'multicultural' experience of how one's own tradition is no better than what appears to us the 'eccentric' traditions of others:

I had been taught, even in my College days, that there is nothing imaginable so strange or so little credible that it has not been maintained by one philosopher or other, and I further recognized in the course of my travels that all those whose sentiments are very contrary to ours are yet not necessarily barbarians or savages, but may be possessed of reason in as great or even a greater degree than ourselves. I also considered how very different the self-same man, identical in mind and spirit, may become, according as he is brought up from childhood amongst the French or Germans, or has passed his whole life amongst Chinese or cannibals. I likewise noticed how even in the fashions of one's clothing the same thing that pleased us ten years ago, and which will perhaps please us once again before ten years are passed, seems at the present time extravagant and ridiculous. I thus concluded that it is much more custom and example that persuade us than any certain knowledge, and yet in spite of this the voice of the majority does not afford a proof of any value in truths a little difficult to discover, because such truths are much more likely to have been discovered by one man than by a nation. I could not, however, put my finger on a single person whose opinions seemed preferable to those of others, and I found that I was, so to speak, constrained myself to undertake the direction of my procedure.[7]

Kojin Karatani is thus justified in emphasizing the insubstantial character of *cogito*: 'It cannot be spoken of positively; no sooner than it is, its function is lost.'[8] *Cogito* is not a substantial entity, but a pure structural function, an empty place (in Lacan, $\$$) – as such, it can only emerge in the interstices of substantial communal systems. The link between the emergence of *cogito* and the disintegration and loss of substantial communal identities is thus inherent, and this holds even more for Spinoza than for Descartes: although Spinoza criticized the Cartesian *cogito*, he criticized it as a positive ontological entity – but he implicitly fully endorsed it as the 'position of enunciated', the one that speaks from radical self-doubting, since, even more than Descartes, Spinoza spoke from the interstice of social space(s), neither a Jew nor a Christian.

Spinoza effectively is a 'philosopher as such', with his subjective stance of a double outcast (excommunicated from the very community of the outcasts of Western civilization); which is why one should use him as a paradigm enabling us to discover the traces of a similar displacement – their communal status of being 'out of joint' – operative in all other great philosophers, up to Nietzsche, who was ashamed of Germans and proudly emphasized his alleged Polish roots. For a philosopher, ethnic roots, national identity, etc. are simply *not a category of truth*, or, to put it in precise Kantian terms, when we reflect upon our ethnic roots, we engage in a *private use of reason*, constrained by contingent dogmatic presuppositions – i.e. we act as 'immature' individuals, not as free human beings who dwell in the dimension of the universality of reason. This, of course, in no way entails that we should be ashamed of our ethnic roots; we can love them, be proud of them, returning home may make us feel the warmth in our hearts – but the fact remains that all this is ultimately irrelevant. The right stance is that of Paul who, while being proud of his particular identity (a Jew and a Roman citizen), was nonetheless aware that, in the proper space of Christian absolute Truth, 'there are no Jews or Greeks ...' The struggle that truly engages him is not simply 'more universal' than that of one ethnic group against another; it is a struggle that obeys an entirely different logic, no longer the logic of one self-identical substantial group fighting another group, but of an antagonism that, in a diagonal way, cuts across all particular groups.

It would be easy to counter here that this Cartesian multiculturalist opening and relativizing of one's own position is just a first step, the abandoning of inherited opinions, which should lead us to acquire the absolute certainty of philosophical knowledge – the abandonment of the false home in order to reach our true home. After all, did not Hegel himself compare Descartes' discovery of the *cogito* to a sailor who, after being adrift at sea, finally catches sight of firm ground? Isn't this Cartesian homelessness thus just a deceitful strategic move? Are we not dealing here with a Hegelian 'negation of negation' – the *Aufhebung* of the false traditional home in the final discovery of the conceptual true home? Was Heidegger, in this sense, not justified in referring approvingly to Novalis' determination of philosophy as a longing for the true lost home? Two things should be added to counter any such misunderstanding. First, Kant himself is effectively unique with regard to this topic: in his transcendental philosophy, home-lessness remains irreducible, and we remain forever split, condemned to a fragile position between the two dimensions and to a 'leap of faith' without any guarantee. Secondly, are things with Hegel really so clear? Is it not that, for Hegel, this new 'home' is in a way *homelessness itself*, the very open movement of negativity?

This point becomes clearer through a particularly morbid joke. A patient in a large hospital room with many beds complains to the doctor about the constant noise that other patients are making, which is driving him crazy. The doctor replies that nothing can be done; one cannot forbid the patients from expressing their despair, since they all know they are dying. The first patient responds: 'Why don't you then put them in a separate room for dying?' The doctor replies calmly and glibly: 'But this *is* a room for those who are dying ...' Why does everyone who knows a little bit about Hegel immediately discern this joke's 'Hegelian' flavour? It is precisely because of the final twist, in which the patient's subjective position is undermined: he finds himself included in the very series from which he wanted to maintain a distance.

The predominant way of asserting the actuality of Hegel, i.e. to save him from the reproach that his system is totally outdated metaphysical madness, is to read him as attempting to establish the normative conditions or presuppositions of our cognitive and ethical claims: Hegel's logic is not a system of universal ontology, but just a systematic deployment of all the ways available to us to make claims about what there is, and of the inherent inconsistencies of these ways. According to this reading, Hegel's starting point is the fact that the fundamental structure of the human mind is self-reflective: a human being does not simply act, it (can) act(s) upon rational freely assumed norms and motivations; this means that, in order to account for our statements and attitudes, one can never simply refer to some positive data (natural laws and processes, divine Reason, God's Will, etc.) – each of these references has to be *justified*, its normative binding power has to be somehow *accounted for*. The problem with this elegant solution is that, in contrast to the robust direct metaphysical reading of Hegel as rendering the structure of the Absolute, it is far too modest: it silently reduces Hegel's logic to a system of global epistemology, of all possible epistemological stances, and what gets lost is the intersection between the epistemological and ontological aspects, the way 'reality' itself is caught in the movement of our knowing of it (or, vice versa, how our knowing of reality is embedded in reality itself, like journalists embedded with the US Army units progressing into Iraq).

Along the lines of this constitutive 'homelessness' of philosophy, one should rehabilitate Kant's idea of the cosmopolitan 'world-civil-society' (*Weltburgergesellschaft*), which is not simply an expansion of the citizenship of a nation state to the citizenship of a global trans-national state; instead, it involves a shift from the principle of identification with one's 'organic' ethnic substance actualized in a particular tradition to a radically different principle of identification. Recall Deleuze's notion of universal singularity as opposed to the triad of Individuality–Particularity–Universality – this opposition is precisely the opposition between Kant and Hegel. For Hegel, 'world-civil-society' is an abstract notion without substantial content, lacking the mediation of the particular and thus the force of full actuality, i.e., it involves an abstract identification which does not substantially grasp the subject; the only way for an individual effectively to participate in universal humanity is therefore through a full identification with a particular Nation-State (I am 'human' only insofar as I am German, English ...).[9] For Kant, on the contrary, 'world-civil-society' designates the paradox of the universal singularity, of a singular subject who, in a kind of short-circuit, bypasses the mediation of the particular by directly participating in the Universal. This identification with the Universal is not the identification with an encompassing global Substance ('humanity'), but an identification with a universal ethico-political principle – a universal religious collective, a scientific collective, a global revolutionary organization, all of which are in principle accessible to everyone. This is what Kant, in the famous passage of his 'What is Enlightenment?', means by 'public' as opposed to 'private': 'private' is not one's individuality as opposed to one's communal ties, but the very communal-institutional order of one's particular identification; while 'public' is the trans-national universality of the exercise of one's Reason. The paradox is thus that one participates in the universal dimension of the 'public' sphere precisely as singular individual extracted from or even opposed to one's substantial communal identification – one is truly universal only as radically singular, in the interstices of communal identities. And what we find at the end of this road is atheism – not the ridiculously pathetic spectacle of the heroic defiance of God, but insight into the irrelevance of the divine, along the lines of Brecht's Herr Keuner:

> Someone asked Herr Keuner if there is a God. Herr Keuner said: I advise you to think about how your behaviour would change with regard to the answer to this question. If it would not change, then we can drop the question. If it would change, then I can help you at least insofar as I can tell you: You already decided: You need a God.[10]

Brecht is right here: we are never in a position directly to choose between theism and atheism, since the choice as such is already located within the field of belief. 'Atheism' (in the sense of deciding not to believe in God) is a miserable, pathetic stance of those who long for God but cannot find him (or who 'rebel against God'). A true atheist does not choose atheism: for him, the question itself is irrelevant – *this* is the stance of a truly atheistic *subject*.

The standard critical procedure today is to mobilize the opposition of human and subject: the notion of subjectivity (self-consciousness, self-positing autonomy, etc.) stands for a dangerous *hubris*, a will to power, which obfuscates and distorts the authentic essence of humanity; the task is thus to think the essence of humanity outside the domain of subjectivity. What Lacan tries to accomplish seems to be the exact opposite of this standard procedure: in all his great literary interpretations – from Oedipus and Antigone through Sade to Claudel – he is in search of a point at which we enter the dimension of the 'inhuman', the point at which 'humanity' disintegrates, so that all that remains is the pure subject. Sophocles' Antigone, Sade's Juliette, Claudel's Sygne – they are all these figures of such an 'inhuman' subject (in contrast to their 'human' counterpoint: Ismene, Justine . . .). To paraphrase Nietzsche, what one should render problematic is what in us is 'human, all too human'. One should not be afraid to apply this insight also to politics: it is all too simple to dismiss Nazis as inhuman and bestial – what if the real problem with the Nazis was precisely that they remained 'human, all too human'?

* * *

The fate of an old Slovene Communist revolutionary stands out as a perfect metaphor for the twists of Stalinism. In 1943, when Italy capitulated, he led a rebellion of Yugoslav prisoners in a concentration camp on the Adriatic island of Rab: under his leadership, 2000 starved prisoners disarmed 2200 Italian soldiers. After the war, he was arrested and put in a prison on a nearby small Goli otok ['naked island'], a notorious Communist concentration camp. While there, he was mobilized in 1953, together with other prisoners, to build a monument to celebrate the tenth anniversary of the 1943 rebellion on Rab – in short, as a prisoner of Communists, he was building a monument *to himself*, to the rebellion led by him . . . If poetic (not justice, but rather) injustice means anything, this was it: is the fate of this revolutionary not the fate of the entire people under the Stalinist dictatorship, of the millions who, first, heroically overthrew the *ancien régime* in the revolution, and, then, enslaved to the new rules, were forced to build monuments to their own revolutionary past? This revolutionary is thus effectively a 'universal singular', an individual whose fate stands for the fate of all.

My gratitude towards Rex Butler and Scott Stephens for their work on this volume is boundless. But I would nonetheless like to dedicate it to the old Slovene Communist.

NOTES

1 See Giles Tremlett, 'Anarchists and the fine art of torture', *Guardian*, 27 January 2003.
2 See Stuart Jeffries, 'Did Stalin's killers liquidate Walter Benjamin?', *Observer*, 8 July 2001.
3 Perhaps the most succinct definition of a revolutionary utopia is this: a social order in which this duality, this parallactic gap, would no longer be operative – a space in which Lenin effectively *could* meet and debate the Dadaists.
4 Upon a closer look, it becomes clear how the very relationship between these two stories is that of a parallax: their symmetry is not pure, since the Laurenčič anecdote is clearly about politics (political terror and torture), using modernist art as a comical counterpoint, while the Benjamin anecdote is about 'high theory', using, on the contrary, Stalin as its comical counterpoint.
5 I should acknowledge here my fundamental indebtedness to Kojin Karatani, *Transcritique: On Kant and Marx*, Cambridge MA, MIT Press, 2003.
6 Drive thus emerges as a strategy to gain profit from the very failure to reach the goal of desire.
7 René Descartes, *Discours de la méthode/Discourse on Method: Bilingual Edition with an Interpretive Essay*, trans. George Heffernan, Notre Dame, University of Notre Dame Press, 1994, p. 33.
8 Karatani, *Transcritique*, p. 134.
9 Is, however, Hegelian totality such an 'organic' totality relying on the Particular as mediating between the Universal and the Individual? Is, on the contrary, the (in)famous 'contradiction' that propels the dialectical movement not the very

contradiction between the 'organic' Whole (the structure of U-P-I) and the singularity that directly – without mediation – stands for the Universal?

10   Bertolt Brecht, *Prosa, Band 3*, Frankfurt, Suhrkamp Verlag, 1995, p. 18.

Section I
LACANIAN ORIENTATIONS

1 The Society for Theoretical Psychoanalysis in Yugoslavia: An interview with Éric Laurent

Éric Laurent *What is peculiar about your group?*

Slavoj Žižek Our field of work to date has been a Lacanian rereading of the great philosophical texts, more so those of the past than contemporary. From this standpoint, we have made a significant impact on the university scene. All the leading specialists in Hegel, ancient and analytical philosophy are overtly Lacanian. The same goes for political analysts. Why? Because self-management [*l'autogestion*] lends itself to an explicitly Lacanian political analysis that is far more precise and paradoxical than the theory of really existing socialism [*la théorie du socialisme réel*].[1] One can work wonders with the Lacanian approach. Our impact is also considerable in the wider literary field. Likewise, cinema theory in Slovenia is represented by four persons who, to put it quite simply, are Lacanians. Our position is thus absolutely predominant.

ÉL *When you speak of 'Lacanians', are you referring to people who have read Lacan?*

SŽ Sure, their French connections are people whose fundamental reference is to Lacan, so for cinema, Pascal Bonitzer or Michel Chion. But they interpret their work in a way that is even more Lacanian than Bonitzer or Chion themselves. The dominant position to which I referred a moment ago yields an interesting situation: Lacanianism is found to be engaging in a series of public struggles, concerning social reform or the elections, for instance. We have, along with others, a complete theory of democracy, thanks to Claude Lefort's Lacanian exposition.[2] We thus tried to explain why really existing socialism tends to avoid the traumatic moment of elections, which produce the atomization of society. But our true problem actually concerns the establishment of systematic contacts with the psychiatric milieu. The situation in Yugoslavia is not like that of other countries under Russian socialism – political repression has never made use of the kind of method that one sees in a range of therapies, from transactional analysis to the primal scream. All of these stupidities are permitted by liberalism as a whole. They are all inscribed into the very framework of institutionalized psychiatry, and consequently are funded by social security. And is institutionalization not the condition of possibility of psychoanalysis itself? It is, after all, impossible for the analysand to pay the analyst without the mediation of the institution. Some psychiatrists nevertheless try their hand at a practice similar to that of psychoanalysis.

Already having contacts with at least ten practitioners – in Ljubljana alone, not to mention in other republics – we tried to organize a meeting. We received many letters – for example, one from a military psychiatrist in Zagreb who was very interested in Lacan – expressing some desire to work with us. Why not? Our next step would be to organize a gathering in order to create, under our own conditions, something that would resemble an analytic social link [*un lien social analytique*]. Therein resides the heart [*vif*] of our problematic; one of my colleagues from Ljubljana has stressed that one must never persist [*céder*] in the 'narcissism of a lost cause'.[3] That's it. That was precisely the logic of what we were doing: because our cause is lost, why not persevere in our academic narcissism? We all knew it was necessary to abandon this logic, not maintaining any illusions; we tried to do everything we could, but as soon as it became a matter of taking concrete measures, all kinds of resistance became manifest, whose great commonality, unfortunately objectively true, consisted in the statement that 'these practitioners know nothing about Lacanian theory', and that one must consequently have nothing to do with them. In effect, what is predominant in practical psychiatry is only a revisionist version of what psychoanalysis calls dynamic therapy. It is very characteristic of Yugoslavia that no reference is ever made to either general Soviet psychiatry or psychology, but rather to a mix of American and German authors, such as Schulz-Hencke and Erickson. One of the main aspects of the situation has to do with the fact that psychiatrists consider the treasure of psychiatric knowledge to be an objectively given knowledge, presented in manuals and technically accessible. They are completely oblivious to the fundamental dimension of the Lacanian *passe*, which is also the moment when the analysand themselves must become able, not to convey a theory of their symptoms, but to explain them in a transmittable fashion. And they are entirely incapable of understanding that the symptom is already addressed to the analyst. They are not able to conceive of knowledge otherwise than as objective, technical, totally indifferent to the analysand. For them, the analysand either does or doesn't learn analytic theory from a technical manual; certainly, as Sasha Nacht in France says, the less the analysand thinks he knows, the better. Further, because they consider analytic knowledge to be a field of technical procedures, they have no idea how important it is to distinguish the Freudian tradition as such. This is a terrible situation, because the only thing that concerns them is what is good, confirmed, usable in practice, in Freud, in Lacan, in X or Y ...

ÉL *What is the actual status of your group?*

SŽ Our great success – because Yugoslavia neighbours countries in which really existing socialism is dominant, in which it is extremely difficult to achieve official recognition as an autonomous group – is to have attained this autonomous status. We had to utilize a number of strategies, but we have succeeded: as a result, we have the ability to publish books, to organize public gatherings, colloquia, etc. We receive State grants for our publications. In fact, we publish a review of the Freudian field in the strict sense, *Razpol*, which designates both 'sex' and 'division' at the same time. We also publish a collection, entirely Lacanian, entitled 'Analecta', which appears between two and four times per year. Over twenty volumes have been published to date, the latest being a translation of Lacan's *Seminar XX*, a bestseller that sold out in five and a half months. This is encouraging. Nevertheless, there is no point being too optimistic as long as we seem incapable of developing our contacts with psychiatric circles.

ÉL *How is the core of your group organized?*

SŽ The structure is triple, like any good hierarchy: one part, the inner circle, the 'purest of the pure' [*les 'purs et durs'*], those who are capable of writing books, the 'true' Lacanians – around ten people; next, twenty or so people of diverse education who belong to the

Lacanian orientation; finally, the mostly indifferent multitude whose orientation is basically pro-Lacanian. To give you some idea of what our activity represents in a small town of 250,000 like Ljubljana, this year, at the Department of Philosophy, I delivered a course each week in which I expounded, chapter by chapter, Lacan's *Seminar XX* to around 250 people. The public is clearly very interested. Perhaps it is only fashionable, but all the same I have a lot of confidence in the young generation, in those that are still students. It is also encouraging to know that there are many students of psychology: this is important for our connections to the clinic in the years to come. The legislation in effect is already liberal enough for us: in order to become a clinician, it is not necessary to be a medical doctor, but one must simply have an education in psychology, with a clinical specialization in the second year of study.

ÉL *In your group, have many of you undertaken psychoanalysis?*

SŽ Few, but some have done so, often for personal reasons prior to becoming Lacanians.

ÉL *What was your last colloquium?*

SŽ It was a gathering on the topic of feminism in March 1986. In Slovenia, feminism represents a very strong tendency that some want to oppose to Lacan by resorting to the text of Luce Irigaray. We have succeeded in amply developing, patiently, a number of examples, derived from Otto Weininger's commentary, *Sex and Character*,[4] whose anti-feminist and anti-Semitic theories have played a decisive role in Slovenia and throughout Europe between the two world wars. We have also developed a whole series of examples drawn from detective novels, through an examination of the tradition of female writers in this domain, concerning the style of Patricia Highsmith and the category of the not-all [*pas-tout*] in Ruth Rendell's novel, *A Judgement in Stone*, in which each phrase alludes to what happens at the end, where that which initially gives the impression of a closed universe in which destiny predominates in fact renders visible the radical contingency of the historical process. These examples thus allow us to explicate the formula 'Woman does not exist', or even 'History does not exist'. Now, in the feminist movement, the slogan will be that a woman, in order to liberate herself, must first admit that she does not exist! I'm joking, but nonetheless, it is crucial to clarify that castration does not signify that man has it and woman doesn't, but that the phallus, in its very presence, incarnates the lack. Our particularity is always to use concrete examples, the operas of Mozart or Hitchcock's films, not only for didactic ends but also for our own enjoyment [*jouissance*].

NOTES

This interview was first published in *Ornicar?*, 39 (1986–7), pp. 115–18. Our translation. It can be read as a much more *situated* – which is to say, necessarily *false* – supplement to Žižek's reflections in Slavoj Žižek and Glyn Daly, *Conversations with Žižek*, London, Polity, 2004, pp. 36–9 [eds].

1   Žižek is referring here to the particular Yugoslavian variant of Communism, which was characterized not by direct repression but by the 'repressive toleration' of the Party already criticizing itself. See on this the interview with Žižek and Renata Salecl, 'Lacan in Slovenia', *Radical Philosophy* 58, Summer 1991, pp. 25–31 [eds].

2   Claude Lefort, *L'Invention démocratique: Les limites de la domination totalitaire*, Paris, Librarie Arthème Fayard, 1981 [eds].

3   See Jacques Lacan, 'The Subversion of the Subject and the Dialectic of Desire in the Freudian Unconscious', in *Écrits: A Selection*, trans. Bruce Fink, New York, W. W. Norton, 2002, p. 311 [eds].

4   Otto Weininger, *Sex and Character*, London, William Heinemann, 1906 [eds].

2 Lacan – At What Point is he Hegelian?

1. THE HEGELIAN THING

Michel Foucault once proposed that philosophy as such could be labelled 'anti-Platonism'. All philosophers, beginning with Aristotle, have defined their projects by distancing themselves from Plato, precisely because Plato was the thinker whose enterprise marked off [*dégagea*] the field of philosophy. In the same way, one could say that what defines philosophy in the last two centuries is its dissociation [*un prise de distance*] from Hegel, the incarnate monster of 'panlogicism' (the total dialectical mediation of reality, the complete dissolution of reality in the self-movement of the Idea). Over against this 'monster', various attempts have affirmed that there is, supposedly, some element which escapes the mediation of the concept, a gesture that is already discernible in the three great post-Hegelian inversions [*renversements*][1] that opposed the absolutism of the Idea in the name of the irrational abyss of the Will (Schelling), the paradox of the existence of the individual (Kierkegaard) and the productive processes of life (Marx). Even Hegel's more favourable commentators, despite identifying with him, refuse to trespass the limit that constitutes Absolute Knowledge. Thus, Jean Hyppolite insists that the post-Hegelian tradition allows for the irreducible opening of the historico-temporal process by means of an empty repetition, destroying the framework of the progress of Reason ... To put it simply, each of these relations to the Hegelian system is always that of a 'I know well, but all the same [*je sais bien, mais quand même*]':[2] one knows well that Hegel affirms the fundamentally antagonistic character of actions, the decentring of the subject, etc., but all the same ... this division is eventually overcome in the self-mediation of the absolute Idea that ends up suturing all wounds. The position of Absolute Knowledge, the final reconciliation, plays here the role of the Hegelian Thing: a monster both frightening and ridiculous, from which it is best to keep some distance, something that is at the same time impossible (Absolute Knowledge is of course unachievable, an unrealizable Ideal) and forbidden (Absolute Knowledge must be avoided, for it threatens to mortify all the richness of life through the self-movement of the concept). In other words, any attempt to define oneself within Hegel's sphere of influence requires a point of blocked identification – the Thing must always be sacrificed ...

For us, this figure of Hegel as 'panlogicist', who devours and mortifies the living substance of the particular, is *the Real of his critics*, 'Real' in the Lacanian sense: the construction of a point which effectively does not exist (a monster with no relation to Hegel himself), but which, nonetheless, must be presupposed in order to justify our negative reference to the other, that is to say, our effort at distantiation. Where does the horror felt by post-Hegelians before the monster of Absolute Knowledge come from? What does this fantasmatic construction conceal by means of its fascinating presence? The answer: a hole, a void. The best way to distinguish this hole is by reading Hegel *with Lacan*, that is to say, by reading Hegel in terms of the Lacanian problematic of the lack in the Other, the traumatic void against which the process of signification articulates itself. From this perspective, Absolute Knowledge appears to be the Hegelian name for that which Lacan outlined in his description of the *passe*, the final moment of the analytic process, the experience of lack in the Other. If, according to Lacan's celebrated formula, Sade offers us the truth of Kant,[3] then Lacan himself allows us to approach the elementary matrix that summarizes the entire movement of the Hegelian dialectic: Kant with Sade, Hegel with Lacan. What is implied, then, by this relationship between Hegel and Lacan?

Today, things seem clear: although no one denies that Lacan owed a certain debt to Hegel, it is argued that all Hegelian references are limited to specific theoretical borrowings, and restricted to a well-defined period of Lacan's work. Between the late 1940s and the early 1950s, Lacan tried to articulate the psychoanalytic process in terms of an intersubjective logic of the recognition of desire and/or the desire for recognition. Already at this stage, Lacan was careful to keep his distance from the closure of the Hegelian system, from an Absolute Knowledge that was allied to the unachievable ideal of a perfectly homogeneous discourse, complete and closed in upon itself. Later, the introduction of the logic of the not-all [*pas-tout*] and the concept of the barred Other (Ⱥ) would render this initial reference to Hegel obsolete. Can one imagine any opposition more incompatible than the one between Hegelian Absolute Knowledge – the closed 'circle of circles' – and the Lacanian barred Other – absolutely empty knowledge? Is not Lacan the anti-Hegel par excellence?

But, ironically, it is on the basis of Lacan's debt to Hegel that most critiques proceed: Lacan remains the prisoner of phallogocentrism due to a subterranean Hegelianism that confines textual dissemination within a teleological circle ... To such a critique, Lacanians could respond, rightly, by stressing the rupture of Lacanianism with Hegelianism – trying hard to save Lacan by emphasizing that he is not and never has been a Hegelian. But it is time to approach this debate in a different light, by expressing the relationship between Hegel and Lacan in an original way. From our perspective, Lacan is fundamentally Hegelian, but without knowing it. His Hegelianism is certainly not where one expects it – that is to say, in his explicit references to Hegel – but precisely in the last stage of his teaching, in his logic of the not-all, in the emphasis placed on the Real and the lack in the Other. And, reciprocally, a reading of Hegel in the light of Lacan provides us with a radically different image from that, commonly assumed, of the 'panlogicist' Hegel. It would make visible a Hegel of the logic of the signifier, of a self-referential process articulated as the repetitive positivization of a central void.

Such a reading would thus affect the definition of both terms. It would mark off [*dégageant*] a Hegel freed from the residues of panlogicism and/or historicism, a Hegel of the logic of the signifier. Consequently, it would become possible clearly to perceive the most subversive core of the Lacanian doctrine, that of the constitutive lack in the Other. This is why our argument is, fundamentally, dialogical: it is impossible to develop a positive line of thought without including the theses that are opposed to it, that is to say, in effect, those commonplaces already mentioned concerning Hegel, which would see in Hegelianism the instance par excellence of the 'imperialism of reason', a closed economy in which the self-movement of the Concept sublates all differences and every dispersion of the material process. Such commonplaces can also be found in Lacan, but they are accompanied by another conception of Hegel which one does not find in Lacan's explicit statements about Hegel – for which reason we pass by these statements, for the most part, in silence. For us, Lacan 'does not know at what point he is Hegelian', because his reading of Hegel is inscribed within the tradition of Kojève and Hyppolite.[4] It would therefore be necessary, in order to articulate the connection between the dialectic and the logic of the signifier, to bracket for the moment any explicit reference by Lacan to Hegel. [. . .]

2. THREE STAGES OF THE SYMBOLIC

It is only after clarifying the relationship between the Hegelian dialectic and the logic of the signifier that one is in the position to situate the 'Hegelianism' in Lacan. Let us take the three successive stages of the progression of the concept of the Symbolic in Lacan.

The first stage, that of 'The Function and Field of Speech and Language in Psychoanalysis',[5] places the accent on the intersubjective dimension of *speech*: speech as the medium of the intersubjective recognition of desire. The predominant themes in this stage are symbolization as historicization and symbolic realization: symptoms, traumas, are the blank, empty, non-historicizable spaces of the subject's symbolic universe. Analysis, then, 'realizes in the symbolic' these traumatic traces, including them in the symbolic universe by conferring upon them after the fact, retrospectively, some signification. Basically, a phenomenological conception of language, close to that of Merleau-Ponty, is here retained: the goal of analysis is to produce the recognition of desire through 'full speech', to integrate desire within the universe of signification. In a typically phenomenological way, the order of speech is identified with that of signification, and analysis itself functions at this level: 'All analytical experience is an experience of signification.'[6]

The second stage, exemplified in the interpretation of 'The Purloined Letter', is in some ways complementary to the first, just as *language* is complementary to speech. It places the emphasis on the signifying order as (that of) a closed, differential, synchronous structure: the signifying structure functions as a senseless 'automatism', to which the subject is subjected. The diachronic order of speech, of signification, is thus governed by a senseless, signifying automatism, by a differential and formalizable game that produces the effect of signification. This structure that 'runs the game' is concealed by the Imaginary relationship – one is here at the level of the 'schema L':[7]

> We realize, of course, the importance of these Imaginary impregnations (*Prägung*) in those partializations of the symbolic alternative which give the symbolic chain its appearance. But we maintain that it is the specific law of that chain which governs those psychoanalytic effects that are decisive for the subject: such as foreclosure [*Verwerfung*], repression [*Verdrängung*], denial [*Verneinung*] itself – specifying with appropriate emphasis that these effects follow so faithfully the displacement [*Enstellung*] of the signifier that imaginary factors, despite their inertia, figure only as shadows and reflections in this process.[8]

If the first stage was 'phenomenological', this one is rather more 'structuralist'. The problem of this second stage is that the subject – insofar as it is the subject of the signifier, irreducible to the Imaginary ego – is radically *unthinkable* [*impensable*]: on the one hand, there is the Imaginary ego, the location of blindness and misrecognition, that is to say, of the axis *a–a'*; on the other hand, a subject totally subjected to the structure, alienated without remainder and in this sense de-subjectivized:

> The coming into operation of the symbolic function in its most radical, absolute usage ends up abolishing the action of the individual so completely that by the same token it eliminates his tragic relation to the world ... At the heart of the flow of events, the functioning of reason, the subject from the first move finds himself to be no more than a pawn, forced inside this system, and excluded from any truly dramatic, and consequently tragic, participation in the realization of truth.[9]

The subject that liberates itself completely from the axis a–a' and entirely realizes itself in the Other, accomplishing its symbolic realization, as subject without ego, without Imaginary blindness, will at once be radically de-subjectivized, reduced to a moment in the functioning of the Symbolic machine, the 'structure without subject'.

The third stage is certainly not, it must be understood, some kind of 'synthesis' of the first two, a combination of the phenomenological perspective of speech and the structuralist perspective of language; these two stages are themselves already complementary, two versions of the same theoretical edifice. The third stage must break with this common edifice, this complementary relationship of a speech filled with signification and a self-sufficient structure, by positing a barred Other, incomplete, 'not-all', an Other articulated against a void, an Other which carries within it an ex-timate, non-symbolizable kernel. It is only by working from the barred Other ($Ⱥ$) that one can understand the subject of the signifier ($\$$): if the Other is not fractured, if it is a complete array, the only possible relationship of the subject to the structure is that of total alienation, of a subjection without remainder; but the lack in the Other means that there is a remainder, a non-integratable residuum in the Other, *objet a*, and the subject is able to avoid total alienation only insofar as it posits itself as the correlative of this remainder: $\$ \lozenge a$. In this sense, one is able to conceive of a subject that is distinct from the ego, the place of Imaginary misrecognition: a subject that is not lost in the 'process without subject' of the structural combination.

One can also approach this conjuncture working from the question of desire: the barred Other means an Other that is not simply an anonymous machine, the automatism of a structural combinatory, but rather a desiring Other, an Other that lacks the object-cause of desire, an Other that wants something from the subject (*'Che vuoi?'*). One would want to say that the subject of the signifier ex-sists insofar as this dimension of the question insists in the Other – not as the question of the subject confronted with the enigma of the Other, but rather as a question that emerges from the Other itself.

At first sight, it might appear that the Lacanian reference to Hegel is fundamentally limited to the first stage, with its themes of symbolization as historicization, integration within the symbolic universe, etc. Throughout this period, the Lacanian reading of the Hegelian text is 'mediated' by Kojève and Hyppolite, and the predominant themes are those of struggle and the final reconciliation in the medium of intersubjective recognition, which is speech. In effect, the achievement of symbolic realization, the abolition of the symptom, the integration of every traumatic kernel into the symbolic universe, this final and ideal moment when the subject is finally liberated from Imaginary opacity, when the blanks of its history are filled in [*comblés*] by 'full speech [*parole pleine*]', when the tension between 'subject' and 'substance' are finally resolved by this speech in which the subject is able to assume his desire, etc. – is it not possible to recognize this state of plenitude as a psychoanalytic version of Hegelian 'Absolute Knowledge': a non-barred Other, without symptom, without lack, without traumatic kernel?

It would thus appear that, with the introduction of a barred Other, any overt reference to Hegel is at least relegated to the background: the barred Other means precisely the constitutive impossibility of an Absolute Knowledge, of the achievement of symbolic realization, because there is a void, a lack of the signifier [*un manque du signifiant*] that accompanies the movement of symbolization, or rather, on another level, because there is a nonsense [*il y a un non sens*], which necessarily emerges as soon as there is the advent of sense [*l'avènement du sens*]. The conceptual field of Lacan's third stage would thus be a field of the Other that resists on all sides the achievement of 'realization', an Other emptied out by a hypothetical kernel of a Real-impossible whose inertia blocks the dialecticization, the 'sublation' in and through the symbol – in short, an anti-Hegelian Other par excellence.

3. DAS UNGESCHEHENMACHEN

Before succumbing too quickly to this seductive image of an anti-Hegelian Lacan, it is worth developing the logic of the three stages of Lacanian doctrine. This can be done by means of several determinants [*par plusieurs biais*]. For example, it is possible to demonstrate that each of these three stages corresponds to a specific conception of the end of the analytic process: 1) *symbolic realization*, the achievement of the historicization of symptoms; 2) the experience of *symbolic castration* ('originary repression') as a dimension that opens for the subject access to his desire at the level of the Other; 3) the *traversing of the fantasy*, the loss of the object that plugs the hole in the Other. Nevertheless, the preferable choice of a determinant is that of 'death drive': for the simple reason that the link between 'death drive' and the symbolic order – everything else remaining constant in Lacanian theory – is articulated in a different way in each of the stages:

1) In the 'Hegelian-phenomenological' stage, it acts as a variation on the Hegelian theme of the 'word as the murder of the thing': the word, the symbol, is not a simple reflection, substitution or representation of the thing; it is the thing itself, that is to say, the thing is *aufgehoben*, suppressed-interiorized, in its concept which exists in the form of a word:

> Remember what Hegel says about the concept – *The concept is the time of the thing*. To be sure, the concept is not the thing as it is, for the simple reason that the concept is always where the thing isn't, it is there so as to replace the thing . . . Of the thing, what is it that can be there? Neither its form, nor its reality, since, in the actual state of affairs, all the seats are taken. Hegel puts it with extreme rigour – the concept is what makes the thing be there, while, all the while, it isn't.
>
> This identity in difference, which characterizes the relation of the concept to the thing, that is what also makes the thing a thing and the fact symbolized . . .[10]

'Death drive' thus stands for the annihilation of the thing in its immediate, corporal reality upon its symbolization: the thing is more present in its symbol than in its immediate reality. The unity of the thing, the trait that makes a thing a thing, is decentred in relation to the reality of the thing itself: the thing must 'die' in its reality in order to arrive, by traversing its symbol, at its conceptual unity.

2) In the following, 'structuralist' stage, 'death drive' is identified with the symbolic order insofar as it follows its own laws beyond

the Imaginary experience of the subject, that is to say, 'beyond the pleasure principle' – a mechanism which, by means of its automatism, breaks, disturbs the subject's equilibrium and Imaginary homeostasis. The symbolic order:

> isn't the libidinal order in which the ego is inscribed, along with all the drives. It tends beyond the pleasure principle, beyond the limits of life, and that is why Freud identifies it with the death instinct. . . . The symbolic order is rejected by the libidinal order, which includes the whole of the domain of the imaginary, including the structure of the ego. And the death instinct is only the mask of the symbolic order . . .[11]

3) In the third stage, in which Lacan places the accent on the Real as the impossible/non-symbolizable kernel, 'death drive' becomes the name for that which, following Sade, takes the form of the 'second death': symbolic death, the annihilation of the signifying network, of the text in which the subject is inscribed, through which reality is historicized – the name of that which, in psychotic experience, appears as the 'end of the world', the twilight, the collapse of the symbolic universe.[12] To put it another way, 'death drive' designates the ahistorical possibility implied, exposed by the process of symbolization/historicization: the possibility of its radical effacement.

The Freudian concept which best designates this act of annihilation is *das Ungeschehenmachen*, 'in which one action is cancelled out by a second, so that it is as though neither action had taken place',[13] or more simply, retroactive cancellation. And it is more than coincidence that one finds the same term in Hegel, who defines *das Ungeschehenmachen* as the supreme power of Spirit.[14] This power of 'unmaking [*défaire*]' the past is conceivable only on the symbolic level: in immediate life, in its circuit, the past is only the past and as such is incontestable; but once one is situated at the level of history *qua* text, the network of symbolic traces, one is able to wind back what has already occurred, or erase the past. One is thus able to conceive of *Ungeschehenmachen*, the highest manifestation of negativity, as the Hegelian version of 'death drive': it is not an accidental or marginal element in the Hegelian edifice, but rather designates the crucial moment of the dialectical process, the so-called moment of the 'negation of negation', the inversion of the 'antithesis' into the 'synthesis': the 'reconciliation' proper to synthesis is not a surpassing or suspension (whether it be 'dialectical') of scission on some higher plane, but a retroactive reversal which means that *there never was* any scission to begin with – 'synthesis' *retroactively annuls* this scission. This is how the enigmatic but crucial passage from Hegel's *Encyclopaedia* must be understood:

> The accomplishing of the infinite purpose consists therefore in sublating the illusion that it has not yet been accomplished.[15]

One does not accomplish the end by attaining it, but by proving that one has already attained it, even when the way to its realization is hidden from view. While advancing, one was not yet there, but all of a sudden, one has been there all along – 'too soon' changes suddenly into 'too late' without detecting the exact moment of their transformation. The whole affair thus has the structure of the missed encounter: along the way, the truth, which we have not yet attained, pushes us forward like a phantom, promising that it awaits us at the end of the road; but all of a sudden we perceive that we were always already in the truth. The paradoxical surplus which slips away, which reveals itself as 'impossible' in this missed encounter of the 'opportune moment', is of course *objet a*: the pure semblance which pushes us toward the truth, right up to the moment when it suddenly appears behind us and that we have already arrived ahead of it, a chimerical being that does not have its 'proper time', only ever persisting in the interval between 'too soon' and 'too late'.

NOTES

This selection appeared in *Le plus sublime des hysteriques – Hegel passe*, Paris, Le point hors ligne, 1988, pp. 5–8, 93–100. Our translation [eds].

1 Žižek's language here is also, ironically, that of Louis Althusser, who famously rejects any such materialist 'inversion' [*renversement*] of the Hegelian dialectic. See his 'On the Materialist

Dialectic: On the Unevenness of Origins', in *For Marx*, trans. Ben Brewster, London and New York, Verso, 1969, pp. 161–218 [eds].

2   This formula of the 'fetishist denial' was famously developed by Octave Mannoni in his 'I Know Well, but All the Same ...', in *Perversion and the Social Relation*, ed. Molly Anne Rothenberg, Dennis A. Foster and Slavoj Žižek, Durham, Duke University Press, 2003, pp. 68–92. Žižek further elaborates this formula in Chapter 11 of this volume, 'Between Symbolic Fiction and Fantasmatic Spectre: Towards a Lacanian Theory of Ideology', pages 260 and 268, n. 10 [eds].

3   Lacan's precise formulation is as follows: '*Philosophy in the Bedroom* comes eight years after the *Critique of Practical Reason*. Once we observe their correspondence, then we may demonstrate that one completes the other, and even suggest that [Sade's *Philosophy*] presents the truth of the *Critique*.' Jacques Lacan, 'Kant avec Sade', in *Écrits II*, Paris, Éditions du Seuil, 1966, p. 244. Our translation [eds].

4   See Alexandre Kojève, *Introduction to the Reading of Hegel: Lectures on the 'Phenomenology of Spirit'*, ed. Raymond Queneau and Allan Bloom, trans. James H. Nichols, Jr., Ithaca and London, Cornell University Press, 1969; Jean Hyppolite, *Genesis and Structure of Hegel's 'Phenomenology of Spirit'*, trans. Samuel Cherniak and John Heckman, Evanston, Northwestern University Press, 1974 [eds].

5   Jacques Lacan, 'The Function and Field of Speech and Language in Psychoanalysis', in *Écrits: A Selection*, trans. Bruce Fink, New York, W. W. Norton, 2002, pp. 31–106 [eds].

6   Jacques Lacan, *The Seminar of Jacques Lacan II: The Ego in Freud's Theory and in the Technique of Psychoanalysis, 1954–55*, ed. Jacques-Alain Miller, trans. Sylvana Tomaselli, New York, W. W. Norton, 1988, p. 325.

7   Lacan develops the 'schema L' in the following texts: 'On a Question Prior to any Possible Treatment of Psychosis', in *Écrits: A Selection*, p. 183; *Seminar II*, pp. 321–6; *The Seminar of Jacques Lacan III: The Psychoses, 1955–56*, ed. Jacques-Alain Miller, trans. Russell Grigg, New York, W. W. Norton, 1993, pp. 13–15, 161–2 [eds].

8   Jacques Lacan, 'Seminar on "The Purloined Letter"', trans. Jeffrey Mehlman, in *The Purloined Poe: Lacan, Derrida and Psychoanalytic Reading*, ed. John P. Muller and William J. Richardson, Baltimore, Johns Hopkins University Press, 1988, pp. 28–9.

9   Lacan, *Seminar II*, 168.

10 Jacques Lacan, *The Seminar of Jacques Lacan I: Freud's Papers on Technique, 1953–54*, ed. Jacques-Alain Miller, trans. John Forrester, Cambridge, Cambridge University Press, 1988, pp. 242–3.

11 Lacan, *Seminar II*, p. 326.

12 Jacques Lacan, *The Seminar of Jacques Lacan VII: The Ethics of Psychoanalysis, 1959–60*, ed. Jacques-Alain Miller, trans. Dennis Porter, London and New York, Routledge, 1992, pp. 209–12 [eds].

13 Sigmund Freud, 'Inhibitions, Symptoms and Anxiety', in *The Penguin Freud Library, 10: On Psychopathology*, ed. and trans. James Strachey, Harmondsworth, Penguin, 1979, p. 274.

14 See G. W. F. Hegel, *Phenomenology of Spirit*, trans. A. V. Miller, Oxford, Oxford University Press, 1977, p. 402.

15 G. W. F. Hegel, *The Encyclopedia of Logic: Part I of the Encyclopedia of Philosophical Sciences with the Zusätze*, trans. T. F. Geraets, W. A. Suchting and H. S. Harris, Indianapolis, Hackett, 1991, p. 286.

3 'The Most Sublime of Hysterics': Hegel with Lacan

1. THE LACK IN THE OTHER

It would be a complete misunderstanding of the dialectical relationship between Knowledge and Truth if this relationship were viewed as a progressive approximation whereby the subject, driven by the operation of Truth, passes from one figure of knowledge (having proved its 'falsity', its insufficiency) to another that is much closer to the Truth, etc., until a final agreement between knowledge and Truth is achieved in the form of Absolute Knowledge. From this perspective, Truth is conceived of as a substantial entity, an In-Itself, and the dialectical process is reduced to a simple, asymptotic movement, a progressive approximation to the Truth, in the sense of Victor Hugo's famous saying: 'Science is an asymptote of Truth. It ever approaches but never touches it.' On the contrary, the Hegelian coincidence of the movement toward truth with truth itself implies that *there already has been contact with the truth*: truth itself must change with the changing of knowledge, which is to say that, once knowledge no longer corresponds to truth, we must not merely adjust knowledge accordingly but rather transform both poles – the insufficiency of knowledge, its lack apropos of the truth, radically indicates a lack, a non-achievement at the heart of truth itself.

We should thus abandon the standard notion that the dialectical process advances by moving from particular (limited and 'unilateral') elements toward some final totality: in fact, the truth at which one arrives is not 'complete' [*n'est pas 'toute'*]; the question remains open, but is transposed into a question addressed to the Other. Lacan's formula that Hegel is 'the most sublime of hysterics'[1] should be interpreted along these lines: the hysteric, by his very questioning, 'burrows a hole in the Other'; his desire is experienced precisely as the

Other's desire. Which is to say, the hysterical subject is fundamentally a subject who poses himself a question all the while presupposing that the Other has the key to the answer, that the Other knows the secret. But this question posed to the Other is in fact resolved, in the dialectical process, by a reflexive turn – namely, by regarding the question as *its own answer*.

Take an example from Adorno:[2] today, it is impossible to find a single definition of society; it is always a matter of a multitude of definitions that are more or less contradictory, even exclusive (for example, on the one hand there are those who conceive of society as an organic Whole that transcends particular individuals, and on the other those who conceive of society as a relationship between atomized individuals – 'organicism' versus 'individualism'). At first glance, these contradictions would seem to block any knowledge of society 'in itself', so that whoever presupposes society as a 'thing in itself' can only approach it by way of a multitude of partial, relative conceptions that are incapable of grasping it. The dialectical turn takes place when this very contradiction becomes the answer: the different definitions of society do not function as an obstacle, but are inherent to the 'thing itself'; they become indicators of actual social contradictions – the antagonism between society as an organic Whole as opposed to atomized individuals is not simply gnoseological; *it is the fundamental antagonism which constitutes the very thing that one wants to comprehend*. Here is the fundamental wager of the Hegelian strategy: 'inappropriateness as such' (in our case, that of opposing definitions) 'gives away the secret' [*l'inappropriation comme telle fait tomber le secret'*][3] – whatever presents itself initially as an obstacle becomes, in the dialectical turn, the very proof that we have made contact with the truth. We are thus thrust into the thing by that which appears to obscure it, that which suggests that 'the thing itself' is hidden, constituted around some lack. Examples of such a paradoxical logic in which the problem functions as its own solution are plentiful in the work of Lacan; besides 'The Subversion of the Subject and the Dialectic of Desire in the Freudian Unconscious', recall two other passages in which Lacan responds to his critics:

– in 'Science and Truth', Lacan comments on the confusion expressed by Laplanche and Leclaire concerning the problem of 'double inscription', a confusion whereby they 'could have read its solution in their split over how to approach the problem'.[4]

– in *Encore*, the response of Lacan to Nancy and Lacoue-Labarthe, who reproach him for the inconsequentiality of his theory of the signifier:

> Beginning with what distinguishes me from Saussure, and what made me, as they say, distort him, we proceed, little by little, to the impasse I designate concerning analytic discourse's approach to truth and its paradoxes ... It is as if it were precisely upon reaching the impasse to which my discourse is designed to lead them that they considered their work done ...[5]

In both cases, Lacan's procedure is the same: he calls attention to a sort of perspectival error. That which his critics perceive as a problem, an impasse, a matter of inconsequence, a contradiction, is in itself already a solution. One is even tempted to see here an elementary form of the Lacanian refutation of critique: your formulation of the problem already contains its very solution. It is precisely *here*, rather than in those explicit references to Hegel, that Lacan's 'Hegelian' dimension should be sought!

We are dealing with the same structure – that of the logic of the question that acts as its own response – in the well-known *Witz* of Rabinovitch: in a first moment, we are confronted with a problem, and our objection is invalidated by the objection of our adversary; but in a second moment, this very objection is revealed as the true argument.[6] Hegel himself cites, in his *Philosophy of History*, the good French saying: 'In pushing away the truth, one embraces it',[7] which suggests a paradoxical space in which the essence of 'the thing itself' encounters its exteriority. This structure is illustrated, in its most elementary form, by the famous Hegelian witticism that the secrets of the Egyptians are secrets for the Egyptians themselves: the solution of the enigma is its redoubling, the same enigma displaced onto the Other. The solution to the enigma consists in understanding it as a question that the Other poses to itself: it is even by that which appears at first to exclude us from the Other – our question by which we conceive of it as enigmatic, inaccessible, transcendental – that we rejoin the Other, precisely because the question becomes the question of the Other itself, *because substance becomes subject* (that which defines the subject, let us not forget, is precisely the question).

Would it not be possible to situate Hegelian 'de-alienation' as an element of Lacanian *separation*? Lacan defines separation as the overlapping of two lacks: when the subject encounters a lack in the Other, he responds with a prior lack, with his own lack.[8] If, in alienation, the subject is confronted with a full and substantial Other, supposedly hiding in its depths some 'secret', its inaccessible treasure, 'de-alienation' has nothing to do with an attainment of this secret: far from managing to penetrate right into the Other's hidden kernel, the subject simply experiences this 'hidden treasure' (*agalma*, the object-cause of desire) as *already missing from the Other itself*. 'De-alienation' is reduced to a gesture whereby the subject realizes that the secret of the substantial Other is also a secret for the Other – it is thus reduced precisely to the experience of a *separation* between the Other and its secret, *objet petit a*.

2. THE SYMBOLIC ACT

If the field of truth were not 'not-all', if the Other were not lacking, we would not be able to 'grasp subject as substance', and the subject would be merely an epiphenomenon, a secondary moment in the movement of substantial Truth: the subject is interior to substance precisely as its constitutive gap; it *is* this void, the impossibility around which the field of substantial Truth is structured. The response to the question, 'Why is error, illusion, immanent to truth? Why does truth arise through mistakes?', is therefore quite simply: *because substance is already subject*. Substance is always already subjectivized: substantial Truth coincides with its very progression through 'subjective' illusions. At this point, another response to the question 'Why is error immanent to the truth?' emerges: *because there is no metalanguage*. The idea that one is able from the outset to account for error, to take it under consideration *as error*, and therefore to take one's distance from it, is precisely the supreme error of the existence of metalanguage, the illusion that, while taking part in illusion, one is somehow also able to

observe the process from an 'objective' distance. By avoiding identifying oneself with error, we commit the supreme error and miss the
truth, because the place of truth itself is only constituted through
error. To put this another way, we could recall the Hegelian proposition which can be paraphrased as 'the fear of error is error itself': the
true evil is not the evil object but the one who perceives evil as such.

One already finds this logic of the error interior to truth in Rosa
Luxemburg's description of the dialectic of the revolutionary process.
When Eduard Bernstein raised objections apropos of the revisionist
fear of taking power 'too soon', prematurely, before the 'objective
conditions' have reached their maturity, she responded that the first
seizures of power are *necessarily* 'premature': for the proletariat, the
only way of arriving at 'maturity', of waiting for the 'opportune'
moment to seize power, is to form themselves, prepare themselves for
this seizure; and the only way of forming themselves is, of course, these
'premature' attempts ... If we wait for the 'opportune moment', we
will never attain it, because this 'opportune moment' – that which
never occurs without fulfilling the subjective conditions for the
'maturity' of the revolutionary subject – can only occur through a
series of 'premature' attempts. Thus the opposition to the 'premature'
seizure of power is exposed as an opposition to the seizure of power *in
general, as such*: to repeat the celebrated phrase of Robespierre, the
revisionists want 'revolution without revolution'.[9]

Once we examine things more closely, we see that Luxemburg's
fundamental wager is precisely the impossibility of a metalanguage in
the revolutionary process: the revolutionary subject does not 'conduct'
the process from an objective distance, he is himself constituted
through this process; and it is because the time of revolution occurs by
means of subjectivity that no one is able to 'achieve revolution on time
[*faire la révolution à temps*]', following 'premature', insufficient efforts.
The attitude of Luxemburg is exactly that of the hysteric faced with
the obsessional metalanguage of revisionism: strive to act, even if
prematurely, in order to arrive at the correct act through this very
error. One must be duped in one's desire, though it is ultimately
impossible, in order that something real comes about.

The propositions of 'grasping substance as subject' and 'there is no
metalanguage' are merely variations on the same theme. It is therefore

impossible to say: 'Although there must be premature attempts at revolution, have no illusions and remain conscious that they are doomed in advance to failure.' The idea that we are able to act and yet retain some distance with regard to the 'objective' – making possible some consideration of the act's 'objective signification' (namely, its destiny to fail) during the act itself – misperceives the way that the 'subjective illusion' of the agents is part of the 'objective' process itself. This is why the revolution must be repeated: the 'meaning' of those premature attempts is literally to be found in their failure – or rather, as one says with Hegel, 'a political revolution is, in general, only sanctioned by popular opinion after it has been repeated'.

The Hegelian theory of historical repetition (developed in his *Philosophy of History*) consists, in brief, in this: 'By repetition that which at first appeared merely a matter of chance and contingency becomes a real and ratified existence.'[10] Hegel develops this apropos of the death of Caesar: when Caesar consolidated his personal power, he acted 'objectively' (in itself) in relation to the historical truth that 'in the Republic . . . there was no longer any security; *that* could be looked for only in a single will'.[11] However, it is the Republic that still rules formally (for itself, in the 'opinion of the people') – the Republic 'is still alive only because it has forgotten that it is already dead', to paraphrase the Freudian dream of the father who did not know that he was dead. To this 'opinion' that still believes in the Republic, Caesar's action can only seem to be an arbitrary act, something accidental; it would appear to this opinion that, 'if this one individual were out of the way, the Republic would be *ipso facto* restored'.[12] However, it would be precisely the conspirators against Caesar who – conforming to the 'cunning of reason' – confirm the truth of Caesar: the final result of his murder would be the reign of Augustus, the first *caesar*. Thus, the truth emerges here from its very failure:

> The murder of Caesar, by completely missing its immediate goal, fulfilled the function it had, in a Machiavellian way, been assigned by history: to exhibit the truth of history in exposing its own non-truth.[13]

The whole problem of repetition is here: in this passage from Caesar – the name of a person – to *caesar* – the title of the Roman emperor.

The murder of Caesar – as historical persona – would produce, as its final result, the establishment of *caesarism*: the Caesar-persona repeats itself as caesar-title. But what is the reason, the 'drive [*mobile*]' behind this repetition? Paul-Laurent Assoun has developed in detail the double stakes of the Hegelian repetition: it signifies simultaneously the passage from contingency to necessity and the passage from unconscious substance to consciousness – in short, from the in-itself to the for-itself: 'The event that occurs only once seems by definition *incapable of occurring at all.*'[14] It seems, however, that Assoun interprets this conjunction in too 'mechanistic' a manner: as if it operates simply – by virtue of the event repeating itself – in being made up of 'two instances of the same general law',[15] which would attempt to convince 'popular opinion' of its necessity. At bottom, Assoun's interpretation is that the end of the Republic and the advent of imperial power was an objective necessity that asserted itself by its repetition. But Assoun's own formulation already belies this simplistic interpretation:

> It is in effect through *recognizing* an event that has already *occurred* that historical consciousness must experience the necessity of the generative process.[16]

If one reads literally here: the difference between the 'original' and its repetition is the intervention of the signifying network in which the event is inscribed. Initially, the event is experienced as a contingent trauma, as an eruption of the non-symbolized; it is only by passing through [*à travers*] repetition that it is 'recognized', which can only signify here: realized in the symbolic order. And this recognition-by-passing-through-repetition necessarily presupposes (much like Moses in Freud's analysis) a crime, an act of murder: Caesar must die as an 'empirical' person in order to be realized in his necessity, as the *title-holder* of power, precisely because the 'necessity' in question is a *symbolic* necessity.

It is not merely that the people 'need time to comprehend', or that the event in its initial form of appearance is too 'traumatic': the *misrecognition* of its first occurrence is 'inherent' to its symbolic necessity, and an immediate constituent of its recognition. To put this in its classical version: the first murder (the 'parricide' of Caesar) gives rise to a 'culpability', and it is this that 'supplies energy' to the repetition. The thing is not repeated because of some 'objective' necessity, 'independent of our subjective will' and in this way 'irresistible' – it is rather the 'culpability' itself that gives rise to the symbolic debt and thus initiates the compulsion to repeat. Repetition announces the emergence of the law, of the Name-of-the-Father instead of the assassinated father: the event that repeats itself retroactively receives, through its repetition, its law. To put this another way, we could conceptualize Hegelian repetition precisely as the passage from the 'lawless' to the 'law-like',[17] as the interpretive gesture par excellence (Lacan says somewhere that interpretation always proceeds under the sign of the Name-of-the-Father): the symbolic appropriation of the traumatic event.

Hegel has thus already succeeded in formulating the constitutive delay of the interpretive gesture: interpretation arrives only by repetition, while the event is incapable of becoming 'law-like' right from the start. We should connect this necessity of repetition to the famous preface to the *Philosophy of Right* on the owl of Minerva who is able to take flight only in the evening, after the fact.[18] Contrary to the Marxist critique which sees this as a sign of the impotence of the contemplative position of interpretation *post festum*, we should grasp this delay as inherent to the 'objective' process itself: the fact that 'popular opinion' sees the act of Caesar as something accidental and not as the manifestation of historical necessity is not a simple case of the 'delay of consciousness with regard to effectivity' – historical necessity itself, missed by 'opinion' during its initial appearance, mistaken for something arbitrary, *is only able to constitute itself, to achieve itself, by means of this mistake.*

There is a crucial distinction between this Hegelian position and the Marxist dialectic of the revolutionary process: for Rosa Luxemburg, the failures of premature attempts create the conditions for the final victory, while for Hegel, the dialectical reversal consists in the change of perspective whereby *failure as such* appears as victory – the symbolic act, the act precisely as symbolic, *succeeds in its very failure.* The Hegelian proposition that the 'true beginning only arrives at the end' should thus be understood in a literal fashion: the act – the 'thesis' – is necessarily 'premature'; it is a 'hypothesis' condemned to failure, and the dialectical reversal takes place when the failure of this 'thesis' – the 'antithesis' – reveals the true 'thesis'. 'Synthesis' is the 'signification' of the thesis emerging from its failure. All the same, Goethe had it right, as opposed to Scripture [Écriture]: in the beginning was the act;[19] the act implies a constitutive blunder, it misses, it 'falls into a void'; and the original gesture of *symbolization* is to posit this pure expenditure as something positive, to experience the loss as a process which opens up a free space, which 'lets things be'.

This is why the standard reproach – according to which Hegelian dialectics reduces the procedure to its purely logical structure, omitting the contingency of delays and overtakings, all the massive weight and inertia of the real which troubles and spoils the dialectical game, that is, which does not allow itself to be absorbed in the movement of *Aufhebung* – completely misses the point: this game of delays and overtaking is included in the dialectical process, not merely on the accidental, non-essential level, but absolutely as its central component. The dialectical process always takes the paradoxical form of over-taking/delay, the form of the reversal of a 'not yet' into an 'always already', of a 'too soon' and an 'after the fact' – its true motor is the structural impossibility of a 'right moment', the irreducible difference between a thing and its 'proper time'. Initially, the 'thesis' arrives by definition too soon to attain its proper identity, and it can only realize 'itself', become 'itself', after the fact, retroactively, by means of its repetition in the 'synthesis'.

3. '… THIS INTEGRAL VOID THAT IS ALSO CALLED THE SACRED'

Let us be precise: it is not a matter of understanding the link between the failure of the act and its symbolization by reducing it to an alleged 'imaginary compensation' ('when the act, the effective intervention into reality, fails, one attempts to make up for this loss by a symbolic compensation, in keeping with the deeper meaning [*signification profonde*] of such events') – for example, when the powerless victim of natural forces divinizes them, understands them as personified spiritual forces ... In such a rapid passage from the act to its 'deeper meaning', we miss the intermediate articulation which is the essence of its symbolization: the very moment of defeat, before it is redeemed by an 'imaginary compensation' and one obtains a 'deeper meaning', becomes in itself a positive gesture, a moment that would be defined by the distinction between the *Symbolic* in the strict sense and what one calls 'symbolic signification', or simply the *symbolic order*.

Normally, we pass directly from the real to the symbolic order: a thing is either itself, self-identical in the inertia of its bare presence, or else it possesses a 'symbolic signification'. So where does the Symbolic fit? It is necessary to introduce the crucial distinction between 'symbolic signification' and its own place, the empty place filled by signification: the Symbolic is above all a place, a place that was originally empty and subsequently filled with the bric-a-brac of the symbolic order. The crucial dimension of the Lacanian concept of the Symbolic is this logical priority, the precedence of the (empty) place with respect to the elements that fill it: before being a collection of 'symbols', bearers of some 'signification', the Symbolic is a differential network structured around an empty, traumatic place, described by Lacan as that of *das Ding*, the 'sacred' place of impossible *jouissance*.[20] As he demonstrates apropos of the vase, with reference to Heidegger, *das Ding* is above all an empty place surrounded by a signifying articulation – an empty place filled up by whatever one wants, right up to Jungian 'archetypes'. This priority of the 'sacred' as an empty place in relation to its content has already been emphasized by Hegel:

> [I]n order, then, that in this *complete void* [*in diesen so* ganz Leeren], which is even called the *holy of holies*, there may yet be something, we must fill it up with reveries [Träumereien], *appearances*, produced by consciousness itself ... since even reveries are better than its own emptiness.[21]

This is why the Hegelian 'loss of the loss' is definitively not the return to a full identity, lacking nothing [*sans perte*]: the 'loss of the loss' is the moment in which loss ceases to be the loss *of* 'something' and becomes the opening of the empty place that the object ('something') can occupy, the moment in which the empty place is conceived as prior to that which fills it – the loss opens up a space for the appearance of the object. In the 'loss of the loss', the loss *remains* a loss, it is not 'cancelled' in the ordinary sense: the regained 'positivity' is that of the loss as such, the experience of loss as a 'positive', indeed 'productive', condition.

Would it not be possible to define the final moment of the analytic process, the *passe*, as precisely this experience of the 'positive' character of loss, of the original void filled by the dazzling and fascinating experience of the fantasmatic object, the experience that the object as such, in its fundamental dimension, is the positivization of a void? Is this not the traversing of the fantasy [*la traversée du fantasme*], this experience of the priority of place in relation to the fantasmatic object, in the moment when, recalling the formula of Mallarmé, 'nothing takes place but the place [*rien n'aura eu lieu que le lieu*]'?

The desire of the analyst (insofar as it is 'pure' desire) is consequently not a particular desire (for example, the desire of interpretation, the desire to reveal the analysand's symptomal knot by way of interpretation), but – according to the Kantian formulation – quite simply non-pathological desire, a desire which is not tied to any fantasmatic 'pathological' object, but which is supported only by the empty place in the Other.

This is why it is so important clearly to distinguish the *passe* from any 'resignation' or 'assent to renunciation'; according to such a reading, analysis would be finished once the analysand 'accepts symbolic castration', when they resign themselves to the necessity of a radical Loss as part of their condition as a speaking-being [*parlêtre*] . . . Such a reading makes of Lacan a kind of 'sage' preaching a 'fundamental renunciation'. At first glance, such a reading would appear well founded: is not fantasy, in the last resort, the fantasy that the sexual relationship is ultimately possible, fully achievable; and would not the end of analysis, the traversing of the fantasy, be precisely the equivalent of the experience of the impossibility of the sexual relationship, and thus the irreducibly discordant, blocked, deficient character of the 'human condition'? But this reading is empty: if one adopts as the fundamental ethical rule of analysis 'not to concede one's desire [*ne pas céder sur son désir*]'[22] – from which it follows that the symptom is, as Jacques-Alain Miller emphasizes, precisely a specific mode of the 'conceding one's desire' – one must define the *passe* as the moment in which the subject takes upon themselves their desire in its pure, 'non-pathological' state, beyond its historicity/ hystericity [*son historicité/hystéricité*] – the exemplary case of the 'post-analytic' subject is not the dubious figure of the 'sage' but that of Oedipus at Colonnus, a rancorous old man who demands everything but renounces nothing! If the traversing of the fantasy overlaps with the experience of any lack, *it is the lack of the Other* and not that of the subject themselves: in the *passe*, the subject gets proof that the *agalma*, the 'hidden treasure', is already wanting in the Other; this object is separate from the point of symbolic identification [*l'objet se sépare de l'I*], from the signifying trait in the Other. After locating the subject in relation to *objet a*,

> the experience of the fundamental fantasy becomes the drive. What, then, does he who has passed through the experience of this opaque relation to the origin, to the drive, become? How can a subject who has traversed the radical fantasy experience the drive? This is the beyond of analysis, and has never been approached. Up to now, it has been approachable only at the level of the analyst, in as much as it would be required of him to have specifically traversed the cycle of the analytic experience in its totality.[23]

Is not Hegel's 'Absolute Knowledge', this incessant pulsation, this traversing of a path already taken repeated to infinity, the exemplary case of how 'to live out the drive [*vivre la pulsion*]' once history/hysteria is over? It is therefore not surprising that Lacan, in Chapter XIV of *Seminar XI*, articulates the circuit of the drive in terms that directly evoke the Hegelian distinction between 'finite' and 'infinite' ends. Lacan recalls the difference, distinctive to the English language, between *aim* and *goal*: '*The aim* is the way taken [*le trajet*]. The end [*le but*] has a different term in English, *goal*.'[24] The circuit of the drive is perhaps best defined as the pulsation [*la pulsation*] between *goal* and *aim*: initially, the drive is on the path towards a certain goal; subsequently, this goal coincides with the experience of the path itself, whose 'aim is nothing else but the return of this circuit'[25] – in short, the true end ('infinite', *aim*) achieves itself by traversing its incessant failure to achieve the 'finite' end (*goal*); in the very failure to achieve our intended goal, the true aim is always already achieved.

4. DIFFERENTIATING 'ABSOLUTE KNOWLEDGE'

'Absolute Knowledge' is undeniably not a position of 'omniscience', in which, ultimately, the subject 'knows everything'; we must first take into consideration the exact point at which it emerges in Hegel: at the end of the 'phenomenology of the spirit', the point where consciousness 'de-fetishizes' itself and, through this, becomes capable of knowing the truth, knowing the place of truth, and thus capable of 'science' in the Hegelian sense. As such, 'Absolute Knowledge' is only a 'that is to say [*scilicet*]', a 'you are permitted to know', which opens up a place for the advance of science (logic, etc.).

What does the fetish represent, in the final analysis? It is an object that fills the constitutive lack in the Other, the empty place of 'primary repression', the place where the signifier must of necessity be lacking in order for the signifying network to articulate itself; in this sense, 'de-fetishization' is equivalent to the experience of this constitutive lack, which is to say, of the Other as barred. It is perhaps for this reason that 'de-fetishization' is all the more difficult to achieve because the fetish reverses the standard relationship between the 'sign' and the 'thing': we usually understand the 'sign' as something that represents, that replaces the absent object, whereas the fetish is an object, a thing that replaces the missing 'sign'. It is easy to detect absence, the structure of signifying deferrals, when one expects the full presence of a thing, but it is more difficult to detect the inert presence of an object when one expects to find 'signs', the game of representational deferrals, traces ... This is why we are able clearly to distinguish Lacan from any tradition called 'post-structuralist', whose objective is to 'deconstruct' the 'metaphysics of presence': to denounce full presence, detecting there the traces of absence, dissolving fixed identity amidst a bundle of deferrals and traces ... Lacan is here much closer to Kafka: it is, of course, well known that Kafka is a 'writer of absence', describing a world that remains religious in its structure but in which the central place belonging to God is empty; however, it remains to be demonstrated how this Absence itself conceals an inert, nightmarish presence, that of an obscene Superegoic object, the 'Supreme-Being-in-Evilness [*Être-Suprême-en-Méchanceté*]'.[26]

It is from this perspective that we would need to reinterpret the two characteristics of Absolute Knowledge that may, at first glance, possess an 'idealist' association: Absolute Knowledge as the 'abolition of the object', the suppression of objectivity as opposed to or outside of the subject; and Absolute Knowledge as the abolition of the Other (understood here as the dependence of the subject vis-à-vis an instance in relation to which he is exterior and decentred). The Hegelian 'sublation of the Other' does not equate either to a fusion of the subject with its Other, or to the appropriation, on the part of the subject, of any substantial content; it is rather a specifically Hegelian way of saying that 'the Other does not exist' (Lacan), in other words, that the Other does not exist as the Guarantor of Truth, as the Other of the Other, and thus this statement posits the lack in the Other, the Other as barred. It is in this hole within [*au sein de*] the substantial Other that the subject must recognize its place: the subject is interior to the substantial Other insofar as it is identified with an obstruction in the Other, with the impossibility of achieving its identity by means of self-closure [*close avec lui-même*]. The 'abolition of the object', in turn, represents the flip-side: it is not a fusion of the subject and the object into a subject-object, but rather a radical shift in the status of the object itself – the object here neither conceals nor fills the hole in the Other. Such is the post-fantasmatic relationship with the object: the object is 'abolished', 'suppressed', it loses its fascinating aura. That which at first dazzles us with its charm is exposed as a sticky and disgusting remainder, the gift given 'is changed inexplicably into a gift of shit'.[27]

Apropos of Joyce, Lacan has stressed that he had very good reason for refusing analysis (the condition stipulated by a wealthy American patron in exchange for financial support); he had no need of it because, in his artistic practice, he had already attained the subjective position corresponding to the final moment in analysis, as is evident, for example, in his celebrated play on words *letter/litter* – that is to say, the transformation of the object of desire into shit, the post-fantasmatic relationship to the object.[28] In the field of philosophy,

Hegelian Absolute Knowledge – and perhaps only Hegelian Absolute Knowledge – designates the same subjective position, that of the traversing of the fantasy, the post-fantasmatic relationship to the object, the experience of the lack in the Other. Perhaps the unique status of Hegelian Absolute Knowledge is due to the question that can be posed to proponents of the so-called 'post-Hegelian inversion',[29] whether the likes of Marx or Schelling: is this 'inversion' not, in the last resort, a flight in the face of the unbearability of the Hegelian procedure? The price of their 'inversion' seems to be a reading of Hegel that is totally blind to the dimension evoked by the traversing of the fantasy and the lack in the Other: in this reading, Absolute Knowledge becomes the culminating moment of so-called 'idealist panlogicism', against which one is able, of course, to affirm without any problem the 'process of effective life'.

One usually understands Absolute Knowledge as the fantasy of a full discourse, without fault or discord, the fantasy of an Identity inclusive of all divisions, whereas our reading, by way of contrast, sees in Absolute Knowledge the exact opposite of this, the dimension of the *traversing* of the fantasy. The defining trait of Absolute Knowledge is not a finally achieved Identity where for 'finite consciousness' there is only division (between the subject and the object, knowledge and truth, etc.), but rather the experience of distance, *separation*, where for 'finite consciousness' there is only fusion and identity (between *objet a* and the Other). Absolute Knowledge, far from filling the lack sensed by 'finite consciousness' separated from the Absolute, transfers this lack into the Other itself. The twist introduced by Absolute Knowledge thus concerns the very status of lack: the 'finite', 'alienated' consciousness suffers from the loss of the object, while 'de-alienation' consists of the realization that this object *was lost from the beginning*, and that any given object is simply an attempt to fill in the empty place of this loss.

The 'loss of loss' marks the point at which the subject recognizes the priority of the loss over the object: in the course of the dialectical process, the subject always loses anew that which it never possessed, while it continues to succumb to the necessary illusion that 'it would otherwise possess it'. This illusion – according to which Absolute Knowledge would be the name given to the complete correspondence of subject and object, knowledge and truth, that is to say, the name of the filling of a lack in an absolute identity which suppresses all differences – is sustained by a perspectival error entirely homologous with the interpretation that understands the end of analytic process, which is the emergence of a non-relationship [*non-rapport*], as the establishment of a complete genital sexual relationship, which is the exact opposite of its actual end:

> It is a fact that psychoanalysis is not able to produce the sexual relationship. Freud despaired over it. The post-Freudians have engaged themselves in finding its remedy by elaborating a genital formula. Even Lacan took note of it: the end of the analytic process does not hinge on the emergence of the sexual relationship. Instead, it depends entirely on the emergence of the non-relationship ... At this point, the end of analysis is resolved in a manner that formerly would have been unthinkable, rejected as pre-genital by the post-Freudian trend: to remain confined to the level of the object ... The object is not what prevents the advent of the sexual relationship, as a perspectival error would have us believe. The object is on the contrary that which fills a relationship that does not exist, and gives it its fantasmatic consistency ... From now on, the end of analysis as such assumes an encounter with absence through the traversing of the fantasy and the separation from the object.[30]

The pre-genital object is the very thing that, by its inert fantasmatic presence, obstructs entry into the full, mature, genital sexual relationship, thus concealing, by the sheer weight of its presence, the fundamental obstacle, the void of the impossibility of the sexual relationship: far from concealing another presence, it instead distracts us, by its presence, from the *place* that it fills. But where does this perspectival error come from? From the fact that *the void is strictly consubstantial with the very movement of its concealment.* It is true that the fantasy *disguises* the void signified by the formula 'there is no sexual relationship', but at the same time it *stands in place of* [tient lieu] this void: the fantasmatic object conceals the gaping void *which is also sustained by it.*

And the same thing goes for the Hegelian object, the objectal figure-fetish: far from being a 'premature' figure of the true dialectical

synthesis, it disguises, by its 'non-dialectical', 'non-mediated' given-
ness, the impossibility of any final synthesis of the subject and the
object. To put it another way, the perspectival error consists in
thinking that at the end of the dialectical process, the subject *finally*
obtains that for which they are searching – the perspectival error is
here, because the Hegelian solution is not that they are not able to
obtain that for which they are searching, but that *they already possess*
that for which they are searching under the very form of its loss. The
formula proposed by Gérard Miller to mark the difference between
Marxism and psychoanalysis ('In Marxism, a man knows what he
wants and does not possess it; in psychoanalysis, a man does not know
what he wants and already possesses it') at the same time delineates
the distance between Hegel and Marxism, the blindness of Marxism to
the properly dialectical inversion of the impasse into the *passe*. The
passe as the final moment of the analytic process does not say that one
has finally resolved the impasse (the snaring of the unconscious in the
transference, for example), overcoming its obstacles – the *passe* can be
reduced to the retroactive experience that the impasse is already its
own 'resolution'. To put it another way, the *passe* is *exactly the same
thing as the impasse* (the impossibility of the sexual relationship), just
as the synthesis is exactly the same thing as the antithesis: what
changes is only the 'perspective', the position of the subject. In Lacan's
early seminars, one can nevertheless find a conception of Absolute
Knowledge that seems directly to contradict ours: Absolute Knowledge as the impossible ideal of attaining a definitive closure of the field
of discourse:

> Absolute knowledge is this moment in which the totality of
> discourse closes in on itself in a perfect non-contradiction, up to
> and including the fact that it posits, explains and justifies itself.
> We are some way from this ideal![31]

The reason is simply that Lacan does not yet have at his disposal
during this period any concept of the lack in the Other, nor does he
appreciate the way this is at work in Hegel: his problematic is here
that of symbolization-historicization, the symbolic realization of the
traumatic kernel, along with the non-integration of the subject into

the symbolic universe. For Lacan, therefore, the ideal end of analysis is to achieve a symbolization which reintegrates all traumatic ruptures within the symbolic field – an ideal incarnated in Hegelian Absolute Knowledge, but one whose true nature is instead Kantian: Absolute Knowledge is conceived as belonging to the species of the 'regulative idea', supposedly guiding the 'progress of the realization of the subject in the symbolic order':[32]

> That is the ideal of analysis, which, of course, remains virtual. There is never a subject without an ego, a fully realized subject, but that in fact is what one must aim to obtain from the subject in analysis.[33]

Against such a conception, one must insist on the decisive fact that Hegelian Absolute Knowledge *has absolutely nothing to do with some kind of ideal*: the specific twist of Absolute Knowledge comes about when one perceives that the field of the Other is already 'closed' *in on its own disorder*. To put it another way, the subject as barred is to be posited as *correlative* to the inert remainder which forms the obstacle to its full symbolic realization, to its full subjectivization: $\$ \diamond a$.

This is why, in the matheme for Absolute Knowledge [*savoir absolu (SA)*], the two terms must be barred – it works by the conjunction of $\$$ and $\cancel{A}$.

NOTES

This selection appeared in *Le plus sublime des hysteriques – Hegel passe*, trans. Our translation, Paris, Le point hors ligne, 1988, pp. 143–62 [eds].

1   See, e.g., Jacques Lacan, *Le Séminaire de Jacques Lacan XVII: L'envers de la psychoanalyse, 1969–70*, ed. Jacques-Alain Miller, Paris, Éditions du Seuil, 1991, p. 38 [eds].

2   See Theodor Adorno et al., *Aspects of Sociology*, trans. John Viertel, Boston, Beacon, 1972, pp. 23–33.

3   Jacques Lacan, 'The Subversion of the Subject and the Dialectic of Desire in the Freudian Unconscious', in *Écrits: A Selection*, trans. Bruce Fink, New York, W. W. Norton, 2002, p. 306. Translation modified [eds].

4   Jacques Lacan, 'Science and Truth', trans. Bruce Fink, *Newsletter of the Freudian Field*, 3, 1989, p. 13.

5   Jacques Lacan, *The Seminar of Jacques Lacan XX: On Feminine Sexuality, the Limits of Love and Knowledge, 1972–73 (Encore)*, ed. Jacques-Alain Miller, trans. Bruce Fink, New York, W. W. Norton, 1998, p. 65.

6   In the opening paragraph of *For They Know Not What They Do: Enjoyment as a Political Factor* (London and New York, Verso, 1991), Žižek tells the joke about Rabinovitch, 'a Jew who wants to emigrate. The bureaucrat at the emigration office asks him why. Rabinovitch answers: "There are two reasons why. The first is that I'm afraid that the Communists will lose power in the Soviet Union, and the new forces will blame us Jews for the Communist crimes ..." "But," interrupts the bureaucrat, "this is pure nonsense, the power of the Communists will last for ever!" "Well," responds Rabinovitch calmly, "that's my second reason."' The same joke also appears in *The Puppet and the Dwarf: The Perverse Core of Christianity* (Cambridge MA, MIT Press, 2003), p. 77 [eds].

7   G. W. F. Hegel, *Philosophy of History*, trans. J. Sibree, New York, Dover Publications, 1956, p. 355 [eds].

8   Jacques Lacan, *The Seminar of Jacques Lacan XI: The Four Fundamental Concepts of Psycho-Analysis, 1964*, ed. Jacques-Alain Miller, trans. Alan Sheridan, New York, W. W. Norton, 1977, p. 204.

9   See Rosa Luxemburg, *Social Reform or Revolution*, 2nd edn, trans. Integer, New York, Pathfinder Press, 1973.

10   Hegel, *Philosophy of History*, p. 313 [eds].

11   *Ibid.*, p. 312 [eds].

12   *Ibid.*, p. 313 [eds].

13   Paul-Laurent Assoun, *Marx et la répétition historique*, Paris, Presses Universitaires de France, 1978, p. 68.

14   *Ibid.*, pp. 69–70.

15   *Ibid.*, p. 70.

16   *Ibid.*, p. 70.

17   See Jacques-Alain Miller, 'Algorithmes de psychoanalyse', *Ornicar?*, 16, 1978.

18   G. W. F. Hegel, *Elements of the Philosophy of Right*, ed. Allen W. Wood, trans. H. B. Nisbet, Cambridge, Cambridge University Press, 1991, p. 23 [eds].

19   Žižek is referring here to the line from Goethe's *Faust* (Part I, Scene 3) – 'in the beginning was the Deed [*Im Anfang war die Tat*]' – with which Freud also concludes his 'Totem and Taboo: Some Points of Agreement between the Mental Lives of Savages and Neurotics', in *The Penguin Freud Library, 13: The Origins of Religion*, ed. and trans. James Strachey, Harmondsworth, Penguin, 1985, p. 224 [eds].

20   Jacques Lacan, *The Seminar of Jacques Lacan VII: The Ethics of Psychoanalysis, 1959–60*, ed. Jacques-Alain Miller, trans. Dennis Porter, London and New York, Routledge, 1992, pp. 119–20, 129–30 [eds].

21   G. W. F. Hegel, *Phenomenology of Spirit*, trans. A.V. Miller, Oxford, Oxford University Press, 1977, pp. 88–9.

22   Lacan, *Seminar VII*, pp. 319–21. Dennis Porter renders the phrase *ne pas céder sur son désir* as 'giving ground relative to one's desire'. Bruce Fink, alternatively, opts for 'not to give up on his or her desire' or 'not to give in when it comes to his or her desire', in the sense that the analysand must not 'let the Other's desire take precedence over his or her own'. See his *A Clinical Introduction to Lacanian Psychoanalysis: Theory and Practice*, Cambridge MA, Harvard University Press, 1997, p. 206 [eds].

23   Lacan, *Seminar XI*, pp. 273–4.

24   *Ibid.*, p. 179 Translation modified [eds].

25   *Ibid.*, p. 179.

26   Lacan refers to this precise expression from Sade in his *Seminar VII*, p. 215, and again in 'Kant avec Sade', in *Écrits II*, Paris: Éditions du Seuil, 1966, p. 251. See also Chapter 6 of this volume, 'The Limits of the Semiotic Approach to Psychoanalysis', p. 135 [eds].

27   Lacan, *Seminar XI*, p. 268.

28   I owe this formulation to Jacques-Alain Miller.

29   Žižek seems to be referring here to Louis Althusser's well-known rejection of a Marxist 'inversion' [*renversement*] of the Hegelian dialectic in his 'On the Materialist Dialectic: On the Unevenness

of Origins', in *For Marx*, trans. Ben Brewster, London and New York, Verso, 1969, 161–218 [eds].

30   Jacques-Alain Miller, 'D'un autre Lacan', *Ornicar?* 28, 1984, pp. 51–2. Žižek cites a portion of this same passage in *Enjoy Your Symptom! Jacques Lacan in Hollywood and Out*, London and New York, Routledge, 1992, p. 89 [eds].

31   Jacques Lacan, *The Seminar of Jacques Lacan I: Freud's Papers on Technique, 1953–54*, ed. Jacques-Alain Miller, trans. John Forrester, Cambridge, Cambridge University Press, 1988, p. 264.

32   Jacques Lacan, *The Seminar of Jacques Lacan II: The Ego in Freud's Theory and in the Technique of Psychoanalysis, 1954–55*, ed. Jacques-Alain Miller, trans. Sylvana Tomaselli, New York, W. W. Norton, 1988, p. 319.

33   *Ibid.*, p. 246.

4 Connections of the Freudian Field to Philosophy and Popular Culture

I would like to begin with an almost narcissistic reflection. Why do I resort so often to examples from popular culture? The simple answer is in order to avoid a kind of jargon, and to achieve the greatest possible clarity, not only for my readers but also for myself. That is to say, the idiot for whom I endeavour to formulate a theoretical point as clearly as possible is ultimately myself: I am not patronizing my readers. An example from popular culture has for me the same fundamental role as the Lacanian procedure of *passe* – the passage of analysand into the analyst; the same role as the two mediators, the two *passeurs*. I think it's not an accident that the Lacanian popular quarterly in France, as you probably know, is called *L'âne* – the Donkey. The idea is that in a way you must accept a total externalization: you must renounce even the last bit of any kind of initiated closed circuit of knowledge. And precisely this is for me the role of my reference to popular culture. In this full acceptance of the externalization in an imbecilic medium, in this radical refusal of any initiated secrecy, this is how I, at least, understand the Lacanian ethics of finding a proper worth.

I think that the way I refer to popular culture, this necessity that I feel that we must go through this radical, if you want, imbecilic, external medium, is a version of what Lacan, in his last phase at least, referred to as the 'subjective destitution' that is involved in the position of the analyst, of the analyst as occupying the place of the *objet petit a*. This position, I think, is far more radical and paradoxical than it may appear.

Let me illustrate it by an example in rather bad taste, a story from the American South before the Civil War. I read in some novel by James Baldwin, I think, that in the whore houses of the old South, of the old New Orleans before the Civil War, the African-American, the black servant, was not perceived as a person, so that, for example, the white couple – the prostitute and her client – were not at all disturbed when the servant entered the room to deliver drinks. They simply went on doing their job, with copulation and so on, since the servant's gaze did not count as the gaze of another person. And in a sense, I think, it is the same with that black servant as with the analyst.

We rid ourselves of all our shame when we talk to the analyst. We are able to confide the innermost secrets of our loves, our hatreds, etc., although our relationship to them is entirely impersonal, lacking the intimacy of true friendship. This is absolutely crucial, I think. The relationship with the analyst, as you probably know, is not an inter-subjective relationship precisely because the analyst in the analytic disposition is not another subject. In this sense, the analyst occupies the role of an object. We can confide ourselves in them without any intimate relationship of friendship.

Another aspect of this subjective destitution can be grasped via a reference to the recently published autobiography, already translated into English, of Louis Althusser.[1] Althusser writes that he was beset all his adult life with the notion that he did not exist: by the fear that others would become aware of his non-existence, that others, for example readers of his books, would become aware of the fact that he is an impostor who only feigns to exist. For example, his great anxiety after the publication of *Lire Capital* [*Reading Capital*] was that some critic would reveal the scandalous fact that the main author of this book doesn't exist.[2] I think, in a sense, that this is what psycho-analysis is about. The psychoanalytic cure is effectively over when the subject loses this anxiety, as it were, and freely assumes their own non-existence.

And I think that here, if you want to put it in a slightly funny, cynical way, resides the difference between psychoanalysis and, let's say, the standard English empiricist-subjectivist solipsism. The stand-ard empiricist-solipsist notion is that we can only be absolutely certain of ideas in our mind, whereas the existence of reality outside is already an inconclusive inference. I think that psychoanalysis claims that reality outside myself definitely exists. The problem is that I myself do not exist.

Now, my next point, of course, is that Lacan arrived at this paradoxical position only towards the end of his teaching. Before this last phase, in the 1950s and 1960s, the end of the psychoanalytic process for Lacan involved almost exactly the opposite movement – the subjectivization, subjective realization, subjective accomplishment, the subjectivizing of one's destiny, etc. So we have this radical shift: one of the series of shifts in Lacan.

So, in this subjective destitution, in accepting my non-existence as subject, I have to renounce the fetish of the hidden treasure responsible for my unique worth. I have to accept my radical externalization in the symbolic medium. As is well known, the ultimate support of what I experience as the uniqueness of my personality is provided by my fundamental fantasy, by this absolutely particular, non-universalizable formation.

Now, what's the problem with fantasy? I think that the key point, usually overlooked, is the way that Lacan articulated the notion of fantasy which is, 'OK, fantasy stages a desire, but whose desire?' My point is: not the subject's desire, not their own desire. What we encounter in the very core of the fantasy formation is the relationship to the desire of the Other: to the opacity of the Other's desire. The desire staged in fantasy, in my fantasy, is precisely not my own, not mine, but the desire of the Other. Fantasy is a way for the subject to answer the question of what object they are for the Other, in the eyes of the Other, for the Other's desire. That is to say, what does the Other see in them? What role do they play in the Other's desire?

A child, for example, endeavours to dissolve, by way of their fantasy, the enigma of the role they play as the medium of interactions between their mother, their father, all their relatives, etc.: the enigma of how mother, father and others fight their battles, settle their accounts through them. This is, I think, the crucial point that, for example, a child experiences their situation as a series of obvious investments in them. Parents fight their battles through them, but it is not clear to them what their role is in this complex, intersubjective network into which they are thrown. And precisely through fantasy they try to clarify this point. Not, 'What is their desire?' but, 'What is their role in the desire of the Other?' This is, I think, absolutely crucial, which is why, as you probably know, in Lacan's graph of desire, fantasy comes as an answer to that question beyond the level of meaning, 'What do you want?', precisely as an answer to the enigma of the Other's desire.[3] Here, again, I think we must be very precise.

Everybody knows this phrase, repeated again and again, 'Desire is the desire of the Other.' But I think that to each crucial stage of Lacan's teaching a different reading of this well-known formula corresponds. First, already in the 1940s, 'Desire is the desire of the Other' alludes simply to the paranoiac structure of desire, to the structure of envy, to put it simply. Here, the desire of the subject is the desire of the Other; it is simply this kind of transitive, imaginary relationship. It's basically the structure of envy – I desire an object only insofar as it is desired by the Other, and so on. This is the first level, let us say the imaginary level.

Then we have the symbolic level where 'Desire is the desire of the Other' involves this dialectic of the recognition and, at the same time, the fact that what I desire is determined by the symbolic network within which I articulate my subjective position, and so on. So it is simply the determination of my desire: the way my desire is structured through the order of the big Other. This is well known.

But I think Lacan's crucial final formulation arrives only when the position of the analyst is no longer defined as starting from the place of the big Other (A), that is to say, the analyst as embodiment of symbolic order, but when the analyst is identified with the small other (a), with the fantasmatic object. In other words, when the analyst gives body to the enigma of the impenetrability of the Other's desire. Here, 'Desire is the desire of the Other' means I can arrive at my desire only through the complication of the Other's desire precisely insofar as this desire is impenetrable, enigmatic for me. I think this is the first crucial point, usually forgotten, about fantasy: how true fantasy is an attempt to resolve the enigma of the Other's desire. That's the desire that is staged in fantasy. It's not simply that I desire something, that I make a fantasy. No.

Another point seems to me crucial, apropos of the notion of fantasy. A very naïve, almost, I'm tempted to say, pre-theoretical observation – but I found it interesting enough – is how not only in

Lacan but generally in psychoanalysis (as is the case, by the way, with the whole series of Lacanian notions) the concept of fantasy is a nice case of the dialectical coincidence of opposites: namely, does not the notion of fantasy designate almost two opposites?

On the one hand, it is, let's call it naïvely, the blissful, beatific aspect of fantasy. You know, fantasy, as, let's say, some kind of idea of an idealized state without disturbances, etc. For example, in politics, the corporatist, usually totalitarian fantasy of society as an organic body in which all members collaborate, etc. This is a kind of beatific, harmonious site of fantasy. Or, to put it naïvely, in private life, fantasy as fantasy of the successful sexual relationship, etc.

But, on the other hand, there is another aspect no less radical and original: the notion of fantasy which is the exact opposite, which is precisely fantasy whose fundamental form is jealousy. Not beatific, blissful fantasy but the dirty fantasy. For example, when you are jealous you are all the time bothered by, 'How is the other treating me?', 'How are they enjoying themselves?', etc. My point being that if there is something to be learned from the so-called (and I'm developing here notions at a very elementary level) totalitarian ideologies, it is precisely that these two notions of fantasy are two sides of the same coin. That the price you must pay for sticking, clinging to the first fantasy is the second, dirty fantasy.

It's not an accident that (and I'm reasoning in a very naïve way here) those political systems that cling to the fantasy in the sense of some harmonious society – for example, in Nazism, of a 'community of the people', etc., or, in Stalinism, building 'new men', a new harmonious socialist society – in order to maintain this fantasy, had, at the same time, to develop to the extreme the other fantasy: obsession with the Jewish blood, obsession with traitors, with what the other is doing, etc. So what is crucial, I think, is that the fantasy is necessarily split in this way. I am tempted to say that with fantasy it is almost the way it is with ideology: there are always two fantasies.

What do I mean by this reference to ideology? What is absolutely crucial is that ideology is always double. OK, I know that today the notion of ideology is somehow out of fashion, proclaimed naïve, etc., but I will try to explain at the end why, how, precisely as Lacanians, we not only have to stick to the notion of ideology but can develop further this notion in a very useful way. My good American Marxist friend, Fredric Jameson, whom I'm in the process of brainwashing into a good Lacanian, with some success, I hope, gave me a very good example of how ideology is at work.

Do you remember up to, let us say, 20 years ago, what we usually call in the standard philosophical and anthropological terminology, the relationship of man with nature, the complex of production, exploitation of nature, etc.? This was perceived as a kind of constant. Nobody doubted that this could go on and on. Work production will go on; the human species will somehow continue to exploit nature, etc. Where possibilities were perceived as open was at the level of social organization itself. Will capitalism prevail? Will fascism? Will there be socialism? So social imagination was active at the level of different possibilities of social organization. The idea was maybe we would have fascism, totalitarianism, maybe some Orwellian closed society, maybe the Huxleyan 'Brave New World', maybe liberal capitalism, state capitalism, whatever. Here it was possible to imagine a change. Somehow production would go on, it would continue to exploit nature – this was conceived as a constant.

Whereas today, 20 or 30 years later, it is, I claim, exactly the opposite. It's very easy to imagine, everybody's doing it, that somehow all of nature will disintegrate, there will be ecological catastrophe, or whatever: the human race will not go on. What is no longer possible to imagine is that there will be no liberal capitalism: there is no change at that level. So the dream is that maybe there will be no nature, maybe there will be a total catastrophe, but liberal capitalism will still somehow exist even if the Earth no longer exists. So precisely scenes like this, where you can see how what is visible, what is invisible, what can be imagined, what cannot be imagined, change. This is, I think, to put it in very naïve terms, a kind of, if you want, empirical proof that ideology is at work.

And again, my claim is that in the same way as the notion of fantasy, the notion of ideology is also always a two-level notion. My point is that the way to recognize ideology at work is always through a denunciation of another ideology. There is never pure, naïve ideology. Ideology is always a gesture of denouncing another position as being naïve ideology. Again, I'm speaking from my own political experience.

For example, how did we experience the moment of the disintegration of communism when finally we got rid of this totalitarian ideological indoctrination and returned to some 'natural' state of things? What was this natural state of things? The free market, multi-party elections, etc.? Precisely, this most spontaneous self-experience of how you are getting rid of some imposed artificial order and returning to some kind of, let us say, non-ideological natural state of things, I think, is the basic, as it were, gesture of ideology. OK, so that I don't get lost, maybe I'll return to this later.

Now, as to this notion of fantasy, I'm not playing the easy game of saying, yes, we can also traverse the fantasy in the political field, etc., but I nonetheless think that one of the lessons of psychoanalysis is that even in politics it is necessary to at least acquire some distance towards the fantasmatic frame. To exemplify this I would like to mention a very simple and, for me, very nice example.

Aldous Huxley's book, *The Grey Eminence,* as you maybe know, is a biography of Père Joseph, who was the political advisor to Cardinal Richelieu. I think this book should be on the reading list for anyone who wants to shed some light on the obscure relationship between ethics and fantasy. Why is this figure – Père Joseph – so interesting? If, in the fictional reconstruction (let's play this game) of modern European history, one wishes to isolate the episode that derailed the so-called normal course of events, the episode that introduced the imbalance the final consequence of which was the two world wars in our century, what could it be? Of course, the main candidate for this crucial disturbance, derailment, is the partitioning of the German kingdom – *Reich* – in the Thirty Years War, from 1618 to 1648, I think – in the first half of the seventeenth century, that is to say. As you probably know, on account of this partitioning of the German empire, the assertion of Germany as a nation state was delayed, and so on. This is, then, the course of the fundamental imbalance in European history. Let's take this fictional, retroactive reconstruction a step further. If there is a person who within this fictitious reconstruction can be made responsible for these catastrophic results, the main candidate for this role was precisely this unfortunate Père Joseph who, as an advisor to Richelieu, through his phenomenal capacity for intrigue, succeeded in introducing – what was his big achievement? – a rupture, a splitting, into the Protestant camp, concluding in a pact between Catholic France and Protestant Sweden against Austria, thus shifting the centre of war to German territory. So, Père Joseph is the ultimate embodiment of the plotting, Machiavellian politician, ready to sacrifice thousands of lives, ready to resort to spying, lies, murder, extortion. OK, nothing new. But, and this was the feature that fascinated Aldous Huxley, there is another side to this same Père Joseph. He was, OK, during the day, horrible, a plotter, the worst politician; but after doing the dirty job during the day, every evening he was not only a priest but a mystic of the most authentic kind. Every evening, after a day full of painful diplomatic intrigue, he plunged into deep meditations. His mystical visions bear witness to an authenticity worthy of St Teresa, St John of the Cross, and so on. He corresponded regularly with the sisters of a small French convent, giving them advice as to their spiritual distress, and so on. This was the enigma for Huxley. How are we to reconcile these two sides?

At this crucial point, I think, Huxley himself avoids the true paradox and opts for an easy way out: by putting the blame on the alleged weak points of Père Joseph's mystical experience. According to Huxley, the excessive centring on Jesus Christ – Père Joseph's obsession with Christ's suffering on the Way of the Cross – is made responsible for rendering possible the reckless manipulation of other people's suffering, and so on.

As you probably know, for that reason, Huxley turned away from Christianity. He sought spiritual salvation in Eastern wisdom, and so on. But I think one of the lessons of psychoanalysis is precisely that we must fully accept this paradox. Yes, you can be, at the same time, an absolutely authentic mystic – that is, of course, not a reproach – and the most horrible plotting politician. There is no guarantee, in your authentic private experience, what the political effects will be. I think this is the illusion we must renounce. There is no guarantee what the political effects of your subjective experience will be.

Let me return now to my main point, which is fantasy. Of course, as we know from Lacan, the ultimate fantasy is the fantasy of sexual relationship. So, of course, the way to traverse the fantasy is to elaborate what Lacan means by saying there is no sexual relationship, that is to say, via Lacan's theorization of sexual difference, the so-called formulae of sexuation. What's my point here? My point is the following one. What is usually not perceived here is that Lacan's assertion, '*La femme n'existe pas*', 'Woman does not exist', in no way refers to some kind of ineffable feminine essence outside the symbolic order, non-integrated into the symbolic order, beyond the domain of discourse.

You know, what I like very much about Lacan is, I don't know if you notice this, he is very much a Leninist in his style. What do I mean? Something very precise. How do you recognise a true Leninist? The typical Leninist twist is that, for example, when somebody says 'freedom', the Leninist question is 'Freedom for whom? To do what?' That is to say, for example, freedom for the bourgeoisie to exploit workers, etc. Do you notice in *Ethics of Psychoanalysis,* Lacan has almost the same twist apropos of 'the good'? Yes, supreme good, but whose good, to do what, etc? So here, I think, when Lacan says 'Woman does not exist' we must also do this Leninist *tour*, and ask ourselves, 'Which woman?', 'For whom does woman not exist?' And, again, the point is that it is not the way woman is usually conceived, which is that woman does not exist within the symbolic order, that woman somehow resists being integrated within the symbolic order. I am tempted to say it is almost the opposite.

To simplify things, I will first present my thesis. A lot of popular introductions, especially feminist introductions to Lacan, usually centre only on this formula and say, 'Yes, not all of woman is integrated into the phallic order, so there is something in woman as if woman is with one leg within the phallic order, and with the other one in some kind of mystical feminine enjoyment, I don't know what'. My thesis, to simplify very much, is that the whole point of Lacan is precisely that since we cannot totalize woman there is no exception. So, in other words, I think that the ultimate example of male logic is precisely this notion of some feminine essence, eternally feminine, excluded outside the symbolic order, beyond. This is the ultimate male fantasy. And when Lacan says, 'Woman does not exist', I think precisely this ineffable, mysterious 'beyond', excluded from the symbolic order, is what does not exist. What do I mean by this?

$\forall x \quad \Phi x$	$\overline{\forall x} \quad \Phi x$
$\exists x \quad \overline{\Phi x}$	$\overline{\exists x} \quad \overline{\Phi x}$
MASCULINE Universal function. All are submitted to the phallic function with one exception. There is one which is not.	FEMININE Not all are submitted to the phallic function. But there is no exception. There is none which is not submitted to the phallic function.

Let me elaborate a little bit, first, in a rather popular way, and then I will slowly approach philosophy. To put my cards on the table, I have already developed my final thesis in my last published book, *Tarrying with the Negative*. The same work is done by my friend from the United States, Joan Copjec, in her book *Read my Desire*, which is probably already in the bookstores in the United States – I think the subtitle is 'Lacan against the New Historicism'.

I don't know how well acquainted you are with the philosophy of Immanuel Kant. Kant's idea is that human reason, applied beyond experience to the domain of the infinite, gets necessarily involved in antinomies. And, as you may know, Kant speaks about two kinds of antinomies of pure reason. On the one hand, so-called mathematical antinomies. On the other hand, so-called dynamic antinomies. To simplify a little bit, we can say that mathematical antinomies correspond to the paradoxes of infinite divisibility, indivisibility, and so on. Whereas dynamic antinomies correspond in their structure to the other set of paradoxes because mainly, as you probably know in logic, we have two matrixes, two sets of paradoxes. On the one hand, the paradoxes of infinite divisibility, indivisibility; on the other hand, the paradoxes of this kind of abnormal set, you know, the kind of famous Russellian paradoxes, 'Can an element be a class of itself?' You know the boring examples like the barber in Seville shaving himself or not. This kind of abnormal element, this kind of self-referential paradox.

Now, my idea, to put it very simply, as has Joan Copjec and others, is that on the feminine side we have precisely the structure of the mathematical antinomies – infinite divisibility versus indivisibility.

Here on the masculine side, we have precisely the structure of a Kantian dynamic antinomy. Why is this so important? Because, as you maybe know, the official Kantian theory of sexual difference is elaborated in his early essay on the beautiful and the sublime, the idea being, to put it somewhat simply, that women are beautiful, men are sublime. No? My thesis, and Joan Copjec's also, is that we must read here Kant against Kant himself. That is to say that when Kant is speaking about two modes of the sublime – mathematical sublime when we are dealing with this kind of quantitative infinity, and on the other hand dynamic sublime – that there already with these two modes of the sublime we encounter sexual difference. But I will return to this later. Let me first explain things the way I understand them at least.

So, first we have the feminine position. The feminine division consists in assuming the inconsistency of desire. It's Lacan's famous, 'I demand you to refuse my demand since this is not that', 'C'est ne pas, ça'. That is to say, the male dread of woman which so deeply branded the spirit of the times, the Zeitgeist, of the turn of the century, from Edvard Munch, August Strindberg, up to Franz Kafka – what is this horror of woman? It is precisely the horror of feminine incon-sistency: horror at what was called, at that time, feminine hysteria – hysteria which traumatized these men, and which also, as you know, marked the birthplace of psychoanalysis – and which confronted them with an inconsistent multitude of masks. A hysterical woman immediately moves from desperate pleas to cruel virago, derision, and so on. What causes such uneasiness is the impossibility of discerning behind these masks a consistent subject manipulating them.

Let me mention here, briefly, Edvard Munch's encounter with hysteria, which left such a deep mark upon him. In 1893, Munch was in love with the beautiful daughter of an Oslo wine merchant. She clung to him but he was afraid of such a tie and anxious about his work, and so he left her. One stormy night, a sailing boat came to fetch him. The report was that the young woman was on the point of death and wanted to speak to him for the last time. Munch was deeply moved and without question went to her place where he found her lying on a bed between two lit candles. But when he approached her bed, she rose and started to laugh. The whole scene was nothing but a hoax. Munch turned, started to leave. At that point, she threatened to shoot herself if he left her and, drawing a revolver, she pointed it at her breast. When Munch bent to wrench the weapon away, convinced that this, too, was only part of the game, the gun went off, wounded him in the hand, and so on.

So here we encounter hysterical theatre at its purest. The subject is caught in a masquerade in which what appears to be deadly serious reveals itself as fraud, and what appears to be an empty gesture reveals itself as deadly serious. The panic that seizes the male subject confronted with this theatre expresses a dread that behind the many masks which fall away from each other like the layers of an onion there is nothing – no ultimate feminine secret.

Here, however, we must avoid a fatal misunderstanding. Insofar as these hysterical masks are the way for a woman to captivate the male gaze, the inevitable conclusion seems to be that the feminine secret inaccessible to the male phallic economy – the famous eternally feminine, and so on – consists of a feminine subject that eludes the reign of what is usually referred to as phallogocentric reason, phallic function, and so on. The complementary conclusion is that, insofar as there is nothing behind the masks, woman is wholly subordinated to the phallic function. But according to Lacan, the exact opposite is true. This is how I read the feminine side of the formulae of sexuation. The presymbolic, eternally feminine is a retroactive, patriarchal fantasy. It is the exception which grounds the reign of the phallus. The same, by the way, as with the anthropological notion of an original, matriarchal paradise. I think that this construction that originally there was a matriarchal paradise gradually replaced by patriarchy is strictly a patriarchal myth. I think the first gesture of true, radical feminism must be to renounce this myth, which from the very beginning served as the support of retroactive legitimization of the male rule.

It is thus the very lack of any exception to the phallus that renders the feminine libidinal economy inconsistent and thus in a way undermines the reign of the phallic function. That's my central point. When Lacan says there is something beyond phallus, feminine *jouissance,* etc., this doesn't mean that on the one hand we get part of the woman caught in what Lacan calls, I hope I don't offend anybody listening, the phallic function, and part of it outside. Let me put it this way, this is the ultimate paradox that I'm trying to get to. It is precisely because there is no exception, precisely because woman is entirely within the phallic function that paradoxically the rule of the phallic function is undermined, that we are caught in inconsistency. What do I mean by this? I will try to explain it further.

As you probably know, Lacan's most famous *écrit*, 'The Subversion of the Subject and the Dialectic of Desire', ends with the ambiguous, 'I won't go any further here.'[4] It's ambiguous since it can be taken to imply that later, somewhere else, Lacan will go further, and this lure enticed some feminist critics of Lacan to reproach him with coming to a halt at the very point at which he should have accomplished the crucial step beyond Freud's phallocentrism. Although Lacan does talk about feminine enjoyment, *jouissance*, that eludes the phallic domain, he conceives of it as an ineffable dark continent, separated from male discourse by a frontier impossible to trespass.

Now, for feminists like Irigaray or Kristeva, this refusal to trespass the frontier, this, as Lacan puts it, 'I won't go any further here', signals the continued tabooing of women. What they want, this kind of feminist, is precisely to go further, to deploy the contours of a feminine discourse beyond the phallic order. Now, why does this operation that from the standpoint of common sense cannot but appear fully justified miss its mark?

In traditional philosophical terms, the limit that defines woman is not epistemological, but ontological. That is to say, yes, there is a limit but beyond it there is nothing. That is to say, woman is not-all, yes, but this means precisely that woman is not-all caught in the phallic function. This does not mean that there is part of her which is not caught in the phallic function. It means precisely that there is nothing beyond. In other words, the feminine is this structure of the limit as such, a limit that precedes what may or may not lie in its beyond. All that we perceive in this beyond, the eternal feminine, for example, or, in more modern terms, semiotic, feminine discourse, whatever, are, basically, male fantasy projections.

In other words, we should not oppose woman as she is for the other, for man, woman as male narcissistic projection, male image of woman, and, on the other hand, the true woman in herself, beyond male discourse. I'm almost tempted to assert the exact opposite. Woman in herself is ultimately a male fantasy, whereas we get much closer to, let's call it the true woman, by simply following to their end the inherent deadlocks of the male discourse on woman. I think that, again, precisely when we are aiming at woman as that ineffable beyond the male symbolic order as opposed to the semiotic, etc., precisely this notion of a beyond is the ultimate male fantasy, if you want. Now let me pass to the other side. In the case of man, on the male side, the split is, at it were, externalized. Man escapes the inconsistency of his desire by establishing a line of separation between the phallic domain – let's call it simply the domain of sexual enjoyment, the relationship to a sexual partner – and the non-phallic – let's say the domain of non-sexual public activity. What we encounter here, I think, are the paradoxes of what is called, in the theory of rational choice, states that are essentially by-products. Man subordinates his relationship to a woman to the domain of ethical goals: when forced to choose between woman and ethical duty, profession, his mission, whatever, man immediately opts for duty; yet he is simultaneously aware that only a relationship to a woman can bring him genuine happiness, personal fulfilment, and so on. So I think, to put it somewhat simply, the dirty trick of the male economy is to say, what? I think you encounter it in every good Hollywood melodrama. What is the basic trick of melo-drama? I could go on with numerous examples, but I don't want to take too much of your time. The logic is the following one: the man sacrifices his love for the woman for some superior cause – revolution, job, something allegedly non-sexual – but the message between the lines is precisely that sacrificing his love is the supreme proof of his love for her, of how she is everything to him, so that the sublime moment in melodrama (and they're crucial, I think, to learn about the male sexual position) is the sublime moment of recognition when the woman finally realizes that the man betrayed her, that he has left, but precisely his sacrificing her is the ultimate proof of his love for her. The ultimate melodramatic phrase is 'I really did it for you', precisely when you drop her. I think this is the male trick: woman is your supreme good, but precisely in order to be worthy of her you must betray her. I believe in melodramas. My basic motto is that melodramas structure our lives, I mean, you find your structure in them. So, again, I think it's precisely man who posits an exception that is far more according to the phallic structure, and so on.

Let me further explain, in a more abstract way, this rather pre-theoretical description that I gave you. What is meant by this non-all which then cannot be universalized? Let me give you a very orthodox and maybe surprising example, as an old-fashioned Marxist. I think that – this is the provocation that I usually try to sell in Paris, but Jacques-Alain Miller usually buys it because he himself is an old Maoist, etc. – the perfect example of what Lacan means by not-all, no exception but precisely for this reason you cannot totalize it is, OK, the Marxist notion of class struggle. What does class struggle mean? Every position we assume towards the class struggle, even a theoretical one, is already a moment of the class struggle. It involves taking sides in the class struggle, which is why there is no impartial objective standpoint enabling us to delineate class struggle. In this precise sense, we can say the same as with woman, class struggle doesn't exist since there is no exception, no element eluding it. We cannot conceive or apprehend class struggle as such, since what we are dealing with are always partial effects whose *accent gros* is the class struggle.

I think that's the structure precisely when you say nothing is out, every position that you take is already part of the class struggle, which is precisely why you cannot totalize it. Or, to give you a less dogmatic, more abstract philosophical example, a quick glance at every manual of philosophy makes it clear how every universal or all-embracing notion of philosophy is rooted in a particular philosophy, how it involves the standpoint of a particular philosophy. There is no neutral notion of philosophy to be then sub-divided into analytical philosophy, hermeneutic philosophy, structuralist philosophy, etc. This is the crucial thing to grasp. Every particular philosophy encompasses itself and all other philosophies, that is to say, its view on all other philosophies. Or, as Hegel put it in his *Lectures on the History of Philosophy*, every crucial epochal philosophy is, in a way, the whole of philosophy. It is not a sub-division of the whole, but the whole itself apprehended in a specific modality.

What we have here is thus not a simple reduction of the universal to the particular, but a kind of surplus of the universal. No single universal encompasses the entire particular content, since each particular has its own universal, each contains a specific perspective on the entire field.

The point is thus rather refined. It's not a kind of primitive nominalism in the sense that there are only particular philosophies. There are only particular universals. Every universal is a universal attached to a certain particularity. For example, the feminine not-all and the masculine position designate precisely an attempt to resolve this deadlock of too many universals by way of excluding one paradoxical particular. This exceptional particular then immediately gives body to the universal, as such.

What do I mean by this? Let's think about an exemplary case of, I think, this precise male logic of exception – the figure of the lady in courtly love. In the figure of the lady, this inaccessible absolute other, woman as sexual object, reaches existence. There woman exists, yet at the price of being posited as an inaccessible thing. Sexualized, she is transformed into an object that precisely insofar as it gives body to sexuality as such renders the masculine subject impotent.

Or another example: a reference to Eurocentrism. It's very fashionable today in the name of multiculturalism to criticize Eurocentrism, etc. I think the situation is rather more complicated. Actual multiculturalism can only emerge in a culture within which its own tradition, the tradition of this culture, its own communal heritage, appears as contingent. That is to say, in a culture that is indifferent towards itself, towards its own specificities. Multiculturalism is for that reason – my radical thesis – always strictly Eurocentric. Only within modern-age Cartesian subjectivity is it possible to experience one's own tradition as a contingent ingredient to be methodologically bracketed. Here resides the paradox of the universal and its constitutive exception. The universal notion of the multiplicity of peoples, each of them embedded in each particular tradition, presupposes an exception, a tradition that experiences itself as contingent.

Again, I think that the crucial point is that this multiculturalism is possible only if you experience your own tradition as radically contingent: if you relate to your own tradition as contingent. And I don't believe this is possible outside this empty point of reference which is the Cartesian subject.

Or to put it differently, at a different level: the catch, as it were, the trap, of the universal resides in what it secretly excludes. As you know, the classical example, the 'man' of universal human rights, excludes those who are – what is the catch of universal human rights? – of course, they are universal, every man has rights to them, but the catch is, then, who are those who are considered not fully human? First, you exclude, for example, savages. You exclude madmen. You exclude non-civilized barbarians. And you can go on: you exclude criminals, you exclude children, you exclude women, you exclude poor people, and so on.

So human rights belong to everybody: the catch is purely tautological usually, no? Human rights are the rights of everybody, but of everybody who is really fully human. And then you can build the trick which can go up to the end so that everybody is an exception to this set [reference to formulae on board]. The nicest case – my favourite one, old leftist terrorist that I am – is the Jacobinical terror in the French Revolution. Practically every concrete individual is potentially excluded, is potentially conceived as an egotist, can be executed by guillotine, etc. So, rights are universal but every concrete individual somehow doesn't fit the universal. My heart is here, but let's go on.

Another nice example of this tension between universal and particular, I think, is precisely the antinomy of the liberal democratic project. This antinomy concerns the relationship between universal and particular. The liberal democratic universalist right to difference encounters its limit the moment it stumbles against an actual difference. Let me go again to my tasteless level, and recall, how do you call it, clitoridectomy, the cutting out of the clitoris to mark a woman's sexual maturity, a practice, as you probably know, that holds out in parts of Eastern Africa. Or, a less extreme case, the insistence of Muslim women in France, for example, to wear the veil in public schools, and so on. Now, this seems a very clear-cut case, but how should we as good liberals approach this problem?

I think there is a dilemma which simply cannot be solved. Namely, what if – and this is not a fiction, this does happen – what if a minority group claims that this difference, their right to clitoridectomy, to forcing women to wear veils in public, etc., that this difference, their specific custom is an indispensable part of the cultural identity of this group and consequently what if this group denounces opposition to, for example, cutting out the clitoris as an exercise in cultural imperialism, as the violent imposition of Eurocentric standards?

What would you say, for example, if not only men but even women themselves, if you tried to teach them, to explain to them how this is part of their primitive patriarchal character, if they say, 'No, this is part of my very cultural identity'? How are we to decide between the competing claims of an individual's rights and group identity when, this is the catch, the group identity accounts for a substantial part of the individual's self identity?

The standard liberal answer is, what? Let the woman choose whatever she wants. If she wants her clitoris cut out, let it be done, on condition that she has been properly informed, acquainted with the span of alternative choices, so that she's fully aware of the wider context of her choice. That's the standard liberal answer, no? We must just inform her objectively – let's put it naïvely – of the global situation. But delusion resides here in the underlying implication that there is a neutral, non-violent way of informing the individual, of acquainting him or her with the full range of alternatives.

The threatened, particular community necessarily experiences the concrete mode of this acquisition of knowledge about alternative lifestyles, for example, through obligatory education, state education, as a violent intervention that disrupts its identity. So that's the catch. Here, I think, the usual liberal approach is a little bit naïve. The whole point is that there is no neutral medium, no neutral way to inform the individual. How will you attempt, for example, to inform the poor woman in a so-called primitive (not my view) African society that cutting out the clitoris is barbaric, etc.? The very form of informing her is already experienced by that community as a certain minimal violence.

By the way, don't misunderstand me. My point is not this kind of false, western neutrality: OK, so let them do whatever they want, etc. My point is simply more pessimistic and [gesturing to the formulae of sexuation] I think this is the truth of this male side that there is no neutral non-exclusive universality. That whatever you do, you must accept a certain degree, a certain level, of violence.

Now, my final part, which is more philosophical: what is Lacan really trying to achieve with these formulae of sexuation? I think something very radical, almost unheard of, which is usually misrecognized, misunderstood. I think that Lacan was the only one, at least as far as I know, who tried to elaborate a notion of sexual difference that would be at the level of the Cartesian subject, the subject of modern science.

That is to say, the Cartesian subject, the abstract subject of 'I think, therefore I am', this abstract, empty subject emerges, as you probably know, of the radical desexualization of man's relationship to the universe. That is to say, traditional wisdom was always anthropomorphic and sexualized. The traditional, pre-modern comprehension of the universe was structured by oppositions which bear an indelible sexual connotation: yin/yang; light/dark; active/passive. There is a kind of anthropomorphic universalization of sexual opposition. This anthropomorphic foundation makes possible the metaphoric correspondence, the mirror relationship, between microcosm and macrocosm: the establishment of structural cosmologies between man, society and the universe. Society as an organism with a monarch at its head, and so on. The birth of the universe through the coupling of earth and sun, etc.

In the modern world, on the contrary, reality confronts us as inherently non-anthropomorphic, as a blind mechanism that, as we usually say, speaks the language of mathematics, and can consequently only be expressed in meaningless formulae. Every search for a deeper meaning of the phenomena is now experienced as the left-over of traditional anthropomorphism. This is the modern approach: the universe does not have meaning.

(I'm sorry that I don't have time to enter into this because what I am currently working on – it may be a surprise to you – is a detailed reading of quantum physics. Why? Because it is a very important field of battle where the New Age obscurantists usually counter-attack. You know, this kind of 'quantum physics opens up a new way to combine western science with oriental wisdom', and so on. I think, absolutely not, even quite the contrary. I think that quantum physics is the peak of modernity, but, OK, we can maybe enter into it in discussion. Let me go on.)

Now, it is against this background that we can measure Lacan's achievement. He was the first, as far as I know even the only, to outline the contours of a, let's say, non-imaginary, non-naturalized – I'm even tempted to say, non-anthropomorphic, non-human – theory of sexual difference. That is to say, a theory that radically breaks with any kind of anthropomorphic sexualization: male/female as the two cosmic principles, yin/yang, active/passive, and so on.

The problem that confronted Lacan was the following: how do we pass from animal coupling led by instinctual knowledge, regulated by natural rhythms, to human sexuality possessed by an eternalized desire for the very reason it cannot be satisfied – it is inherently perturbed, doomed to failure, and so on? So, again, how do we pass from natural coupling to human sexuality? Lacan's answer is, I think, we enter human sexuality through the intervention, of course, of the symbolic order as a kind of heterogeneous parasite that derails the natural rhythm of coupling. OK, everybody seems to know this, but what does this mean?

Apropos of these two asymmetric antinomies of symbolization – we have the masculine side: universality with exception; the feminine side: a not-all field which precisely for that reason has no exception – a question imposes itself, the most naïve question. What we have here is simply a certain inherent deadlock of symbolization which is also expressed in two main sets of logical paradoxes, and so on. Now, you are fully justified in asking yourself a very simple, naïve question. What constitutes the link that connects these two purely logical antinomies with the opposition of female and male which, however symbolically mediated, however culturally conditioned, remains ultimately an obvious biological fact? What's the link between this [gesturing toward the formulae] and the still almost experiential fact that there is something biological about male, female, and so on?

I think Lacan's answer to this question is, there is none. There is precisely no link. That is to say, what we experience as a sexuality – human sexuality perturbed, there is no sexual relation, and so on – is precisely the effect of the contingent act of, let's say, grafting the fundamental deadlock of symbolization on to the biological opposition of male and female. So, the answer to the question, 'Isn't this link between the two logical paradoxes of universalization and sexuality illicit?' is, therefore, that that's precisely Lacan's point. What Lacan does is simply to transpose this illicit character from, let us say, the epistemological to the ontological level. Sexuality itself, what we experience as the highest, most intense assertion of our being, is, let me put it this way, a bricolage – a montage of two totally heterogeneous elements. So this parasitic grafting of the symbolic deadlock on to animal coupling is what undermines the instinctual rhythm of animal coupling, and so on.

Now what Lacan does here is something very precise. In Lacan, masculine and feminine as defined by these formulae of sexuation are not predicates providing positive information about the subject, designating some positive properties. I don't know how well you know Kant's philosophy, but my thesis is that they are a case of what Kant conceives as a purely negative determination, a determination which merely designates, registers, a certain deadlock, a certain limit, a specific modality of how the subject fails in their bid for an identity that would constitute them as an object fully constituted, fully realized, and so on. So, here Lacan is again far more subversive than may appear.

As you probably know, the whole point of Kantian ethics and philosophy is the search for so-called formal, *a priori* structures independent of empirical, contingent entities, entities that are encountered within our sensible experience. I think that those who try to suggest that what Lacan did is, in a way, to elaborate in a Kantian mode a critique of pure desire, the *a priori* conditions of desire, do something like this.

What Lacan calls 'object small a' [*objet petit a*] is precisely a kind of non-pathological *a priori* object-cause of desire, precisely a kind of quasi-transcendental object. The problem – I cannot elaborate this, just give you a hint – as Lacan points out again and again, where it goes wrong with Kant, is the following one. Here it would be productive, I think, to read Kant's philosophy with Edgar Allan Poe. For example, in his two stories, 'Black Cat' and 'Imp of the Perverse', Poe refers to a so-called 'imp of the perverse', which is what? Let me return to Kant. For Kant, we have, on the one hand, pathological acts, acts which are caused by our pathological desires, that is to say, by desires whose object is some sensible, contingent, empirical object; and then we have ethical activity, which is defined as non-pathological, that is to say, as an activity whose mobile motive is some *a priori*, purely formal, empty rule. Now, the nice paradox where things get complicated and here, I think, is one of Lacan's critiques of Kant, is that, of course, Kant aimed at purifying ethical activity of every pathological element, of defining pure ethical activity. But what he inadvertently did was to open up a new kind of evil, which is what Kant himself referred to as diabolical evil, which is a far more radical evil, that is a paradoxical evil that perfectly fits the Kantian conditions of good, of a good act. That is to say, of a non-pathological act, of an act unconditioned by any empirical, contingent object. Let's now briefly go to Edgar Allan Poe's 'Imp of the Perverse'.

As you probably know, in these two stories, 'Black Cat' and 'Imp of the Perverse', Poe speaks about a strange impulse in every man to accomplish an act for no positive reason but, simply, the formula is you must do it precisely because it is prohibited. It is pure negative motivation. Now think about it and you will see that this purely negative motivation is *a priori* formal in the purest Kantian sense. It's purely grounded in itself with no empirical reference. That's the problem, that a new domain of evil opened up ... OK, but that's a further development.

My point here is that what Lacan tries with his formulae of sexuation is precisely at the same level to provide a kind of non-empirical, but purely formal, transcendental, *a priori* in Kantian terms, logic of sexual difference. In a very precise, paradoxical way, Kant says that there are two main types of antinomies in which human reason necessarily *a priori* gets involved. And I think, to simplify it a little bit, according to Lacan, they correspond to the two forms of the sublime, etc. These two types of antinomies precisely designate, structure the two sexual positions. So, let me again be very precise here. For that reason, Lacan is as far as possible from the notion of sexual difference as the relationship of two opposite poles which supplement each other, which together form the whole of man. You know, this mythology of masculine, feminine, as the two poles, the two opposites, which together form the fullness of the genus of man, and so on. On this point, according to Lacan, we cannot say that with this and this together [referring to parts of the formulae on the board] we have the full totality of man, if we put man and woman together. Why not? Because we only get two failures. Each of these two attempts is precisely already in itself a failure. These are precisely two attempts to arrive at the universality but which fail.

Here, I think, we can draw a distinction in a very clear way. (I always like, as an old Stalinist, to draw the line of distinction between us and them, the enemies, the enemy here being the Foucauldian constructionists who say, you know, sexual difference is not something naturally given.) Sex – you know Foucault developed this in the first volume of his *History of Sexuality* – is a bricolage, an artificial unification of heterogeneous discursive practices, etc. Lacan rejects this. For him, sex, sexual positions, is not something simply discursively constructed. But for all that, Lacan, of course, does not return to a naïve position of sex as something substantially pre-discursively given. Sex is not a symbolic discursive construction. What is it? It emerges precisely where symbolization fails. That's Lacan's point. That, in other words, we are sexed beings precisely because symbolization necessarily fails. And sexuality means two versions of this failure.

In other words, to put it very precisely, if it were possible to symbolize sexual difference, we would not have two sexes, but only one. There are two sexes precisely because each of them is, if you want, its own kind of failure. I think that I would advise you to read, to grasp the logic of this, one of the best articles/essays of Lévi-Strauss. It's a marvellous one. There he is, really, I think, a Lacanian (although he rather hated Lacan). In his *Structural Anthropology*, he reports on an experiment. He noticed that the members of some tribe, I think in Brazil, the Amazon, were divided into two groups. He asked each of the members of the two groups a very simple question: could you draw me, on paper, the map of the houses of your village? The paradox was that each of the two groups, although they were depicting the same village, drew a totally different map. One of them drew houses around some centre. This is how they saw the disposition, the map of the village. The other group drew a series of houses with a divide in the middle. Now, of course, you would say, not a problem: we rent a helicopter, we take a photo from above, and we get the true picture. But that's not the point: we miss the point this way. The whole point, as Lévi-Strauss points out very nicely, is that the problem was there was some fundamental deadlock, some structural imbalance, and that each of the groups perceived in its own way this imbalance and tried to symbolize it, to mend it ... And that's how we have to comprehend the logic of sexual difference. Again, it's not [referring to formulae] half here, half there. It's one failed way to grasp the whole of man; another way to grasp the whole, the entire man.

In other words, my next point is that, for example, what we must avoid apropos of sexual difference is the formulation of sexual difference as a kind of complementary polarity of opposites. I think this is the ultimate ideological operation.

For example, and here I am against a certain kind of feminism which tries to oppose to male discourse another special, separate feminine discourse. I think that they are repeating the same mistake that is usually denounced, that was usually made in the good old times of Stalinism by the most radical Stalinist who claims that, as you know, we have bourgeois science and proletarian science. We all laugh at them as primitive but I think they are making the same mistake. The same as, precisely insofar as we stick to class struggle, we must say, yes, there is no neutral position, but precisely because there is only one science, and this science is split from within. I think it's absolutely crucial that we stick to the same point with regard to discourse. I'm not saying discourse is simply sex-neutral, not gendered. It's not neutral but it is discourse which is, as it were, split from within.

Let me put it another way. Again, if you'll pardon me my last reference to Louis Althusser, I think that everything hinges on the status of the word 'and' as a category. If you've read Althusser – he is still worth reading, I think – in a whole series of his texts, of his essays, in the title this word 'and' appears. For example, you have one title, 'Ideology and Ideological State Apparatuses', or you have, for example, 'Contradiction and Overdetermination'. What is the logic of this 'and'? The first term before this 'and' is some general ideological notion: the notion of ideology, the notion of contradiction. Then, the second term, 'ideological state apparatuses' or 'overdetermination', provides the concrete material conditions so that this notion begins to function as non-ideological. If you want to avoid idealist dialectics, and stick to materialist dialectics, you must conceive of contradiction as part of a concrete, overdetermining, complex totality, and so on. So, again, this 'and' is in a sense tautological. It conjoins the same content in its two modalities. First, in its ideological evidence the abstract universal notion, and then, the extra-ideological, the concrete, material conditions of its existence. Ideology exists only in ideological state apparatuses. Contradiction exists materially only in overdetermination. So, no first term is needed here to mediate between the two points of the end because the second term is already the concrete existence of the first term.

Here, by the way – and now you'll say, what has this to do with psychoanalysis? – is one of the ways to grasp the difference between Freud and Jung, because what Jung does is, precisely, in opposition to Freud. For example, apropos of the notion of libido, for Jung libido is precisely a kind of neutral universal notion and then you have the concrete forms of libido – different metamorphoses, as he says. You have sexual, creative, destructive libido, and so on. Whereas Freud insists that libido, in its concrete existence, is irreducibly sexual. So, the Althusserian title of Freud would be 'Libido and its Sexual Existence', or whatever. My point is what, here? My point is that with Lacan, sexual difference, man and woman, has to be conceived precisely in terms of this Althusserian 'and'. Man is this universal, woman is the concrete existence, to put it this way. There are two ways. Either we do it this way: man and woman as ideology and ideological state apparatuses. Or we do it in this abstract, obscurantist way: man and woman, two polarities, complementing each other, etc., and we are very quickly in some kind of New Age obscurantism.

Let me finish very quickly now. To put this paradox in another way: when Lacan says woman doesn't exist, this is another consequence of what I was saying. We must absolutely not grasp this as following the logic according to which no empirical element fully corresponds to its symbolic place. It's clear that this is the basic thesis of Lacan. For example, father – the empirical, the real as part of reality, the empirical person of father – never lives up to, never fully fits its symbolic mandate. There is always a gap between the symbolic place of the father and the empirical father. The empirical person is somebody who refers to, literally acts in the name of, his paternal authority. He is not immediately the authority. Now, you would say, but what if he is? OK, I hope you don't have this kind of father because then you have a psychotic father. I mean, the father of Schreber was fully a father: there was no gap of this kind. So my point is that you must grasp the difference, must avoid another trap, here. And this is, by the way, what the notion of castration means, I think. The notion of castration means precisely that for you to exert, let us say, paternal authority, you must undergo a kind of transubstantiation and you must accept that you no longer act as fully yourself but as an embodiment, as an agent, of some transcendent symbolic agency. That you are not fully yourself. It's the big Other, as it were, that speaks through you. Precisely insofar as you are an agent of authority you are always decentred, you are not immediately the authority. You are a stand-in for the absent symbolic authority. This would be how the father pays the price for his authority, precisely by this castration as the gap between his empirical existence and his symbolic place.

Now my point is that when Lacan says woman doesn't exist, this absolutely does not mean the same gap. It doesn't mean that, in the same way as no empirical father fully fits the symbolic place of the father, no empirical woman fully fits the capitalized Woman. I think it's not the same logic. Why? In what sense not?

Let me make the last quick detour. It's the same as the Jew. You know, in anti-Semitism you also have this kind of gap. You have what is usually referred to as the so-called conceptual Jew, that is to say, the fantasmatic image of the Jew as the plotter, etc. Of course, no empirical Jew that you encounter fully fits the image of this horrible, plotting Jew, but the point is that this gap between the empirical Jew and the notional Jew, this gap is not the same as the gap that separates the father from the Name-of-the-Father. The logic is different because I think that with the father we have the structure of castration. With the Jew, it's the opposite. The paradox with the way the Jew functions is that the more they are empirically destroyed, humiliated, the more they are all-powerful.

That's the basic paradox of the Jew and I can give you an example of the same logic from my own country, where now the right-wing populists are attacking communists, even though the communists have lost power. The way they construct the communist danger is they claim that although the communists have lost power, the more invisible they are, the more they are the all-powerful, secret power who really have all the power in their hands, etc. So this is the logic of the Jew: the more you ruin him empirically, the more they are killed, the more they acquire some kind of spectral, fantasmatic presence which is all-powerful. In other words, precisely the more you kill them, the less they can be castrated. So, in opposition to paternal castration, the Jew precisely, and that's the horror of the Jew within Nazi anti-Semitism, the Jew precisely, in a way, cannot be castrated. So, in what does this difference consist? I think it can be formulated in a very precise way. The name-of-the-father is a symbolic fiction. Here we are in the order of what was called in a very nice way yesterday, 'the noble lie'. It's the symbolic fiction. Whereas the Jew is not a symbolic fiction but a fantasmatic spectre, a spectral apparition. And this is absolutely crucial if we are to grasp Lacanian theory. The spectral apparitions – these fantastic horrors, like the living dead, father's ghost in *Hamlet*, and so on – they are not of the order of the symbolic fiction, but quite the contrary. What do I mean by 'quite the contrary'? The point is, what does Lacan mean when he insists again and again that truth has the structure of a fiction, etc.? I mean this is already a commonplace from every stupid sociological manual. There are books written about the symbolic social construction of reality, etc. The point being that there is always – just think about the example from Lévi-Strauss – the failure of the symbolic fiction which tries to patch up a certain fundamental deadlock: the failure of the fiction to cope with some fundamental social antagonism, either sexual difference or class struggle, or whatever. This failure is then posited in spectral apparitions, in ghosts, in living dead. They are always here as the embodiment of what Lacan would have called a certain symbolic deadlock.

To conclude, my point is that if we approach Lacan in this way we can really, I think, elaborate a whole theory of ideology based on Lacan. The basic constituents of this theory of ideology being that what this spectral, fantasmatic apparition conceals is not reality, social reality. Here we must leave behind this naïve Marxist approach – ideological construction simply conceals some social reality. No. The whole point of Lacan is that in order for social reality to establish itself – by social reality I mean social order, social symbolic reality – something must be primordially repressed. Something cannot be symbolized, and the spectral apparition emerges to fill up the gap of what cannot be symbolized. So, again, the spectre conceals not social reality but what must be primordially repressed in order for social reality to emerge.

So I think that the Lacanian notion of the Real as that rock which resists symbolization is extremely useful for a non-naïve notion of ideology. By non-naïve notion of ideology I mean a notion of ideology which avoids the usual traps of, if you say ideology, false consciousness, then you automatically imply some kind of natural direct approach to what reality truly is, etc. You don't need this. What you need is precisely the notion that reality itself is never fully constituted, and that this is what ideological spectral fantasies try to mask. Not some positive reality but precisely the fact that what we usually call in sociology the 'social construction of reality' always fails.

NOTES

This is an edited transcript of the second of Žižek's series of public lectures delivered at the Eighth Annual Conference of the Australian Centre for Psychoanalysis in the Freudian Field, Melbourne, 13 August 1994. It was originally published in *Agenda: Australian Contemporary Art* 44, 1995, pp. 11–34 [eds].

1   Louis Althusser, *The Future Lasts Forever: A Memoir*, ed. Olivier Corpet and Yann Moulier Boutang, trans. Richard Veasey, London, Chatto and Windus, 1993 [eds].

2   *Ibid.*, pp. 147–8 [eds].

3   Jacques Lacan, 'The Subversion of the Subject and the Dialectic of Desire in the Freudian Unconscious', in *Écrits: A Selection*, trans. Bruce Fink, New York and London, W. W. Norton, 2002, pp. 300–1. See Slavoj Žižek, *The Sublime Object of Ideology*, London and New York, Verso, 1989, pp. 110–14 [eds].

4   Lacan, 'The Subversion of the Subject and the Dialectic of Desire', p. 311 [eds].

5 Lacan between Cultural Studies
and Cognitivism

1. CULTURAL STUDIES VERSUS THE
'THIRD CULTURE'

(a)   *The Struggle for Intellectual Hegemony*

We are witnessing today the struggle for intellectual hegemony – for who will occupy the universal place of the 'public intellectual' – between postmodern-deconstructionist cultural studies and the cognitivist popularizers of 'hard' sciences, that is, the proponents of the so-called 'third culture'. This struggle, which caught the attention of the general public first through the so-called 'de Man affair' (where opponents endeavoured to prove the proto-Fascist irrationalist tendencies of deconstruction), reached its peak in the Sokal-*Social Text* affair. In cultural studies, 'theory' usually refers to a mixture of literary/cinema criticism, mass culture, ideology, queer studies, and so on. It is worth quoting here the surprised reaction of Dawkins:

> I noticed, the other day, an article by a literary critic called 'Theory: What Is It?' Would you believe it? 'Theory' turned out to mean 'theory in literary criticism' ... The very word 'theory' has been hijacked for some extremely narrow parochial literary purpose – as though Einstein didn't have theories; as though Darwin didn't have theories.[1]

Dawkins is here in deep solidarity with his great opponent Stephen Jay Gould, who also complains that 'there's something of a conspiracy among literary intellectuals to think they own the intellectual landscape and the reviewing sources, when in fact there are a group of nonfiction writers, largely from sciences, who have a whole host of fascinating ideas that people want to read about'.[2] These quotes clearly stake the terms of the debate as the fight for ideological hegemony in the precise sense this term acquired in Ernesto Laclau's writings: the fight over a particular content that always 'hegemonizes' the apparently neutral universal term. The third culture comprises the vast field that reaches from the evolutionary theory debate (Dawkins and Dennett versus Gould) through physicists dealing with quantum physics and cosmology (Hawking, Weinberg, Capra), cognitive scientists (Dennett again, Marvin Minsky), neurologists (Sacks), the theorists of chaos (Mandelbrot, Stewart), authors dealing with the cognitive and general social impact of the digitalization of our daily lives, up to the theorists of auto-poetic systems, who endeavour to develop a universal formal notion of self-organizing emerging systems that can be applied to 'natural' living organisms and species as well as social 'organisms' (the behaviour of markets and other large groups of interacting social agents). Three things should be noted here: (1) as a rule, we are not dealing with scientists themselves (although they are often the same individuals), but with authors who address a large public in such a way that their success outdoes by far the public appeal of cultural studies (suffice it to recall the big bestsellers of Sacks, Hawking, Dawkins and Gould); (2) as in the case of cultural studies, we are not dealing with a homogenized field, but with a rhizomatic multitude connected through 'family resemblances', within which authors are often engaged in violent polemics, but where interdisci-plinary connections also flourish (between evolutionary biology and cognitive sciences, and so on); (3) as a rule, authors active in this domain are sustained by a kind of missionary zeal, by a shared awareness that they all participate in a unique shift in the global paradigm of knowledge.

As a kind of manifesto of this orientation, one could quote the 'Introduction' to *The Third Culture: Beyond the Scientific Revolution,* in which the editor (John Brockman) nicely presents the large narrative that sustains the collective identification of the various scientists interviewed in the book.[3] According to Brockman, back in the 1940s and 1950s, the idea of a public intellectual was identified with an academic versed in 'soft' human (or social) sciences who addressed issues of common interest, took a stance on the great issues of the day and thus triggered or participated in large and passionate public debates. What then occurred, with the onslaught of 'French' postmodern deconstructionist theory, was the passing of that generation of public thinkers and their replacement by 'bloodless academics', that is, by cultural scientists whose pseudo-radical stance against 'power' or 'hegemonic discourse' effectively involves the growing disappearance of direct and actual political engagements outside the narrow confines of academia, as well as the increasing self-enclosure in an elitist jargon that precludes the very possibility of functioning as an intellectual engaged in public debates. Happily, however, this retreat of the 'public intellectual' was counteracted by the surge of the third culture, by the emergence of a new type of public intellectual, the third culture author, who, in the eyes of the general public, more and more stands for the one 'supposed to know', trusted to reveal the keys to the great secrets that concern us all. The problem is here again the gap between effective 'hard' sciences and their third culture ideological proponents who elevate scientists into subjects supposed to know, not only for ordinary people who buy these volumes in masses, but also for postmodern theorists themselves who are intrigued by it, 'in love with it', and suppose that these scientists 'really know something about the ultimate mystery of being'. The encounter here is failed. No, popular third-culturalists do *not* possess the solution that would solve the crisis of cultural studies; they do not have what cultural studies is lacking. The love encounter is thus failed: the beloved does not stretch his or her hand back and return love.

(b) *The 'Third Culture' as Ideology*

It is thus crucial to distinguish here between science itself and its inherent ideologization, its sometimes subtle transformation into a new holistic 'paradigm' (the new code name for 'world view'). A series of notions (complementarity, anthropic principle, and so on) are here doubly inscribed, functioning as scientific *and* ideological terms. It is difficult effectively to estimate the extent to which the third culture is infested with ideology. Among its obvious ideological appropriations (but are they merely secondary appropriations?), one should, again, note at least two obvious cases: first, the often present New Age inscription, in which the shift in paradigm is interpreted as an advance beyond the Cartesian mechanistic-materialist paradigm toward a new holistic approach that brings us back to the wisdom of ancient oriental thought (the Tao of physics, and so on). Sometimes, this is even radicalized into the assertion that the scientific shift in the predominant paradigm is an epiphenomenon of the fact that humanity is on the verge of the biggest spiritual shift in its entire history, that we are entering a new epoch in which egoistic individualism will be replaced by a transindividual cosmic awareness. The second case is the 'naturalization' of certain specific social phenomena, clearly discernible in so-called cyber-revolutionism, which relies on the notion of cyberspace (or the Internet) as a self-evolving 'natural' organism; the 'naturalization of culture' (market, society, and so on, as living organisms) overlaps here with the 'culturalization of nature' (life itself is conceived as a set of self-reproducing information – 'genes are memes'). This new notion of life is thus neutral with respect to the distinction between natural and cultural (or 'artificial') processes – the Earth (as Gaia) as well as the global market both appear as gigantic self-regulated living systems whose basic structure is defined in terms of the process of coding and decoding, of passing information, and so on. So, while cyberspace ideologists can dream about the next step of evolution in which we will no longer be mechanically interacting 'Cartesian' individuals, in which individuals will cut their substantial links to their bodies and conceive of themselves as part of the new holistic mind that lives and acts through them, what is obfuscated in such a direct 'naturalization' of the Internet or market is the set of power relations – of political decisions, of institutional conditions – which 'organisms' like the Internet (or the market, or capitalism) require to thrive. We are dealing here with an all too fast metaphoric transposition of certain biological-evolutionist concepts to the study of the history of human civilization, like the jump from 'genes' to 'memes', that is, the idea that not only do human beings use language to reproduce themselves, multiply their power and knowledge, and so on, but also, at perhaps a more fundamental level, language itself uses human beings to replicate and expand itself, to gain a new wealth of meanings, and so on.

The standard counter-argument cultural studies' proponents make to third culture criticism is that the loss of the public intellectual bemoaned in these complaints is effectively the loss of the traditional type (usually white and male) of modernist intellectual. In our postmodernist era, that intellectual was replaced by a proliferation of theoreticians who operate in a different mode (replacing concern with one big issue with a series of localized strategic interventions), and who effectively do address issues that concern the public at large (racism and multiculturalism, sexism, how to overcome the Eurocentrist curriculum, and so on) and thus trigger public debates (like the 'political correctness' or sexual harassment controversies). Although this answer is all too easy, the fact remains that themes addressed by cultural studies do stand at the centre of public politico-ideological debates (hybrid multiculturalism versus the need for a close community identification, abortion and queer rights versus Moral Majority fundamentalism, and so on), while the first thing that strikes one apropos of the third culture is how their proponents, busy as they are clarifying the ultimate enigmas ('reading the mind of God', as Hawking once designated it), silently pass over the burning questions that effectively occupy the centre stage of current politico-ideological debates.

Finally, one should note that, in spite of the necessary distinction between science and ideology, the obscurantist New Age ideology is *an immanent outgrowth of modern science itself* – from David Bohm to Fritjof Capra, examples abound of different versions of 'dancing Wu Li masters', teaching us about the Tao of physics, the 'end of the Cartesian paradigm', the significance of the anthropic principle and holistic approach, and so on.[4] To avoid any misunderstanding, as an old-fashioned dialectical materialist, I am ferociously opposed to these obscurantist appropriations of quantum physics and astronomy. These obscurantist sprouts, I believe, are not simply imposed from outside, but function as what Louis Althusser would have called a 'spontaneous ideology' among scientists themselves, as a kind of spiritualist supplement to the predominant reductionist-proceduralist attitude of 'only what can be precisely defined and measured counts'. What is much more worrying than cultural studies' 'excesses' are the

New Age obscurantist appropriations of today's 'hard' sciences that, in order to legitimize their position, invoke the authority of science itself ('today's science has outgrown mechanistic materialism and points toward a new spiritual holistic stance ...'). Significantly, the defenders of scientific realism (like Brichmont and Sokal) only briefly refer to some 'subjectivist' formulations of Heisenberg and Bohr that can give rise to relativist/historicist misappropriations, qualifying them as the expression of their authors' philosophy, not part of the scientific edifice of quantum physics itself. Here, however, problems begin: Bohr's and Heisenberg's 'subjectivist' formulations are not a marginal phenomenon, but were canonized as 'Copenhagen orthodoxy', that is, as the 'official' interpretation of the ontological consequences of quantum physics. The fact is, the moment one wants to provide an ontological account of quantum physics (which notion of reality fits its results), paradoxes emerge that undermine standard commonsense scientistic objectivism. This fact is constantly emphasized by scientists themselves, who oscillate between the simple suspension of the ontological question (quantum physics functions, so do not try to understand it, just do the calculations ...) and different ways out of the deadlock (Copenhagen orthodoxy, the Many Worlds Interpretation, some version of the 'hidden variable' theory that would save the notion of a singular and unique objective reality, like the one proposed by David Bohm, which nonetheless involves paradoxes of its own, like the notion of causality that runs backwards in time).

The more fundamental problem beneath these perplexities is: can we simply renounce the ontological question and limit ourselves to the mere functioning of the scientific apparatus, its calculations and measurements? A further impasse concerns the necessity somehow to relate scientific discoveries to everyday language, to translate them into it. It can be argued that problems emerge only when we try to translate the results of quantum physics back into our commonsense notions of reality. But is it possible to resist this temptation? All these topics are widely discussed in the literature on quantum physics, so they have nothing to do with cultural studies' (mis)appropriation of sciences. It was Richard Feynman himself who, in his famous statement, claimed that 'nobody really understands quantum physics', implying that one can no longer translate its mathematical-theoretical edifice into the terms of our everyday notions of reality. The impact of modern physics *was* the shattering of the traditional naïve-realist epistemological edifice: the sciences themselves opened up a gap in which obscurantist sprouts were able to grow. So, instead of pouring scorn on poor cultural studies, it would be much more productive to approach anew the old topic of the precise epistemological and ontological implications of the shifts in the 'hard' sciences themselves.

(c)   The Impasse of Historicism

On the other hand, the problem with cultural studies, at least in its predominant form, is that it *does* involve a kind of cognitive suspension (the abandonment of the consideration of the inherent truth-value of the theory under consideration), characteristic of historicist relativism. When a typical cultural theorist deals with a philosophical or psychoanalytic edifice, the analysis focuses exclusively on unearthing its hidden patriarchal, Eurocentrist, identitarian 'bias', without ever asking the naïve, but nonetheless necessary questions: 'OK, but what *is* the structure of the universe? How *is* the human psyche "really" working?' Such questions are not even taken seriously in cultural studies, since it simply tends to reduce them to the historicist reflection upon the conditions in which certain notions emerged as the result of historically specific power relations. Furthermore, in a typically rhetorical move, cultural studies denounces the very attempt to draw a clear line of distinction between, say, true science and pre-scientific mythology, as part of the Eurocentrist procedure to impose its own hegemony by devaluating the Other as not-yet-scientific. In this way, we end up arranging and analysing science proper, premodern 'wisdom' and other forms of knowledge as different discursive formations evaluated not with regard to their inherent truth-value, but with regard to their socio-political status and impact (a native 'holistic' wisdom can thus be considered much more 'progressive' than the 'mechanistic' western science responsible for the forms of modern domination). The problem with such a procedure of historicist relativism is that it continues to rely on a set of silent (non-thematized) ontological and epistemological presuppositions about the nature of human knowledge and reality – usually a proto-Nietzschean notion that knowledge is not only embedded in, but also generated by, a complex set of discursive strategies of power (re)production. So it is crucial to emphasize that, at this point, Lacan parts with cultural studies' historicism. For Lacan, modern science is resolutely *not* one of the 'narratives' comparable in principle to other modes of 'cognitive mapping'. Modern science touches the Real in a way totally absent in premodern discourses.

Cultural studies here needs to be put in its proper context. After the demise of the great philosophical schools in the late 1970s, European academic philosophy itself, with its basic hermeneutical-historical stance, paradoxically shares with cultural studies the stance of cognitive suspension. Excellent studies have recently been produced on great past authors, yet they focus on the correct reading of the author in question, while mostly ignoring the naïve, but unavoidable, question of truth-value – not only questions such as 'Is this the right reading of Descartes' notion of the body? Is this what Descartes' notion of the body has to repress in order to retain its consistency?', and so on, but also 'Which, then, *is* the true status of the body? How do *we* stand towards Descartes' notion of the body?' And it seems as if these prohibited 'ontological' questions are returning with a vengeance in today's third culture. What signals the recent rise of quantum physics and cosmology if not a violent and aggressive rehabilitation of the most fundamental metaphysical questions (e.g., what is the origin and putative end of the universe)? The explicit goal of people like Hawking is a version of TOE (Theory of Everything), that is, the endeavour to discover the basic formula of the structure of the universe that one could print and wear on a T-shirt (or, for a human being, the genome that identifies what I objectively am). So, in clear contrast to cultural studies' strict prohibition of direct 'ontological' questions, third culture proponents unabashedly approach the most fundamental pre-Kantian metaphysical issues – the ultimate constituents of reality, the origins and end of the universe, what consciousness is, how life emerged, and so on – as if the old dream, which died with the demise of Hegelianism, of a large synthesis of metaphysics and science, the dream of a global theory of *all* grounded in exact scientific insights, is coming alive again.

In contrast to these two versions of cognitive suspension, the cognitivist approach opts for a naïve, direct inquiry into 'the nature of things' (What is perception? How did language emerge?). However, to use a worn-out phrase, by throwing out the bath water, it also loses the baby, that is, the dimension of proper philosophico-transcendental reflection. That is to say, is historicist relativism (which ultimately leads to the untenable position of solipsism) really the only alternative to naïve scientific realism (according to which, in sciences and in our knowledge in general, we are gradually approaching the proper image of the way things really are out there, independent of our consciousness of them)? From the standpoint of a proper philosophical reflection, it can easily be shown that both of these positions miss the properly transcendental-hermeneutical level. Where does this level reside? Let us take the classical line of realist reasoning, which claims that the passage from premodern mythical thought to the modern scientific approach to reality cannot simply be interpreted as the replacement of one predominant 'narrative' with another, in that the modern scientific approach definitely brings us closer to what 'reality' (the 'hard' reality existing independently of the scientific researcher) effectively is. A hermeneutic philosopher's basic response to this stance would be to insist that, with the passage from the premodern mythic universe to the universe of modern science, *the very notion of what 'reality' (or 'effectively to exist') means or what 'counts' as reality has also changed*, so that we cannot simply presuppose a neutral external measure that allows us to judge that, with modern science, we come closer to the 'same' reality as that with which premodern mythology was dealing. As Hegel would have put it, with the passage from the premodern mythical universe to the modern scientific universe, the measure, the standard that we implicitly use or apply in order to measure how 'real' what we are dealing with is, has itself undergone a fundamental change. The modern scientific outlook involves a series of distinctions (between 'objective' reality and 'subjective' ideas/impressions of it; between hard neutral facts and 'values' that we, the judging subjects, impose onto the facts; and so on) which are *stricto sensu* meaningless in the premodern universe. Of course, a realist can retort that this is the whole point: only with the passage to the modern scientific universe did we get an appropriate notion of what 'objective reality' is, in contrast to the premodern outlook that confused 'facts' and 'values'. Against this, the transcendental-hermeneutic philosopher would be fully justified in insisting that, nonetheless, we cannot get out of the vicious circle of presupposing our result: the most fundamental way reality 'appears' to us, the most fundamental way we experience what 'really counts as effectively existing', is always already presupposed in our judgements of what 'really exists'. This transcendental level was very nicely indicated by Kuhn himself when, in his *Structure of Scientific Revolutions*, he claimed that the shift in a scientific paradigm is *more* than a mere shift in our (external) perspective on/ perception of reality, but nonetheless *less* than our effectively 'creating' another new reality. For that reason, the standard distinction between the social or psychological contingent conditions of a scientific invention and its objective truth-value falls short here: the very distinction between the (empirical, contingent socio-psychological) genesis of a certain scientific formation and its objective truth-value, independent of the conditions of this genesis, already presupposes a set of distinctions (e.g. between genesis and truth-value) that are by no means self-evident. So, again, one should insist here that the hermeneutic-transcendental questioning of the implicit presuppositions in no way endorses the historicist relativism typical of cultural studies.

(d)   *Knowledge and Truth*

In what, then, does the ultimate difference between cognitivism and cultural studies consist? On the one hand, there is neutral objective knowledge, that is, the patient empirical examination of reality. Cognitivists like to emphasize that, politically, they are not against the Left – their aim is precisely to liberate the Left from the irrationalist-relativist-elitist postmodern imposter; nonetheless, they accept the distinction between the neutral theoretical (scientific) insight and the eventual ideologico-political bias of the author. In contrast, cultural studies involves the properly dialectical paradox of a truth that relies on an engaged subjective position. This distinction between knowledge inherent to the academic institution, defined by the standards of 'professionalism', and, on the other hand, the truth of a (collective) subject engaged in a struggle (elaborated, among others, by philosophers from Theodor Adorno to Alain Badiou), enables us to explain how the difference between cognitivists and proponents of cultural studies functions as a shibboleth: it is properly visible only from the side of cultural studies. So, on the one hand, one should fully acknowledge the solid scholarly status of much of the cognitivist endeavour – often, it is academia at its best; on the other hand, there is a dimension that simply eludes its grasp. Let me elaborate this relationship between truth and the accuracy of knowledge by means of a marvellous thought experiment evoked by Daniel Dennett in his *Darwin's Dangerous Idea*: you and your best friend are about to be captured by hostile forces, who know English but do not know much about your world. You both know Morse code, and hit upon the following impromptu encryption scheme: for a dash, speak a truth; for a dot, speak a falsehood. Your captors, of course, listen to you two speak: 'Birds lay eggs, and toads fly. Chicago is a city, and my feet are not made of tin, and baseball is played in August', you say, answering 'No' (dash-dot; dash-dash-dash) to whatever your friend has just asked. Even if your captors know Morse code, unless they can determine the truth and falsity of these sentences, they cannot detect the properties that stand for the dot and dash.[5] Dennett himself uses this example to make the point that meaning cannot be accounted for in purely syntactic inherent terms: the only way ultimately to gain access to the meaning of a statement is to situate it in its life-world context, that is, to take into account its semantic dimension, the objects and processes to which it refers. My point is rather different. As Dennett himself puts it, the two prisoners, in this case, use the world itself as a 'one-time pad'. Although the truth-value of their statements is not indifferent but crucial, it is not this truth-value as such, in itself, that matters; what matters is the translation of truth-value into a differential series of pluses and minuses (dashes and dots) that delivers the true message in Morse code. And is something similar not going on in the psychoanalytic process? Although the truth-value of the patient's statements is not indifferent, what really matters is not this truth-value as such, but the way the very alternation of truths and lies discloses the patient's desire – a patient also uses reality itself (the way they relate to it) as a 'one-time pad' to encrypt their desire. And, in the same way, theory uses the very truth-value (accuracy) of post-theoretical knowledge as a medium to articulate its own truth-message.

On the other hand, politically correct proponents of cultural studies often pay for their arrogance and lack of a serious approach by confusing truth (the engaged subjective position) and knowledge, that is, by disavowing the gap that separates them, by directly subordinating knowledge to truth (say, a quick socio-critical dismissal of a specific science like quantum physics or biology without proper acquaintance with the inherent conceptual structure of this field of knowledge). Essentially, the problem of cultural studies is often the lack of specific disciplinary skills: a literary theorist without proper knowledge of philosophy can write disparaging remarks on Hegel's phallogocentrism, on film, and so on. What we are dealing with here is a kind of false universal critical capacity to pass judgements on everything without proper knowledge. With all its criticism of traditional philosophical universalism, cultural studies effectively functions as a kind of *ersatz*-philosophy, and notions are thus transformed into ideological universals. In postcolonial studies, for instance, the notion of 'colonization' starts to function as a hegemonic notion and is elevated to a universal paradigm, so that in relations between the sexes, the male sex colonizes the female sex, the upper classes colonize the lower classes, and so on. Especially with some 'progressive' interpreters of contemporary biology, it is popular to focus on the way the opposing positions are overdetermined by the politico-ideological stance of their authors. Does Dawkins' 'Chicago gangster theory of life', this reductionist determinist theory about 'selfish genes' caught in a deadly struggle for survival, not express the stance of a competitive, bourgeois individualist society? Is Gould's emphasis on sudden genetic change and ex-aptation not a sign of the more supple, dialectical and 'revolutionary' Leftist stance of its author? Do those who emphasize spontaneous cooperation and emerging order (like Lynn Margulis) not express the longing for a stable organic order, for a society that functions as a 'corporate body'? Do we thus not have here the scientific expression of the basic triad of Right, Centre and Left – of the organicist conservative notion of society as a whole, of the bourgeois individualist notion of society as the space of competition between individuals, and of the revolutionary theorist notion of sudden change? (Of course, the insistence on a holistic approach and emerging order can be given a different accent: it can display the conservative longing for a stable order, or the progressive utopian belief in a new society of solidary cooperation where order grows spontaneously from below and is not imposed from above.) The standard form of the opposition is the one between the 'cold' mechanist probing into causality, displaying the attitude of the scientific manipulator in the service of the exploitative domination of nature, and the new 'holistic' approach focused on spontaneously emerging order and cooperation, pointing toward what Andrew Ross called a 'kinder, gentler science'. The mistake here is the same as that of Stalinist Marxism, which opposed 'bourgeois' to 'proletarian' science, or that of pseudo-radical feminism, which opposes 'masculine' to 'feminine' discourse as two self-enclosed wholes engaged in warfare. We do not have *two* sciences, but *one* universal science split from within, that is, caught in the battle for hegemony.[6]

(e)   *Theoretical State Apparatuses*

The academically recognized 'radical thought' in the liberal West does not operate in a void, but is indeed a part of power relations. Apropos of cultural studies, one has to ask again the old Benjaminian question: not 'How does one explicitly *relate* to power?' but 'How is one *situated within* predominant power relations?' Does cultural studies not also function as a discourse that pretends to be critically self-reflective, to render visible the predominant power relations, while it effectively obfuscates its own mode of participating in them? So it would be productive to apply to cultural studies itself the Foucauldian notion of productive 'bio-power' as opposed to 'repressive'/prohibitory legal power: what if the field of cultural studies, far from effectively threatening today's global relations of domination, fits within this framework perfectly, in the same way that sexuality and the 'repressive' discourses that regulate it are fully complementary? What if the criticism of patriarchal/identitarian ideology betrays an ambiguous fascination with it, rather than a will committed to undermining it? There is a way to *avoid* responsibility and/or guilt precisely by emphasizing one's responsibility or too readily assuming guilt in an exaggerated way, as in the case of the politically correct white male academic who emphasizes the guilt of racist phallogocentrism, and uses this admission of guilt as a stratagem *not* to confront the way he, as a 'radical' intellectual, perfectly fits the existing power relations of which he pretends to be thoroughly critical. Crucial here is the shift from British to American cultural studies. Even if we find the same themes and notions in both, the socio-ideological functioning is thoroughly different: we shift from the effective engagement with working-class culture to academic radical chic.

However, despite these critical remarks, the very fact that there is resistance to cultural studies proves that it remains a foreign body unable to fit fully into the existing academy. Cognitivism is ultimately the attempt to get rid of this intruder, to re-establish the standard functioning of academic knowledge – 'professional', rational, empirical, problem-solving, and so on. The distinction between cognitivism and cultural studies is thus not simply the distinction between two doctrines or two theoretical approaches; it is ultimately a much more radical distinction between two totally different modalities or, rather, *practices* of knowledge, inclusive of two different institutional apparatuses of knowledge. This dimension of 'theoretical state apparatuses', to use the Althusserian formulation, is crucial: if we do not take it into account, we simply miss the point of the antagonism between cognitivism and cultural studies. It is no wonder that cognitivists like to emphasize their opposition to psychoanalysis: two exemplary cases of such non-academic knowledge are, of course, Marxism and psychoanalysis. Psychoanalysis differs from cognitivist psychology and psychotherapy in at least three crucial features: (1) since it does not present itself as empirically tested objective knowledge, there is the perennial problem (in the United States, where psychiatric care is sometimes covered by medical insurance) of the extent to which the state or insurance will reimburse the patient; (2) for the same reason, psychoanalysis has inherent difficulties in integrating itself into the academic edifice of psychology or medical psychiatry departments, so it usually functions as a parasitic entity that attaches itself to cultural studies, comparative literature or psychology departments; (3) as to their inherent organization, psychoanalytic communities do not function as 'normal' academic societies (like sociological, mathematical or other societies). From the standpoint of 'normal' academic societies, the psychoanalytic society cannot but appear as a 'dogmatic' discipline engaged in eternal factional struggles between sub-groups dominated by a strong authoritarian or charismatic leader; conflicts within psychoanalytic communities are not resolved through rational argumentation and empirical testing, but rather resemble sectarian religious struggles. In short, the phenomenon of (personal) transference functions here in an entirely different way than in the 'standard' academic community. (The dynamics in Marxist communities are somewhat similar.) In the same way that Marxism interprets the resistance against its insights as the 'result of the class struggle in theory', as accounted for by its very object, psychoanalysis also interprets the resistance against itself to be the result of the very unconscious processes that are its topic. In both cases, theory is caught in a self-referential loop: it is in a way *the theory about the resistance against itself*. Concerning this crucial point, the situation today is entirely different than, almost the opposite of, that of the 1960s and early 1970s when 'marginal' disciplines (like the cultural studies' version of psychoanalysis) were perceived as 'anarchic', as liberating us from the 'repressive' authoritarian regime of the standard academic discipline. What cognitivist critics of cultural studies play upon is the common perception that, today, (what remains of) the cultural studies' version of psychoanalysis is perceived as sectarian, Stalinist, authoritarian, engaged in ridiculous pseudo-theological factional struggles in which problems over the party line prevail over open empirical research and rational argumentation. Cognitivists present themselves as the fresh air that does away with this close and stuffy atmosphere – finally, one is free to formulate and test different hypotheses, no longer 'terrorized' by some dogmatically imposed global party line. We are thus far from the anti-academic/establishment logic of the 1960s: today, academia presents itself as the place of open, free discussion, as liberating us from the stuffy constraints of 'subversive' cultural studies. And although, of course, the 'regression' into authoritarian prophetic discourse is one of the dangers that threatens cultural studies, its inherent temptation, one should nonetheless focus attention on how the cognitivist stance succeeds in unproblematically presenting the framework of the institutional academic university discourse as the very locus of intellectual freedom.

2. IS FREEDOM NOTHING BUT A CONCEIVED NECESSITY?

(a)   *You Cannot, Because You Should Not!*

So, how does Lacanian theory enable us to avoid the impasse of cultural studies and to confront the challenge of the cognitivist and/or evolutionary naturalization of the human subject? In Andrew Niccol's futuristic thriller *Gatacca* (1998), Ethan Hawke and Uma Thurman prove their love for each other by throwing away the hair each partner provides to be analyzed in order to establish his or her genetic quality. In this futuristic society, authority (access to the privileged elite) is established 'objectively', through genetic analysis of the newborn – we no longer have symbolic authority proper, since authority is directly grounded in the real of the genome. As such, *Gatacca* merely extrapolates the prospect, opened up today, of the direct legitimization of social authority and power in the real of the genetic code: 'By eliminating artificial forms of inequality, founded on power and culture, socially egalitarian programs could eventually highlight and crystallize natural forms of inequality far more dramatically than ever before, in a new hierarchical order founded on the genetic code'.[7] Against this prospect, it is not enough to insist that the democratic principle of what Étienne Balibar calls *egaliberté* has nothing to do with the genetic-biological similarity of human individuals, but aims instead at the principal equality of subjects *qua* participants in the symbolic space. *Gatacca* confronts us with the following dilemma: is the only way to retain our dignity as humans by way of accepting some limitation, of stopping short of full insight into our genome, short of our full naturalization, that is, by way of a gesture of 'I do not want to know what you objectively/really are, I accept you for what you are'?

Among the modern philosophers, it was Kant who most forcefully confronted this predicament, constraining our knowledge of the causal interconnection of objects to the domain of phenomena in order to make a place for noumenal freedom, which is why the hidden truth of

Kant's 'You can, therefore you must!' is its reversal: 'You cannot, because you should not!' The ethical problems of cloning seem to point in this direction. Those who oppose cloning argue that we *should not* pursue it, at least not on human beings, because it is *not possible* to reduce a human being to a positive entity whose innermost psychic properties can be manipulated – biogenetic manipulation *cannot* touch the core of human personality, so we should prohibit it. Is this not another variation on Wittgenstein's paradox of *prohibiting the impossible*: 'What we cannot speak about we must pass over in silence'? The underlying fear that gains expression in this prohibition, of course, is that the order of reason is actually inverted, that is, that the ontological impossibility is grounded in ethics: we should claim that we cannot do it, because otherwise *we may well do it*, with catastrophic ethical consequences. If conservative Catholics effectively believe in the immortality of the human soul and the uniqueness of human personality, if they insist we are not just the result of the interaction between our genetic code and our environs, then why do they oppose cloning and genetic manipulations? In other words, is it not that *these Christian opponents of cloning themselves secretly believe in the power of scientific manipulation, in its capacity to stir up the very core of our personality*? Of course, their answer would be that human beings, by treating themselves as just the result of the interaction between their genetic codes and their environs, freely renounce their dignity: the problem is not genetic manipulation as such, but the fact that its acceptance signals how human beings conceive of themselves as just another biological machine and thus rob themselves of their unique spirituality. However, the answer to this is, again: but why should we not endorse genetic manipulation *and* simultaneously insist that human beings are free responsible agents, since we accept the proviso that these manipulations do not really affect the core of our soul? Why do Christians still talk about the 'unfathomable mystery of conception' that man should not meddle with, as if, nonetheless, by pursuing our biogenetic explorations, we may touch some secret better left in shadow – in short, as if, by cloning our bodies, we *at the same time also clone our immortal souls*?

So, again, we are back at the well-known conservative wisdom that claims that the only way to save human freedom and ethical dignity is to restrain our cognitive capacities and renounce probing too deeply into the nature of things. Today's sciences themselves seem to point toward a way out of this predicament. Does contemporary cognitivism not often produce formulations that sound uncannily familiar to those acquainted with different versions of ancient and modern philosophy, from the Buddhist notion of Void and the German Idealist notion of reflexivity as constitutive of the subject, up to the Heideggerian notion of 'being-in-the-world' or the deconstructionist one of *différance*? The temptation arises here to fill in the gap by either reducing philosophy to science, claiming that modern naturalizing cognitivism 'realizes' philosophical insights, translating them into acceptable scientific form, or, on the contrary, by claiming that, with these insights, postmodern science breaks out of the 'Cartesian paradigm' and approaches the level of authentic philosophical thought. This short-circuit between science and philosophy appears today in a multitude of guises: Heideggerian cognitivism (Hubert Dreyfuss), cognitivist Buddhism (Francisco Varela), the combination of oriental thought with quantum physics (Capra's 'Tao of physics'), up to deconstructionist evolutionism. Let's take a brief look at the two main versions of this short-circuit.

(b) *Deconstructionist Evolutionism*

There are obvious parallels between the recent popularized readings of Darwin (from Gould to Dawkins and Dennett) and Derridean deconstruction. Does Darwinism not practise a kind of 'deconstruction', not only of natural teleology, but also of the very idea of nature as a well-ordered positive system of species? Does the strict Darwinian notion of 'adaptation' not claim that, precisely, *organisms do not directly 'adapt'*, that there is *stricto sensu* no 'adaptation' in the teleological sense of the term? Contingent genetic changes occur, and some of them enable some organisms to function better and survive in an environment that is itself fluctuating and articulated in a complex way, but there is no linear adaptation to a stable environment: when something unexpectedly changes in the environment, a feature which hitherto prevented full 'adaptation' can suddenly become crucial for the organism's survival. So Darwinism effectively prefigures a version of Derridean *différance* or of Freudian *Nachträglichkeit*, according to which contingent and meaningless genetic changes are retroactively used (or 'exapted', as Gould would have put it) in a manner appropriate for survival. In other words, what Darwin provides is a model explanation of how a state of things which appears to involve a well-ordered teleological economy (animals doing things 'in order to . . .'), is effectively the outcome of a series of meaningless changes. The temporality here is future anterior, that is, 'adaptation' is something that always and by definition 'will have been'. And is this enigma of how (the semblance of) teleological and meaningful order can emerge from contingent and meaningless occurrences not also central to deconstruction?

One can thus effectively claim that Darwinism (of course, in its true radical dimension, not as a vulgarized evolutionism) 'deconstructs' not only teleology or divine intervention in nature, but also the very notion of nature as a stable positive order – this makes the silence of deconstruction about Darwinism, the absence of deconstructionist attempts to 'appropriate' it, all the more enigmatic. Dennett, the great proponent of cognitivist evolutionism, himself acknowledges (ironically, no doubt, but nonetheless with an underlying serious intent) the closeness of his 'pandemonium' theory of human mind to cultural studies deconstructionism in his *Consciousness Explained*: 'Imagine my mixed emotions when I discovered that before I could get my version of the idea of "the self as the centre of narrative gravity" properly published in a book, it had already been satirized in a novel, David Lodge's *Nice Work*. It is apparently a hot theme among the deconstructionists.'[8] Furthermore, a whole school of cyberspace theorists (the best known among them is Sherry Turkle) advocate the notion that cyberspace-phenomena render palpable in our everyday experience the deconstructionist 'decentred subject'. According to these theorists, one should endorse the 'dissemination' of the unique self into a multiplicity of competing agents, into a 'collective mind', a plurality of self-images without a global coordinating centre, that is operative in cyberspace, and disconnect it from pathological trauma – playing in virtual spaces enables individuals to discover new aspects of 'self', a wealth of shifting identities, and thus to experience the ideological mechanism of the production of self, the immanent violence and arbitrariness of this production/construction.

However, the temptation to be avoided here is precisely the hasty conclusion that Dennett is a kind of deconstructionist wolf in the sheep's clothing of empirical science. There is a gap that forever separates Dennett's evolutionary naturalization of consciousness from the deconstructionist 'meta-transcendental' probing into the conditions of (im)possibility of philosophical discourse. As Derrida argues exemplarily in his 'White Mythology', it is insufficient to claim that 'all concepts are metaphors', that there is no pure epistemological cut, since the umbilical cord connecting abstract concepts with everyday metaphors is irreducible. First, the point is not simply that 'all concepts are metaphors', but that the very difference between a concept and a metaphor is always minimally metaphorical, relying on some metaphor. Even more important is the opposite conclusion, that the very reduction of a concept to a bundle of metaphors already has to rely on some implicit *philosophical, conceptual* determination of the difference between concept and metaphor, that is to say, on the very opposition it tries to undermine.[9] We are thus forever caught in a vicious circle: true, it is impossible to adopt a philosophical stance freed from the constraints of naïve, everyday life-world attitudes and notions; however, although *impossible*, this philosophical stance is at the same time *unavoidable*. Derrida makes the same point apropos of the well-known historicist thesis that the entire Aristotelian ontology of the ten modes of being is an effect/expression of Greek grammar. The problem is that *this reduction of ontology (of ontological categories) to an effect of grammar presupposes a certain notion (categorical determination) of the relationship between grammar and ontological concepts which is itself already metaphysical-Greek.*[10]

We should always bear in mind this delicate Derridean stance, through which the twin pitfalls of naïve realism and direct philosophical foundationalism are avoided: a 'philosophical foundation' for our experience is *impossible*, and yet *necessary* – although all we perceive, understand and articulate is, of course, overdetermined by a horizon of pre-understanding, this horizon itself remains ultimately impenetrable. Derrida is thus a kind of meta-transcendentalist, in search of the conditions of possibility of this very philosophical discourse. If we miss this precise way in which Derrida undermines philosophical discourse *from within*, we reduce deconstruction to just another naïve historicist relativism. Derrida's position here is thus the opposite of Foucault's. In answer to a criticism that he speaks from a position whose possibility is not accounted for within the framework of his theory, Foucault cheerfully retorted: 'These kinds of questions do not concern me: they belong to the police discourse with its files constructing the subject's identity!' In other words, the ultimate lesson of deconstruction seems to be that one cannot postpone *ad infinitum* the *ontological* question; and what is deeply symptomatic in Derrida is his oscillation between, on the one hand, the hyper-self-reflective approach that denounces in advance the question of 'how things really are' and limits itself to third-level deconstructive comments on the inconsistencies of philosopher B's reading of philosopher A, and, on the other hand, direct 'ontological' assertions about how *différance* and arche-trace designate the structure of all living things and are, as such, already operative in animal nature. One should not miss here the paradoxical interconnection between these two levels: the very feature that prevents us from forever directly grasping our intended object (the fact that our grasping is always refracted, 'mediated', by a decentred otherness) is the feature that connects us with the basic proto-ontological structure of the universe.

Deconstructionism thus involves two prohibitions: it prohibits the 'naïve' empiricist approach ('let us examine carefully the material in question and then generalize hypotheses about it . . .'), as well as global ahistorical metaphysical theses about the origin and structure of the universe. This double prohibition that defines deconstructionism clearly and unambiguously bears witness to its Kantian transcendental origins. Is not the same double prohibition characteristic of Kant's philosophical revolution? On the one hand, the notion of the transcendental constitution of reality involves the loss of a direct naïve empiricist approach to reality; on the other hand, it involves the prohibition of metaphysics, that is, of an all-encompassing world-view providing the noumenal structure of the universe as a whole. In other words, one should always bear in mind that, far from simply expressing a belief in the constitutive power of the (transcendental) subject, Kant introduces the notion of the transcendental dimension in order to answer the fundamental and unsurpassable deadlock of human existence: a human being compulsorily strives toward a global notion of truth, of a universal and necessary cognition, yet this cognition is simultaneously forever inaccessible to them.

(c) Cognitivist Buddhism

Is the outcome any better in the emerging alliance between the cognitivist approach to mind and the proponents of Buddhist thought, where the point is not to naturalize philosophy, but rather the opposite, that is, to use the results of cognitivism in order to (re)gain access to ancient wisdom? The contemporary cognitivist denial of a unitary, stable, self-identical self – that is, the notion of the human mind as a pandemonic playground of multiple agencies, that some authors (most notably Francisco Varela)[11] link to the Buddhist denial of the self as the permanent substance underlying our mental acts/events – seems persuasive in its critical rejection of the substantial notion of self. The paradox upon which cognitivists and neo-Buddhists build is the gap between our common experience that automatically relies on and/or involves a reference to some notion of self as the underlying substance that 'has' feelings and volitions and to which these mental states and acts 'happen', and the fact, well known even in Europe at least from Hume onwards, that, no matter how deeply and carefully we search our self-experience, we encounter only passing, elusive mental events, and never the self as such (that is, a substance to which these events could be attributed). The conclusion drawn by cognitivists and Buddhists alike is, of course, that the notion of self is the result of an epistemological (or, in the case of Buddhism, ethico-epistemological) mistake inherent to human nature as such. The thing to do is to get rid of this delusive notion and to fully assume that there is no self, that 'I' am nothing but that groundless bundle of elusive and heterogeneous (mental) events.

Is, however, this conclusion really unavoidable? Varela also rejects the Kantian solution of the self, the subject of pure apperception, as the transcendental subject nowhere to be found in our empirical experience. Here, though, one should introduce the distinction between egoless/selfless mind events or aggregates and the subject as identical to this void, to this lack of substance, itself. What if the conclusion that there is no self is too quickly drawn from the fact that there is no representation or positive idea of self? What if the self is precisely the 'I of the storm', the void in the centre of the incessant vortex/whirlpool of elusive mental events, something like the 'vacuola' in biology, the void that is nothing in itself, that has no substantial positive identity, but which nonetheless serves as the unrepresentable point of reference, as the 'I' to which mental events are attributed? In Lacanian terms, one has to distinguish between the 'self' as the pattern of behavioural and other imaginary and symbolic identifications (as the 'self-image', as that what I perceive myself to be) and the empty point of pure negativity, the 'barred' subject ($). Varela himself comes close to this when he distinguishes between: (1) the self *qua* the series of mental and bodily formations that has a certain degree of causal coherence and integrity through time; (2) the capitalized Self *qua* the hidden substantial kernel of the subject's identity (the 'ego-self'); and, finally, (3) the desperate craving/grasping of the human mind for/to the self, for/to some kind of firm bedrock. From the Lacanian perspective, however, is this 'endless craving' not *the subject itself*, the void that 'is' subjectivity?

Neo-Buddhists are justified in criticizing cognitivist proponents of the 'society of mind' notion for endorsing the irreducible split between our scientific cognition (which tells us that there is no self or free will) and the everyday experience in which we simply cannot function without presupposing a consistent self endowed with free will. Cognitivists have thus condemned themselves to a nihilistic stance of endorsing beliefs they know are wrong. The effort of neo-Buddhists is to bridge this gap by translating/transposing the very insight that there is no substantial self into our daily human experience (this is ultimately what Buddhist meditative reflection is about). When Ray Jackendoff, author of one of the ultimate cognitivist attempts to explain consciousness, suggests that our awareness-consciousness emerges from the fact that we are, precisely, *not* aware of the way awareness-consciousness itself is generated by worldly processes – that there is consciousness only insofar as its biological-organic origins remain opaque[12] – he comes very close to the Kantian insight that there is self-consciousness, that I think, only insofar as '*das Ich oder Er oder Es (das Ding), welches denkt*'[13] remains impenetrable for me. Varela's counter-argument that Jackendoff's reasoning is confused, that these

processes we are unaware of are just that – processes that are not part
of our daily human experience but totally beyond it, hypostatized by
the cognitivist scientific practice[14] – thus misses the point. This
inaccessibility of the substantial-natural self (or, rather, of the
substantial-natural base to my self) *is* part of our daily non-scientific
experience, precisely in the guise of our ultimate failure to find a
positive element in our experience that would directly 'be' our self
(the experience, formulated already by Hume, that no matter how
deeply we analyse our mental processes, we never find anything
that would be our self). So what if one should here apply to Varela
the joke about the madman who was looking for his lost key under a
street light and not in the dark corner where he lost it, because
it was easier to search under the light? What if we are looking for
the self in the wrong place, in the false evidence of positive empirical facts?

(d)   *The Inaccessible Phenomenon*

Our result is thus that there is effectively no way to overcome the abyss
that separates the transcendental *a priori* horizon from the domain of
positive scientific discoveries. On the one hand, the standard 'philosophical reflection of science' (positive sciences 'do not think'; they are
unable to reflect on their horizon of pre-understanding accessible only
to philosophy) more and more resembles an old automatic trick losing
its efficiency; on the other hand, the idea that some 'postmodern'
science will attain the level of philosophical reflection (say, that
quantum physics, by including the observer in the observed material
objectivity, breaks out of the frame of scientific objectivism/naturalism
and reaches the level of the transcendental constitution of reality)
clearly misses the proper level of transcendental *a priori*.

It is true that modern philosophy is in a way 'on the defensive'
against the onslaught of science. Kant's transcendental turn is linked
to the rise of modern science not only in the obvious way (providing
the *a priori* of Newtonian physics), but in the more radical way of
taking into account how, with the rise of modern empirical science, a
direct metaphysical 'theory of everything' is no longer viable and
cannot be combined with science. So the only thing philosophy can do

is to 'phenomenalize' scientific knowledge and then to provide its *a priori* hermeneutic horizon, given the ultimate inscrutability of the universe and man. It was Adorno who had already emphasized the thorough ambiguity of Kant's notion of transcendental constitution: far from simply asserting the subject's constitutive power, it can also be read as the resigned acceptance of the *a priori limitation* of our approach to the real. And it is our contention that, if we think to the end the consequences of this notion of the transcendental subject, we can nonetheless avoid this debilitating deadlock and 'save freedom'. How? By reading this deadlock as its own solution, that is, by yet again displacing the epistemological obstacle into a positive ontological condition.

To avoid any misunderstanding: we are not aiming here at illegitimate short-circuits in the style of 'the ontological undecidability of the quantum fluctuation grounds human freedom', but at a much more radical pre-ontological openness/gap, a 'bar' of impossibility in the midst of 'reality' itself. What if *there is no 'universe'* in the sense of an ontologically fully constituted cosmos? That is to say, the mistake of identifying (self)consciousness with misrecognition, with an epistemological obstacle, is that it stealthily (re)introduces the standard, premodern, 'cosmological' notion of reality as a positive order of being. In such a fully constituted, positive 'chain of being', there is, of course, no place for the subject, so the dimension of subjectivity can only be conceived of as something which is strictly codependent with the epistemological misrecognition of the true positivity of being. Consequently, the only way effectively to account for the status of (self)consciousness is to assert *the ontological incompleteness of 'reality' itself*: there is 'reality' only insofar as there is an ontological gap, a crack, in its very heart. It is only this gap that accounts for the mysterious 'fact' of transcendental freedom, that is, for a (self)consciousness that is effectively 'spontaneous' and whose spontaneity is not an effect of the misrecognition of some 'objective' causal process, no matter how complex and chaotic this process is. And where does *psychoanalysis* stand with regard to this deadlock? In a first approach, it may seem that psychoanalysis is the ultimate attempt to fill in the gap, to re-establish the complete causal chain that generated the 'inexplicable' symptom. However, does Lacan's strict opposition between cause and the law (of causality) not point in a wholly different direction? Lacan states:

> Cause is to be distinguished from that which is determinate in a chain, in other words from the *law*. By way of example, think of what is pictured in the law of action and reaction. There is here, one might say, a single principle. One does not go without the other ... There is no gap here ... Whenever we speak of cause, on the other hand, there is always something anti-conceptual, something indefinite ... In short, there is a cause only in something that doesn't work ... The Freudian unconscious is situated at that point, where, between cause and that which it affects, there is always something wrong. The important thing is not that the unconscious determines neurosis – of that one Freud can quite happily, like Pontius Pilate, wash his hands. Sooner or later, something would have been found, humoural determinates, for example – for Freud, it would be quite immaterial. For what the unconscious does is to show the gap through which neurosis recreates a harmony with a real – a real that may well not be determined.[15]

The unconscious intervenes when something 'goes wrong' in the order of causality that encompasses our daily activity: a slip of the tongue introduces a gap in the connection between intention-to-signify and words, a failed gesture frustrates my act. However, Lacan's point is, precisely, that psychoanalytic interpretation does not simply fill in this gap by way of providing the hidden complete network of causality that 'explains' the slip: the cause whose 'insistence' interrupts the normal functioning of the order of causality is not another positive entity. As Lacan emphasizes, it belongs rather to the order of the *nonrealized* or *thwarted*, that is, it is *in itself structured as a gap*, a void insisting indefinitely on its fulfilment. (The psychoanalytic name for this gap, of course, is the death drive, while its philosophical name in German Idealism is 'abstract negativity', the point of absolute self-contraction that constitutes the subject as the void of pure self-relating.)

And the psychoanalytic notion of fantasy accounts precisely for the illusory/failed attempt to fill in this ontological gap. The basic paradox of the Freudian notion of fantasy resides in the fact that it subverts the standard opposition between 'subjective' and 'objective'. Of course, fantasy is by definition not 'objective' (in the naïve sense of 'existing' independently of the subject's perceptions); however, it is also not 'subjective' (in the sense of being reducible to the subject's consciously experienced intuitions). Fantasy rather belongs to the 'bizarre category of the objectively subjective – the way things actually, objectively seem to you even if they don't seem that way to you'.[16] When, for example, the subject actually experiences a series of fantasmatic formations that interrelate as so many permutations of each other, this series is never complete; rather, it is always as if the actually experienced series presents so many variations of some underlying 'fundamental' fantasy that is never actually experienced by the subject. (In Freud's 'A Child Is Being Beaten', the two consciously experienced fantasies pre-suppose, and thus relate to, a third one, 'My father is beating me', which was never actually experienced and can only be retroactively reconstructed as the presupposed reference of – or, in this case, the intermediate term between – the other two fantasies.[17]) One can go even further and claim that, in this sense, the Freudian unconscious itself is 'objectively subjective'. When, for example, we claim that someone who is consciously well-disposed toward Jews nonetheless harbours profound anti-Semitic prejudices he is not consciously aware of, do we not claim that (insofar as these prejudices do not render the way Jews really are, but the way they appear to him) *he is not aware how Jews really seem to him?*

Furthermore, does this not allow us to throw a new light on the mystery of Marxian commodity fetishism? What the fetish objectivizes is 'my true belief', the way things 'truly seem to me', although I never effectively experience them this way – Marx himself here uses the term *'objektiv-notwendiges Schein* [a necessarily objective appearance]'.[18] So, when a critical Marxist encounters a bourgeois subject immersed in commodity fetishism, the Marxist's reproach to him is not, 'A commodity may seem to you a magical object endowed with special powers, but it really is just a reified expression of relations between people'; the Marxist's actual reproach is rather, 'You may think that the commodity appears to you as a simple embodiment of social relations (that, for example, money is just a kind of voucher entitling you to a part of the social product), but *this is not how things really seem to you* – in your social reality, by means of your participation in social exchange, you bear witness to the uncanny fact that a commodity really appears to you as a magical object endowed with special powers.'

This is also one of the ways of specifying the meaning of Lacan's assertion of the subject's constitutive 'decentrement'. The point is not that my subjective experience is regulated by objective unconscious mechanisms that are 'decentred' with regard to my self-experience and, as such, beyond my control (a point asserted by every materialist), but rather something much more unsettling: I am deprived of even my most intimate 'subjective' experience, of the way things 'really seem to me', of the fundamental fantasy that constitutes and guarantees the core of my being, since I can never consciously experience it and assume it. According to the standard view, the dimension that is constitutive of subjectivity is that of the phenomenal (self)experience. In other words, I am a subject the moment I can say to myself: 'No matter what unknown mechanism governs my acts, perceptions and thoughts, nobody can take from me what I see and feel now.' Say, when I am passionately in love, and a biochemist informs me that all my intense sentiments are just the result of biochemical processes in my body, I can answer him by clinging to the appearance: 'All you're saying may be true, but, nonetheless, nothing can take from me the intensity of the passion that I am experiencing now . . .' Lacan's point, however, is that the psychoanalyst is the one who, precisely, *can* take this from the subject, insofar as his or her ultimate aim is to deprive the subject of the very fundamental fantasy that regulates the universe of the subject's (self)experience. The Freudian subject of the unconscious emerges only when a key aspect of the subject's *phenomenal* (self)experience (his or her fundamental fantasy) becomes *inaccessible* (that is, is primordially repressed). At its most radical, the unconscious is the *inaccessible phenomenon*, not the objective mechanism, that regulates my phenomenal experience. So, in contrast to the commonplace that we are dealing with a subject the moment an entity displays signs of 'inner life' – that is, of a fantasmatic self-experience that cannot be reduced to external behaviour – one should claim that what characterizes human subjectivity proper is rather the gap that separates the two, that is, the fact that fantasy, at its most elementary, becomes inaccessible to the subject; it is this inaccessibility that makes the subject 'empty' ($). We thus obtain a relationship that totally subverts the standard notion of the subject who directly experiences themselves and their 'inner states': an 'impossible' relationship between the *empty, nonphenomenal subject* and the *phenomena that remain inaccessible to the subject* – the very relation registered by Lacan's formula of fantasy, $\$\lozenge a$.

Geneticists predict that in about ten to fifteen years, they will be able to identify and manipulate each individual's exact genome. Potentially, at least, each individual will thus have at their disposal the complete formula of what they 'objectively are'. How will this 'knowledge in the Real', the fact that I will be able to locate and identify myself completely as an object in reality, affect the status of subjectivity? Will it lead to the end of human subjectivity? Lacan's answer is negative: what will continue to elude the geneticist is not my phenomenal self-experience (say, the experience of a love passion that no knowledge of the genetic and other material mechanisms determining it can take from me), but the 'objectively subjective' fundamental fantasy, the fantasmatic core inaccessible to my conscious experience. Even if science formulates the genetic formula of what I objectively am, it will still be unable to formulate my 'objectively subjective' fantasmatic identity, this objectal counterpoint to my subjectivity, which is neither subjective (experienced) nor objective.

NOTES

Published in *UMBR(a): A Journal of the Unconscious* 4, 2000, pp. 9–32 [eds].

1   Richard Dawkins, 'A Survival Machine', in *The Third Culture: Beyond the Scientific Revolution*, ed. John Brockman, New York, Simon and Schuster, 1996, p. 23.
2   Stephen Jay Gould, 'The Pattern of Life's History', in *The Third Culture*, p. 21.
3   John Brockman, 'Introduction: The Emerging Third Culture', in *The Third Culture*, pp. 17–34.
4   See, as one among the thousand paradigmatic passages: 'Is there, as David Bohm says, an "implicate order" to matter that is

beyond our present comprehension and presumes a "wholeness" to all things? Can we conceive of a "Tao of physics", as Fritjof Capra's million-selling book terms it, in which Eastern philosophies parallel the mind-wrenching paradoxes of the quantum world?' Pat Kane, 'There's Method in the Magic', in *The Politics of Risk Society,* ed. Jane Franklin, Oxford, Polity, 1998, pp. 78–9.

5   See Daniel C. Dennett, *Darwin's Dangerous Idea: Evolution and the Meanings of Life,* Harmondsworth, Penguin, 1995, p. 421.

6   It is interesting to note how the opposition of 'hard' science, whose conceptual structure embodies the stance of domination, and 'gentle' science bent on collaboration, and so on, comes dangerously close to the New Age ideology of two mental universes, masculine and feminine, competitive and cooperative, rational-dissecting and intuitive-encompassing. In short, we come dangerously close to the premodern sexualization of the universe, which is conceived of as the tension between the two principles, Masculine and Feminine.

7   Perry Anderson, 'A Sense of the Left', *New Left Review* 231, September/October 1998, p. 76.

8   Daniel C. Dennett, *Consciousness Explained,* Harmondsworth, Penguin, 1991, p. 410.

9   See Jacques Derrida, 'White Mythology: Metaphor in the Text of Philosophy', in *Margins of Philosophy,* trans. Alan Bass, Chicago, University of Chicago Press, 1984, pp. 207–71.

10   See Jacques Derrida, 'The Supplement of the Copula: Philosophy before Linguistics', in *Margins of Philosophy,* pp. 175–205.

11   See Francisco Varela, Evan Thompson and Eleanor Rosh, *The Embodied Mind,* Cambridge MA, MIT Press, 1993.

12   See Ray Jackendoff, *Consciousness and the Computational Mind,* Cambridge MA, MIT Press, 1987.

13   'The I/Ego or He or It (the Thing), which thinks.'

14   See Varela, Thompson and Rosh, *The Embodied Mind,* p. 126.

15   Jacques Lacan, *The Seminar of Jacques Lacan XI: The Four Fundamental Concepts of Psycho-Analysis, 1964,* ed. Jacques-Alain Miller, trans. Alan Sheridan, New York, W. W. Norton, 1977, p. 22.

16 Dennett, *Consciousness Explained*, p. 132. (Dennett, of course, evokes this concept in a purely negative way, as a nonsensical *contradictio in adjecto*.)

17 Sigmund Freud, ' "A Child Is Being Beaten" (A Contribution to the Study of the Origin of Sexual Perversions)', in *The Penguin Freud Library, 10: On Psychopathology*, ed. and trans. James Strachey, Harmondsworth, Penguin, 1979, pp. 169–71 [eds].

18 Karl Marx, *Capital: A Critique of Political Economy, Volume 1*, trans. Ben Fowkes, London, Penguin/New Left Books, 1976, pp. 166–7 [eds].

Section II

PHILOSOPHY TRAVERSED BY PSYCHOANALYSIS

6 *The Limits of the Semiotic Approach to Psychoanalysis*

1. LE POINT DE CAPITON

Lacan's best-known proposition is surely the famous 'the unconscious is structured like a language', which is usually understood as pointing toward a semiotic reinterpretation of psychoanalytical theory and practice. The aim of the present paper is to demonstrate that, contrary to this widely assumed proposition, Lacan's theory, at least in its last period, is far from endorsing any such linguistic reductionism: his central effort is precisely to articulate the different modes of the real kernel (*das Ding, objet petit a*) which presents an irreducible obstacle to the movement of symbolization. We will try to exemplify this deadlock of symbolization by some ideological and artistic phenomena.

Let's begin on the opposite end: with the elementary semiotic operation as it is articulated by Lacan – that of the *point de capiton*. Lacan introduces this concept in his *Seminar III*, with regard to the first act of *Athalie* by Racine: in response to the lamentations of Abner about the sad fate which awaits the partisans of God under the reign of Athalia, Jehoiada replies with these famous lines:

> He who can still the raging seas
> can also thwart the wicked in their plots.
> In respectful submission to His holy will,
> I fear God, dear Abner, and have no other fear.[1]

This brings about a true conversion of Abner: from an impatient zealot [*zélé*], and precisely for that reason uncertain, these words create a calm believer [*fidélé*] assured of himself and of a greater divine power. But how does this evocation of the 'fear of God' succeed in effecting such a miraculous conversion? Before his conversion, Abner sees in the earthly world only a multitude of dangers that fill him with fear, and he waits for the opposite pole, that of God and his representatives, to lend him their help and allow him to overcome the many difficulties of this world. Faced with this opposition between the earthly realm of dangers, uncertainty, fear, etc., and the divine realm of peace, love and assurance, Jehoiada does not simply try to convince Abner that divine forces are, despite everything, powerful enough to have the upper hand over earthly disarray; he appeases his fears in a quite different way: by presenting him with their very opposite – God – as a more frightening thing than all earthly fears. And – this is the 'miracle' of the *point de capiton* – this supplemental fear, the fear of God, retroactively changes the character of all other fears. It:

> transforms, from one minute to the next, all fears into perfect courage. All fears – *I have no other fear* – are exchanged for what is called the fear of God.[2]

The common Marxist formula – religious consolation as compensation for or, more precisely, an 'imaginary supplement' to earthly misery – should thus be taken literally. In this case we are dealing with a dual imaginary relation between the earthly below and the celestial beyond, without the intervention of the moment of symbolic 'mediation'. The religious operation would consist, according to this conception, in compensating us for earthly horrors and uncertainties by the beatitude that awaits us in the other world – all the famous formulas of Feuerbach on the divine beyond as an inverted, specular image of earthly misery. For this operation to work, a third moment must intervene, which somehow 'mediates' between the two, opposite poles. Behind the multitude of earthly horrors, the infinitely more frightening horror of God's anger must show through, so that earthly horrors take on a new dimension and become so many manifestations of divine anger. One has the same operation, for example, in Fascism: what does Hitler do in *Mein Kampf* to explain to the Germans the misfortunes of this epoch (e.g. economic crisis, moral 'decadence', etc.)? Behind the multitude of these miseries he constructs a new terrifying subject, a unique cause of evil: the Jew. The so-called 'Jewish plot' *explains everything*, so that all earthly miseries – from the economic crisis to the family crisis – become manifestations of the 'Jewish plot': the Jew is thus Hitler's *point de capiton*.

The 'Dreyfus Affair' develops the effect of this 'miraculous curve' of the discursive field, produced by the intervention of the *point de capiton*, in a paradigmatic fashion. Its role in French and European political history already resembles that of a *point de capiton*, for it restructured the entire field and released, directly or indirectly, a whole series of displacements which even today determine the political scene: for example, the final separation of Church and State in bourgeois democracies, the socialist collaboration in bourgeois government and the split of social democracy into Socialism and Communism. One could also point to the birth of Zionism and the elevation of anti-Semitism to this key moment of 'right wing populism'.

But here we will only try to indicate the decisive turn in its unfolding: an intervention which produced a judicial row concerning the equity and legality of a verdict, the stake of a political battle which shook national life in its entirety. This turning point is not to be sought, as one usually believes, in the famous *J'accuse* that appeared in the *Aurore*, 13 January 1898, where Émile Zola took up once again all the arguments for Dreyfus's defence and denounced the corruption of official circles. Zola's intervention remained in the cadre of bourgeois liberalism, that of the defence of liberties and rights of the citizen, etc. The real upset took place in the second half of the year 1898. On 30 August, Lieutenant Colonel Henry, the new Chief of the Second Bureau, was arrested. He was suspected of having forged one of the secret documents on the basis of which Dreyfus had been condemned for high treason. The next day, Henry committed suicide with a razor in his cell. This news provoked a shock in public opinion. If Henry confessed his guilt – and what other meaning could one give to his suicide? – the act of accusation against Dreyfus must, in its entirety, lack solidity. Everyone expected a retrial and the acquittal of Dreyfus. For the moment, let us repeat the poetic description of Ernest Nolte:

> Then in the midst of the confusion and consternation, a newspaper article appeared which altered the situation. Its author was Maurras, a thirty-year-old writer hitherto known only in limited

circles. The article was entitled 'The first blood'. It looked at things in a way which no one had thought or dared to look.[3]

What did Maurras do? He did not present any supplementary evidence, nor did he refute any fact. He simply produced a global reinterpretation of the whole 'affair' which cast it in a different light. He made a heroic victim of Lieutenant Colonel Henry, who had preferred patriotic duty to abstract 'justice'. That is to say, Henry, after having seen how the Jewish 'Syndicate of Treason' exploited an insignificant judicial error in order to denigrate and undermine the foundation of French life for the purpose of breaking the force of the Army, did not hesitate to commit a small patriotic falsity in order to stop this race towards the precipice. The true stake in the 'affair' is no longer the fairness of a sentence but the shock, the degeneration of the vital French power from the Jewish financiers who hid behind corrupt liberalism, freedom of the press, autonomy of justice, etc. As a result, its true victim is not Dreyfus but Henry himself, the solitary patriot who risked everything for the salvation of France and on whom his superiors, at the decisive moment, turned their backs: the 'first blood' spilled by the Jewish plot.

Maurras' intervention altered the situation: the right wing united its forces, and 'patriotic' unity rapidly took the upper hand over the disarray. He provoked this upset by creating triumph, the myth of the 'first victim', from the very elements which, before his intervention, roused disorientation and amazement (the falsification of documents, the inequity of the sentence, etc.), and which he was far from contesting. It is not surprising that up until his death he considered this article as the best work of his life.

The elementary operation of the *point de capiton* should be sought in this 'miraculous' turn, in this *quid pro quo* by means of which what was previously the very source of disarray becomes proof and testimony of a triumph – as in the first act of *Athalie* where the intervention of 'supplementary fear', that of God, suddenly changes all other fears into their opposites. Here we are dealing with the act of 'creation' in its strictest sense: the act which turns chaos into a 'new harmony' and suddenly makes 'comprehensible' what was up to then only a senseless and even terrifying disturbance. It is impossible not to recall Christianity – not so much the act of God that made an ordered world out of chaos, but rather this decisive turning from which the definitive form of Christian religion, the form that showed its worth in our tradition, resulted. This is, of course, the Paulinian cut. St Paul centred the whole Christian edifice precisely on the point which previously appeared, to Christ's disciples, as a horrifying trauma, 'impossible', non-symbolizable, non-integrable in their field of signification: his shameful death on the cross between two bandits. St Paul made of this final defeat of his earthly mission which annihilated the hope of deliverance (of Jews from the Roman domination) the very act of salvation. By his death Christ has redeemed, saved humankind.

2. TAUTOLOGY AND ITS FORBIDDEN

Further light can be shed on the logic of this operation by a small detour through the detective story. What is its principal charm apropos of the relationship between law and its transgression, the criminal adventure? We have on one side the reign of law, tranquillity, certainty, but also the triteness, the boredom of everyday life, and on the other side crime as – Brecht was already saying it – the only possible adventure in the bourgeois world. Detective stories, however, effect a terrific twist in this relationship, one already uncovered by Gilbert Keith Chesterton:

> While it is the constant tendency of the Old Adam to rebel against so universal and automatic a thing as civilization, to preach departure and rebellion, the romance of police activity keeps in some sense before the mind the fact that civilization itself is the most sensational of departures and the most romantic of rebellions ... When the detective in a police romance stands alone, and somewhat fatuously fearless amid the knives and fists of a thieves' kitchen, it does certainly serve to make us remember that it is the agent of social justice who is the original and poetic figure, while the burglars and footpads are merely placid old cosmic conservatives, happy in the immemorial respectability of apes and wolves. The

romance of the police force is thus the whole romance of man. It is based on the fact that morality is the most dark and daring of conspiracies.[4]

The fundamental operation of the detective story thus consists in presenting the detective himself – the one who works for the defence of the law, in the name of the law, in order to restore the reign of the law – as the greatest adventurer, as a person in comparison to whom it is the criminals themselves who appear like indolent, petit-bourgeois conservatives ... This is a truly miraculous trick: there are, of course, a great number of transgressions of the law, crimes, adventures that break the monotony of everyday loyal and tranquil life, but the only true transgression, the only true adventure, the one which changes all the other adventures into petit-bourgeois prudence, is the adventure of civilization, of the defence of the law itself.

And it is the same with Lacan. For him also, the greatest transgression, the most traumatic, the most senseless thing, is law itself: the mad, superegotistical law which both inflicts and commands *jouissance*. We do not have on one side a plurality of transgressions, perversions, aggressivities, etc., and on the other side a universal law which regulates, normalizes the cul-de-sac of transgressions and makes possible the pacific co-existence of subjects. The maddest thing is the other side of the appeasing law itself, the law as a misunderstood, dumb injunction to *jouissance*. We can say that law divides itself necessarily into an appeasing law and a mad law. Thus the opposition between the law and its transgressions repeats itself within law itself. Here we have the same operation as the one in *Athalie*: in Chesterton, law appears, in the face of ordinary criminal transgressions, as the only true transgression; in *Athalie*, God appears, in face of earthly fears, as the only thing which is really to be feared. God thus divides himself into an appeasing God, a God of love, tranquillity and grace, and into a fierce, enraged God, the one who provokes in humans the most terrible fear.

This turn, this point of reversal where the law itself appears as the only true transgression, corresponds exactly to what one calls, in Hegelian terminology, the 'negation of the negation'. First, we have the simple opposition between a position and its negation, in our case between the positive, appeasing law, and the multitude of its particular transgressions, crimes. The 'negation of the negation' is the moment when one notices that the only true transgression, the only true negativity, is that of the law itself which changes all of the ordinary, criminal transgressions, into indolent positivity. That is why Lacanian theory is irreducible to any variant of transgressism, of anti-Oedipism, etc. The only true anti-Oedipism is Oedipus himself, his super-egotistical reverse ... One can follow this 'Hegelian' economy up to Lacan's organizing decisions. The dissolution of the *École freudienne de Paris* and the constitution of the *Cause freudienne* could have given the impression of a liberating act – an end to the bureaucratization and regimentation of the school. From now on, one would worry only about the Cause itself, liberated from all the earthly hindrances ... But, very quickly, it can be observed that this act enhanced the restoration of an *École de la Cause elle-même*, much more severe than all the other schools, just as surpassing earthly fears by divine love implicates the fear of God, something more terrible than all earthly fears.

The most appropriate form to indicate this curve of the *point de capiton*, of the 'negation of the negation', in ordinary language is, paradoxically, that of the tautology: 'law is law', 'God is God'. Here the tautology functions precisely in the Hegelian sense, as one's identity which reveals the supreme contradiction. In the tautology 'God is God', the first 'God' is the one of tranquillity, grace and love, while the second 'God' is the one of an unsustainable rage and ferocity. Likewise, the tautology 'law is law' shows the illegal and illegitimate character of the establishment of the reign of the law. Blaise Pascal was probably the first to detect this subversive content of the tautology 'law is law':

Custom is the whole of equity for the sole reason that it is accepted. That is the mystic basis of its authority. Anyone who tries to bring it back to its first principle destroys it. Nothing is so defective as those laws which correct defects. Anyone obeying them because they are just is obeying an imaginary justice, not the essence of the law, which is completely self-contained: it is law and nothing more ... That is why the wisest of legislators used to say that men must often be deceived for their own good, and another sound politician: *When he asks about the truth that is to bring him freedom, it is a good thing that he should be deceived.* The truth about the usurpation must not be made apparent; it came about originally without reason and has become reasonable. We must see that it is regarded as authentic and eternal, and its origins must be hidden if we do not want it soon to end.[5]

There is no need to emphasize the scandalous character of these propositions: they subvert the foundations of power, of its authority, at the very moment when they give the impression of supporting them. The illegitimate violence by which law sustains itself must be concealed at any price, because this concealment is the positive condition of the functioning of law. Law functions only insofar as its subjects are fooled, insofar as they experience the authority of law as 'authentic and eternal' and do not realize 'the truth about the usurpation'. That is why Kant is forced, in his *Metaphysics of Morals*, to forbid any question concerning the origins of legal power: it is by means of precisely such questioning that the stain of this illegitimate violence appears which always soils, like original sin, the purity of the reign of law. It is not surprising, then, that in Kant this prohibition assumes the paradoxical form well known in psychoanalysis: it forbids something which is at the same time given as impossible:

A people should not *inquire* with any practical aim in view into the origin of the supreme authority to which it is subject, that is, a subject *ought not to reason subtly* for the sake of action about the origin of this authority, as a right that can still be called into question with regard to the obedience he owes it ... [F]or a people already subject to civil law these subtle reasonings are altogether pointless and, moreover, threaten a state with danger. It is *futile* to inquire into the *historical documentation* of the mechanism of government, that is, one cannot reach back to the time at which civil society began ... But it is *culpable* to undertake this inquiry with a view to possibly changing by force the constitution that now exists.[6]

Notice here that one cannot go back to the origin of law because one must not do it. The Kantian formula of duty is well-known: 'You can because you must [*Du kannst, denn du sollst*].' This so-called prohibition is an exact inversion of this famous formula: 'You cannot because you must not.' The elementary model of such a prohibition is, of course, that of incest. It is, nevertheless, not foreign to philosophical discourse, as could be demonstrated by a whole series of examples, up to the famous proposition which concludes Wittgenstein's *Tractatus*: 'Whereof one cannot speak, thereof one must be silent.'[7] One must ask a totally naïve question here: if one declares that one cannot, at any rate, say anything about the ineffable, why add again the totally redundant statement that one must not say anything about it, that one must be quiet? Where does such a fear of not saying too much about the inexpressible come from? The paradox of this 'nothing', of this pure semblance, is, of course, the very paradox of the object-cause of desire in the Lacanian sense of the *objet petit a*.

3. KANT WITH SADE

'At the beginning' of law, there is a transgression, a certain reality of violence, which coincides with the very act of the establishment of law.[8] The whole of classical politico-philosophical thought rests on the refusal of an overturning of law; this is why one must read 'Kant with Sade'. Even though Kant was unable to articulate the lack in the Other (A̶), he did nonetheless – taking Jacques-Alain Miller's formulation – formulate the *B barré* under the form of inaccessibility, of the absolute transcendence of the supreme Good [*le Bon suprême*] as the only object and legitimate, non-pathological motivation of our moral activity. Every given, determined, represented object which functions as a motivation of our will is already pathological in the Kantian sense: an empirical object, related to the conditions of our finished experience and not having an *a priori* necessity. That is why the only legitimate motivation of our will remains the very form of law, the universal form of the moral maxim. The fundamental thesis of Lacan is that this impossible object is nevertheless given to us in a specific experience, that of the *objet petit a*, object-cause of desire, which is not 'patho-logical', which does not reduce itself to an object of need or demand. And *that* is why Sade is to be taken as the truth of Kant. This object whose experience is eluded by Kant appears precisely in Sade's work under the appearance of the hangman, the executioner, the agent who practises his sadistic activity on the victim.

The Sadean executioner has nothing to do with pleasure. His activity is therefore ethical in the strictest sense: beyond each 'pathological' motivation, he simply fulfils his duty, as is demonstrated by the lack of wit in Sade's work. The executioner always works for the Other's *jouissance* and not for his own. He thus becomes an instrument solely of the will of the Other. In the Sadean scene, near to the executioner and his victim, there is always a third, the Other for which the sadist practises his activity, the Other whose pure form is that of the voice of a law which addresses itself to the subject in the second person, with the imperative 'Fulfil your duty!'

The greatness of Kantian ethics is thus to have formulated for the first time the 'beyond of the pleasure principle'. Kant's categorical imperative is a superegotistical law which goes against the subject's well-being. Or, more precisely, it is totally indifferent to his well-being, which, from the view-point of the 'pleasure principle' as it prolongs the 'reality principle', is totally non-economical and non-economizable, senseless. Moral law is a fierce order which does not admit excuses – 'you can because you must' – and which in this way acquires an air of mischievous neutrality, of mean indifference.

According to Lacan, Kant ignores the other side of this neutrality of moral law, its meanness and obscenity, its mischievousness which goes back to the *jouissance* behind law's command; Lacan relates this suppression to the fact that Kant avoids the split of the subject (subject of enunciation/subject of the enunciated) implied in moral law. That is the meaning of Lacan's criticism of the Kantian example of the deposit [*dépôt*] and the depositary [*dépositaire*].[9] The subject of enunciation is here reduced to the subject of the enunciated, and the depositary to his function as depositary: Kant presupposes that we are dealing with a trustee 'doing his duty', with a subject who lets himself be taken with-out remainder into the abstract determination of being the deposi-tary.[10] A brief Lacanian joke goes in the same direction: 'My fiancée never misses the rendezvous, because as soon as she misses it, she would no longer be my fiancée.' Here too, the fiancée is reduced to her function of fiancée. Hegel had already detected the terrorist potential of this reduction of the subject to an abstract determination.

The presupposition of revolutionary terror is precisely that the subject lets themselves be reduced to their determination as Citizen who is 'doing their duty', which brings about the liquidation of subjects who are not doing their duty. Therefore, Jacobinical terror is really the consequence of Kantian ethics. It is the same with the command of real socialism: 'All people support the Party.' Such a proposition is not an empirical declaration and as such refutable; it functions, on the contrary, performatively, as the definition of the true People, of the People who live 'up to their duty'. The true People are those who support the Party. The logic is thus exactly the same as that of the joke about the fiancée: 'All the people support the Party because the constituents of the People who agitate against the Party have in that way excluded themselves from the community of the People.' One is dealing after all with what Lacan, in his first seminars, called 'foundational speech',[11] the symbolic mandate, etc. (the 'you are my fiancée, my depositary, the citizen . . .'). This should be read again from the perspective of the ulterior conceptualization of the S_1, the master-signifier. The wager of Lacanian criticism is that there is always an excess in the subject who takes on themselves the symbolic mandate, who agrees to incarnate an S_1, a side which does not let itself be taken into the S_1, the mandate. This excess is precisely the side of the *objet*.[12] As long as they escape being caught in the signifier, the mandate which is conferred on them by the socio-symbolic tie, the subject of enunciation functions as an object.

That, then, is the split between the subject of the enunciated and the subject of enunciation of law. Behind the S_1 – law in its neutral, pacifying, solemn and sublime form – there is always the presence of the object which reveals mischievousness, meanness and obscenity. Another well-known example illustrates perfectly this split of the subject of law. In response to the question of explorers researching cannibalism, the native answers: 'No, there aren't any more cannibals in our region. Yesterday, we ate the last one.' At the level of the subject of the enunciated, there are no more cannibals, and the subject of enunciation is precisely this 'we' who have eaten the last cannibal. That, then, is the intrusion of the 'subject of enunciation' of law, elided by Kant: this obscene agent who ate the last cannibal in order to ensure the order of law. Now we can specify the status of paradoxical prohibition which concerns the question of the origin of law, of legal power. It aims at the object of law in the sense of its 'subject of enunciation', of the subject who becomes the obscene and fierce agent-instrument of law.

4. KANT WITH McCULLOUGH

This is precisely what Kant misses, this philosopher of unconditional Duty, the greatest of obsessions of the history of philosophy. But what Kant did not understand is realized by the vulgar, sentimental literature, the *kitsch*, of today. This is not surprising if one realises that it is precisely in the universe of such literature that the tradition of *amour courtois* has survived, whose fundamental trait consists in considering the love of the Lady as a supreme Duty. Let us take an exemplary case of this genre, *An Indecent Obsession* by Colleen McCullough (a novel completely unreadable and for that reason, published in France in the collection *J'ai lu*), the story of a nurse in charge of psychiatric patients in a small hospital in the Pacific around the end of the Second World War, divided between her professional duty and her love for one of her patients. At the end of the book, she perceives things concerning her desire, gives up love and goes back to her duty. At first glance, then, this is the most insipid moralism: the victory of duty over passionate love, the renunciation of 'pathological' love in the name of duty. The presentation of her motives for this renunciation is nevertheless a little more delicate. Here are the last sentences of the novel:

> She had a duty here ... This wasn't just a job – her heart was in it, fathoms deep in it! This was what she truly wanted ... Nurse Langtry began to walk again, briskly and without any fear, under-standing herself at last. And understanding that duty, the most indecent of all obsessions, was only another name for love.

One is dealing then with a true dialectical Hegelian twist: the opposition of love and duty is surpassed when one feels duty itself to be the 'other name for love'. By means of this reversal – the 'negation of the negation' – duty, at first the negation of love, coincides with supreme love which abolishes all other 'pathological' loves, or, in order to express oneself in Lacanian terms, it functions as the *point de capiton* in relation to all other 'ordinary' loves. The tension between duty and love, between the purity of duty and indecency (the pathological obscenity of love/passion), is resolved at the moment when one has experienced the radically obscene character of duty itself.

The essential part rests in this change of place of the 'indecent obsession' in relation to the opposition between duty and love. Initially, it is duty that appears as pure, universal, contrary to the pathological, particular, indecent, love/passion. It is then duty itself which is revealed as being '*the most indecent of all obsessions*'. That is the Hegelian logic of 'reconciliation' between the Universal and the Particular. The most radical, absolute Particularity is indeed that of the Universal itself as far as it has a negative *rapport* of exclusion towards the Particular: in other words, inasmuch as it opposes itself to the Particular and excludes the wealth of its concrete content. And that is how one should also take the Lacanian thesis according to which Good is only the mask of radical, absolute Evil, the mask of 'indecent obsession' by *das Ding*, the atrocious-obscene thing.[13] Behind Good, there is radical Evil; Supreme Good is the other name for an Evil which does not have a particular, 'pathological' status. Insofar as it obsesses us in an indecent, obscene way, *das Ding* makes it possible for us to untie ourselves, to free ourselves from our 'pathological' attachment to particular, earthly objects. The 'Good' is only one way to keep the distance towards this evil Thing, the distance which makes it bearable.

That is what Kant did not understand, unlike the *kitsch* literature of our century: this other, obscene side of Duty itself. And that is why it was only possible for him to evoke the concept of *das Ding* in its negative form, as an absurd (im)possibility – in his treatise on negative grandiosities, for example, apropos of the difference between logical contradiction and real opposition. Contradiction is a logical relationship that does not have a real existence while, in the real opposition, the two poles are equally positive. In other words, their relationship is not that of something and its lack but indeed that of the two positive givens which constitute the opposition. For example – an example which is not accidental at all, insofar as it shows directly the level at which we are, namely that of enjoyment, the pleasure principle – enjoyment and pain: 'Enjoyment and pain are opposed to each other not as profit and lack of profit (+ and 0), but as profit and loss (+ and –): that is, one is opposed to the other not merely as its *contradictory* [*contradictorie s. logice oppositum*] but also as its *contrary* [*contrarie s. realiter oppositum*].'[14] Enjoyment and pain are then like poles of a real opposition, in themselves positive facts. One is negative only in relation to the other, while Good and Evil are contradictory, their *rapport* being that of + and 0. That is why Evil is not a positive entity. It is only the lack, the absence of Good. It would be an absurdity to want to take the negative pole of a contradiction as something positive, thus, 'to think of a particular sort of object and to call them negative things'. Furthermore, *das Ding*, in its Lacanian conceptualization, is precisely such a negative thing, a paradoxical Thing which is only the positivization of a lack, of a hole in the symbolic Other. *Das Ding* as an 'incarnated Evil' is indeed an irreducible object at the level of the pleasure principle, of the opposition between pleasure and pain. In other words, it is a 'non-pathological' object in the strict sense, also the unthinkable paradox of the 'critical' step for Kant, for which reason he is to be thought along 'with Sade'.

5. THE 'TOTALITARIAN OBJECT'

Now, here is our fundamental thesis: the advent of contemporary 'totalitarianism' introduces a decisive cut in this – let's say – classical conjuncture, a cut which corresponds precisely to the passage from Kant to Sade. In 'totalitarianism', this illegal agent-instrument of the law, the Sadean executioner, is no longer hidden. He *appears as such* – for example, in the shape of the Party, as an agent-instrument of historical will. The Stalinist Party is quite literally an executor of great creations: executor of the creation of Communism, the greatest of all creations. That is the meaning of Stalin's famous proposition: 'We are, us, Communists, people of a different sort. We are carved out of a different material.' This 'different material' (the right stuff, one could say) is precisely the incarnation, the apparition of the *objet*. Here, one should return to the Lacanian definition of the structure of perversion as an inverted effect of the fantasy. It is the subject who determines himself as object, in his encounter with the division of subjectivity.[15]

The formula for fantasy is written as $\$ \lozenge a$. In other words, the barred subject is divided in its encounter with the object-cause of its desire. The sadist inverts this structure, which gives $a \lozenge \$$. In a way, he avoids this division by occupying the place of the object himself, of the agent-executor, before his victim, the divided-hystericized subject: for example, the Stalinist before the 'traitor', the hysterical petit-bourgeois who did not want completely to renounce his subjectivity, who continues to 'desire in vain' (Lacan). In the same passage, Lacan returns to his 'Kant avec Sade' in order to recall that 'the sadist himself occupies the place of the object, but without knowing it, to the benefit of another, for whose *jouissance* he exercises his action as sadistic pervert'.[16]

The Other of 'totalitarianism' – for example, the 'inevitable necessity of laws of historical development' to which the Sadean figure of the great Other refers itself, for which the Stalinist executor practises his act – would then be conceived as a new version of the 'Supreme-Being-in-Evilness [*Être-Suprême-en-Méchanceté*]'.[17] It is this radical objectivization-instrumentization of his own subjective position which confers on the Stalinist, beyond the deceptive appearance of a cynical detachment, his unshakeable conviction of only being the instrument of the production of historical necessity. The Stalinist Party, this 'historical subject', is thus the exact opposite of a subject. The distinctive trait of the 'totalitarian subject' is to be sought precisely in this radical refusal of subjectivity in the sense of $\$$, the hysterical-bourgeois subject, by means of the radical instrumentalization of the subject in relation to the Other. By making himself the transparent instrument of the Will of the Other, the subject tries to avoid his constitutive division, for which he pays through the total alienation of his *jouissance*. If the advent of the bourgeois subject is defined by his right to free *jouissance*, the 'totalitarian' subject shows this freedom as belonging to the Other, the 'Supreme-Being-in-Evilness'.

One could then conceptualize the difference between the classical, pre-liberal Master and the totalitarian Leader as that between S_1 and *objet petit a*. The authority of the classical Master is that of a certain S_1, a signifier-without-signified, an auto-referential signifier which incarnates the performative function of the word. The 'liberalism' of the Enlightenment wants to do without this instance of 'irrational' authority. Its project is that of an authority founded entirely in effective '*savoir(-faire)*'. In this frame, the Master reappears as the totalitarian Leader. Excluded like S_1, he takes the shape of the object-incarnation of an S_1 (for example the 'objective knowledge of the laws of history'), instrument of the superegotistical Will which takes on itself the 'responsibility' of producing historical necessity in its cannibalistic cruelty. The formula, the matheme of the 'totalitarian subject', would thus be S_2/a, the semblance of a neutral 'objective' knowledge, under which the obscene object-agent of a superegotistical Will hides.

6. THE KING AND HIS BUREAUCRACY

Hegel was probably the last classical thinker to have developed, in his *Philosophy of Right*, the necessary function of a purely formal symbolic point, of an unfounded, 'irrational' authority. Constitutional monarchy is a rational Whole, at whose head there is a strictly 'irrational' moment: the person of the monarch. The essential thing, here, is the irreducible abyss between the organically articulated rational Whole of the constitution of the State, and the 'irrationality' of the person who incarnates supreme Power, by which the Power receives the form of subjectivity. To the reproach that the destiny of the State is abandoned here to the eventuality of the psychic disposition of the monarch (to his wisdom, honesty, courage, etc.), Hegel replies:

But this objection is based on the invalid assumption that the monarch's particular character is of vital importance. In a fully organized state, it is only a question of the highest instance of formal decision, and all that is required in a monarch is someone to say 'yes' and dot the 'i'; for the supreme office should be such that the particular character of its occupant is of no significance ... In a well-ordered monarchy, the objective aspect is solely the concern of the law, to which the monarchy merely has to add his subjective 'I will'.[18]

The nature of the monarch's act is thus completely formal. The frame of his decisions is determined by the constitution. The concrete content of his decisions is proposed to him by his expert advisers, so that often he has nothing to do but to sign his name. 'But this *name* is important: it is the ultimate instance and *non plus ultra*'.[19]

Really, this example contains everything. The monarch is the 'pure' signifier, the master-signifier 'without signified'. His entire 'reality' (and authority) rests on the name, and that is why his 'effectiveness in reality' is arbitrary; it can be abandoned to the biological contingency of heredity. The monarch is the One who – as the exception, the 'irrational' apex of the amorphous mass ('not-all') of the people – makes the totality of customs concrete. With his ex-sistence as 'pure' signifier, he constitutes the Whole in its 'organic articulation' (*organische Gliederung*). He is the 'irrational' supplement as the condition of the rational Totality, the 'pure' signifier without signified as condition of the organic Whole of the signifier-signified:

> *Without* its monarch and that *articulation* of the whole which is necessarily and immediately associated with monarchy, *the* people is a formless mass. The latter is no longer a state, and *none* of those determinations which are encountered only in an *internally organised* whole (such as sovereignty, government, courts of law, public authorities, estates, etc.) is applicable to it.[20]

Here, the Hegelian wager is much more ambiguous, even cynical, than we think. His conclusion is almost the following: if the Master is indispensable within politics, one must not condescend to the reasoning of good sense which tells us 'that he may at least be the most capable, wise, courageous'. One must, on the contrary, preserve as much as possible of the distance between symbolic legitimations and 'real' skills, localize the function of the Master in a point rejected from the Whole where it really does not matter if he is dumb. In other words, Hegel says the same thing here as Lacan in his *Seminar XVII*.[21] The gap between State bureaucracy and the monarch corresponds to that between the battery of 'knowledge' (S_2, the bureaucratic *savoir-faire*) and the *point de capiton* (S_1, the 'unary' master-signifier) who 'quilts' (*capitonne*) his discourse, who 'totalizes' it from outside, who takes on himself the moment of 'decision' and confers to this discourse the 'performative' dimension. Our only chance is thus to isolate as much as possible S_1, to make of it the empty point of formal 'decision' without any concrete weight; in other words, to keep a maximum distance between S_1 and the register of 'skill qualifications', which is that of the bureaucratic '*savoir(-faire)*'. If this point of exception fails, bureaucratic knowledge 'becomes mad'. The 'neutrality' proper to the knowledge, in the absence of the *capitonnage*, appears to be 'evil'. Its very 'indifference' provokes in the subject the effect of a superegotistical imperative. In other words, we come to the reign of 'totalitarian' bureaucracy.

The decisive thing is thus not to confuse the 'irrational' authority of pre-liberal monarchy with that of the post-liberal 'totalitarian' regime. The first one is based on the gap of S_1 in relation to S_2, while 'totalitarianism' comes precisely from the *non-capitonne* bureaucratic discourse of S_2 without S_1. This difference comes out better when one considers the justification of obedience. The 'totalitarian' leader demands submission in the name of his supposed 'effective' capacities, his wisdom, his courage, his adherence to the Cause, etc. While, if one says 'I obey the king because he is wise and just', it is already a crime of *lèse majesté*. The only appropriate justification for this is the tautology: 'I obey the king because he is king'. Kierkegaard has developed it in a magnificent passage which stretches, in an extended arc, from divine authority, through the highest secular authority (the king), up to school and family authority (the father):

To ask whether Christ is profound is blasphemy and an attempt (whether consciously or unconsciously) to annihilate him, for in the question is contained a doubt about his authority ... To ask whether the king is a genius, with the implication that in such case he is to be obeyed, is really *lèse majesté*, for the question contains a doubt concerning subjection to authority. To be willing to obey a board in case it is able to say witty things is at bottom to make a fool of the board. To honour one's father because he is a distinguished pate is impiety.[22]

Horkheimer, who cites these lines in 'Authority and the Family', sees in them an indication of the passage of the liberal-bourgeois principle of 'rational authority' to the post-liberal 'totalitarian' principle of 'irrational' and unconditional authority. Against such a reading, one must insist on the gap between symbolic authority and those 'effective' capacities which alone hold open the non-'totalitarian' space. In other words, Kierkegaard moves here on the terrain of pre-liberal Hegelian argumentation, while post-liberal 'totalitarianism' is to be taken as an effect of the interior reversal of 'liberalism' itself. Namely: when and in what conditions does State bureaucracy become 'totalitarian'? Not where S_1, the point of 'irrational' authority, would exert a pressure 'too strong', excessive, on the bureaucratic *savoir(-faire)*, but on the contrary, where this 'unary' point which 'quilts' and 'totalizes' from outside the field of S_2 fails. Bureaucratic 'knowledge' here 'becomes mad': it operates 'by itself', without reference to a decentred point which would confer upon it a 'performative' dimension. In a word, it starts to function as a superego.

7. THE 'MISCHIEVOUS NEUTRALITY' OF BUREAUCRACY

When knowledge itself assumes the moment of 'authority' (i.e. summons, command, imperative), a short-circuit between the 'neutral' field of knowledge and the 'performative' dimension is produced. Far from limiting itself to a kind of 'neutral' declaration of the given objectivity, the discourse 'becomes mad' and starts to behave in a 'performative' way towards the given of the facts themselves. More precisely, it conceals its own 'performative force' under the shape of 'objective knowledge', of the neutral 'declaration' of the 'facts'. The example that comes to mind immediately is that of Stalinist bureaucratic discourse, the supposed 'knowledge of objective laws' as the ulterior legitimation of its decisions: a true 'uncontrolled knowledge' capable of 'founding' any decision after the fact. And it is, of course, the subject who pays for this 'short-circuit' between S_1 and S_2. In a 'pure' case, the accused, through great political trials, finds himself confronted by an impossible choice. The confession demanded from him is obviously in conflict with the 'reality' of the facts since the Party asks him to declare himself guilty of 'false accusations'. Furthermore, this demand of the Party functions as a superegotistical imperative, which means that it constitutes the symbolic 'reality' of the subject. Lacan insisted many times on this link between the superego and the supposed 'sentiment of reality': 'When the feeling of foreignness, strangeness, strikes somewhere, it's never on the side of the superego – it's always the ego that loses its bearings ...'[23]

Does he not indicate by this an answer to the question: where does the confession come from in the Stalinist trials? Since there was not any 'reality' outside of the superego of the Party for the accused, outside its obscene and mean imperative – the only alternative to this superegotistical imperative being the emptiness of an abominable reality – the confession demanded by the Party was in fact the only way for the accused to avoid the 'loss of reality'. Stalinist 'confessions' are to be conceived as an extreme consequence which ensues from the 'totalitarian' short-circuit between S_1 and S_2. In other words, in the way that S_1 himself takes on the 'performative' dimension on itself, one is dealing with a 'mad' variant of the discourse's own 'performativity'. The signifying work can indeed 'change reality', namely, the symbolic reality, by transforming retroactively the signifying network which determines the symbolic significance of the 'facts'. But here, signifying work 'falls into the Real', as if language could change extralinguistic facts in their own very real 'massiveness'.

The fundamental fact of the advent of 'totalitarianism' would consist then of social Law beginning to function as a superego. Here it is no longer that which 'forbids' and, on the basis of this prohibition, opens, supports and guarantees the field of co-existence of 'free' bourgeois subjects, the field of their diverse pleasures. By becoming 'mad', it begins directly to command *jouissance*: the turning point where a permitted freedom-to-enjoy is reversed into an obligatory *jouissance* which is, one must add, the most effective way to block the access of the subject to *jouissance*. One finds in Kafka's work a perfect staging of bureaucracy under the rule of an obscene, fierce, 'mad' law, a law which immediately inflicts *jouissance* – in short, the superego:

> 'Thus I belong to justice', says the priest. 'So then, what could I want from you? The Court makes no claims upon you. It receives you when you come and relinquishes you when you go.'[24]

How can one not recognize, in these lines with which the interview between Josef K. and the priest ends in Chapter IX of *The Trial*, the 'mischievous neutrality' of the superego? Already the starting point of his two great novels, *The Trial* and *The Castle*, is the call of a superior instance (the Law, the Castle) to the subject – aren't we dealing with a law which 'would give the order, "*Jouis!*" ["Enjoy!" or "Come!"], and the subject could only reply "*J'ouïs*" ["I hear"], in which the *jouissance* would no longer be anything but understood?'[25] The 'misunderstanding', the 'confusion' of the subject confronting this instance, isn't it precisely due to the fact that he misunderstands the imperative of *jouissance* which resounds here and which perspires through all the pores of its 'neutral' surface? When Josef K., in the empty chamber, glances at the judges' books, he finds 'an indecent picture' in the first book. 'A man and woman were sitting naked on a sofa, the obscene intention of the draughtsman was evident enough.'[26] That is the superego: a solemn 'indifference' impregnated in parts by obscenities.

That is why, for Kafka, bureaucracy is 'closer to original human nature than any other social institution' (letter to Oscar Baum, June 1922): what is this 'original human nature' if not the fact that man is from the start a '*parlêtre* [speaking-being]'? And what is the superego – the functioning mode of bureaucratic knowledge – if not, according to Jacques-Alain Miller, what 'presentifies' under the pure form of the signifier as the cause of the division of the subject; in other words, the intervention of the signifier-command under its chaotic, senseless aspect?

8. POSTMODERNISM I:
ANTONIONI VERSUS HITCHCOCK

This reference to Kafka is by no means accidental. Kafka was in a way the first postmodernist. It is precisely postmodernism that, in the field of art, embodies the limits of the semiotic, 'textual' approach characteristic of modernism.

'Postmodernism' is a theme of theoretical discussions from Germany to the United States, with the quite surprising effect that it evokes a totally incompatible problematic in the different countries. In Germany, by 'postmodernism' one understands the devalorization of universal Reason, of the 'modern' tradition of Enlightenment, in the current which starts with Nietzsche and whose most recent offspring would be the French 'post-structuralism' of Foucault, Deleuze, etc. (cf. the many texts by Habermas). In the United States, it designates particularly the aesthetic stage which follows the expiration of the modernist avant-garde: in other words the different forms of 'retro' movements. In all of this diversity, there is, however, the same matrix. One conceives of 'postmodernism' as a reaction to modernist 'intellectualism', as a return of the metonymy of the interpretative movement to the fullness of the Thing itself, to the instilment in vital experience, to the baroque wealth of the *Erlebnis* before the supposed 'prison-house of language'.

Now, here is our thesis. It is only the Lacanian passage from the signifier to the object, 'from the symptom to the fantasy' (Jacques-Alain Miller), which makes it possible to remove the advent of postmodernism from the field of an ideology of authenticity, instilment, etc. Postmodernism marks the rising in the middle of the modernist space of language and its interpretative auto-movement to the infinite of a 'hard' nucleus, of the inertia of a non-symbolizable Real. Lacan enables us to see this place outside the symbolic as an emptiness opened by the hole in the symbolic Other. The inert object is always the presentification, the filling of the hole around which the symbolic command articulates itself, of the hole retroactively constituted by this command itself and in no way a 'pre-linguistic' fact.

Let's start with *Blow-Up* (1966) by Antonioni, perhaps the last great modernist film. When the hero (the photographer) develops the photographs of a park in the laboratory, his attention is attracted to the stain in the bushes on the side of a photograph. He enlarges the detail, and one discovers the contours of a body there. Immediately, in the middle of the night, he goes back to the park and indeed finds the body. But the next day, when he goes back to see the scene of the crime again, the body has disappeared without leaving a trace. It is useless to stress the fact that the body is, according to the detective novel's code, the object of desire par excellence, the cause which starts the interpretative desire. The key to the film is given to us, however, by the final scene. The hero, resigned because of the cul-de-sac where his investigation has ended, takes a walk near a tennis court where a group of hippies pretend to play tennis (without a ball, they simulate the hits, run and jump, etc.). In the frame of this supposed game, the imagined ball jumps through the court's fence and stops near the hero. He hesitates a moment and then accepts the game. He bends over, makes the gesture of picking up the ball, and throws it back into the court ... This scene has, of course, a metaphorical function in relation to the totality of the film. It makes the hero sensitive to consenting to the fact that 'the game works without an object'. The hippies do not need a ball for their game, just as in his own adventure everything works without a body.

The 'postmodernist' way is the exact reverse of this process. It consists not in showing the game which also works without an object and which is put into movement by a central emptiness, but directly in showing the object, making visible the indifferent and arbitrary character of the object itself. The same object can function successively as disgusting shit and as a sublime, charismatic apparition. The difference is strictly structural. It is not tied to the 'effective proprieties' of the object, but only to its place, to its tie to a symbolic identification (I).[27] One can grasp this difference between modernism and postmodernism with regard to horror in Hitchcock's films. At first, it seems that Hitchcock simply respects the classical rule (already known by Aeschylus in the *Oresteia*) according to which one must place the terrifying event outside of the scene and only show its reflections and its effects on the stage. If one does not see it directly, terror rises as the emptiness of its absence is filled by fantasmatic projections ('one sees it as more horrible than it actually is ...'). The most simple process of evoking horror would be, then, to limit oneself to the reflections of the terrifying object on its witnesses or victims. For example, the horror is only visible by means of the frightened faces of the victims on the screen.

However, Hitchcock, when he is 'doing his duty', inverts this traditional process. Let's take a small detail from his *Lifeboat* (1944), the scene where the group of allied castaways welcome on to their boat a German sailor from a destroyed submarine: the castaways' surprise when they discover that the person they saved is an enemy. The traditional way of rendering this scene would be to let us hear the screams for help, to show the hands of an unknown person who grips the side of the boat, and then, rather than showing the German sailor, focus the camera on the shipwrecked survivors. It is the perplexed expression on their faces which must show us that they have pulled something unexpected out of the water. What? At that moment, when one has already created the suspense, the camera can finally show us the German sailor. But Hitchcock does the exact opposite of this traditional process: what he does is precisely not to show the shipwrecked survivors. Instead, he depicts the German sailor climbing on board and saying, with a friendly smile, 'Danke schön!' But then he does not show the surprised faces of the survivors. The camera remains on the German. If his appearance provoked a terrifying effect, one can only detect it by his reaction to the survivors' reaction: his smile dies out, his look becomes perplexed.

This confirms what Pascal Bonitzer observed as Hitchcock's Proustian side:[28] this Hitchcockian procedure corresponds perfectly to that of Proust in *Un amour de Swann*. When Odette confesses to Swann her lesbian adventures, Proust describes only Odette. If her story has a terrifying effect on Swann, Proust only presents it through the changed tone of the narrative when she observes its disastrous effect. One shows an object or an activity which is presented as an everyday, even common, thing, but suddenly, through the reactions of this object's milieu being reflected back on to the object itself, we realize that one is confronting a terrifying object, the source of an inexplicable terror. The horror is intensified by the fact that this object is, according to its appearance, completely ordinary. What we perceived only a moment ago as being a totally common thing is revealed as Evil incarnated.

9. POSTMODERNISM II: JOYCE VERSUS KAFKA

Such a postmodernist procedure is much more subversive than the usual modernist procedure, because the latter, by not representing the Thing, leaves open the possibility of apprehending this central emptiness from within the theological perspective of the 'absent God'. If the modernist lesson is that the structure, the intersubjective machine, worked just as well if the Thing is missing, if the machine turned around an emptiness, then the postmodernist reversal shows the Thing itself as incarnated, positivized emptiness, by representing the terrifying object directly and then denouncing its frightening effect as a simple effect of its place within the structure. The terrifying object is an everyday object that begins to function, by chance, as an occupant of the hole in the Other. The prototype of the modernist work would thus be *Waiting for Godot*. The whole futile, senseless activity takes place while waiting for Godot's arrival when, finally, 'something might happen'. But one knows very well that 'Godot' can never arrive. What would the 'postmodernist' way of rewriting the same story be? On the contrary, one would have directly to represent Godot himself: a dumb guy who makes fun of us, who is, that is to say, exactly like us, who lives a futile life full of boredom and foolish pleasures – the only difference being that, by chance, not knowing it himself, he found himself occupying the place of the Thing. He began to incarnate the Thing whose arrival one is awaiting.

There is another, less well-known film by Fritz Lang, *Secret Beyond the Door* (1947), which stages in a pure (one is almost tempted to say distilled) form this logic of an everyday object which is found in the place of *das Ding*. Celia Barrett, a young businesswoman, travels to Mexico after her older brother's death, where she meets Mark Lamphere. She marries him and moves with him to Lavender Falls. Some time later, the couple hosts Mark's close friends and he shows them his gallery of historical rooms which have been reconstituted in his own house, but he forbids anyone access to Room 7, which is locked. Fascinated by his reservation vis-à-vis this room, Celia gets a key made and enters it. It is the exact replica of her room. The most familiar things receive a dimension of disquieting strangeness because of the fact that one finds oneself in a place out of place, a place that 'is not right'. And the thrill effect results exactly from the familiar, domestic character of what one finds in this Thing's forbidden place. That is the perfect illustration of the fundamental ambiguity of the Freudian notion of *das Unheimliche*.

From this problematic, one can also approach the chief motif of the 'hard-boiled' detective novel: that the femme fatale is 'a bad object' par excellence, the object which eats men, which leaves many broken lives as a trace of its presence. In the best novels of this genre, a certain reversal takes place when the femme fatale as 'a bad object' is subjectivized. First she is presented as a terrifying, devouring, exploitative object. But when, suddenly, one is placed in the perspective which is hers, one finds out that she is only a sickly, broken being, one who is not in control of her effects on the milieu (masculine), who, especially when she thinks she 'masters the game', is no less a victim than her own victims. What gives her the power of fascination as the femme fatale is exclusively her place within masculine fantasy. She is only 'mastering the game' as an object of masculine fantasy. The theoretical lesson that one should get from this is that subjectivization coincides with the experience of one's own powerlessness, of one's own position as that of a victim of destiny. It is the moment detected by Adorno in his superb text on *Carmen* (in *Quasi una fantasia*), concerning the melody on the 'unmerciful card' of the third act, the nodal point of the whole opera, where Carmen, this bad-fatal object, is subjectivized, is felt as a victim of her own game.

That is how the beautiful Adornian sentence on the 'original passivity of the subject' should be grasped. It is to be taken literally. In other words, one is not dealing with the fact that the subject – this centre and origin of activity – of the remaking and appropriation of the world should in some way recognize their own limit, their subordination to the objective world. One must, on the contrary, affirm a certain passivity as an original dimension of subjectivity itself. The structure of this passivity is given to us by the Lacanian formula of fantasy ($ \$ \diamond a $). The fascination of the subject in front of *das Ding*, in front of the 'bad Thing' which occupies the hole in the Other, and the exceptional character of the subjectivization of the femme fatale, comes from the fact that she is indeed herself this object in relation to which she feels her original passivity.

However, one must suspend this series of variations in order to notice the socio-political correlation of this passage from modernism to postmodernism: the advent of what we call post-industrial society where all the coordinates of art change, including the status of art itself. The modernist work of art loses its 'will have' [*aura*].[29] It functions as a reject without charisma insofar as the 'everyday' world of merchandise becomes itself 'will-have-like' [*auratique*] (publicity, etc.). The postmodernist work regains the 'will have'. Furthermore, it does so at the expense of a radical renunciation, contrary to the modernist utopia ('fusion of art and life') detectable even in its most 'elitist' projects. Postmodernism reaffirms art as a social institution, the irreducible distance between art and 'everyday' life. One is tempted to conceive of postmodernism as one of the phenomena of global ideological change which includes the end of the great eschatological projects. As such it is at the same time post-Marxist.

This opposition of modernism and postmodernism is, however, far from being reduced to a simple diachronic. One finds it already articulated at the beginning of the century in the opposition between Joyce and Kafka. If Joyce is the modernist par excellence, the writer of the symptom (Lacan), of interpretative delirium taken to the infinite, of the time (to interpret) when each stable moment is revealed to be only a freezing effect of a plural signifying process, Kafka is in a certain way already postmodernist, the antipode of Joyce, the writer of fantasy, of the space of a painful, inert presence. If Joyce's text provokes interpretation, Kafka's blocks it. It is precisely this dimension of a non-dialectizable, inert presence which is misperceived by a modernist reading of Kafka, with its accent on the inaccessible, absent, transcendent instance (the Castle, the Court Room), holding the place of the lack, of the absence as such. From this perspective, the secret of Kafka would be that at the heart of the bureaucratic machinery, there is only an emptiness, the Nothing. Bureaucracy would be a mad machine which 'works by itself', like the game in *Blow-Up* which can function without a body-object. One can read this conjuncture in two different ways which share the same theoretical frame: theological and immanentist. Either one can take the inaccessible, transcendent character of the Centre (of the Castle, of the Court Room) as a mark of an 'absent God' – the universe of Kafka as an anguished universe, abandoned by God – or one can take the emptiness of this transcendence as an 'illusion of perspective', as a form of a reversed apparition of the immanence of desire. The inaccessible transcendence, its emptiness, its lack, is only the negative of the supplement (surplus) of the productive movement of desire on its object (Deleuze–Guattari). The two readings, although opposed, miss the same point: the way that this absence, this empty place, is found always already filled by an inert, obscene, dirty, revolting presence. The Court Room in *The Trial* is not only absent, it is indeed present under the figures of the obscene judges who, during the night trials, glance through pornographic books. The Castle is indeed present under the figure of subservient, lascivious and corrupted civil servants. Here, the formula of the 'absent God' in Kafka does not work at all: on the contrary Kafka's problem is that in his universe God is too present, under a shape – of course, which is not at all comforting – of obscene, disgusting phenomena. Kafka's universe is a world where God – who up to this point has held himself at an assured distance – got too close to us. One must read the thesis of the exegetes, according to whom Kafka's would be a universe of anxiety, based on the Lacanian definition of anxiety. We are too close to *das Ding*. That is the theological lesson of post-modernism. The mad, obscene God, the Supreme-Being-in-Evilness, is exactly the same as the God taken as the Supreme Good. The difference lies only in the fact that we got too close to Him.

NOTES

Published in *Psychoanalysis and ...*, ed. Richard Feldstein and Henry Sussman, London and New York, Routledge, 1990, pp. 89–110. We have revised the translation and made corrections to certain grammatical and terminological errors [eds].

1 See Jacques Lacan, *The Seminar of Jacques Lacan III: The Psychoses, 1955–56*, ed. Jacques-Alain Miller, trans. Russell Grigg, New York, W. W. Norton, 1993, p. 265 [eds].

2 Lacan, *Seminar III*, p. 267.

3 Ernest Nolte, *Three Faces of Fascism*, Toronto, University of Toronto Press, 1969, p. 85.

4 Gilbert Keith Chesterton, 'A Defence of Detective Stories', in *The Defendant*, London, J. M. Dent and Sons, 1940, pp. 161–2.

5   Blaise Pascal, *Pensées*, revised edn, trans. A. J. Krailsheimer, Harmondsworth, Penguin, 1995, p. 17.

6   Immanuel Kant, *The Metaphysics of Morals*, in *Practical Philosophy*, trans. and ed. Mary J. Gregor, Cambridge, Cambridge University Press, 1996, pp. 461–2 and 480, respectively.

7   Ludwig Wittgenstein, *Tractatus Logico-Philosophicus*, London, Kegan Paul, 1922, p. 189 [eds].

8   Žižek is referring here to the famous line from Goethe – 'in the beginning was the Deed [*Im Anfang war die Tat*]' – with which Freud concludes his 'Totem and Taboo: Some Points of Agreement between the Mental Lives of Savages and Neurotics', in *The Penguin Freud Library, 13: The Origins of Religion*, ed. and trans. James Strachey, Harmondsworth, Penguin, 1985, p. 224. See also Chapter 3 of this volume, '"The Most Sublime of Hysterics": Hegel with Lacan', p. 46 [eds].

9   See Immanuel Kant, *Critique of Practical Reason*, trans. Mary Gregor, Cambridge, Cambridge University Press, 1997, p. 25 [eds].

10 See Jacques Lacan, 'Kant avec Sade', in *Écrits II*, Paris, Éditions du Seuil, 1966, p. 245.

11 See, for example, Jacques Lacan, *The Seminar of Jacques Lacan II: The Ego in Freud's Theory and in the Technique of Psychoanalysis, 1954–55*, ed. Jacques-Alain Miller, trans. Sylvana Tomaselli, New York, W. W. Norton, 1988, pp. 20, 324; and *The Seminar of Jacques Lacan III: The Psychoses, 1955–56*, ed. Jacques-Alain Miller, trans. Russell Grigg, New York, W. W. Norton, 1993, p. 229 [eds].

12 Žižek's unusual language here presumes some knowledge of the 'four discourses' that Lacan develops at considerable length in his *Seminar XVII*. See Jacques Lacan, *Le Séminaire de Jacques Lacan XVII: L'envers de la psychanalyse, 1969–70*, ed. Jacques-Alain Miller, Paris, Éditions du Seuil, 1991, pp. 9–95; and 'Radiophonie', in *Autres écrits*, ed. Jacques-Alain Miller, Paris, Éditions du Seuil, 1991, pp. 444–7. Žižek's most sustained exposition of the four discourses is in his 'Four Discourses, Four Subjects', in *Cogito and the Unconscious*, ed. Slavoj Žižek, Durham, Duke University Press, 1998, pp. 74–113. In the Lacanian formula for

the Master's discourse ($S_1/\$ \rightarrow S_2/a$), the *objet petit a* occupies the position of the 'product', the 'unassimilable excess', of the master-signifier's (S_1) determination of the symbolic field (S_2) [eds].

13   Jacques Lacan, *The Seminar of Jacques Lacan VII: The Ethics of Psychoanalysis, 1959–60*, ed. Jacques-Alain Miller, trans. Dennis Porter, London and New York, Routledge, 1992, pp. 115–27 [eds].

14   Immanuel Kant, *Anthropology from a Pragmatic Point of View*, trans. Mary J. Gregor, The Hague, Martinus Nijhoff, 1974, p. 99.

15   Jacques Lacan, *The Seminar of Jacques Lacan XI: The Four Fundamental Concepts of Psycho-Analysis, 1964*, ed. Jacques-Alain Miller, trans. Alan Sheridan, New York, W. W. Norton, 1977, p. 185.

16   *Ibid.*

17   Lacan, 'Kant avec Sade', p. 251. See also Chapter 3 of this volume, '"The Most Sublime of Hysterics": Hegel with Lacan', p. 51 [eds].

18   G. W. F. Hegel, *Elements of the Philosophy of Right*, ed. Allen W. Wood, trans. H.B. Nisbet, Cambridge, Cambridge University Press, 1991, pp. 322–3.

19   *Ibid.*, p. 321.

20   *Ibid.*, p. 319.

21   Jacques Lacan, *Séminaire XVII*, pp. 11–12, 33–5 [eds].

22   Søren Kierkegaard, *On Authority and Revelation*, cited in Max Horkheimer, 'Authority and the Family', in *Critical Theory: Selected Essays*, trans. M. J. O'Connell *et al.*, New York, Herder and Herder, 1972, pp. 103–4.

23   Lacan, *Seminar III*, p. 277.

24   Franz Kafka, *The Trial*, trans. Willa and Edwin Muir, Harmondsworth, Penguin, 1953, p. 244 [eds].

25   Jacques Lacan, 'The Subversion of the Subject and the Dialectic of Desire in the Freudian Unconscious', in *Écrits: A Selection*, trans. Bruce Fink, New York, W. W. Norton, 2002, p. 306.

26   Kafka, *The Trial*, p. 61.

27   Žižek further develops this line of thought in some detail in his *The Fragile Absolute – or, Why is the Christian Legacy Worth Fighting For?*, London and New York, Verso, 2000, pp. 25–40 [eds].

28   Pascal Bonitzer, 'Longs feux', *L'âne* 16, 1984 [eds].
29   Walter Benjamin, 'The Work of Art in the Age of Mechanical Reproduction', in *Illuminations*, ed. Hannah Arendt, trans. Harry Zohn, New York, Schocken, 1968, pp. 222–3 [eds].

7 *A Hair of the Dog that Bit You*

Jacques Lacan formulates the elementary dialectical structure of the symbolic order by stating that 'speech is able to recover the debt it engenders',[1] a thesis in which one must recognize all its Hegelian connotation. The debt, the 'wound', opened up by the symbolic order is a philosophical commonplace, at least from Hegel onward: with entry into the symbolic order, our immersion into the immediacy of the real is forever lost, we are forced to assume an irreducible loss, the word entails the (symbolic) murder of the thing, etc. In short, what we are dealing with here is the negative-abstractive power that pertains to what Hegel called *Verstand* (the analytical mortification-dismembering of what organically belongs together). How, then, precisely, are we to conceive the thesis that *logos* is able to recover its own constitutive debt, or, even more pointedly, that it is only speech itself, the very tool of disintegration, that can heal the wound it incises into the real ('only the spear that smote you / can heal your wound', as Wagner puts it in *Parsifal*)? It would be easy to provide examples here, first among them the ecological crisis: if there is one thing that is clear today, it is that a return to any kind of natural balance is forever precluded; only technology and science themselves can get us out of the deadlock into which they brought us. Let us, however, remain at the level of the notion. According to the postmodern *doxa*, the very idea that the symbolic order is able to square its debt in full epitomizes the illusion of the Hegelian *Aufhebung*: language compensates us for the loss of immediate reality (the replacement of 'things' with 'words') with sense, which renders present the essence of things, that is, in which reality is preserved in its notion. However – so the *doxa* goes on – the problem consists in the fact that the symbolic debt is constitutive and as such unredeemable: the emergence of the symbolic order opens up a *béance* that can never be wholly filled up by sense; for that reason, sense is never 'all'; it is always truncated, marked by a stain of non-sense.

Yet, contrary to the common opinion, Lacan does not follow this path; the most appropriate way to track down his orientation is to take as our starting point the relationship between 'empty speech' [*parole vide*] and 'full speech' [*parole pleine*]. Here, we immediately encounter one of the standard misapprehensions of Lacanian theory: as a rule, empty speech is conceived of as empty, nonauthentic prattle in which the speaker's subjective position of enunciation is not disclosed, whereas in full speech the subject is supposed to express their authentic existential position of enunciation; the relationship between empty and full speech is thus conceived as homologous to the duality of 'subject of the enunciated' and 'subject of the enunciation'. Such a reading, however (even if it does not absolutely devalue empty speech but conceives it also as 'free associations' in the psychoanalytical process, i.e. as a speech emptied of imaginary identifications), misses entirely Lacan's point, which becomes manifest the moment we take into account the crucial fact that for Lacan the exemplary case of empty speech is the password [*mot-de-passage*]. How does a password function? As a pure gesture of recognition, of admission into a certain symbolic space, whose enunciated content is totally indifferent. If, say, I arrange with my gangster-colleague that the password that gives me access to his hideout is 'Aunt has baked the apple pie', it can easily be changed into 'Long live comrade Stalin!' or whatever else. Therein consists the 'emptiness' of empty speech: in this ultimate nullity of its enunciated content. And Lacan's point is that human speech in its most radical, fundamental dimension functions as a password: prior to its being a means of communication, of transmitting the signified content, speech is the medium of the mutual recognition of the speakers. In other words, it is precisely the password *qua* empty speech that reduces the subject to the punctuality of the 'subject of the enunciation': in it, he is present *qua* a pure symbolic point freed of all enunciated content. For that reason, full speech is never to be conceived as a simple and immediate filling out of the void that characterizes the empty speech (as in the usual opposition of 'authentic' and 'nonauthentic' speech). Quite the contrary, one must say that it is only empty speech that, by way of its very emptiness (of its distance from the enunciated content that is posited in it as totally indifferent), creates the space for 'full speech', for speech in which the subject can articulate their position of enunciation.

Or, in Hegelese: it is only the subject's radical estrangement from immediate substantial wealth that opens up the space for the articulation of their subjective content. In order to posit the substantial content as 'my own', I must first establish myself as a pure, empty form of subjectivity devoid of all positive content.

And insofar as the symbolic wound is the ultimate paradigm of Evil, the same holds also for the relationship between Evil and Good: radical Evil opens up the space for Good precisely the same way as empty speech opens up the space for full speech. What we come across here, of course, is the problem of 'radical Evil' first articulated by Kant in his *Religion within the Boundaries of Mere Reason*.[2] By conceiving the relationship Evil–Good as contrary, as 'real opposition', Kant is forced to accept a hypothesis on 'radical Evil', on the presence, in man, of a positive counterforce to his tendency toward Good. The ultimate proof of the positive existence of this counterforce is the fact that the subject experiences moral Law in himself as an unbearable traumatic pressure that humiliates his self-esteem and self-love – so there must be something in the very nature of the Self that resists the moral Law, that is, that gives preference to the egotistical, 'pathological' leanings over following the moral Law. Kant emphasizes the *a priori* character of this propensity toward Evil (the moment that was later developed by Schelling): insofar as I am a free being, I cannot simply objectify that which in me resists the Good (by saying, for example, that it is part of my nature for which I am not responsible). The very fact that I feel morally responsible for my evil bears witness to the fact that, in a timeless transcendental act, I had to choose freely my eternal character by giving preference to Evil over Good. This is how Kant conceives 'radical Evil': as an *a priori*, not just an empirical, contingent propensity of human nature toward Evil. However, by rejecting the hypothesis of 'diabolical Evil', Kant recoils from the ultimate paradox of radical Evil, from the uncanny domain of those acts that, although 'evil' as to their content, thoroughly fulfil the formal criteria of an ethical act: they are not motivated by any pathological considerations, that is, their sole motivating ground is Evil as a principle, which is why they can involve the radical abrogation of one's pathological interests, up to the sacrifice of one's life.

Let us recall Mozart's *Don Giovanni*: when, in the final confrontation with the statue of the Commendatore, Don Giovanni refuses to repent, to renounce his sinful past, he accomplishes something the only proper designation of which is a radical ethical stance. It is as if his tenacity mockingly reverses Kant's own example from the *Critique of Practical Reason*, wherein the libertine is quickly prepared to renounce the satisfaction of his passion as soon as he learns that the price to be paid for it is the gallows:[3] Don Giovanni persists in his libertine attitude at the very moment when he knows very well that what awaits him is *only* the gallows and none of the satisfactions. That is to say, from the standpoint of pathological interests, the thing to do would be to accomplish the formal gesture of penitence: Don Giovanni knows that death is close, so that by atoning for his deeds he stands to lose nothing, only to gain (i.e., to save himself from posthumous torments), and yet 'on principle' he chooses to persist in his defiant stance of the libertine. How can one avoid experiencing Don Giovanni's unyielding 'No!' to the statue, to this living dead, as the model of an intransigent *ethical* attitude, notwithstanding its 'evil' content?

If we accept the possibility of such an 'evil' ethical act, then it is not sufficient to conceive radical Evil as something that pertains to the very notion of subjectivity on a par with a disposition toward Good; one is compelled to advance a step further and to conceive radical Evil as something that ontologically precedes Good by way of opening up the space for it. That is to say, in what, precisely, does Evil consist? Evil is another name for the 'death drive', for the fixation on some Thing that derails our customary life circuit. By way of Evil, man wrests himself from the animal instinctual rhythm; that is, Evil introduces the radical reversal of the 'natural' relationship.[4] Here, therefore, is revealed the insufficiency of Kant's and Schelling's standard formula (the possibility of Evil is grounded in man's freedom of choice, on account of which he can invert the 'normal' relationship between universal principles of Reason and his pathological nature by way of subordinating his suprasensible nature to his egotistical inclinations). Hegel, who, in his *Lectures on the Philosophy of Religion*, conceives the very act of becoming human, of the passage from animal into man, as the Fall into sin,[5] is here more penetrating: the possible space for Good is opened up by the original choice of radical Evil, which disrupts the pattern of the organic substantial Whole. The choice between Good and Evil is thus in a sense not the true, original choice. The truly first choice is the choice between (what will later be perceived as) yielding to one's pathological leanings or embracing radical Evil, an act of suicidal egoism that 'makes place' for the Good, that is, that overcomes the domination of pathological natural impulses by way of a purely negative gesture of suspending the life circuit. Or, to refer to Kierkegaard's terms, Evil is Good itself 'in the mode of becoming'. It 'becomes' as a radical disruption of the life circuit; the difference between them concerns a purely formal conversion from the mode of 'becoming' into the mode of 'being'.[6] This is how 'only the spear that smote you can heal the wound': the wound is healed when the place of Evil is filled out by a 'good' content. Good *qua* 'the mask of the Thing (i.e. of the radical Evil)' (Lacan) is thus an ontologically secondary, supplementary attempt to re-establish the lost balance. Its ultimate paradigm in the social sphere is the corporatist endeavour to (re)construct society as a harmonious, organic, non-antagonistic edifice.

The thesis according to which the possibility to choose Evil pertains to the very notion of subjectivity has therefore to be radicalized by a kind of self-reflective inversion: *the status of the subject as such is evil*. That is, insofar as we are 'human', in a sense we *always already* have chosen Evil. Far more than by his direct references to Hegel, the Hegelian stance of the early Lacan is attested to by the rhetorical figures that give body to this logic of the 'negation of negation'. Lacan's answer to the ego-psychological notion of the ego's 'maturity' as the capability to endure frustrations, for example, is that 'the ego . . . is frustration in its very essence':[7] insofar as the ego emerges in the process of imaginary identification with its mirror double who is at the same time its rival, its potential paranoid persecutor, the frustration on the part of the mirror double is constitutive of the ego. The logic of this reversal is strictly Hegelian: what first appears as an external hindrance frustrating the ego's striving for satisfaction is thereupon experienced as the ultimate support of its being.[8]

Why, then, does Kant hold back from bringing out all the consequences of the thesis on radical Evil? The answer is here clear, albeit paradoxical: what prevents him is the very logic that compelled him to articulate the thesis on radical Evil in the first place, namely, the logic of 'real opposition', which, as suggested by Monique David-Menard, constitutes a kind of ultimate fantasmatic frame of Kant's thought. If moral struggle is conceived as the conflict of two opposing positive forces striving for mutual annihilation, it becomes unthinkable for one of the forces, Evil, not only to oppose the other, endeavouring to annihilate it, but also to undermine it from within, by way of assuming the very form of its opposite. Whenever Kant approaches this possibility (apropos of 'diabolical Evil' in practical philosophy; apropos of the trial against the monarch in the doctrine of law), he quickly dismisses it as unthinkable, as an object of ultimate abhorrence. It is only with Hegel's logic of negative self-relating that this step can be accomplished.

This dialectical coincidence of Good and radical Evil that is the 'unthought' of Kant can be further clarified by reference to the relationship between the Beautiful and the Sublime. That is to say, Kant, as is well known, conceives of beauty as the symbol of the Good. At the same time, in his *Critique of the Power of Judgment*, he points out that what is truly sublime is not the object that arouses the feeling of sublimity but the moral Law in us, our suprasensible nature.[9] Are then beauty and sublimity simply to be conceived of as two different symbols of the Good? Is it not, on the contrary, that this duality points toward a certain chasm that must pertain to the moral Law itself? Lacan draws a line of demarcation between the two facets of law. On the one hand, there is Law *qua* symbolic Ego-Ideal, that is, Law in its pacifying function, Law *qua* guarantee of the social pact, *qua* the intermediary Third that dissolves the impasse of imaginary aggressivity. On the other hand, there is law in its superego dimension, that is, law *qua* 'irrational' pressure, the force of culpability, totally incommensurable with our actual responsibility, the agency in the eyes of which we are *a priori* guilty and that gives body to the impossible imperative of enjoyment. It is this distinction between Ego-Ideal and superego that enables us to specify the difference in the way Beauty and Sublimity are related to the domain of ethics. Beauty is the symbol of the Good, that is, of the moral Law as the pacifying agency that bridles our egotism and renders possible harmonious social

co-existence. The dynamical sublime, on the contrary – volcanic erup-
tions, stormy seas, mountain precipices, etc. – by its very failure to
symbolize (to represent symbolically) the suprasensible moral Law,
evokes its superego dimension. The logic at work in the experience of
the dynamical sublime is therefore as follows: true, I may be powerless in the face of the raging forces of nature, a tiny particle of dust
thrown around by wind and sea, yet all this fury of nature pales in
comparison with the absolute pressure exerted on me by the superego,
which humiliates me and compels me to act contrary to my fundamental interests!

(What we encounter here is the basic paradox of the Kantian
autonomy: I am a free and autonomous subject, delivered from the
constraints of my pathological nature precisely and only insofar as my
feeling of self-esteem is crushed by the humiliating pressure of the
moral Law.) Therein consists also the superego dimension of the Jewish
God evoked by the high priest Abner in Racine's *Athalie*: 'I fear God
and have no other fear [*Je crains Dieu et n'ai point d'autre crainte*].'[10]
The fear of raging nature and of the pain other men can inflict on me
converts into sublime peace not simply by my becoming aware of the
suprasensible nature in me out of reach of the forces of nature but by
my taking cognisance of how the pressure of the moral law is stronger
than even the mightiest exercise of the forces of nature.

The unavoidable conclusion to be drawn from all this is that if
Beauty is the symbol of the Good, the Sublime is the symbol of ...
Here, already, the homology gets stuck. The problem with the sublime
object (more precisely: with the object that arouses in us the feeling of
the sublime) is that it *fails* as a symbol – it evokes its Beyond by the
very failure of its symbolic representation. So, if Beauty is the symbol
of the Good, the Sublime evokes – what? There is only one answer
possible: the nonpathological, ethical, suprasensible dimension, for
sure, but *that dimension precisely insofar as it eludes the domain of the
Good* – in short: radical Evil, Evil as an ethical attitude. In today's
popular ideology, this paradox of the Kantian Sublime is what
perhaps enables us to detect the roots of the public fascination with
figures like Hannibal Lecter, the cannibal serial killer from Thomas
Harris' novels: what this fascination ultimately bears witness to is a
deep longing for a Lacanian psychoanalyst. That is to say, Hannibal

Lecter is a sublime figure in the strict Kantian sense: a desperate, ultimately failed attempt by the popular imagination to represent to itself the idea of a Lacanian analyst. The relationship between Lecter and the Lacanian analyst corresponds perfectly to the relationship that, according to Kant, defines the experience of the 'dynamic sublime': the relationship between wild, chaotic, untamed, raging nature and the suprasensible Idea of Reason beyond any natural constraints. True, Lecter's evil – he not only kills his victims but then goes on to eat parts of their entrails – strains to its limits our capacity to imagine the horrors we can inflict on our fellow creatures; yet even the utmost effort to represent Lecter's cruelty to ourselves fails to capture the true dimension of the act of the analyst: by bringing about *la traversée du fantasme* [the going-through of our fundamental fantasy], he literally 'steals the kernel of our being', the *objet a*, the secret treasure, *agalma*, what we consider most precious in ourselves, denouncing it as a mere semblance. Lacan defines the *objet a* as the fantasmatic '"stuff" of the *I*',[11] as that which confers on $, on the fissure in the symbolic order, on the ontological void that we call 'subject', the ontological consistency of a 'person', the semblance of a fullness of being. And it is precisely this 'stuff' that the analyst 'swallows', pulverizes. This is the reason for the unexpected 'eucharistic' element at work in Lacan's definition of the analyst, namely his repeated ironic allusion to Heidegger: 'Mange ton *Dasein*!' ('Eat your being there!').[12] Therein consists the power of fascination that pertains to the figure of Hannibal Lecter: by its very failure to attain the absolute limit of what Lacan calls 'subjective destitution', it enables us to get a presentiment of the Idea of the analyst. So, in *The Silence of the Lambs*, Lecter is truly cannibalistic not in relation to his victims but also in relation to Clarice Sterling: their relationship is a mocking imitation of the analytic situation, since in exchange for his helping her to capture 'Buffalo Bill', he wants her to confide in him – what? Precisely what the analysand confides to the analyst, the kernel of her being, her fundamental fantasy (the crying of the lambs). The *quid pro quo* proposed by Lecter to Clarice is therefore, 'I'll help you if you let me eat your *Dasein*!' The inversion of the proper analytic relation consists in the fact that Lecter compensates her for it by helping her in tracking down 'Buffalo Bill'. As such, he is not cruel enough to be a Lacanian analyst, since in psychoanalysis, we must pay the analyst so that they will allow us to offer them our *Dasein* on a plate.

What opens up the space for such sublime monstrous apparitions is the breakdown of the logic of representation, that is, the radical incommensurability between the field of representation and the un-representable Thing, which emerges with Kant. The pages that describe the first encounter of Madame Bovary and her lover[13] condense the entire problematic that, according to Foucault, determines the post-Kantian episteme of the nineteenth century: the new configuration of the axis power–knowledge caused by the incommensurability between the field of representation and the Thing, as well as the elevation of sexuality to the dignity of the unrepresentable Thing. After the two lovers enter the coach and tell the driver just to circulate around the city, we hear nothing about what goes on behind its safely closed curtains: with an attention to detail reminiscent of the later *nouveau roman*, Flaubert limits himself to lengthy descriptions of the city environment through which the coach wanders aimlessly, the stone-paved streets, the church arches, etc.; only in one short sentence does he mention that, for a brief moment, a naked hand pierces through the curtain. This scene is made as if to illustrate Foucault's thesis, from the first volume of his *History of Sexuality*, that the very speech whose 'official' function is to conceal sexuality engenders the appearance of its secret, that is, that (to make use of the very terms of psychoanalysis against which Foucault's thesis is aimed) the 'repressed' content is an effect of repression.[14] The more the writer's gaze is restricted to boring architectural details, the more we, the readers, are tormented, greedy to learn what goes on in the closed space behind the curtains of the coach. The public prosecutor walked into this trap in the trial against *Madame Bovary* in which it was precisely this passage that was quoted as one of the proofs of the obscene character of the book: it was easy for Flaubert's defence lawyer to point out that there is nothing obscene in the neutral descriptions of paved streets and old house – the obscenity is entirely constrained to the reader's (in this case, the prosecutor's) imagination obsessed by the 'real thing' behind the curtain. It is perhaps no mere accident that today this procedure of Flaubert cannot but strike us as eminently *cinematic*: it is as if it plays upon what cinema theory designates as *hors-champ*, the externality of the field of vision, which, in its very absence, organizes the economy of what can be seen: if (as was long ago proven by the classical analyses of Eisenstein) Dickens introduced into the literary discourse the correlates of what later became the elementary cinematic procedures – the triad of establishing shots, 'American' pans and close-ups, parallel montage, etc. – Flaubert went a step further toward an externality that eludes the standard exchange of field and counterfield, that is, that has to remain excluded if the field of what can be represented is to retain its consistency.[15]

The crucial point, however, is not to mistake *this* incommensurability between the field of representation and sexuality for the censorship in the description of sexuality already at work in the preceding epochs. If *Madame Bovary* had been written a century earlier, the details of sexual activity would also have remained unmentioned, for sure, yet what we would have got after the two lovers' entry into the secluded space of the coach would have been a simple, short statement like: 'Finally alone and hidden behind the curtains of the coach, the lovers were able to gratify their passion.' The lengthy descriptions of streets and buildings would have been totally out of place; they would have been perceived as lacking any function, since, in this pre-Kantian universe of representations, no radical tension could arise between the represented content and the traumatic Thing behind the curtain. Against this background, one is tempted to propose one of the possible definitions of 'realism': a naïve belief that, behind the curtain of representations, there actually exists some full, substantial reality (in the case of *Madame Bovary*, the reality of sexual superfluity). 'Post-realism' begins when a doubt emerges as to the existence of this reality 'behind the curtain', that is, when the foreboding arises that the very gesture of concealment creates what it pretends to conceal.

An exemplary case of such a 'post-realist' playing, of course, is found in the paintings of René Magritte. His notorious *Ceçi n'est pas une pipe* is today part of common knowledge: a drawing of a pipe with an inscription below it stating, 'This is not a pipe'. Taking as a starting point the paradoxes implied by this painting, Michel Foucault wrote a perspicacious little book of the same title.[16] Yet perhaps there is another of Magritte's paintings that can serve even more appropriately to establish the elementary matrix that generates the uncanny effects that pertain to his work: *La lunette d'approche* from 1963, the painting of a half-open window where, through the windowpane, we see the external reality (blue sky with some dispersed white clouds). Yet what we see in the narrow opening that gives direct access to the reality beyond the pane is nothing, just a nondescript black mass. The translation of this painting into Lacanese goes by itself: the frame of the windowpane is the fantasy frame that constitutes reality, whereas through the crack we get an insight into the 'impossible' Real, the Thing-in-itself.[17]

This painting renders the elementary matrix of the Magrittean paradoxes by way of staging the 'Kantian' split between (symbolized, categorized, transcendentally constituted) reality and the void of the Thing-in-itself, of the Real, which gapes in the midst of reality and confers upon it a fantasmatic character. The first variation that can be generated from this matrix is the presence of some strange, inconsistent element that is 'extraneous' to the depicted reality, that is, that, uncannily, has its place in it, although it does not 'fit' in it: the gigantic rock that floats in the air close to a cloud as its heavy counterpart, its double, in *La Bataille de l'Argonne* (1959); or the unnaturally large bloom that fills out the entire room in *Tombeau des lutteurs* (1960). This strange element 'out of joint' is precisely the fantasy object filling out the blackness of the real that we perceived in the crack of the open window in *La lunette d'approche*. The effect of uncanniness is even stronger when the 'same' object is redoubled, as in *Les deux mystères*, a later variation (from 1966) on the famous *Ceçi n'est pas une pipe*: the pipe and the inscription underneath it, 'Ceçi n'est pas une pipe', are both depicted as drawings on a blackboard; yet, on the left of the blackboard, the apparition of another gigantic and massive pipe floats freely in a non-specified space. The title of this painting could also have been 'A pipe is a pipe', for what is it if not a perfect illustration of the Hegelian thesis on tautology as the ultimate contradiction: the coincidence between the pipe located in a clearly defined symbolic reality and its fantasmatic, uncanny, shadowy double. The inscription under the pipe on the blackboard bears witness to the fact that the split between the two pipes, the pipe that forms part of reality and the pipe as real, that is, as a fantasy apparition, results from the intervention of the symbolic order: it is the emergence of the symbolic order that splits reality into itself and the enigmatic surplus of the real, each of them 'derealizing' its counterpart. (The Marx brothers' version of this painting would be something like, 'This looks like a pipe and works like a pipe, but this should not deceive you – this *is* a pipe!'[18]) The massive presence of the free-floating pipe, of course, turns the depicted pipe into a 'mere painting', yet, simultaneously, the free-floating pipe is opposed to the 'domesticated' symbolic reality of the pipe on the blackboard and as such acquires a phantom-like, 'surreal' presence, like the emergence of the 'real' Laura in Otto Preminger's *Laura*: the police detective (Dana Andrews) falls asleep staring at the portrait of the allegedly dead Laura; upon awakening, he finds at the side of the portrait the 'real' Laura, alive and well. This presence of the 'real' Laura accentuates the fact that the portrait is a mere 'imitation'; on the other hand, the very 'real' Laura emerges as a non-symbolized fantasmatic surplus, a ghost – like the inscription, 'This is not Laura'. A somewhat homologous effect of the real occurs at the beginning of Sergio Leone's *Once upon a Time in America*: a phone goes on ringing endlessly; when, finally, a hand picks up the receiver, it continues to ring. The first sound belongs to 'reality', whereas the ringing that goes on even after the receiver is picked up comes out of the non-specified void of the Real.[19]

This splitting between symbolized reality and the surplus of the Real, however, renders only the most elementary matrix of the way the Symbolic and the Real are intertwined; a further dialectical 'turn of the screw' is introduced by what Freud called *Vorstellungs-Repräsentanz*, the symbolic representative of an originally missing, excluded ('primordially repressed') representation. This paradox of the *Vorstellungs-Repräsentanz* is perfectly staged by Magritte's *Person-nage marchant vers l'horizon* (1928–9): the portrait of his usual elderly gentleman in a bowler hat, seen from behind, situated near five thick, formless blobs that bear the italicized words 'nuage', 'cheval', 'fusil', etc. Words are here signifiers' representatives that stand in for the absent representation of the things. Foucault is quite right in remarking that this painting functions as a kind of inverted rebus: in a rebus, pictorial representations of things stand for the words that designate these things, whereas here words themselves fill out the void of absent things. It would be possible for us to continue *ad infinitum* with the variations generated by the elementary matrix (one thinks of *The Fall of the Evening*, for example, where the evening literally falls through the window and breaks the pane – a case of realized metaphor, i.e. of the intrusion of the Symbolic into the Real). Yet it suffices to ascertain how behind all these paradoxes the same matrix can be discerned, the same basic fissure whose nature is ultimately Kantian: reality is never given in its totality; there is always a void gaping in its midst, filled out by monstrous apparitions.

The impenetrable blackness that can be glimpsed through the crack of the half-opened window thus opens up the space for the uncanny apparitions of an Other who precedes the Other of 'normal' intersubjectivity. Let us recall here a detail from Hitchcock's *Frenzy* that bears witness to his genius. In a scene that leads to the second murder, Babs, its victim, a young girl who works in a Covent Garden pub, leaves her workplace after a quarrel with the owner and steps out onto the busy market street. The street noise that hits us for a brief moment is quickly suspended (in a totally 'nonrealistic' way) when the camera approaches Babs for a closeup, and the mysterious silence is then broken by an uncanny voice coming from an indefinite point of absolute proximity, as if from behind her and at the same time from within her, a man's voice softly saying, 'Need a place to stay?' Babs moves off and looks back. Standing behind her is her old acquaintance who, unbeknownst to her, is the 'necktie murderer'. After a couple of seconds, the magic again evaporates and we hear the sound tapestry of 'reality', of the market street bustling with life. This voice that emerges on the suspension of reality is none other than the *objet petit a*, and the figure that appears behind Babs is experienced by the spectator as supplementary with regard to this voice: it gives body to it, and, simultaneously, it is strangely intertwined with Babs's body, as its shadowy protuberance (not unlike the strange double body of Leonardo's Madonna, analysed by Freud; or, in *Total Recall*, the body of the leader of the underground resistance movement on Mars, a kind of parasitic protuberance on another person's belly). It would be easy to produce a long list of homologous effects. For instance, in one of the key scenes of *Silence of the Lambs*, Clarice and Lecter occupy the same positions when engaged in a conversation in Lecter's prison: in the foreground, the closeup of Clarice staring into the camera, and on the glass partition wall behind her, the reflection of Lecter's head germinating behind – out of her – as her shadowy double, simultaneously less and more real than she. The supreme case of this effect, however, is found in one of the most mysterious shots of Hitchcock's *Vertigo*, when Scottie peers at Madeleine through the crack in the half-opened back door of the florist's shop. For a brief moment, Madeleine watches herself in a mirror close to this door, so that the screen is vertically split: the left half is occupied by the mirror in which we see Madeleine's reflection, while the right half is carved by a series of vertical lines (the doors); in the vertical dark band (the crack of the half-opened door) we see a fragment of Scottie, his gaze transfixed on the 'original' whose mirror reflection we see in the left half. There is a truly 'Magrittean' quality to this unique shot. Although, as to the disposition of the diegetic space, Scottie is here 'in reality', whereas what we see of Madeleine is only her mirror image, the effect of the shot is exactly the reverse: Madeleine is perceived as part of reality and Scottie as a phantom-like protuberance who (like the legendary dwarf in the Grimms' *Snow White*) lurks from behind the mirror. This shot is Magrittean in a very precise sense: the dwarf-like mirage of Scottie peeps out of the very impenetrable darkness that gapes in the crack of the half-open window in *La lunette d'approche* (the mirror in *Vertigo*, of course, corresponds to the windowpane in Magritte's painting). In both cases, the framed space of the mirrored reality is traversed by a vertical black rift.[20] As Kant puts it, there is no positive knowledge of the Thing-in-itself; one can only designate its place, 'make room' for it. This is what Magritte accomplishes on a quite literal level: the crack of the half-open door, its impenetrable blackness, makes room for the Thing. And by locating in this crack a gaze, Hitchcock supplements Magrite in a Hegelian-Lacanian way: the Thing-in-itself beyond appearance is ultimately the gaze itself, as Lacan puts it in his *Seminar XI*.[21]

In his Bayreuth production of *Tristan und Isolde*, Jean-Pierre Ponelle changed Wagner's original plot, interpreting all that follows Tristan's death – the arrival of Isolde and King Mark, Isolde's death – as Tristan's mortal delirium: the final appearance of Isolde is staged so that the dazzlingly illuminated Isolde grows luxuriantly *behind* him, while Tristan stares at us, the spectators, who are able to perceive his sublime double, the protuberance of his lethal enjoyment. This is also how Bergman, in his version of *The Magic Flute*, often shot Pamina and Monostatos: a close-up of Pamina, who stares intensely into the camera, with Monostatos appearing behind her as her shadowy double, as if belonging to a different level of reality (illuminated with pointedly 'unnatural' dark violet colours), with his gaze also directed into the camera. This disposition, in which the subject and their shadowy, extimate double stare into a common third point (materialized in us, spectators), epitomizes the relationship of the subject to an Otherness that is prior to intersubjectivity. The field of intersubjectivity wherein subjects, within their shared *reality*, 'look into each other's eyes', is sustained by the paternal metaphor, whereas the reference to the absent third point that attracts the two gazes changes the status of one of the two partners – the one in the background – into the sublime embodiment of the *Real* of enjoyment.

What all these scenes have in common on the level of purely cinematic procedure is a kind of formal correlate of the reversal of face-to-face intersubjectivity into the relationship of the subject to his shadowy double that emerges behind them as a kind of sublime protuberance: the condensation of the field and counterfield within the same shot. What we have here is a paradoxical kind of communication: not a 'direct' communication of the subject with his fellow creature *in front of* him, but a communication with the excrescence *behind* him, mediated by a third gaze, as if the counterfield were to be mirrored back into the field itself. It is this third gaze that confers upon the scene its hypnotic dimension: the subject is enthralled by the gaze that sees 'what is in himself more than himself'. And the analytical situation itself – the relationship between analyst and analysand – does it not ultimately also designate a kind of return to this pre-intersubjective relationship of the subject (analysand) to his shadowy other, to the externalized object in himself? Is not this the whole point of its spatial disposition: after the so-called preliminary encounters, that is, with the beginning of the analysis proper, the analyst and the analysand are *not* confronted face to face, but the analyst sits *behind* the analysand who, stretched on the divan, stares into the void in front of him? Does not this very disposition locate the analyst as the analysand's *objet a*, not his dialogical partner, not another subject?

At this point, we should return to Kant: in his philosophy, this crack, this space where such monstrous apparitions can emerge, is opened up by the distinction between negative and indefinite judgment. The very example used by Kant to illustrate this distinction is telling: the positive judgement by means of which a predicate is ascribed to the (logical) subject – 'The soul is mortal', the negative judgement by means of which a predicate is denied to the subject – 'The soul is not mortal', the indefinite judgement by means of which, instead of negating a predicate (i.e., the copula that ascribes it to the subject), we affirm a certain non-predicate – 'The soul is not-mortal'.[22] (In German also, the difference is solely a matter of spacing: '*Die Seele ist nicht sterbliche*' versus '*Die Seele ist nichtsterbliche*'; Kant enigmatically does not use the standard '*unsterbliche*'.)

In this line of thought, Kant introduces in the second edition of the *Critique of Pure Reason* the distinction between positive and negative meanings of 'noumenon': in the positive meaning of the term, 'noumenon' is 'an object of a nonsensible intuition', whereas, in the negative meaning, it is 'a thing insofar as it is not an object of our sensible intuition'.[23] The grammatical form should not deceive us here: the positive meaning is expressed by the negative judgement and the negative meaning by the indefinite judgement. In other words, when one determines the Thing as 'an object of a nonsensible intuition', one immediately negates the positive judgement that determines the Thing as 'an object of a sensible intuition': one accepts intuition as the unquestioned base or genus; against this background, one opposes its two species, sensible and nonsensible intuition. Negative judgement is thus not only limiting; it also delineates a domain beyond phenomena where it locates the Thing – the domain of the nonsensible intuition – whereas in the case of the negative determination, the Thing is excluded from the domain of our sensible intuition, without being posited in an implicit way as the object of a nonsensible intuition; by leaving in suspense the positive status of the Thing, negative determination saps the very genus common to affirmation and negation of the predicate.

Therein consists also the difference between 'is not mortal' and 'is not-mortal': what we have in the first case is a simple negation, whereas in the second case, a *nonpredicate is affirmed*. The only 'legitimate' definition of the noumenon is that it is 'not an object of our sensible intuition', that is, a wholly negative definition that excludes it from the phenomenal domain; this judgement is 'infinite' since it does not imply any conclusions as to where, in the infinite space of what remains outside the phenomenal domain, the noumenon is located. What Kant calls 'transcendental illusion' ultimately consists in the very (mis)reading of infinite judgement as negative judgement: when we conceive the noumenon as an 'object of a nonsensible intuition', the subject of the judgement remains the same (the 'object of an intuition'); what changes is only the character (nonsensible instead of sensible) of this intuition, so that a minimal 'commensurability' between the subject and the predicate (i.e., in this case, between the noumenon and its phenomenal determinations) is still maintained.

A Hegelian corollary to Kant here is that limitation is to be conceived of as prior to what lies 'beyond' it, so that it is ultimately Kant himself whose notion of the Thing-in-itself remains too 'reified'. Hegel's position as to this point is subtle: what he claims by stating that the Suprasensible is 'appearance *qua* appearance' is precisely that the Thing-in-itself is *the limitation of the phenomena as such.* 'Suprasensible objects (objects of suprasensible intuition)' belong to the chimerical 'topsy-turvy world'. They are nothing but an inverted presentation, a projection, of the very content of sensible intuition in the form of another, nonsensible intuition. Or, to recall Marx's ironic critique of Proudhon in *The Poverty of Philosophy*: 'Instead of the ordinary individual with his ordinary manner of speaking and thinking we have nothing but this ordinary manner itself – without the individual.'[24] (The double irony of it, of course, is that Marx intended these lines as a mocking rejection of Proudhon's Hegelianism, i.e. of his effort to supply economic theory with the form of speculative dialectics!) This is what the chimera of 'nonsensible intuition' is about: instead of ordinary objects of sensible intuition, we get the same ordinary objects of intuition, without their sensible character.

This subtle difference between negative and indefinite judgement is at work in a certain type of witticism wherein the second part does not immediately invert the first part by negating its predicate but instead repeats it with the negation displaced on to the subject. The judgement, 'He is an individual full of idiotic features', for example, can be negated in a standard mirror way, that is, replaced by its contrary,

'He is an individual with no idiotic features'; yet its negation can also be given the form of, 'He is full of idiotic features without being an individual.' This displacement of the negation from the predicate on to the subject provides the logical matrix of what is often the unforeseen result of our educational efforts to liberate the pupil from the constraint of prejudices and clichés: not a person capable of expressing themselves in a relaxed, unconstrained way, but an automatized bundle of (new) clichés behind which we no longer sense the presence of a 'real person'. Let us just recall the usual outcome of psychological training intended to deliver the individual from the constraints of their everyday frame of mind and to set free their 'true self', their authentic creative potentials (transcendental meditation, etc.): once they get rid of the old clichés that were still able to sustain the dialectical tension between themselves and the 'personality' behind them, what take their place are new clichés that abrogate the very 'depth' of personality behind them. In short, they become a true monster, a kind of 'living dead'. Samuel Goldwyn, the old Hollywood mogul, was right: what we need are indeed some new, original clichés.

The mention of the 'living dead' is by no means accidental here: in our ordinary language, we resort to indefinite judgements precisely when we endeavour to comprehend those borderline phenomena that undermine established differences such as that between living and being dead. In the texts of popular culture, the uncanny creatures that are neither alive nor dead, the 'living dead' (vampires, etc.), are referred to as 'the undead': although they are not dead, they are clearly not alive like us ordinary mortals. The judgement, 'he is undead', is therefore an indefinite-limiting judgement in the precise sense of a purely negative gesture of excluding vampires from the domain of the dead, without for that reason locating them in the domain of the living (as in the case of the simple negation, 'he is not dead'). The fact that vampires and other 'living dead' are usually referred to as 'things' has to be rendered with its full Kantian meaning: a vampire is a Thing that looks and acts like us, yet is not one of us. In short, the difference between the vampire and a living person is that between indefinite and negative judgement: a dead person loses the predicates of a living being, yet they remain the same person. An undead, on the contrary, retains all the predicates of a living being without being one. As in the above-quoted Marxian joke, what we get with the vampire is 'this ordinary manner itself – without the individual'.

This intermediate space of the unrepresentable Thing, filled out by the 'undead', is what Lacan has in mind when he speaks of 'l'entre-deux-morts'.[25] To delineate more precisely the contours of this uncanny space, let us take as our starting point a new book on Lacan, Richard Boothby's *Death and Desire*.[26] Its central thesis, although ultimately false, is very consequential and at the same time deeply satisfying in the sense of fulfilling a demand for symmetry: it is as if it provides the missing element of a puzzle. The triad Imaginary–Real–Symbolic renders the fundamental coordinates of the Lacanian theoretical space. But these three dimensions can never be conceived simultaneously, in pure synchronicity. One is always forced to choose between two of them (as with Kierkegaard's triad of the aesthetical–ethical–religious): Symbolic versus Imaginary, Real versus Symbolic. The hitherto predominating interpretations of Lacan in effect put the accent on one of these axes: symbolization (Symbolic realization) against Imaginary self-deception in the Lacan of the 1950s; the traumatic encounter of the Real as the point at which symbolization fails in the late Lacan. What Boothby offers as a key to the entire Lacanian theoretical edifice is simply the third, not yet exploited, axis: Imaginary versus Real. That is to say, according to Boothby, the theory of the mirror stage not only is chronologically Lacan's first contribution to psychoanalysis but also designates the original fact that defines the status of man. The alienation in the mirror image due to the human's premature birth and their ensuing helplessness in the first years of life, this fixation on an imago, interrupts the supple life flow, introducing an irreducible *béance*, a gap, separating forever the Imaginary ego – the wholesome yet immobile mirror image, a kind of halted cinematic picture – from the polymorphous, chaotic sprout of bodily drives, the Real Id. In this perspective, the Symbolic is of a strictly secondary nature with regard to the original tension between Imaginary and Real: its place is the void opened up by the exclusion of the polymorphous wealth of bodily drives. Symbolization designates the subject's endeavour, always fragmentary and ultimately doomed to fail, to bring into the light of the day, by way of Symbolic representatives, the Real of bodily drives excluded by Imaginary identification; it is therefore a kind of compromise formation by way of which the subject integrates fragments of the ostracized Real. In this sense, Boothby interprets the death drive as the re-emergence of what was ostracized when the ego constituted itself by way of imaginary identification: the return of the polymorphous impulses is experienced by the ego as a mortal threat, since it actually entails the dissolution of its Imaginary identity. The foreclosed Real thus returns in two modes: either as a wild, destructive, non-symbolized raging or in the form of Symbolic mediation, that is, 'sublated' [*aufgehoben*] in the Symbolic medium. The elegance of Boothby is here to interpret the death drive as its very opposite: as the return of the life force, of the part of it excluded by the imposition of the petrified mask of the ego. What re-emerges in the 'death drive' is ultimately *life itself*, and the fact that the ego perceives this return as a death threat precisely confirms its perverted 'repressive' character. The 'death drive' means that life itself rebels against the ego: the true representative of death is Ego itself, as the petrified imago that interrupts the flow of life. Boothby also reinterprets against this background Lacan's distinction between the two deaths: the first death is the death of the ego, the dissolution of its imaginary identifications, whereas the second death designates the interruption of the pre-symbolic life flow itself. Here, however, problems begin with this otherwise simple and elegant construct: the price to be paid for it is that Lacan's theoretical edifice is ultimately reduced to the opposition between an original polymorphous life force and its later coagulation, confining to the Procrustean bed of imagos the opposition that characterizes the field of *Lebensphilosophie*. For that reason, there is no place in Boothby's scheme for the fundamental Lacanian insight according to which the Symbolic order 'stands for death' in the precise sense of 'mortifying' the Real of the body, of subordinating it to a foreign automatism, of perturbing its 'natural' instinctual rhythm, thereby producing the surplus of desire, that is, desire *as* a surplus: the very Symbolic machine that 'mortifies' the living body produces by the same token its opposite, the immortal desire, the Real of 'pure life' that eludes symbolization. To clarify this point, let us bring to mind an example that, in a first approach, may appear to confirm Boothby's thesis: Wagner's *Tristan und Isolde*. In what, precisely, consists the effect on the (future) lovers of the philtre provided by Isolde's faithful maid Brangaene?

> Wagner never intends to imply that the love of Tristan and Isolde is the *physical consequence* of the philtre, but only that the pair, having drunk what they imagine to be the draught of Death and believing that they have looked upon earth and sea and sky for the last time, feel themselves free to confess, when the potion begins its work within them, the love they have so long felt but have concealed from each other and almost from themselves.[27]

The point is therefore that after drinking the philtre, Tristan and Isolde find themselves in the domain 'between the two deaths', alive, yet delivered of all symbolic ties. *In this domain*, they are able to confess their love. In other words, the 'magical effect' of the philtre is simply to suspend the 'big Other', the Symbolic reality of social obligations (honours, vows). Does this not fully accord with Boothby's thesis on the domain 'between the two deaths' as the space where Imaginary identification, as well as the Symbolic identities attached to it, are all invalidated, so that the excluded Real (pure life drive) can emerge in all its force, although in the form of its opposite, the death drive? According to Wagner himself, the passion of Tristan and Isolde expresses the longing for the 'eternal peace' of death. The trap to be avoided here, however, is that of conceiving this pure life drive as a substantial entity subsisting prior to its being captured in the Symbolic network: this 'optical illusion' renders invisible that it is the very mediation of the Symbolic order that transforms the organic 'instinct' into an unquenchable longing that can find solace only in death. In other words, this 'pure life' beyond death, this longing that reaches beyond the circuit of generation and corruption, is it not the *product* of symbolization, so that symbolization itself engenders the surplus that escapes it? By conceiving the Symbolic order as an agency that fills out the gap between the Imaginary and the Real opened up by the mirror identification, Boothby avoids its constitutive paradox: the Symbolic itself opens up the wound it professes to heal. In lieu of a more detailed theoretical elaboration, it is appropriate at this point to approach the relationship of Lacan to Heidegger in a new way. In the 1950s, Lacan endeavoured to read 'death drive' against the background of Heidegger's 'being-toward-death' [*Sein-zum-Tode*], conceiving death as the inherent and ultimate limit of symbolization that provides for its irreducible temporal character. With the shift of accent toward the Real from the 1960s onward, however, it is rather the 'undead' lamella, the indestructible-immortal life that dwells in the domain 'between the two deaths', that emerges as the ultimate object of horror. Lacan delineates the contours of this 'undead' object toward the end of Chapter XV of his *Seminar XI*, where he proposes his own myth, constructed upon the model of Aristophanes' fable from Plato's *Symposium*, the myth of *l'hommelette* [little female-man omelette]:

> Whenever the membranes of the egg in which the foetus emerges on its way to becoming a newborn are broken, imagine for a moment that something flies off, and that one can do it with an egg as easily as with a man, namely the *hommelette*, or the lamella.
>
> The lamella is something extra-flat, which moves like the amoeba. It is just a little more complicated. But it goes everywhere. And as it is something ... that is related to what the sexed being loses in sexuality, it is, like the amoeba in relation to sexed beings, immortal – because it survives any division, any scissiparous intervention. And it can run around.
>
> Well! This is not very reassuring. But suppose it comes and envelops your face while you are quietly asleep ...
>
> I can't see how we would not join battle with a being capable of these properties. But it would not be a very convenient battle. This lamella, this organ, whose characteristic is not to exist, but which is nevertheless an organ ... is the libido.
>
> It is the libido, *qua* pure life instinct, that is to say, immortal life, or irrepressible life, life that has need of no organ, simplified, indestructible life. It is precisely what is subtracted from the living being by virtue of the fact that it is subject to the cycle of sexed reproduction. And it is of this that all the forms of the *objet a* that can be enumerated are the representatives, the equivalents. The *objets a* are merely its representatives, its figures. The breast – as

equivocal, as an element characteristic of the mammiferous organization, the placenta for example – certainly represents that part
of himself that the individual loses at birth, and which may serve to
symbolize the most profound lost object.[28]

What we have here, again, is an Otherness prior to intersubjectivity:
the subject's 'impossible' relationship to this amoeba-like creature is
what Lacan is ultimately aiming at by way of his formula $\text{\$} \lozenge a$. The
best way to clarify this point is perhaps to allow ourselves the string of
associations that Lacan's description must evoke insofar as we like
horror movies. Is not the alien from Ridley Scott's film of that title the
'lamella' in its purest form? Are not all the key elements of Lacan's
myth contained already in the first truly horrifying scene of the film
when, in the womblike cave of the unknown planet, the 'alien' leaps
from the egg-like globe when its lid splits off and sticks to John Hurt's
face? This amoeba-like flattened creature that envelops the subject's
face stands for the irrepressible life beyond all the finite forms that are
merely its representatives, its figures (later in the film, the 'alien' is able
to assume a multitude of different shapes), immortal and indestructible. It suffices to recall the unpleasant thrill of the moment when a
scientist cuts with a scalpel into a leg of the creature that envelops
Hurt's face: the liquid that drips from it falls on to the metal floor and
corrodes it immediately; nothing can resist it.[29]

The second association here, of course, is with a detail from
Syberberg's film version of *Parsifal*, in which Syberberg depicts
Amfortas's wound – externalized, carried by the servants on a pillow
in front of him, in the form of a vagina-like partial object out of which
blood is dripping in a continuous flow (like, *vulgari eloquentia*, a
vagina in an unending period). This palpitating opening – an organ
that is at the same time the entire organism (let us just recall a
homologous motif in a series of science fiction stories, like the gigantic
eye living a life of its own) – epitomizes life in its indestructibility:
Amfortas's pain consists in the very fact that he is unable to die, that
he is condemned to an eternal life of suffering; when, at the end,
Parsifal heals his wound with 'the spear that smote it', Amfortas is
finally able to rest and die. This wound of Amfortas, which persists
outside himself as an *undead* thing, is the 'object of psychoanalysis'.

And – to conclude – it is precisely the reference to this indestructible, mythical object-libido that enables us to throw some light on one of the most obscure points of Lacanian theory: what, precisely, is the role of *objet petit a* in a drive – say, in the scopic drive – as opposed to desire? The key is provided by Lacan's clarification, in his *Seminar XI*, that the essential feature of the scopic drive consists in '*making oneself seen [se faire voir]*'.[30] However, as Lacan immediately points out, this 'making oneself seen' that characterizes the circularity, the constitutive loop, of the drive, is in no way to be confused with the narcissistic 'looking at oneself through the other', that is, through the eyes of the big Other, from the point of the Ego-Ideal in the Other, in the form in which I appear to myself worthy of love: what is lost when I 'look at myself through the other' is the radical heterogeneity of the object *qua* gaze to whom I expose myself in 'making oneself seen'. In the ideological space proper, an exemplary case of this narcissistic satisfaction provided by 'looking at oneself through the other' (Ego-Ideal) is the reporting on one's own country as seen through the foreign gaze (see the obsession of American media today by the way America is perceived – admired or despised – by the Other: Japanese, Russians, etc.). The first exemplary case of it, of course, is Aeschylus's *Persians*, where the Persian defeat is rendered as seen through the eyes of the Persian royal court: the amazement of King Darius at what a magnificent people the Greeks are, etc., provides for the deep narcissistic satisfaction of the Greek spectators. Yet this is not what 'making oneself seen' is about. In what, then, does it consist?

Let us recall Hitchcock's *Rear Window*, which is often quoted as an exemplary staging of the scopic drive. Throughout most of the film, it is the logic of desire that predominates: this desire is fascinated, propelled, by its object-cause, the dark window opposite the courtyard that gazes back at the subject. When, in the course of the film, does 'the arrow come back toward the subject'? At the moment, of course, when the murderer in the house opposite Stewart's rear window returns the gaze and catches him red-handed in his act of voyeurism: at this precise moment when James Stewart does not 'see himself seeing himself', but *makes himself seen to the object of his seeing*, that is, to that stain that attracted his gaze in the dark room across the courtyard, we pass from the register of desire into that of drive. That is to say, we remain within the register of desire as long as, by way of assuming the inquisitive attitude of a voyeur, we are looking in what we see for the fascinating X, for some trace of what is hidden 'behind the curtain'; we 'change the gear' into drive the moment we make ourselves seen to this stain in the picture, to this impervious foreign body in it, to this point that attracted our gaze. Therein consists the reversal that defines drive: insofar as I cannot see the point in the other from which I'm gazed at, the only thing that remains for me to do is to make myself visible to that point. The difference between this and the narcissistic looking at oneself from the point of the Ego-Ideal is clear: the point to which the subject makes himself seen retains its traumatic heterogeneity and non-transparency; it remains an object in a strict Lacanian sense, not a symbolic feature. This point to which I make myself visible in my very capacity of looking is the object of drive, and in this way one can perhaps clarify a little bit the difference between the status of *objet a* in desire and in drive. (As we all know, when Jacques-Alain Miller asks Lacan about this point in *Seminar XI*, the answer he gets is chiaroscuro at its best.)

What can further clarify this crucial distinction is another feature of the final scene of *Rear Window* that stages in its purest this transmutation of desire into drive: the desperate defence of Jefferies, who attempts to stop the murderer's advance by letting off his flashbulbs. This apparently nonsensical gesture must be read precisely as a *defence against drive*, against 'making oneself seen'. Jefferies endeavours frantically to blur the other's gaze.[31] What befalls him when the murderer throws him through the window is precisely the inversion that defines drive: by falling through the window, Jefferies in a radical sense falls into his own picture, into the field of his own visibility. In Lacanian terms, he changes into a stain in his own picture, he makes himself seen in it, that is, within the space defined as his own field of vision.[32]

Those magnificent scenes toward the end of *Who Framed Roger Rabbit* are another variant on the same motif, where the hard-boiled detective falls into the universe of cartoons: he is thereby confined to the domain 'between the two deaths' where there is no death proper, just unending devouring and/or destruction. Yet another left-paranoiac variant of it is to be found in *Dreamscape*, a sci-fi movie about an American president troubled by bad dreams about the nuclear catastrophe he may trigger: the dark militarist plotters try to prevent his pacifist plans by making use of a criminal with a paranormal capacity to transpose himself into another person's dream and act in it. The idea is to scare the president so much in his dream that he dies of a heart attack.

The apparent melodramatic simplicity of the final scene of Chaplin's *Limelight* should not deceive us: here, also, we have the reversal of desire into drive. This scene is centred on a magnificent backward tracking shot that moves from the close-up of the dead clown Calvero behind the stage to the establishing shot of the entire stage where the young girl, now a successful ballerina and his great love, is performing. Just before this scene, the dying Calvero expresses to the attending doctor his desire to see his love dancing; the doctor taps him gently on the shoulders and comforts him: 'You shall see her!' Thereupon Calvero dies, his body is covered by a white sheet, and the camera withdraws so that it comprises the dancing girl on the stage, while Calvero is reduced to a tiny, barely visible white stain in the background. What is here of special significance is the way the ballerina enters the frame: from behind the camera, like the birds in the famous 'God's-view' shot of Bodega Bay in Hitchcock's *Birds* – yet another white stain that materializes out of the mysterious intermediate space separating the spectator from the diegetic reality on the screen. We encounter here the function of the gaze *qua* object-stain in its purest: the doctor's forecast is fulfilled, precisely as dead – that is, insofar as he cannot *see* her any more – Calvero *looks at her*. For that reason, the logic of this backward tracking shot is thoroughly Hitchcockian: by way of it, a piece of reality is transformed into an amorphous stain (a white blot in the background), yet a stain around which the entire field of vision turns, a stain that 'smears over' the entire field (as in the backward tracking shot in *Frenzy*). In other words, what confers upon this scene its melodramatic beauty is our – the spectators' – awareness that without knowing that he is already dead, the ballerina is dancing for it, for that stain (the melodramatic effect always hinges on such an ignorance of the agent). It is this stain, this white smudge in the background, that guarantees the sense of the scene. Where, precisely, is the transmutation of desire into drive here? We remain within the register of desire as long as the field of vision is organized, supported, by Calvero's desire to see for the last time his love dancing; we enter the register of drive the moment Calvero is reduced to a stain-object in his own picture. For that precise reason, it is not sufficient to say that it is simply she, the ballerina, his love, who makes herself seen to him; the point is rather that, simultaneously, he acquires the presence of a stain, so that both of them appear within the same field of vision.[33]

The scopic drive always designates such a closing of the loop whereby I get caught in the picture I'm looking at, lose distance toward it; as such, it is never a simple reversal of desire to see into a passive mode. 'Making oneself seen' is inherent to the very act of seeing: drive is the loop that connects them. The ultimate exemplifications of drive are therefore the visual and temporal paradoxes that materialize the nonsensical, 'impossible' vicious circle: Escher's two hands drawing each other, or the waterfall that runs in a closed perpetuum-mobile, or the time-travel loop whereby I visit the past in order to create myself (to couple my parents).

Perhaps even better than by the arrow mentioned by Lacan, this loop formed by the outward and return movement of the drive[34] can be exemplified by the first free association that this formulation resuscitates, namely, the boomerang, where 'hitting the animal' changes over into 'making oneself hit'. That is to say, when I throw the boomerang, the 'goal' of it, of course, is to hit the animal; yet the true artifice of it consists in being able to catch it when, upon my missing the goal, the boomerang flies back – the true aim is precisely to miss the goal, so that the boomerang returns to me (the most difficult part of learning how to handle the boomerang is therefore to master the art of catching it properly, i.e., of avoiding being hit by it, of blocking the potentially suicidal dimension of throwing it). The boomerang thus designates the very moment of the emergence of 'culture', the moment when instinct is transformed into drive: the moment of splitting between goal and aim, the moment when the true aim is no longer to hit the goal but to maintain the very circular movement of repeatedly missing it.

NOTES

Published in *Lacanian Theory of Discourse: Subject, Structure, and Society*, ed. Mark Bracher, Marshall W. Alcorn, Jr., Ronald J. Corthell and Françoise Massardier-Kenney, New York, New York University Press, 1994, pp. 46–73 [eds].

1 Jacques Lacan, *Écrits: A Selection*, trans. Bruce Fink, New York, W. W. Norton, 2002, p. 136.

2 Immanuel Kant, *Religion within the Boundaries of Mere Reason and Other Writings*, trans. and ed. Allen Wood and George di Giovanni, Cambridge, Cambridge University Press, 1998, pp. 45–73 [eds].

3 Immanuel Kant, *Critique of Practical Reason*, trans. and ed. Mary Gregor, Cambridge, Cambridge University Press, 1997, p. 27 [eds].

4 In this sense, the femme fatale who, in the film noir universe, derails man's daily routine, is one of the personifications of Evil: the sexual relationship becomes impossible the moment woman is elevated to the dignity of the Thing.

5 G. W. F. Hegel, *Lectures on the Philosophy of Religion, Volume III: The Consummate Religion*, ed. P. C. Hodgson, trans. R. F. Brown, P. C. Hodgson, J. M. Stewart and H. S. Harris, Berkeley, University of California Press, 1985, p. 207 [eds].

6 We must be careful here to avoid the trap of retroactive projection: Milton's Satan in his *Paradise Lost* is not yet the Kantian radical Evil – it appeared as such only to the Romantic gaze of Shelley and Blake. When Satan says, 'Evil, be thou my Good', this is not yet radical Evil, but remains simply a case of wrongly putting some Evil in the place of Good. The logic of radical Evil consists rather in its exact opposite, that is, in saying 'Good, be thou my Evil' – in filling out the place of Evil, of the Thing, of the traumatic element that derails the closed circuit of organic life, by some (secondary) Good.

7 Lacan, *Écrits: A Selection*, p. 42.

8 Lacan often makes use of the same rhetorical inversion to delineate the relationship of the ego to its symptoms: it is not

sufficient to say that ego forms its symptoms in order to maintain its precarious balance with the forces of Id. Ego itself is, as to its essence, a symptom, a compromise-formation, a tool enabling the subject to regulate their desire. In other words, the subject desires by means of their ego-symptom.

9   Immanuel Kant, *Critique of the Power of Judgment*, ed. Paul Guyer, trans. Paul Guyer and Eric Matthews, Cambridge, Cambridge University Press, 2000, pp. 149–52 [eds].

10   Cited in Jacques Lacan, *The Seminar of Jacques Lacan III: The Psychoses, 1955–56*, ed. Jacques-Alain Miller, trans. Russell Grigg, New York, W. W. Norton, 1993, p. 265 [eds].

11   Lacan, *Écrits: A Selection*, p. 302 [eds].

12   Jacques Lacan, *The Seminar of Jacques Lacan II: The Ego in Freud's Theory and in the Technique of Psychoanalysis, 1954–55*, ed. Jacques-Alain Miller, trans. Sylvana Tomaselli, New York, W. W. Norton, 1988, p. 205 [eds].

13   Cf. Alain Abelhauser's analysis, 'D'un manque à saisir', in *Razpol* 3, 1987.

14   Michel Foucault, *The Will to Knowledge: The History of Sexuality, Volume I*, trans. Robert Hurley, Harmondsworth, Penguin, 1978 [eds].

15   One can imagine how the cinematic version of this scene would be able to rely on the contrapuntal use of sound: the camera would show the coach running along the empty streets, the fronts of old palaces and churches, whereas the soundtrack would be allowed to retain the absolute proximity to the Thing and to render the real of what goes on in the coach: the gasping and groaning that bear witness to the intensity of the sexual encounter.

16   Cf. Michel Foucault, *This Is Not a Pipe*, trans. James Harkness, Berkeley, University of California Press, 1973, pp. 13–15.

17   One encounters the same paradox in Robert Heinlein's science-fiction novel *The Unpleasant Profession of Jonathan Hoag*: upon opening a window, the reality previously seen through it dissolves and all we see is the dense, non-transparent slime of the Real; for a more detailed Lacanian reading of this scene, cf. Slavoj Žižek, *Looking Awry: An Introduction to Jacques Lacan through Popular Culture*, Cambridge MA, MIT Press, 1991, pp. 13–15.

18   In Marx brothers films, we encounter three variations on this paradox of identity, that is, of the uncanny relationship between existence and attribute. (1) Groucho Marx, upon being introduced to a stranger: 'Say, you remind me of Emmanuel Ravelli.' 'But I *am* Emmanuel Ravelli.' 'No wonder, then, that you look like him!' (2) Groucho, defending a client in court: 'This man looks like an idiot and acts as an idiot, yet all this should not deceive you – he *is* an idiot!' (3) Groucho, courting a lady: 'Everything on you reminds me of you, your nose, your eyes, your lips, your hands – everything except you!'

19   What we have in this scene, of course, is a kind of reflective redoubling of the external stimulus (sound, organic need, etc.), which triggers the activity of dreaming: one invents a dream integrating this element in order to prolong the sleep, yet the content encountered in the dream is so traumatic that, finally, one escapes into reality and awakens. The ringing of the phone while we are asleep is such a stimulus par excellence; its duration even after the source in reality ceased to emit it exemplifies what Lacan calls the insistence of the Real.

20   A similar shot is found in Fritz Lang's *Blue Gardenia*, when Anne Baxter peeps out of the crack of half-opened doors.

21   Jacques Lacan, *The Seminar of Jacques Lacan XI: The Four Fundamental Concepts of Psychoanalysis, 1964*, ed. Jacques-Alain Miller, trans. Alan Sheridan, New York, W. W. Norton, 1977, pp. 76–7 [eds].

22   Immanuel Kant, *Critique of Pure Reason*, trans. and ed. Paul Guyer and Allen W. Wood, Cambridge, Cambridge University Press, 1998, pp. 207–8 [eds].

23   *Ibid.*, pp. 360–1 [eds].

24   Karl Marx, *The Poverty of Philosophy*, New York, International Publishers, 1963, p. 105 [eds].

25   Jacques Lacan, *The Seminar of Jacques Lacan VII: The Ethics of Psychoanalysis, 1959–60*, ed. Jacques-Alain Miller, trans. Dennis Porter, London and New York, Routledge, 1992, pp. 270–83 [eds].

26   Richard Boothby, *Death and Desire: Psychoanalytic Theory in Lacan's Return to Freud*, New York and London, Routledge, 1991.

27   Ernest Newman, *Wagner Nights*, London, Bodley Head, 1988, p. 221.
28   Lacan, *Seminar XI*, pp. 197–8.
29   It is precisely this physical, tangible impact of 'lamella' that gets lost in *Aliens 2*, which is why this sequel is infinitely inferior to *Alien*.
30   Lacan, *Seminar XI*, p. 195.
31   The same defence against the drive is at work in the famous tracking shot from Hitchcock's *Young and Innocent*: the nervous blinking of the drummer is ultimately a defence-reaction to being seen, an attempt to avoid being seen, a resistance to being drawn into the picture. The paradox, of course, is that by his very defence-reaction he inadvertently draws attention to himself and thus exposes himself, divulges, that is, literally 'renders public by the beat of the drum', his guilt. He is unable to endure the other's (camera's) gaze.
32   We get a hint of this even in the first scene of the film where we see for a brief moment the last snapshot taken by Jefferies prior to his accident, depicting the cause of his broken leg. This shot is a true Hitchcockian counterpart to Holbein's *Ambassadors*: the oblique stain in its centre is a racing-car wheel flying toward the camera, captured the split second before Jefferies was hit by it. The moment rendered by this shot is the very moment when Jefferies lost his distance and was, so to speak, caught into his own picture; cf. Miran Božovič's article on *Rear Window*, 'The Man Behind His Own Retina', in *Everything You Always Wanted to Know about Lacan (But Were Afraid to Ask Hitchcock)*, ed. Slavoj Žižek, London and New York, Verso, 1992, pp. 161–77.
33   What we encounter here, again, is the condensation of field and counterfield within the same shot. Desire delineates the field of ordinary intersubjectivity in which we look at each other face to face, whereas we enter the register of drive when, together with our shadowy double, we find ourselves on the same side, both of us staring at the same third point. Where here is the 'making oneself seen' constitutive of the drive? One makes oneself seen precisely to this third point, to the gaze capable of embracing field in counterfield, that is, capable of perceiving in me also my shadowy double, what is in me more than myself, the *objet a*.
34   Lacan, *Seminar XI*, pp. 177–8 [eds].

8 Hegel, Lacan, Deleuze: Three Strange Bedfellows

1. THE PURE SURFACE OF THE SENSE EVENT

In his *The Logic of Sense*, Deleuze aims at displacing the opposition that defines the Platonic space, that of suprasensible Ideas and their sensible-material copies, into the opposition of substantial/opaque depth of the Body and the pure surface of the Sense-Event.[1] This surface depends on the emergence of language: it is the non-substantial void that separates Things from Words. As such, it has two faces: one face is turned towards Things, i.e., it is the pure, non-substantial surface of Becoming, of Events heterogeneous with regard to substantial Things to which these Events happen; the other face is turned towards Language, i.e., it is the pure flux of Sense in contrast to representational Signification, to the referring of a sign to bodily objects. Deleuze, of course, remains a materialist: the surface of Sense is an effect of the interplay of bodily causes – it is, however, a hetero-geneous effect, an effect of a radically different order than that of (corporeal) Being. We thus have, on the one hand, the generative bodily mixture of causes and effects and, on the other, the incorporeal surface of pure effects: events that are 'sterile', 'asexual', neither active nor passive.

This other, anti-Platonic, line emerged for the first time in Stoicism, with the Stoic perversion (rather than subversion) of Platonism through the theory of Sense *qua* incorporeal Event (our principal, although scarce, source is here Chrysippos' fragments on logic); it reappeared triumphantly in the 'anti-ontological' turn of philosophy at the turn of the century. The Deleuzian opposition of bodies and sense-effect thus opens up a new approach not only to Husserl's phenomen-ology but also to its less known double, Alexis Meinong's 'theory of objects' (*Gegenstandstheorie*). Both aim at *setting phenomena free from the constraints of substantial being*. Husserl's 'phenomenological reduction' brackets the substantial bodily depth – what remain are 'phenomena' *qua* the pure surface of Sense. Meinong's philosophy similarly deals with 'objects in general'. According to Meinong, an object is everything that is possible to conceive intellectually, irrespective of its existence or non-existence. Meinong thus admits not only Bertrand Russell's notorious 'present French king who is bald' but also objects like 'wooden iron' or 'round square'. Apropos of every object, Meinong distinguishes between its *Sosein* [being-thus] and its *Sein* [being]: a round square has its *Sosein*, since it is defined by the two properties of being round and square, yet it does not have *Sein*, since, due to its self-contradictory nature, such an object cannot exist. Meinong's name for such objects is 'homeless' objects: there is no place for them, neither in reality nor in the domain of the possible. More precisely, Meinong classifies objects into those that have being, that exist in reality; those that are formally possible (since they are not self-contradictory), although they do not exist in reality, like the 'golden mountain' – in this case, it is their non-being that exists; and, finally, 'homeless' objects that do not exist *tout court*. Meinong furthermore claims that every subject's attitude, and not only the assertoric attitude of knowledge, possesses its objective correlative. The correlative of representation is object [*Gegenstand*], the correlative of thought is 'objective' [*Objektiv*], the correlative of feeling, dignity, and the correlative of drive, desiderative. A new field of objects thus opens up that is not only 'wider' than reality but constitutes a separate level of its own: objects are determined only by their quality, *Sosein*, irrespective of their real existence or even of their mere possibility – in a sense, they 'take off' from reality.

Does not Wittgenstein's *Tractatus* also belong to the same 'Stoicist' line? In its very first proposition, Wittgenstein establishes a distinction between things [*Dinge*] and the world [*die Welt*] as the entirety of facts [*Tatsachen*], of everything that is a case [*der Fall*], that can occur: 'The world is the totality of facts, not of things [*Die Welt ist die Gesamtheit der Tatsachen, nicht der Dinge*].'[2] In his Introduction, which is usually reprinted with *Tractatus*, Bertrand Russell endeavours precisely to domesticate this 'homelessness' of the event by way of reinscribing the event back into the order of things.[3] The first association that this tension between presymbolic depth and the surface of events gives rise to in the domain of popular culture is, of course, the 'Alien' from the film of the same name. Our first response is to conceive of it as a creature of the chaotic depth of the maternal body, as the primordial Thing. However, the 'Alien's' incessant changing of its form, the utter 'plasticity' of its being, does it not point also in the very opposite direction: are we not dealing with a being whose entire consistency resides in the fantasmatic surface, with a series of pure events-effects devoid of any substantial support?

Perhaps this difference of the two levels also offers the key to Mozart's *Così fan tutte*. One of the commonplaces about this opera is that it constantly subverts the line that separates sincere from feigned emotions: not only is pathetic heroism (that of Fiordiligi who wants to rejoin her fiancé at the battlefield, for example) again and again denounced as empty posture, the subversion goes also in the opposite direction – the philosopher Alfonso, this supreme cynic, from time to time becomes the dupe of his own manipulation and is carried away by his feigned emotions which unexpectedly prove sincere (in the trio 'Soave sia il vento', for example). This pseudo-dialectics of sincere and feigned emotions, although not entirely out of place, nonetheless fails to take into account the gap that separates the bodily machine from the surface of its effects-events. The point of view of the philosopher Alfonso is that of mechanical materialism: the human is a machine, a puppet; their emotions – love, in this case – do not express some spontaneous authentic freedom but can be brought about automatically, by way of submitting them to proper causes. Mozart's answer to this cynicism of the philosopher is the autonomy of the 'effect' *qua* pure event: emotions are effects of the bodily machine, but they are also effects in the sense of an effect-of-emotion (as when we speak about an 'effect-of-beauty'), and this surface of the effect *qua* event possesses its own authenticity and autonomy. Or, to put it in contemporary terms: even if biochemistry succeeds in isolating the hormones that regulate the rise, the intensity and the duration of sexual love, the actual experience of love *qua* event will maintain its autonomy, its radical heterogeneity with regard to its bodily cause.

This opposition of bodily machine and surface event is personified in the couple of Alfonso and Despina. Alfonso is a mechanicist-materialist cynic who believes only in the bodily machine, while Despina stands for love *qua* pure surface-event. The lesson of the philosopher Alfonso is – as usual – 'Renounce your desire, acknowledge its vanity!' If it were possible, by way of a carefully conducted experiment, to induce the two sisters to forget their fiancés and to fall in love anew with unequalled passion in the span of a single day, then it is useless to ask which love is true and which is false – one love equals the other, all of them result from the bodily mechanism to which man is enslaved. Despina, on the contrary, maintains that in spite of all this it is still worthy to remain faithful to one's desire – hers is the ethics displayed by Sam Spade who, in a well-known passage from Hammett's *Maltese Falcon*, reports how he was hired to find a man who had suddenly left his settled job and family and vanished. Spade is unable to track him down, but a few years later he stumbles into him in a bar in another city where the man lives under an assumed name and leads a life remarkably similar to the one from which he had fled. The man is nonetheless convinced that the change was not in vain ... One of the key arias of the entire opera, Despina's 'Una donna a quindici anni' from the beginning of Act II – if one pays proper attention to it, as was done by Peter Sellars in his deservedly famous staging – attests to an unexpected ambiguity of Despina's character: what lurks beneath the mask of a jovial intriguer is the melancholic ethic of persisting in one's desire notwithstanding its fragility and fickleness.

2. DELEUZE'S MATERIALISM

Perhaps the most acute experience of the gap that separates the surface from the bodily depth concerns our relationship to our partner's naked body: we can take this body as a pure object of knowledge (and concentrate on flesh, bones and glands beneath the skin), as an object of disinterested aesthetic pleasure, as an object of sexual desire ... To put it in a somewhat simplified way, the 'wager' of phenomenology is that each of these attitudes and/or its objective correlative possesses an autonomy of its own: it is not possible to 'translate' our experience of the partner's body as the object of sexual desire into the terms of a biochemical process. The surface, of course, is an effect of bodily causes – but an effect that is irreducible to its cause since it belongs to a radically heterogeneous order. The fundamental problem of Deleuze in *The Logic of Sense*, but also of Lacan, is how we are to conceive theoretically the passage from bodily depth to the surface event, the rupture that had to occur at the level of bodily depth if the effect-of-sense is to emerge. In short: *how are we to articulate the 'materialist' genesis of Sense*? 'Idealism' denies that the sense-effect is an effect of bodily depth, it fetishizes the sense-effect into a self-generated entity; the price it pays for this denial is the *substantialization* of the sense-effect: idealism covertly qualifies the sense-effect as a new Body (the immaterial body of Platonic Forms, for example). Paradoxical as it may sound, Deleuze's thesis is that only materialism can think the effect of Sense, sense *qua* event, in its specific autonomy, without a substantialist reduction.

The universe of Sense *qua* 'autonomous' forms a vicious circle: we are always-already part of it, since the moment we assume towards it the attitude of external distance and turn our gaze from the effect to its cause, we lose the effect. The fundamental problem of materialism is therefore: how does this circle of Sense, which allows of no externality, emerge? How can the immixture of bodies give rise to 'neutral' thought, i.e., to the symbolic field that is 'free' in the precise sense of not being bound by the economy of bodily drives, of not functioning as a prolongation of the drive's striving for satisfaction? The Freudian hypothesis is: through the inherent impasse of sexuality. It is not possible to derive the emergence of 'disinterested' thought from other bodily drives (hunger, self-preservation . . .) – why not? Sexuality is the only drive that is in itself hindered, perverted: simultaneously insufficient and excessive, with the excess as the form of appearance of the lack. On the one hand, sexuality is characterized by the universal capacity to provide the metaphorical *meaning* or innuendo of any activity or object – any element, including the most abstract reflection, can be experienced as 'alluding to *that*' (suffice it to recall the proverbial example of the adolescent who, in order to forget his sexual obsessions, takes refuge in pure mathematics and physics – whatever he does here again reminds him of 'that': how much volume is needed to fill out an empty cylinder? how much energy is discharged when two bodies collide? . . .). This universal surplus – this capacity of sexuality to overflow the entire field of human experience so that everything, from eating to excretion, from beating up our fellow-man (or getting beaten up by him) to the exercise of power, can acquire a sexual connotation – is not the sign of its preponderance. It is rather the sign of a certain structural faultiness: sexuality strives outwards and overflows the adjoining domains precisely because it cannot find satisfaction in itself, because it never attains its goal. How, precisely, does an activity that is in itself definitely asexual acquire sexual connotation? It is 'sexualized' when it fails to achieve its asexual goal and gets caught in the vicious circle of futile repetition. We enter sexuality when a gesture that 'officially' serves some instrumental goal becomes an end-in-itself, when we start to enjoy the very 'dysfunctional' repetition of this gesture and thereby suspend its purposefulness.

Sexuality can function as a co-sense that supplements the 'desexualized' neutral-literal meaning precisely insofar as this neutral meaning *is already here*. As Deleuze demonstrates, perversion enters the stage as an inherent reversal of this 'normal' relationship between the asexual literal sense and the sexual co-sense: in perversion, sexuality is made into a direct object of our speech, but the price we pay for it is the desexualization of our attitude towards sexuality: sexuality becomes one desexualized object among others. The exemplary case of such an attitude is the 'scientific' disinterested approach to sexuality or the Sadeian approach that treats sexuality as the object of an instrumental activity. Suffice it to recall the role of Jennifer Jason Leigh in Altman's *Short Cuts*: a housewife who earns supplementary money by paid phone-sex, entertaining customers with pep talk. So well accustomed to her job, she improvizes, receiver tucked into her shoulder, how she is all wet between her thighs, etc., all the while changing her baby or preparing lunch. She maintains a wholly external, instrumental attitude towards her caller's sexual fantasies, they simply do not concern her.[4] What Lacan aims at with the notion of 'symbolic castration' is precisely this *vel*, this choice: *either* we accept the desexualization of the literal sense that entails the displacement of sexuality to a 'co-sense', to the supplementary dimension of sexual connotation-innuendo; *or* we approach sexuality 'directly', we make sexuality the subject of literal speech, which we pay for with the 'desexualization' of our subjective attitude to it. What we lose in every case is a direct approach, a literal talk about sexuality that would remain 'sexualized'.

In this precise sense, phallus is the signifier of castration: far from acting as the potent organ-symbol of sexuality *qua* universal creative power, it is the *signifier and/or organ of the very desexualization*, of the 'impossible' passage of 'body' into symbolic 'thought', the signifier that sustains the neutral surface of 'asexual' sense. Deleuze conceptualizes this passage as the inversion of the 'phallus of coordination' into the 'phallus of castration': 'phallus of coordination' is an imago, a figure the subject refers to in order to coordinate the dispersed erogeneous zones into the totality of a unified body, whereas 'phallus of castration' is a signifier. Those who conceive of the phallic signifier after the model of the mirror stage, as a privileged image or bodily part that provides the central point of reference enabling the subject to totalize the dispersed multitude of erogeneous zones into a unique, hierarchically ordered totality, remain at the level of the 'phallus of coordination' and reproach Lacan with what is actually his fundamental insight: this coordination through the central phallic image necessarily fails. The outcome of this failure, however, is not a return to the uncoordinated plurality of erogeneous zones, but precisely 'symbolic castration': sexuality retains its universal dimension and continues to function as the (potential) connotation of every act, object, etc., only if it 'sacrifices' literal meaning, i.e., only if literal meaning is 'desexualized' – the step from the 'phallus of coordination' to the 'phallus of castration' is the step from the impossible-failed total sexualization, from the state in which 'everything has sexual meaning', to the state in which this sexual meaning becomes secondary, changes into the 'universal innuendo', into the co-sense that potentially supplements every literal, neutral-asexual sense.[5]

How, then, do we pass from the state in which 'the meaning of everything is sexual', in which sexuality functions as the universal *signified*, to the surface of the neutral-desexualized literal sense? The desexualization of the *signified* occurs when the very element that (failed to) coordinate(d) the universal sexual meaning (i.e., phallus) is reduced to a *signifier*. Phallus is the 'organ of desexualization' precisely in its capacity of a signifier without signified: it is the operator of the evacuation of sexual meaning, i.e., of the reduction of sexuality *qua* signified content to an empty signifier. In short, phallus designates the following paradox: sexuality can universalize itself only by way of desexualization, only by undergoing a kind of transubstantiation and changing into a supplement-connotation of the neutral, asexual literal sense.

3. THE PROBLEMS OF 'REAL GENESIS'

The difference between Lacan and someone who, like Habermas, accepts the universal medium of intersubjective communication as the ultimate horizon of subjectivity is therefore not where it is usually sought: it does not reside in the fact that Lacan, in a postmodern fashion, emphasizes the remainder of some particularity that forever prevents our full access to universality and condemns us to the multiple texture of particular language-games. Lacan's basic reproach to someone like Habermas is, on the contrary, that he fails to acknowledge and to thematize *the price the subject has to pay for his access to universality*, to the 'neutral' medium of language: this price, of course, is none other than the traumatism of 'castration', the sacrifice of the object that 'is' the subject, the passage from S (the full 'pathological' subject) to $ (the 'barred' subject). Herein resides also the difference between Heidegger and Gadamer: Gadamer remains an 'idealist' insofar as for him the horizon of language is 'always-already here', whereas Heidegger's problematic of the difference [*Unter-Schied*] as pain [*Schmerz*] that inheres in the very essence of our dwelling in language, 'obscurantist' as it may sound, points towards the materialist problematic of the traumatic cut, 'castration', that marks our entry into language.

The first to formulate this materialist problematic of 'real genesis' as the obverse of the transcendental genesis was Schelling: in his *Die Weltalter* fragments from 1811 to 1815, he deploys the programme of deriving the emergence of the Word, *logos*, out of the abyss of the 'real in God', of the vortex of drives [*Triebe*] that is God prior to the creation of the world. Schelling distinguishes between God's existence and the obscure, impenetrable Ground of Existence, the horrendous presymbolic Thing as 'that in God which is not yet God'. This Ground consists of the antagonistic tension between 'contraction' [*Zusammenziehung, contractio*] – withdrawal-into-self, egotistic rage, all-destructive madness – and 'extension' – God's giving away, pouring out, of his Love. (How can we not recognize in this antagonism Freud's duality of the ego-drives and the love-drives that precedes his duality of libido and death-drive?) This unbearable antagonism is timelessly past – a past that was never 'present', since the present already implies *logos*, the clearing of the spoken Word that transposes the antagonistic pulsation of the drives into symbolic difference.

God is thus first the abyss of 'absolute indifference', the volition that does not want anything, the reign of peace and beatitude: in Lacanian terms, pure feminine *jouissance*, the pure expansion into the void that lacks any consistency, the 'giving away' held together by nothing. God's 'pre-history' proper begins with an act of primordial contraction by means of which God procures himself a firm Ground, constitutes himself as One, a subject, a positive entity. Upon 'contracting' being as an illness, God gets caught in the mad, 'psychotic' alternation of contraction and expansion. He then creates the world, speaks out the Word, gives birth to the Son, in order to escape this madness. Prior to the emergence of the Word, God is a 'manic depressive', and this provides the most perspicuous answer to the enigma of why God created the universe – as a kind of creative therapy that allowed him to pull himself out of madness . . .[6] The late Schelling of the 'philosophy of revelation' recoiled from this previous radicality of his by conceding that God possesses in advance his existence: contraction now no longer concerns God himself, it designates solely the act by means of which God creates the matter that is later formed into the universe of creatures. This way, God himself is no longer involved in the process of 'genesis'. Genesis concerns only creation, whereas God supervises the historical process from a safe place outside history and guarantees its happy outcome. In this withdrawal, in this shift from *Die Weltalter* to the 'philosophy of revelation', the problematic of *Die Weltalter* is translated into traditional Aristotelian ontological terms: the opposition of Existence and its Ground now becomes the opposition of Essence and Existence, i.e., *logos* is conceived as the divine Essence that needs a positive Existence in order to achieve its effectuation, etc.[7]

Therein resides the materialist 'wager' of Deleuze and Lacan: the 'desexualization', the miracle of the advent of the neutral-desexualized surface of Sense-Event, does not rely on the intervention of some transcendent, extra-bodily force, it can be derived from the inherent impasse of the sexualized body itself. Phallus *qua* signifier of 'castration' mediates the emergence of the pure surface of Sense-Event; as such, it is the 'transcendental signifier' – nonsense within the field of sense, that distributes and regulates the series of Sense. Its 'transcendental' status means that there is nothing 'substantial' about it: phallus is the semblance *par excellence*. What the phallus 'causes' is the gap that separates the surface-event from bodily density: it is the 'pseudo-cause' that sustains the autonomy of the field of Sense with regard to its true, effective, bodily cause. One should recall here Adorno's observation on how the notion of transcendental constitution results from a kind of perspectival inversion: what the subject (mis)perceives as their constitutive power is actually their impotence, their incapacity to reach beyond the imposed limitations of their horizon – the transcendental constitutive power is a pseudo-power that is the obverse of the subject's blindness as to true bodily causes. Phallus *qua* cause is the pure semblance of a cause.[8]

There is no structure without the 'phallic' moment as the crossing-point of the two series (of signifier and signified), as the point of the short-circuit at which – as Lacan puts it in a very precise way – 'the signifier falls into the signified'. The point of nonsense within the field of Sense is the point at which the signifier's cause is inscribed into the field of Sense. Without this short-circuit, the signifier's structure would act as an external bodily cause and would be unable to produce the effect of Sense. On that account, the two series (of the signifier and the signified) always contain a paradoxical entity that is 'doubly inscribed', i.e., that is simultaneously surplus and lack – surplus of the signifier over the signified (the empty signifier without a signified) *and* the lack of the signified (the point of nonsense within the field of Sense). That is to say, as soon as the symbolic order emerges, we are dealing with the minimal difference between a structural place and the element that occupies, fills out, this place: an element is always logically preceded by the place in the structure it fills out. The two series can therefore also be described as the 'empty' formal structure (signifier) and the series of elements filling out the empty places in the structure (signified). From this perspective, the paradox consists in the fact that the two series never overlap: we always encounter an entity that is simultaneously – with regard to the structure – an *empty, unoccupied place*, and – with regard to the elements – a rapidly moving, elusive object, an *occupant without a place*.[9] We have thereby produced Lacan's formula of fantasy $\$ \diamond a$, since the matheme for the subject is $\$$, an empty place in the structure, an elided signifier, while *objet a* is by definition an excessive object, an object that lacks its place in the structure. Consequently, the point is not that there is simply the surplus of an element over the places available in the structure or the surplus of a place that has no element to fill it out: an empty place in the structure would still sustain the fantasy of an element that will emerge and fill out this place; an excessive element lacking its place would still sustain the fantasy of a yet unknown place waiting for it. The point is rather that the empty place in the structure is strictly correlative to the errant element lacking its place: they are not two different entities but the front and the obverse of one and the same entity, i.e., one and the same entity inscribed into the two surfaces of a Möbius strip. In short, the subject *qua* $\$$ doesn't belong to the depth: it emerges from a topological twist of the surface itself.

There is, however, a problem with Deleuze as he does not distinguish bodily depth from the symbolic pseudo-depth. That is to say, there are two depths: the opaque impenetrability of the body and the pseudo-depth generated by the 'ply' of the symbolic order itself (the abyss of the 'soul', what one experiences when one looks into another person's eyes ...). The subject is such a pseudo-depth that results from the ply of the surface. Let us recall the very last shot of Ivory's *Remains of the Day*: the slow fade-out of the window of Lord Darlington's castle, passing into the helicopter shot of the entire castle moving away. This fade-out lasts a little bit too long, so that, for a brief moment, the spectator cannot avoid the impression that a third reality emerged, over and above the common reality of the window and the castle: it is as if, instead of the window being simply a small part of the castle, the castle itself in its entirety is reduced to a reflection in the window glass, to a fragile entity that is a pure semblant, neither a being nor a non-being. The subject is such a paradoxical entity that emerges when the Whole itself (the entire castle) appears comprised in its own part (a window).

Deleuze is obliged to ignore this symbolic pseudo-depth: there is no place for it in his dichotomy of body and Sense. What opens up here, of course, is the possibility of a Lacanian critique of Deleuze: is the signifier *qua* differential structure not an entity that, precisely, belongs neither to the bodily depth nor to the surface of the Sense-Event? Concretely, with regard to Mozart's *Così fan tutte*: the 'machine', the automatism on which the philosopher Alfonso relies, is it not the *symbolic* machine, the 'automatism' of the symbolic 'custom', this big motif of Pascal's *Pensées*? Deleuze distinguishes between bodily causality 'proper' and the paradoxical 'phallic' moment, the crossroad of the series of the signifier and the series of the signified, the nonsense *qua* pseudo-cause, i.e., the decentred cause of sense inherent to the surface flux of sense itself. What he fails to take into account here is the radically heterogeneous nature of the series of the signifier with regard to the series of the signified, of the synchrony of a differential structure with regard to the diachrony of the flux of the Sense-Event. What, perhaps, becomes visible here is the limitation of Deleuze who, in the end, remains a *phenomenologist* – it was this limitation that ultimately brought about his theoretical 'regression' into the 'anti-Oedipus', the rebellion against the Symbolic. In this precise sense, one could say that the Stoics, Husserl, etc., are psychotics rather than perverts: it is the psychotic foreclusion of the proper symbolic level that gives rise to the paradoxical short-circuits between sense and reality (the Stoic logic that suggests that 'when you say "carriage", a carriage runs through your mouth', etc.).[10]

4. THE ENIGMA OF 'MECHANICAL MEMORY'

It is this limitation of Deleuze that, perhaps, accounts for his fanatical anti-Hegelianism. Against Deleuze, it is possible to prove that Hegel himself was, at a crucial turning point of his system, 'Deleuzian'. What we have in mind here is the sudden and unexpected appearance of the

so-called 'Mechanical Memory' *after* the fully accomplished 'sublation' of the language-sign in its spiritual content (in the paragraphs on
language in Hegel's *Encyclopedia*).[11]

Hegel develops his theory of language in 'Representation', Section 2
of 'Psychology', which delineates the contours of the transition from
'Intuition' to 'Thinking', that is to say: the process of the subject's
gradual deliverance from externally found and imposed content, as
provided by senses, through its internalization and universalization.
As usual with Hegel, the process occurs in three moments. First, in
'Recollection', an intuition is torn out of the external causal spatio-
temporal context and brought within the subject's own inner space
and time; this way, it is at his disposal as a contingent element that can
be at any time freely recalled. Once an intuition is transposed within
Intelligence, it comes under its power. The Intelligence may do with it
as it pleases: it can decompose an intuition into its ingredients and then
recombine them in a different, 'unnatural' Whole or it can compare it
with other intuitions and set out common markers. All this is the work
of 'Imagination' that gradually leads to the Symbol. First, a particular
image stands for some more complex network of representations or for
some universal feature (the image of a beard, for example, can recall to
one's mind virile masculinity, authority, etc.). This universal feature,
however, is still tainted with the particular sensible image that stands
for it – we reach the true universality only when every resemblance
between the universal feature and the image that represents it is
abolished. This way, we arrive at the *Word*: at an external, arbitrary
sign whose link with its meaning is wholly arbitrary. It is only this
abasement of sign to a pure indifferent externality that enables
meaning to free itself of sensible intuition and thus to purify itself into
true universality. This way, the sign (word) is posited in its truth: as the
pure movement of self-sublation, as an entity that attains its truth by
obliterating itself in front of its meaning.

'Verbal Memory' then internalizes and universalizes the very
external sign that signifies a universal feature. The result at which we
thus arrive is a 'representational language' composed of signs which are
the unity of two ingredients. On the one hand, the universalized name,
mental sound, a type recognized as the same in different utterances; on
the other hand, its meaning, some universal representation. Names in

'representational language' possess a fixed universal content determined not by their relationship to other names but by their relationship
to represented reality. What we are dealing with here is the standard
notion of language as a collection of signs with a fixed universal
meaning that mirrors reality, the notion that involves the triad of sign
itself *qua* body, signified content in the subject's mind and reality
that signs refer to. A simple pre-theoretical sensitivity tells us that
something is missing here: that this is not yet a true, living language.
What is missing is twofold, chiefly: on the one hand, the syntactic and
semantic relations between signs themselves, i.e., the *self-referential
circularity* on account of which one can always say that the meaning of
a word is a series of other words (when asked 'What is a camel?', one
usually answers with a series of words: 'a four-footed mammal resemb-
ling a horse, yet with a high hump on the back', etc.); on the other
hand, the *relationship to the speaking subject*. It is not clear how
the speaker himself is inscribed in 'representational language' as
the mirroring of the three levels of signs, mental ideas and reality.
In Hegelese, the fatal weakness of representational language resides
in its very representational character, in the fact that it remains
stuck at the level of *Vorstellung*, of the external, finite representation that refers to some transcendent, external content. To put it in
contemporary terms: representational language is the self-effacing
medium of representing-transmitting some universal notional Content
that remains external to this medium: the medium itself functions as an
indifferent means of transmitting an independent content. What is
missing here is a word that would not merely represent its external
content but would also constitute it, bring it forth, a word through
which this signified content would become what it is – in short,
a 'performative'.

From here, then, how do we arrive at a speech that acts as the
adequate medium of infinite thought? At this point we come across a
surprise that causes much embarrassment to the interpreters of Hegel.
Between the 'Verbal Memory' that warrants the concrete unity of
meaning and expression and the 'Thought' proper, Hegel somewhat
mysteriously interposes 'Mechanical Memory', a recitation by heart of
the series of words in which one attaches no meaning to one's words,
in short, an 'abandoning of the spirit' (*Geistesverlassen*) as the very

transition to the activity of thinking. After exposing how the sign remains within the confines of representation, i.e., of the external synthesis of meaning and expression, Hegel does not dismantle the 'false' unity of sign by casting off its external side – expression as the external medium of the designated content. On the contrary, he discards, sacrifices, the inner content itself. The outcome of such a radical reduction is that, within the space of language, we 'regress' to the level of Being, the poorest category. Hegel refers to the Intelligence in Mechanical Memory as '*being*, the universal space of names as such, i.e., of meaningless words',[12] that in a way disappear even before they fully arise, of 'utterance' as 'fleeting, vanishing, completely *ideal* realization which proceeds in an unresisting element'.[13] What we have here are no longer representational words as universal types of the fixed connection of an expression with its meaning (the word 'horse' always means ...) but *a pure becoming*, a flux of senseless individuality of utterances – the only thing that unites them is the 'empty connective band' of Intelligence itself. At this level, the meaning of a name can only reside in the fact that it follows on and/or triggers other such names. *It is only here that the true, concrete negativity of the linguistic sign emerges.* For this negativity to emerge, it is not sufficient for the word to be reduced to the pure flux of self-obliteration: its Beyond itself, meaning, has to be 'flattened', it has to lose all its positive content, so that the only thing that remains is the empty negativity that 'is' the subject. The Christological connotation of this sacrificing of the representational-objective meaning is unmistakable: the reduction of the word to the pure flux of becoming is not the word's self-obliteration in front of its Meaning but the death of this Meaning itself, the same as with Christ whose death on the Cross is not the passing of God's terrestrial representative but the death of the God of Beyond himself. Therein resides Hegel's properly dialectical insight: the stumbling block to the true-infinite activity of Thought in the representational name is not its external appearance but the very fixed universality of its inner meaning.

The voidance that occurs here is double. First, the entire objective-representational content is evacuated, so that the only thing that remains is the void of Intelligence (subject) itself – in Lacanese, from sign that represents something (a positive content) for someone, we

pass to signifier that represents the subject itself for other signifiers. However, with the same gesture, the subject (S) itself ceases to be
the fullness of the experienced inner content, of meaning, and is
'barred', hollowed out, reduced to $\math$ – or, as Hegel puts it, the job
of Mechanical Memory is 'to level the ground of the inner life to
pure being or to pure space ... with no antithesis to a subjective
inwardness'.[14] It is only this 'levelling', this reduction to Being, to the
new immediacy of the word, that opens up the performative dimension – why? Let us approach this crucial point via a passage from
Jenaer Realphilosophie in which Hegel describes how 'to the question
"What is this?" we usually answer, "It is a lion, donkey", etc. It is –
that means that it is not a yellow thing that has feet, etc., something
independent on its own, but a name, a tone of my voice – something completely different from what it is in the intuition. And that is
(its) true Being.'[15]

Hegel draws our attention to the paradox of naming, so obvious
that it is generally passed over in silence: when I say 'This is an
elephant', what I literally, at the most elementary, immediate level,
claim is that this gigantic creature with a trunk, etc., really is a sound
in my mouth, the eight letters I have just pronounced. In his *Seminar I*
on Freud's technical writings, Lacan plays on the same paradox:
once the word 'elephant' is pronounced, the elephant is here in all
its massive presence – although it is nowhere to be seen in reality, its
notion is rendered present.[16] We encounter here the unexpected Stoic
aspect of Hegel (and Lacan). What Hegel has in mind, however,
is something else: the simple, apparently symmetrical inversion of
'elephant is ... (a four-footed mammal with a trunk)' into 'this is an
elephant' involves the reversal of a representational constative into a
performative. That is to say, when I say 'elephant is ... (a four-footed
mammal with a trunk)', I treat 'elephant' as a representational name
and point out the external content it designates. However, when I say
'this is an elephant', I thereby confer upon an object its symbolic
identity; I add to the bundle of real properties a symbolic unifying
feature that changes this bundle into One, a self-identical object. The
paradox of symbolization resides in the fact that the object is
constituted as One through a feature that is radically external to the

object itself, to its reality; through a name that bears no resemblance to the object. The object becomes One through the appendage of some completely null, self-obliterating Being, *le peu de réalité* of a couple of sounds – a fly that makes up the elephant, as with the Monarch, this imbecilic contingent body of an individual that not merely 'represents' the State *qua* rational totality but constitutes it, renders it effective. This performative dimension, by means of which the signifier is inscribed into the signified content itself as its constituent (or, as Lacan puts it, by means of which the signifier 'falls into the signified'), is what is lacking in the representational name.

5. HEGEL'S LOGIC OF THE SIGNIFIER

From what we have just said, it is not difficult to ascertain how the Hegelian duality of 'representational names' and 'names as such' that emerge in Mechanical Memory perfectly corresponds to the Lacanian opposition of sign and signifier. The sign is defined by a fixed relationship of the signifier to the signified represented by the signifier – its *signification*. Whereas the signifier, through its incessant sliding, referring to the other signifiers in the chain, brings forth the effect-of-sense. The sign is a body related to other bodies, the signifier is a pure flux, 'event'. The sign refers to the substantial fullness of things, the signifier refers to the subject *qua* the void of negativity that mediates the self-relating of the signifying chain ('a signifier represents the subject for other signifiers'). Although a stronger contrast seems unthinkable than that of Hegel as a Deleuzian, we do encounter in Hegel's 'Mechanical Memory' the notion of Sense *qua* pure Event later articulated by Deleuze in *Logic of Sense*. The proof that Hegel's dialectic truly is the logic of the signifier *avant la lettre* is provided by John McCumber who, in his *The Company of Words*,[17] proposes a provocative and perspicuous reading of the Hegelian dialectical process as a self-relating operation with symbolic 'markers' (Hegel's German term is *Merkmal*; its French equivalent would be *le trait signifiant*, the signifying feature). We arrive at the starting point of the process, the 'thesis', through the operation of 'immediation-abbreviation': a series of markers, $M_1 \ldots M_J$, is abbreviated in the marker M_K whose content (i.e., what this marker designates) is this very series:

$$(M_1 \ldots M_J) - M_K \tag{1}$$

What then follows is the inverse operation of 'explication' in which the series $M_1 \ldots M_J$ explicates the M_K:

$$M_K - (M_1 \ldots M_J) \tag{2}$$

What occurs now is yet another reversal – and the crucial point not to be missed here is that this additional reversal does not bring us back to our starting point, to (1) (or, in Hegelese, that 'negation of negation' does not entail a return to the initial position):

$$(M_1 \ldots M_J)/M_K \tag{3}$$

In order to indicate this shift from (1), McCumber uses a different symbol, / instead of –; he determines / as the 'synthesis' in which explication and abbreviation occur simultaneously. What can this mean? In (3), the marker M_K is *stricto sensu* 'reflective': it no longer stands for immediation that is abstractly opposed to explication, since *it explicates the very series that explicated M_K itself in* (2). In order to explain this 'reflection', let us resort to the logic of anti-Semitism. First, the series of markers that designate real properties are abbreviated-immediated in the marker 'Jew':

$$\text{(avaricious, profiteering, plotting, dirty \ldots) – Jew} \tag{1}$$

We then reverse the order and 'explicate' the marker 'Jew' with the series (avaricious, profiteering, plotting, dirty ...), i.e., this series now provides the answer to the question 'What does "Jew" mean?':

$$\text{Jew – (avaricious, profiteering, plotting, dirty \ldots)} \tag{2}$$

Finally, we reverse the order again and posit 'Jew' as the reflective abbreviation of the series:

$$\text{(avaricious, profiteering, plotting, dirty \ldots)/Jew} \tag{3}$$

In what, precisely, resides the difference between (1) and (3)? In (3), 'Jew' *explicates the very preceding series it immediates/abbreviates*:

in it, abbreviation and explication dialectically coincide. That is to say, within the discursive space of anti-Semitism, a collection of individuals not only pass for Jews because they display the series of properties (avaricious, profiteering, plotting, dirty ...), *they have this series of properties BECAUSE THEY ARE JEWS*. This becomes clear if we translate abbreviation in (1) as

$$(\text{profiteering, plotting, } \dots) \textit{ is called } \text{Jewish} \tag{1}$$

and explication in (2) as

$$\text{X is Jew } \textit{because he is } (\text{profiteering, plotting} \dots) \tag{2}$$

In this perspective, the uniqueness of (3) is that it returns to (1) *while maintaining the copulative of (2)*:

$$\text{X is (profiteering, plotting } \dots) \textit{ because he is } \text{Jewish} \tag{3}$$

In short, 'Jew' designates here the hidden ground of the phenomenal series of actual properties (avaricious, profiteering, plotting, dirty ...). What thus occurs is a kind of 'transubstantiation': 'Jew' starts to function as the marker of the hidden ground, the mysterious *je ne sais quoi*, that accounts for the 'Jewishness' of the Jews. (The *cognoscenti* of Marx, of course, will immediately realize how these inversions are homologous to the development of the form of commodity in *Capital*:[18] the simple inversion of the 'developed' form into the form of 'general equivalent' brings forth a new entity, the general equivalent itself as the exception constitutive of the totality.)

Our ultimate point is therefore a rather technical one: McCumber's formulas gain considerably as to their clarity and power of insight if we replace the series of markers $M_1 \dots M_J$, with Lacan's matheme S_2, the signifier of the chain of knowledge, and M_K, the abbreviation of the series $M_1 \dots M_J$, with S_1, the Master-Signifier. Let us elucidate this point *via* an example that is structurally homologous to that of anti-Semitism, the anti-Socialist cynical witticism from Poland: 'True, we don't have enough food, electricity, flats, books, freedom, but what does it matter in the end, since we do have Socialism!' The underlying Hegelian logic is here the following: first, socialism is posited as the simple abbreviation of a series of markers that designate effective qualities ('When we have enough food, electricity, flats, books, freedom we are in socialism'); one then inverts the relationship and refers to this series of markers in order to 'explicate' socialism ('socialism means enough food, electricity, flats, books, freedom . . .'); however, when we perform another inversion, we are not thrown back to our starting point, since 'socialism' now changes into 'Socialism', the Master-Signifier, i.e., no longer a simple abbreviation that designates a series of markers but the name of the hidden ground of this series of markers that act as so many expressions-effects of this ground. And, since 'Socialism' is now the Cause expressed in the series of phenomenal markers, one can ultimately say 'What does it matter if all these markers disappear – they are not what our struggle is really about! The main thing is that we still have Socialism!'

To summarize: in (1), the marker of abbreviation-immediation is a simple *sign*, an external designation of the given series, whereas in (3), this marker is a *signifier* that performatively establishes the series in its totality. In (1), we are victims of the illusion that the complete series is an In-itself that persists independently of its sign, whereas in (3) it becomes clear that the series is only completed, constituted, through the reflective marker that supplements it, i.e., in (3) the sign is *comprised within the 'thing itself' as its inherent constituent*, the distance that keeps apart the sign and the designated content disappears.

NOTES

Published in *From Phenomenology to Thought, Errancy and Desire: Essays in Honor of William J. Richardson, SJ*, ed. Babette E. Babich, Dordrecht, Kluwer Academic Publishers, 1995, pp. 483–99 [eds].

1   See Gilles Deleuze, *The Logic of Sense*, trans. Mark Lester, ed. Constantin V. Boundas, New York, Columbia University Press, 1990.

2   Ludwig Wittgenstein, *Tractatus Logico-Philosophicus*, London, Kegan Paul, 1922, p. 31 [eds].

3   Bertrand Russell, 'Introduction', Wittgenstein, *Tractatus*, pp. 7–23 [eds].

4   What opens up here is the possibility of 'secondary perverse resexualization' (Deleuze). At a meta-level, such an instrumental, non-sexualized relationship to sexuality can 'turn us on'. Thus

one of the ways to enliven our sexual practice is to feign that we are dealing with an ordinary instrumental activity: with our partner, we approach the sexual act as a difficult technical task, we discuss every step in detail and establish the exact plan of how we shall proceed ...

5   In order to exemplify this logic of sexual connotation, let us take the signifier 'commerce' whose predominant meaning is 'trade, merchandising', yet which is also an (archaic) term for sexual act. The term is 'sexualized' when the two levels of its meaning intermingle. Let us say that 'commerce' evokes in our mind the figure of an elderly merchant who delivers tedious lessons on how we are to conduct commerce, on how we must be careful in our dealings, mind the profit, not take excessive risks, etc.; or, let us suppose that the merchant actually talks about *sexual* commerce – all of a sudden, the entire affair acquires an obscene superego dimension, the poor merchant changes into a dirty old man who gives cyphered advice on sexual enjoyment, accompanied with obscene smiles ...

6   For an unsurpassed presentation of this problematic, see Jean-François Marquet, *Liberté et existence: Étude sur la formation de la philosophie de Schelling*, Paris, Édition Gallimard, 1973.

7   This withdrawal also implies a radical change in the political attitude: in the *Die Weltalter* fragments, the State is denounced as Evil incarnate, as the tyranny of the external machine of Power over individuals (as such, it has to be abolished), whereas the late Schelling conceives of the State as the embodiment of human Sin – precisely insofar as we never fully recognize ourselves in it, i.e., insofar as the State remains an external, alienated force that crushes individuals, it is a divine punishment for human conceit, a reminder of our sinful origins (as such, it has to be obeyed unconditionally). See Jürgen Habermas, 'Dialektischer Idealismus im Ubergang zum Materialismus – Geschichtsphilosophische Folgerungen aus Schellings Idee einer Kontraktion Gottes', in *Theorie und Praxis*, Frankfurt am Main, Suhrkamp, 1966, pp. 108–61.

8   The effort to formulate this 'impossible' intersection between (symbolic) negativity and the body seems also to be the driving

force of Jacqueline Rose's 'return to Melanie Klein'. See Rose's *Why War?*, Oxford, Blackwell, 1993. For that reason, although the author of these lines considers himself a pure 'dogmatic' Lacanian, he feels a deep solidarity with Rose's enterprise.

9 Deleuze, *Logic of Sense*, p. 41.

10 Is, therefore, Deleuze's oversight not correlative to Althusser's? Deleuze confines himself to the axis Imaginary–Real and forecloses the Symbolic, whereas the Althusserian duality of the 'real object' (i.e., the experienced reality, object of imaginary experience) and the 'object of knowledge' (the symbolic structure produced through the process of knowledge) fits the axis Imaginary–Symbolic. Lacan is the only one to thematize the axis Symbolic–Real that founds the other two axes. Furthermore, does this opposition of Deleuze and Althusser not account for the uncanny closeness and fundamental difference of their respective readings of Spinoza? Althusser's Spinoza is the Spinoza of symbolic structure, of subjectless knowledge, freed from imaginary affects, whereas Deleuze's Spinoza is the Spinoza of the real, of 'anarchic' bodily mixtures.

11 See G. W. F. Hegel, *Philosophy of Mind: Part III of the Encyclopedia of Philosophical Sciences*, trans. William Wallace and A. V. Miller, Oxford, Clarendon Press, 1971, pp. 201–23. We are relying here on the excellent, though somewhat one-sided, reconstruction of Hegel's line of argumentation in John McCumber, *The Company of Words: Hegel, Language, and Systematic Philosophy*, Evanston, Northwestern University Press, 1993, pp. 215–49.

12 Hegel, *Philosophy of Mind*, p. 222.

13 *Ibid.*, p. 187 (*Zusätz*).

14 *Ibid.*, p. 223. This is what seems to elude the Derridean reading that conceives of 'Mechanical Memory' as a kind of 'vanishing mediator', an externalization that is subsequently self-sublated in the Inwardness of the Spirit: by obliterating the entire representational inner content, 'Mechanical Memory' opens up and maintains the absolute Void as the medium of the Spirit, as the space filled out by the spiritual content. In short, by performing the radical obliteration of the entire *enunciated* representational

content, 'Mechanical Memory' makes place for the *subject of enunciation*. What is crucial here is the codependence of the reduction of the sign to the senseless externality of the signifier and the emergence of the 'barred' subject *qua* pure void ($): Hegel is here unexpectedly close to Althusser, who also articulates the codependence of Ideological State Apparatuses (ideological practice *qua* pure externality of a 'mechanical' ritual) and the process of subjectivization. The problem with Althusser, however, is that he lacks the concept of the subject of the signifier ($): since he reduces the subject to imaginary recognition in the ideological sense, he fails to notice the correlation of the emergence of the subject to the radical loss of sense in the senseless ritual. At a somewhat different level, the same paradox defines the status of woman in Weininger: woman is the subject *par excellence* precisely insofar as the feminine position involves the evacuation of the entire spiritual content – this voidance confronts us with the subject *qua* empty container of sense ...

15   G. W. F. Hegel, *Jenaer Realphilosophie*, Hamburg, Meiner, 1931, p. 183.

16   Jacques Lacan, *The Seminar of Jacques Lacan I: Freud's Papers on Technique, 1953–54*, ed. Jacques-Alain Miller, trans. John Forrester, Cambridge, Cambridge University Press, 1988, pp. 242–3 [eds].

17   See McCumber, *The Company of Words*, pp. 130–43.

18   Karl Marx, *Capital: A Critique of Political Economy, Volume I*, trans. Ben Fowkes, London, Penguin/New Left Books, 1976, pp. 162–3 [eds].

9 The Eclipse of Meaning: on Lacan and Deconstruction

It seems to me the very thoughtful questions, full of precise and perspicacious observations, posed by *Agenda* circle around one central issue: *'What are the real differences between your approach and deconstruction?'* So, in tackling these questions, I immediately got immersed in the problem of the complex relationship between Lacanian psychoanalysis and Derridean deconstruction. Here are the preliminary results of my endeavour to clarify this relationship.

I

My first point is purely 'transcendental'. It concerns the 'conditions of possibility' of the Derridean deconstructive reading of Lacan: *which* Lacan is addressed in this reading? My hypothesis is that the Derridean deconstructive reading of Lacan[1] reduces the corpus of Lacan's texts to a *doxa* on Lacan which restricts his teaching to the framework of traditional philosophy. Far from being a simple case of false reading, this *doxa* definitely has support in Lacan: Lacan himself often yields to its temptation, since this *doxa* is a kind of 'spontaneous philosophy of (Lacanian) psychoanalysis'. What, then, are its basic contours? The moment we enter the symbolic order, the immediacy of the presymbolic Real is lost forever: the true object of desire ('mother') becomes impossible-unattainable. Every positive object we encounter in reality is already a substitute for this lost original, the incestuous *Ding* rendered inaccessible by the very fact of language – therein resides 'symbolic castration'. The very existence of the human *qua* being-of-language stands thus under the sign of an irreducible and constitutive lack. We are submerged in the universe of signs which forever prevent us from attaining the Thing. So-called 'external reality' itself is already 'structured like a language', i.e., its meaning is always-already overdetermined by the symbolic framework which structures our perception of reality. The symbolic agency of the paternal prohibition (the 'Name-of-the-Father') merely personifies, gives body to, the impossibility which is co-substantial with the very fact of the symbolic order – '*jouissance* is forbidden to him who speaks as such'.

This gap that forever separates the lost Thing from symbolic semblances which are never '*that*' defines the contours of the ethics of desire: 'do not give way as to your desire' can only mean 'do not put up with any of the substitutes of the Thing, keep open the gap of desire'. In our everyday lives, we constantly fall prey to imaginary lures which promise the healing of the original/constitutive wound of symbolization, from Woman with whom full sexual relationship will be possible, to the totalitarian political ideal of a fully realized community. In contrast, the fundamental maxim of the ethics of desire is simply desire as such: one has to maintain desire in its dissatisfaction. What we have here is a kind of heroism of the lack: the aim of the psychoanalytic cure is to induce the subject to assume his constitutive lack heroically; to endure the splitting which propels desire. A productive way out of this deadlock is provided by the possibility of *sublimation*, when one picks out an empirical, positive object and 'elevates it to the dignity of the Thing', i.e., turns it into a kind of stand-in for the impossible Thing. One thereby remains faithful to one's desire without getting drawn into the deadly vortex of the Thing. Such a (mis)reading of Lacan led some German philosophers to interpret Antigone's clinging to her desire as a *negative* attitude, i.e., as the exemplary case of the lethal obsession with the Thing which cannot achieve sublimation and therefore gets lost in a suicidal abyss – as if the whole point of Lacan's reading of *Antigone* is not to present her as an exemplary case of the psychoanalytic ethics of 'not compromising one's desire'!

The political consequences of this reading of Lacan are clear: the field of the political is characterized by the radically ambiguous relationship of the subjects towards the public Thing (*res publica*), the kernel of the Real around which the life of a community turns. The subject, *qua* member of a community, is split not only between their 'pathological' urges and their relationship to the Thing, their relationship to the Thing is also split: on the one hand, the law of desire orders us to neglect our pathological interests and to follow our Thing; on the other hand, an even higher law (Bernard Baas writes it with a capital 'L'[2]) enjoins us to maintain a minimum of distance towards our Thing, i.e., to bear in mind, apropos of every political action which purports to realize our Cause, that 'this is not that' [ce n'est pas ça]. The Thing can appear only in its retreat, as the obscure Ground which motivates our activity, but which dissipates the moment we endeavour to grasp it in its positive ontological consistency. If we neglect this Law, sooner or later we get caught in the 'totalitarian' self-destructive vicious cycle. What lurks in the background, of course, is the Kantian distinction between the constitutive and the regulative aspect: the Thing (freedom, for example) has to remain a regulative ideal – any attempt at its full realization can lead only to the most terrifying tyranny. (It is easy to discern here the contours of Kant's criticism of the perversion of the French Revolution in the revolutionary terror of the Jacobins.) And how can we avoid recognizing here reference to the contemporary political landscape, with its two extremes of unprincipled liberal pragmatism and fundamentalist fanaticism?

In a first approach, this reading of Lacan cannot but appear convincing, almost a matter of course – yet it is the very ease of this translation of Lacanian concepts into the modern structuralist and/or existentialist philosophemes of constitutive lack, etc., that should render it suspect. To put it somewhat bluntly, we are dealing here with an 'idealist' distortion of Lacan. To this 'idealist' problematic of desire, its constitutive lack, etc., one has to oppose the 'materialist' problematic of the Real of drives. That is to say, for Lacan, the 'Real' is not, in the Kantian mode, a purely negative category, a designation of a limit without any specification of what lies beyond. The Real qua drive is, on the contrary, the agens, the 'driving force', of desiring. This 'active' (and not purely negative) status of drives, of the presymbolic 'libido', induces Lacan to elaborate the myth of 'lamella'. In it, he deploys – in the form of a mythical narrative, not of a conceptual articulation – the 'real genesis', i.e., what had to occur prior to symbolization, prior to the emergence of the symbolic order.

Incidentally, what I have just said in no way implies that the Real of drive is, as to its ontological status, a kind of full substantiality, the positive 'stuff' of formal-symbolic structurations. What Lacan did with the notion of drive is strangely similar to what Einstein, in his general theory of relativity, did with the notion of gravity. Einstein 'desubstantialized' gravity by way of reducing it to geometry: gravity is not a substantial force which 'bends' space but the name for the curvature of space itself. In a homologous way, Lacan 'desubstantialized' drives: a drive is not a primordial positive force but a purely geometrical, topological phenomenon, the name for the curvature of the space of desire, i.e. for the paradox that, within this space, the way to attain the object (*a*) is not to go straight for it (the safest way to miss it) but to encircle it, to 'go round in circles'. Drive is this purely topological 'distortion' of the natural instinct which finds satisfaction in a direct consumption of its object.

In short, Lacan's point here is that the passage from the radically 'impossible' Real (the maternal Thing-Body which can be apprehended only in a negative way) to the reign of the symbolic law, to desire which is regulated by Law, sustained by the fundamental Prohibition, is not direct: something happens *between* the 'pure', 'prehuman' nature and the order of symbolic exchanges, and this 'something' is precisely the Real of drives – *no longer* the 'closed circuit' of instincts and of their innate rhythm of satisfaction (drives are already 'derailed nature'), but *not yet* the symbolic desire sustained by Prohibition. The Lacanian Thing is not simply the 'impossible' Real which withdraws into the dim recesses of the Unattainable with the entry of the symbolic order, it is the very universe of drives. Here, the reference to Schelling is of crucial importance, since Schelling was the first to accomplish a homologous step within the domain of philosophy. His mythical narrative on the 'ages of the world' focuses on a process in God which precedes the actuality of the divine Logos, and, as we have already seen, this process is described in terms which clearly pave the way for Lacan's notion of the Real of drives.

II

So in what, exactly, does the difference between Lacan and deconstruction reside? Let me elaborate this crucial point apropos the

Derridean couple, 'supplement/centre'. In a way reminiscent of the Foucauldian endless variations on the complex heterogeneity of power relations (they run upwards, downwards, laterally), Derrida also likes to indulge heavily in exuberant variations on the paradoxical character of the supplement (the excessive element which is neither inside nor outside; it sticks out of the series it belongs to and simultaneously completes it, etc.). Lacan, on the contrary – by means of a gesture which, of course, for Derrida would undoubtedly signal reinscription into traditional philosophical discourse – *directly offers a concept of this element*, namely the concept of the Master-Signifier, S_1, in relation to S_2, the 'ordinary' chain of knowledge. This concept is not a simple unambiguous concept, but the concept of the structural ambiguity itself. That is to say, Lacan reunites in one and the same concept what Derrida keeps apart. In Lacan, S_1 stands for the supplement – the trait which sticks out, but is as such, in its very excess, unavoidable; and, simultaneously, for the totalizing Master-Signifier. Therein, in this 'speculative identity' of the supplement and the Centre, resides the implicit 'Hegelian' move of Lacan: the Centre which Derrida endeavours to 'deconstruct' is ultimately the very supplement which threatens to disrupt its totalizing power, or, to put it in Kierkegaard-ese, supplement is the Centre itself 'in its becoming'. In this precise sense, supplement is the condition of possibility *and* the condition of impossibility of the Centre.

Mutatis mutandis, the same goes for the couple, 'voice/writing'. In his deconstruction of western logo-phono-centrism, Derrida proposed the idea that the metaphysics of presence is ultimately founded upon the illusion of 'hearing-oneself-speaking [*s'entendre-parler*]', upon the illusory experience of the Voice as the transparent medium that enables and guarantees the speaker's immediate self-presence. In his theory of voice as a partial object (on a par with other such objects: breasts, faeces), Lacan supplements Derrida with the Hegelian identity as the coincidence of opposites. True, the experience of *s'entendre-parler* serves to ground the illusion of the transparent self-presence of the speaking subject. However, is not the voice *at the same time* that which undermines most radically the subject's self-presence and self-transparency? Not writing, which undermines the voice as it were from without, from a minimal distance, but the voice itself, one is tempted to say: the voice *as such* in its uncanny presence – I hear myself speaking, yet what I hear is never fully myself but a parasite, a foreign body in my very heart. In short, voice is that on account of which 'I can't hear myself think', so that the subject's basic plea to their voice is, 'Would you please shut up, I can't hear myself think!' This stranger *in myself* acquires positive existence in different guises, from the voice of conscience to the voice of the persecutor in paranoia. The voice's 'self-identity' resides in the fact that the voice *qua* medium of transparent self-presence *coincides* with the voice *qua* foreign body which undercuts my self-presence 'from within'. With regard to this inner friction of the voice, the tension between voice and writing is already secondary: in it, this inner friction is, as it were, displaced into the relationship of the voice to writing *qua* its *external* Other.

Consequently, the status of voice in Lacan does not amount to a simple symmetrical reversal of the Derridean notion of writing as supplement, i.e., it is not that instead of writing supplementing the voice, it is now the voice's turn to supplement writing: the very logic of the relationship is different in each case. In Lacan, voice prior to writing (and to the movement of *différance*) is a drive and, as such, is caught in the antagonism of a closed circular movement. By way of the expulsion of its own opaque materiality into the 'externality' of writing, voice establishes itself as the ideal medium of self-transparency. Perhaps therein resides the abyss that forever separates the Real of an antagonism from Derrida's *différance*: *différance* points towards the constant and constitutive deferral of impossible self-identity; whereas, in Lacan, what the movement of symbolic deferral-substitution forever fails to attain is not Identity but the Real of an antagonism. In social life, for example, what the multitude of (ideological) symbolizations-narrativizations fails to render is not society's *self-identity* but the *antagonism*, the constitutive splitting of the 'body politic'.

To recapitulate: in Derrida, voice is the medium of illusory self-transparency. Consequently, the fact that voice for structural reasons always fails to deliver this self-transparency means that voice is always-already tainted with writing, that it always-already contains the minimum of the materiality of a trace which introduces an inter-space, a gap, into the voice's pure self-presence. In Lacan's 'graph of desire', however, voice is the remainder of the signifying operation, i.e., the meaningless piece of the real which stays behind once the operation of 'quilting' [*capitonnage*] responsible for the stabilization of meaning is performed – in short, *voice is that which, in the signifier, resists meaning*: it stands for the opaque inertia which cannot be recuperated by meaning. It is only the dimension of writing which accounts for the stability of meaning, or, to quote the immortal words of Samuel Goldwyn: 'A verbal agreement isn't worth the paper it's written on.' As such, voice is neither dead nor alive: its status is, rather, that of a 'living dead', of a spectral apparition which somehow survives its own death, i.e., the eclipse of meaning. In other words, it is true that the life of a voice can be opposed to the dead letter of a writing, but this life is the uncanny life of an 'undead' monster, not a 'healthy' living self-presence of Meaning.

As I have already hinted, one could also formulate this paradoxical status of voice in terms of the Hegelian notion of tautology as the highest contradiction. 'Voice is voice' in *s'entendre parler* is a tautology homologous to 'God is ... God': the first voice ('Voice is ...') is the medium of self-transparent presence, whereas the second voice (... voice') is the opaque stain which decentres me from within, a strange body in my very midst: the form of identity contains utter hetero-geneity. My self-identity is sustained by its 'condition of impossibility', by a 'spectral' foreign body in my very heart. 'Supplement is the Centre', on the contrary, has to be read as an 'infinite judgement' in the Hegelian sense of the term. Instead of the tautology giving form to the radical antagonism between the two appearances of the same term, the very juxtaposition of the two terms which seem incompatible renders visible their 'speculative identity' – 'the Spirit is a bone', for example. The ultimate Lacanian 'infinite judgment', of course, is his formula of fantasy, $\$ \diamond a$, positing the codependence of the pure void of subjectivity and the formless remainder of the Real which, precisely, resists subjectivization: *objet a* is not merely the objectal correlative to the subject, it is the subject itself in its 'impossible' objectal existence, a kind of objectal stand-in for the subject. And it is the same with 'Supplement is the Centre'. The point is not merely that there is no Centre without the supplement, that it is only the supplement which, retroactively, constitutes the Centre; the Centre itself is nothing but the supplement perceived from a certain perspective – the shift from the Centre to its supplement concerns the point of view, not the 'thing itself'. We are dealing here with a purely topological shift, homologous to the shift in the status of low-class popular food brought about by the development of industrialized mass food. The cheapest and most elementary kind of food (full-grain, dark bread, for example) gradually disappears from the market, forced out by industrially produced, white, square loaves or hamburger buns, only to return triumphantly as the most expensive 'natural', 'home-made' speciality. The fight against the opaque Voice is therefore the fight against transparent self-identity itself: in endeavouring to contain the supplement, the Centre undermines its own foundations.

To put it in yet another way, Lacan subverts the metaphysics of presence at the very point at which, by way of equating voice with subjectivity, he seems to succumb to one of its basic premises. To the horror and/or delight of deconstructionists, he claims that a signifying chain subjectivizes itself through the voice – there is no subject prior to the voice. Writing is in itself non-subjective, it involves no subjective position of enunciation, no difference between the enunciated content and its process of enunciation. However, the voice through which the signifying chain subjectivizes itself is not the voice *qua* the medium of the transparent self-presence of Meaning, but the voice *qua* a dark spot of non-subjectivizable remainder, the point of the eclipse of meaning, the point at which meaning slides into *jouis-sense*. Or, to put it even more pointedly: we have a chain of (written) signs which transparently designate their signified: when does this chain subjectivize itself? How is its 'flat' meaning (denotation in which no subjectivity reverberates) transformed into Sense? Only when a nonsensical vocal dark spot which, in its very opaqueness, functions as the stand-in for the subject is added to it. The Lacanian paradox is, therefore, that if one is to transform (objective-denotative) Meaning into (subjective-expressive) Sense, one has simply to supplement it with a senseless vocal stain: *Sense = meaning + nonsense*. The presence of this impenetrable vocal supplement effectuates the magic transmutation of a written chain of signifiers into 'subjectivized' speech in which one can discern, beyond its denotative meaning, the reverberation of a subjective position of enunciation. In this precise sense, Lacan can assert that the voice accounts for the minimum of *passage à l'acte* of the signifying chain.

Suffice it to recall the example of 'hate speech', i.e., of speech acts in which the very intention-to-signify, the intention to 'say something', is eclipsed by the intention to attain and destroy the kernel of the Real, *objet a*, in the Other (victim). It is crucial that the term used is 'hate speech', not 'hate writing'.

III

The key point is thus the status of the excessive voice which stands for the eclipse of meaning. In order to render this uncanny voice, it is sufficient to cast a cursory glance at the history of music. It reads as a kind of counter-history to the Derridean history of Western metaphysics as the domination of voice over writing. What we encounter in it, again and again, is a voice that threatens the established order and that, for that reason, has to be brought under control, subordinated to the rational articulation of spoken and written word, fixed into writing. In order to designate the danger that lurks here, Lacan coined the neologism *jouis-sense* – enjoyment-in-meaning – the moment at which the singing voice 'runs amok', cuts loose from its anchoring in meaning, and accelerates into a consuming self-enjoyment. The two exemplary cases of this eclipse of meaning in consuming self-enjoyment are, of course, the climax of the (feminine) operatic aria and the mystical experience. The effort to dominate and regulate this excess runs from ancient China, where the Emperor himself legislated music, to the fear of Elvis Presley that brought together the conservative moral majority in the USA and the Communist hard-liners in the Soviet Union. In his *Republic*, Plato tolerates music only insofar as it is strictly subordinated to the order of Word. Music is located at the very crossroads of Nature and Culture. It seizes us, as it were, 'in the real', far more directly than the meaning of words. For that reason, it can serve as the mightiest weapon of education and discipline, yet the moment it loses its footing and gets caught in the self-propelling vicious circle of enjoyment, it can undermine the very foundations not only of the State, but of the social order as such. In medieval times, Church power confronted the same dilemma: it is amazing to observe how much energy and care the highest ecclesiastic authority (popes) put into the seemingly trifling question of the regulation of music (the problem of polyphony, the 'devil's triton', etc.). The figure that personifies the ambiguous attitude of Power toward the excess of the Voice is, of course, Hildegard von Bingen, who put mystical enjoyment into music and was thus constantly on the verge of excommunication, although she was integrated into the highest level of the hierarchy of power, counselling the emperor, etc. The same matrix is again at work in the French Revolution, whose ideologues endeavoured to assert 'normal' sexual difference under the domination of the male spoken word against decadent aristocratic indulgence in the pleasures of listening to castrati. One of the last episodes in this everlasting struggle is the notorious Soviet campaign, instigated by Stalin himself, against Shostakovich's *Katarina Izmajlova*. Rather curiously, one of the main reproaches was that the opera is a mass of unarticulated screams ... The problem is thus always the same: how are we to prevent the voice from sliding into a consuming self-enjoyment that 'effeminates' the reliable masculine Word? The voice functions here as a 'supplement' in the Derridean sense. One endeavours to restrain it, to regulate it, to subordinate it to the articulated Word, yet one cannot dispense with it altogether, since a proper dosage is vital for the exercise of power. (Suffice to recall the role of patriotic-military songs in the building-up of a totalitarian community, or, an even more flagrant obscenity, the US Marine Corps' mesmeric 'marching chants'. Are their debilitating rhythm and sadistic-nonsensical content not an exemplary case of consuming self-enjoyment in the service of Power?)

IV

This brings us back to the problem of Hegel, of Hegelian dialectics. One of the postmodern commonplaces about Hegel is the reproach of 'restrained economy': in the dialectical process, loss and negativity are contained in advance, accounted for – what gets lost is merely the inessential aspect (and the very fact that a feature has been lost counts as the ultimate proof of its inessential status), whereas one can rest assured that the essential dimension will not only survive, but even be strengthened by the ordeal of negativity. The whole (teleological) point of the process of loss and recuperation is to enable the Absolute to purify itself, to render manifest its essential dimension by getting rid of the inessential, like a snake which, from time to time, has to cast off its skin in order to rejuvenate itself. One can see, now, where this reproach, which imputes to Hegel the obsessional economy of 'I can give you everything *but that*', goes wrong and misses its target. The basic premise of Hegel is that every attempt to distinguish the Essential from the Inessential always proves itself false. Whenever I resort to the strategy of renouncing the Inessential in order to save the Essential, sooner or later (but always when it's already too late) I'm bound to discover that I made a fatal mistake as to what is essential, and that the essential dimension has already slipped through my fingers. The crucial aspect of a proper dialectical reversal is this shift in the very relationship between the Essential and the Inessential. When, for example, I defend my unprincipled flattery of my superiors by claiming that it amounts to mere external accommodation, whereas deep in my heart I stick to my true convictions and despise them, I blind myself to the reality of the situation: I have already given way as to what really matters, since it is my inner conviction, sincere as it may be, which is effectively 'inessential'.

The 'negation of negation' is not a kind of existential sleight of hand by means of which the subject feigns to put everything at stake, but effectively sacrifices only the inessential. Rather, it stands for the horrifying experience which occurs when, after sacrificing everything considered 'inessential', I suddenly perceive that the very essential dimension, for the sake of which I sacrificed the inessential, is already lost. The subject does save his skin, he survives the ordeal, but the price he has to pay for it is the loss of his very substance, of the most precious kernel of his individuality. More precisely, prior to this 'transubstantiation', the subject is not a subject at all, since *'subject' is ultimately the name for this very 'transubstantiation' of substance* which, after its dissemination, 'returns to itself', but not as 'the same'. It is therefore all too easy to be misled by Hegel's notorious propositions concerning Spirit as the power of 'tarrying with the negative', i.e., of resurrecting after its own death. In the ordeal of absolute negativity, the Spirit in its particular selfhood *effectively dies*, is over and done with, so that the Spirit which 'resurrects' *is not the Spirit which previously expired.* The same goes for the Resurrection. Hegel emphasizes again and again that Christ dies on the Cross for real – he returns as the Spirit of the community of believers, not in person. So, again, when, in what is perhaps the most famous single passage from his *Phenomenology,* Hegel asserts that the Spirit is capable of 'tarrying with the negative', of enduring the power of the negative, this does not mean that, in the ordeal of negativity, the subject merely has to clench his teeth and hold out – true, he will lose some plumage, but, magically, everything will somehow turn out OK. Hegel's whole point is that the subject does *not* survive the ordeal of negativity: he *effectively* loses his very essence and passes over into his Other. One is tempted to evoke here the science fiction motif of changed identity, when a subject biologically survives, but is no longer the same person. This is what the Hegelian transubstantiation is about, and, of course, it is this very transubstantiation which distinguishes Subject from Substance. 'Subject' designates that X which is able to survive the loss of its very substantial identity and to continue to live as the 'empty shell of its former self'.

One can also make the same point by way of focusing on the dialectics of In-itself and For-itself. In today's ecological struggles, the position of the 'mute In-itself' of the abstract Universal is best epitomized by an external observer who apprehends 'ecology' as the neutral universality of a genus which then sub-divides itself into a multitude of species (feminist ecology, socialist ecology, New Age ecology, conservative ecology, etc.). However, for a subject who is 'within', engaged in the ecological fight, there is no such neutral universality. Say, for a feminist ecologist, the impending threat of ecological catastrophe *results from* the male attitude of domination and exploitation, so that she is not a feminist *and* an ecologist – feminism provides her with the specific content of her ecological identity, i.e. a 'non-feminist ecologist' is for her not another kind of ecologist, but simply somebody who *is not a true ecologist.* The – properly Hegelian – problem of the 'For-itself' of a Universal is, therefore, how, under what concrete conditions, can the universal dimension become 'for itself'? How can it be posited 'as such', in explicit contrast to its particular qualifications, so that I experience the specific feminist (or conservative or socialist or ...) qualification of my ecological attitude as something contingent with respect to the universal notion of ecology? And, back to the relationship between Derrida and Lacan, therein resides the gap which separates them: for Derrida, the subject always remains substance, whereas for Lacan (as well as for Hegel) subject is precisely that which is not substance. The following passage from *Grammatology* is typical:

> However it [the category of the subject] is modified, however it is endowed with consciousness or unconsciousness, it will refer, by the entire thread of its history, to the substantiality of a presence unperturbed by accidents, or to the identity of the selfsame in the presence of self-relationship.[3]

For Derrida, then, the notion of subject involves a minimum of substantial self-identity, a kernel of self-presence which remains the same beneath the flux of accidental changes. For Hegel, on the contrary, the term 'subject' designates the very fact that the substance, in the kernel of its identity, *is* perturbed by accidents. The 'becoming-subject of substance' stands for the gesture of *hubris* by means of which a mere accident or predicate of the substance, a subordinated moment of its totality, installs itself as the new totalizing principle and subordinates the previous Substance to itself, turning it into its own particular moment. In the passage from feudalism to capitalism, for example, money – in medieval times, a clearly subordinated moment of the totality of economic relations – asserts itself as the very principle of totality (since the aim of capitalist production is profit). The 'becoming-subject' of the Substance involves such a continuous displacement of the Centre. Again and again, the old Centre turns into a subordinate moment of the new totality dominated by a different structuring principle – far from being a 'deeper' underlying agency which 'pulls the strings' of this displacement of the Centre (i.e., of the structuring principle of totality), 'subject' designates the void which serves as the medium and/or operator of this process of displacement.

One should therefore renounce the usual formulas of the Hegelian 'concrete Universal' as the Universal which is the unity of itself and its Other (the Particular), i.e., not abstractly opposed to the wealth of the particular content, but the very movement of self-mediation and self-sublating of the Particular. The problem with this standard 'organic' image of 'concrete Universal' as a living substantial Totality which reproduces itself through the very movement of its particular content is that in it the Universal is not yet 'for itself', i.e., posited as such. In this precise sense, the emergence of the subject is correlative to the positing of the Universal 'as such', in its opposition to the particular content. Let us return to our example of ecology: every attempt to define a substantial core of ecology, the minimum of content every ecologist has to agree with, is necessarily doomed to fail, since this very core shifts in the struggle for ideological hegemony. For a socialist, the ultimate cause of the ecological crisis is to be sought in the profit-oriented capitalist mode of production, which is why anti-capitalism is for him the very core of a true ecological attitude. For a conservative, the ecological crisis is rooted in man's false pride and will to dominate the universe, so that humble respect for tradition forms the very core of a true ecological attitude. For a feminist, the ecological crisis results from male domination, etc., etc. What is at stake in the ideologico-political struggle, of course, is the positive content which will fill out the 'empty' signifier 'ecology': *what will it mean* to be an 'ecologist' (or a 'democrat', or to belong to a 'nation')? And our point is that *the emergence of 'subject' is strictly correlative to the positing of this central signifier as 'empty'*. I become a 'subject' when the universal signifier to which I refer ('ecology', in our case) is no longer connected by an umbilical cord to some particular content, but is experienced as an empty space to be filled out by the particular (feminist, conservative, state, pro-market, socialist) content. This 'empty' signifier whose positive content is the 'stake' of the ideologico-political struggle 'represents the subject for the other signifiers', for the signifiers which stand for its positive content.

V

Lacan deploys the contours of this 'desubstantialization' which gives birth to the subject in his detailed commentary on Paul Claudel's Coûfontaine-trilogy, elevated by him into a contemporary counterpart to *Antigone*.[4] The reference to Lacan's Antigone as the exemplary case of the ethics of desire has become a commonplace in the last few years – in significant contrast to the non-reactions to Lacan's commentary on Claudel's play. This absence of reactions, however, is really not surprising, since in Claudel things are far more disquieting: no flashes of beauty generated by the sublime pathos of the tragic events on the stage, merely a repulsive tic.

I'll limit myself to the first part of the trilogy, *The Hostage*. The play takes place towards the end of the Napoleonic rule, on the estate of the impoverished noble family of Coûfontaine in the French countryside. After long years of assiduous endeavour, Sygne de Coûfontaine, a somewhat faded beauty in her late twenties and the last member of the family to remain there, has succeeded in bringing together what was left of the estate in the revolutionary turmoil. On a stormy night, she is paid an unexpected secret visit by her cousin Georges, the heir of the family and a fervent royalist, who had emigrated to England. Caught in a mystical trance comparable to Wagner's *Tristan*, Sygne and Georges make the vow of eternal love which simultaneously expresses their profound attachment to the family land and title. The two lovers are united in the prospect of marrying and continuing the family tradition: they are dedicated and sacrifice everything, their youth and happiness, to it – the family title and the small piece of land is all they've got. However, new troubles already lurk on the horizon. The cousin returns to France on a very sensitive secret political mission – he has brought the Pope, who is on the run from Napoleon, into their manor. Next morning, Sygne is visited by Toussaint Turelure, the Prefect of the region and a *nouveau riche*, a person she despises thoroughly. Turelure, the son of her servant and wet nurse, has used the Revolution to promote his career: as a Jacobinical local potentate he ordered the execution of Sygne's parents in the presence of their children. This same Turelure, the arch-enemy of the family, now approaches Sygne with the following proposal: his spies have informed him of the presence of Georges and the Pope in the manor, and, of course, he has strict orders from Paris to arrest the two immediately. However, he is ready to let them slip away if only Sygne will marry him and thus transfer to him the Coûfontaine family title. Although Sygne proudly rejects the offer and dismisses Turelure, the ensuing long conversation with the local priest, the confidant of the family, causes her to change her mind. In his paradigmatically modern strategy of inducing her to accept Turelure's offer of marriage and thus save the Pope, the priest renounces any direct appeal to her duty and obligation. He repeats again and again that nobody, not even God Himself, has the right to ask from her such a horrifying sacrifice. The decision is entirely hers: she has the right to say no without any reproach. A year later, Turelure, her husband and now the Prefect of Seine, conducts the negotiations for the surrender of Paris to the advancing Royalists. By means of his negotiating skills, he assures himself one of the most powerful posts in post-Napoleonic France. The chief negotiator for the returning King is none other than Georges, and, moreover, negotiations take place on the very day when a son is born to Sygne and Turelure. Unable to bear that the corrupted and opportunistic Turelure has usurped their family title, Georges gets involved in a violent fight with him. A shoot-out takes place between the two men in the presence of Sygne. Georges is mortally shot, while Sygne shields Turelure with her own body, intercepting Georges's bullet. In an alternative version of the scene which follows this shoot-out, Turelure, standing by the bed of the fatally wounded Sygne, desperately asks her to give a sign which would confer some meaning on her unexpected suicidal gesture of saving the life of her loathed husband – anything, even if she didn't do it for the love of him but merely to save the family name from disgrace. The dying Sygne doesn't utter a sound: she merely signals her rejection of the final reconciliation with her husband by means of a compulsive tic, a kind of convulsed twitching which repeatedly distorts her gentle face. Lacan is here fully justified in reading the very name 'Sygne' as a distorted '*signe*' (French for 'sign').[5] What Sygne refuses to do is to provide a sign which would integrate her absurd act of sacrificing herself for the loathed husband into the symbolic universe of honour and duty, thereby softening its traumatic impact. In the last scene of the play, while Sygne is dying of her wound, Turelure bids a pathetic welcome to the King on behalf of faithful France.

In Claudel's play, the Pope is portrayed as a powerless, sentimental, half-senile old man, definitely out of touch with his time, personifying the hollow ritual and lifeless wisdom of an institution in decay. The restoration of the *ancien régime* after Napoleon's fall is an obscene parody in which the most corrupted parvenus of the Revolution, dressed up as Royalists, run the show. Claudel thus clearly signals that the order for which Sygne makes the ultimate sacrifice is not the authentic old order but its shallow and impotent semblance, a mask under the guise of which the new forces of corruption and degeneration fortify their rule. In spite of this, however, her word obliges her, or, as Lacan puts it, she is the hostage of her Word,[6] so she goes through the empty motions of sacrificing herself for her husband whom she is supposed not only to obey but also to respect and love wholeheartedly. Therein resides the horrifying senselessness of her suicidal gesture: this gesture is empty, there is no substantial Destiny which predetermines the symbolic coordinates of the hero's existence, no guilt they have to assume in a pathetically heroic gesture of self-sacrifice. 'God is dead', the substantial Universal for which the subject is ready to sacrifice the kernel of his being is but an empty form, a ridiculous ritual devoid of any substantial content, which nonetheless holds the subject as its hostage.

The modern subject constitutes themselves by means of such a gesture of redoubled renunciation, i.e., of sacrificing the very kernel of their being, their particular substance for which they are otherwise ready to sacrifice everything. In other words, they sacrifice the substantial kernel of their being on behalf of the universal order which, however, since 'God is dead', reveals itself as an impotent empty shell. The subject thus finds themselves in the void of absolute alienation, deprived even of the beauty of the tragic pathos. Reduced to a state of radical humiliation, turned into an empty shell of themselves, they are compelled to obey the ritual and to feign enthusiastic allegiance to a Cause they no longer believe in, or even utterly despise. The more than obvious fact that *The Hostage* often approaches ridiculous and excessive melodrama is, therefore, not a weakness of the piece. It rather functions as the index of a subjective deadlock which can no longer express itself in tragic pathos: the subject is bereft of even the minimum of tragic dignity. The gap that separates Claudel's piece from *Antigone* is here clearly perceptible. If one were to rewrite *Antigone* as a modern tragedy, one would have to change the story so as to deprive Antigone's suicidal gesture of its sublime dignity and turn it into a case of ridiculously stubborn perseverance which is utterly out of place, and is, in all probability, masterminded by the very state power it pretends to call in question. Lacan's precise formulation of this key point fits like a glove the position of the accused in the Stalinist monster trials. In the modern tragedy, the subject 'is asked to assume with enjoyment the very injustice of which they are horrified ['*il est demandé d'assumer comme une jouissance l'injustice même qui lui fait horreur*']'.[7] Is this not a perfect qualification of the impasse of a Stalinist subject? Not only are they forced to sacrifice everything that really matters to them – tradition, loyalty to their friends, etc. – to the Party, what's more, they are requested to do it with enthusiastic allegiance. One is, therefore, tempted to risk the hypothesis that the Stalinist monster trials with their absolute (self-relating) humiliation of the accused (who is compelled to ask for the death penalty for themselves, etc.) provide the clearest actualization in social reality itself of the fundamental structure of the modern tragedy articulated by Lacan apropos of Claudel.

Insofar as the subject runs out on the kernel of his being, they, as it were, cut off the possibility of a dignified retreat into tragic authenticity. What, then, remains for them but a 'No!', a gesture of denial which, in Claudel, appears in the guise of the dying Sygne's convulsive twitches. Such a grimace, a tic that disfigures the harmony of a beautiful feminine face, registers the dimension of the Real, of the subject *qua* 'answer of the Real'. This tiny, barely perceptible tic – 'a refusal, a *no*, a *non*, this tic, this grimace, in short, this flexion of the body, this psychosomatics'[8] – incomparably more horrifying than the Cyclopean vortex of the Real celebrated by Schelling, is the elementary gesture of hysteria. By means of her symptoms, the hysterical woman says 'No' to the demands of the (social) big Other to 'assume with enjoyment the very injustice of which she is horrified' – say, to pretend to find personal fulfilment and satisfaction in carrying out her 'calling' the way it is defined by the ruling patriarchal order.

One should recall here Lacan's reversal of Dostoevsky's famous proposition from *The Brothers Karamazov*: '*If God doesn't exist*, the father says, *then everything is permitted*. Quite evidently, a naïve notion, for we analysts know full well that if God doesn't exist, then nothing at all is permitted any longer. Neurotics prove that to us every day.'[9] (A somewhat pathetic corroboration of this reversal of

Dostoevsky is the plight of ex-dissident intellectuals in post-Communist East European countries. While the Communist censorship was still operative, it was possible to pass the subversive message between the lines – the very fact of censorship attuned readers' attentiveness to the hidden message, so that everybody understood what a text was about. Now that there is no censorship and everything is permitted, the prohibition is universalized. It is impossible to pass the subversive message: readers simply miss it; critical intellectuals' speech finds no echo ...) In other words, the fact that there is no longer a Destiny preordaining the contours of my guilt in no way allows me to enjoy the innocence of the autonomous subject delivered from any externally imposed standard of guilt. This absence of Destiny rather makes me *absolutely guilty*: I feel guilty without knowing what I am effectively guilty of, and this ignorance makes me even more guilty. It is this 'abstract guilt' that renders the subject vulnerable to the 'totalitarian' trap. So there is an aspect of truth in the conservative claim that the freedom of the modern subject is 'false'. A hysterical disquiet pertains to his very existence on account of his lacking any firm social identity, which can only come from a substantial sense of Tradition. This abstract, indefinite and for that very reason absolute guilt, which weighs down on the subject delivered from the rule of Destiny, is the ultimate object of psychoanalysis, since it lies at the root of all forms of 'psychopathology'. In this precise sense, Lacan maintains that the subject of psychoanalysis is the Cartesian subject of modern science, i.e., the subject characterized by permanent nervous strain and discontent, which come from the lack of support in the big Other of Destiny. Is not the ultimate proof of the pertinence of Lacan's reversal of Dostoevsky the shift from the Law *qua* Prohibition to the rule of 'norms' or 'ideals' we are witnessing today? In all domains of our everyday lives, from eating habits to sexual behaviour and professional success, there are fewer and fewer prohibitions, and more and more norms-ideals to follow. The suspended Law-Prohibition re-emerges in the guise of the ferocious superego that fills the subject with guilt the moment his performance is found lacking with respect to the norm or ideal. Therein resides the lesson of Catholicism much appreciated by Lacan: the function of a clear and explicit external prohibition is not to make us guilty but, on the contrary, to relieve the unbearable pressure of the guilt which weighs upon us when the Prohibition fails to intervene. In our late capitalist universe, the subject is not guilty when he infringes a prohibition. It is far more likely that he feels guilty when (or, rather, because) he is not happy – the command to be happy is perhaps the ultimate superego injunction.

This story about happiness begins with the French Revolution. To what, precisely, does Saint-Just's statement that happiness is a political factor amount? The point is not simply that now that people have escaped the yoke of tyranny they have the right to be happy, and that the new State has the obligation to work for the happiness of its subjects. What lurks behind is a potential 'totalitarian' inversion: it is your *duty* to be happy. If, in the midst of the Revolution when such unheard-of events take place, you are unhappy, it means that you are a counter-revolutionary traitor. Robespierre was the unsurpassed expert at manipulating this guilt of feeling unhappy and ill at ease. In one of his great speeches, after scaring the life out of the members of the National Assembly by claiming that there were numerous traitors among them (nobody could be sure that they were not on his list), Robespierre continued, 'If, at this very moment, anyone in this hall feels frightened, this is irrefutable proof that he is a traitor!' What we are dealing with here is not merely the variation on the well-known theme of 'If you're not guilty, you have nothing to fear!', but also a masterful manipulation of the audience's *desire*: the guilt Robespierre refers to is ultimately guilt of nourishing a perverse desire which makes us resist our own true happiness – in short, the guilt for having a desire *tout court*.

Robespierre's implicit reasoning could also be formulated as follows: the subject who reacts with fear at his accusation that there are traitors in the room thereby gives preference to his individual safety and well-being over the well-being and freedom of the French people, i.e., over the revolutionary Cause. And this attitude in itself is already treacherous: it is treason at its purest, a form of treason prior to any determinate treacherous act. The same logic is at work in the Stalinist's insistence that the accused at the political trial who claims that they are innocent is guilty even if their protestations of innocence are true at the level of facts. By focusing on their individual destiny, they display total indifference to the proletarian Cause, and to the fact that their protestations of innocence seriously undermine the authority of the Party and thereby weaken its unity: in this bourgeois-individualist attitude resides their true guilt.

VI

Incidentally, Slovene literature offers an example which is in no way lacking when compared with Claudel. France Prešeren's *Baptism at Savica* is an epic poem from the 1840s about the ninth-century violent Christianization of the Slovenes. According to the mythical narrative of origins, this poem 'founded' the Slovene nation. The truth is that, up till now, at least, every Slovene schoolboy has had to learn it by heart. A prologue first describes the heroic struggle of the last pagan Slovenes: the place of their last stand is a mountain castle surrounded by Christians. In a sanguinary night battle, they are all slaughtered, with the sole exception of Črtomir, their young leader. Taking advantage of the confusion of the night to slip away, he takes refuge in an isolated pagan sanctuary run by the beautiful priestess Bogomila, his great love. Here, however, a bad surprise awaits Črtomir. While he was fighting his battles, Bogomila has been converted to Christianity. She now tries passionately to persuade him to be baptized himself – the two of them can be united only in Christ. His love for her is so strong that, on its account, he is ready to renounce the pagan mores which form the very substance of his being. However, after Črtomir nods his agreement, expecting that in this way he will win her, he discovers there is another turn of the screw to the affair. Bogomila now asks him to renounce carnal love for her: if he truly loves her, he must accept what matters to her most, a chaste life in the service of Christ. How does Črtomir break down for the second time and renounce Bogomila herself? In Lacanese, how does he fully assume symbolic castration? What intervenes at this precise point is the fascinating image: Črtomir looks at Bogomila and is struck by the beatitude of her heavenly image. The moment this image casts its spell over him, he is lost. This image is the lure *par excellence*, the place-holder of lack, or, in Lacanese, the *objet petit a* (object-cause of desire) standing over minus phi (castration). 'Castration' is generally presented in the guise of a fascinating image. The final scene: the totally broken Črtomir undergoes the ceremony of baptism at the waterfall of Savica, in what are now the Slovene Alps. The last lines of the poem tersely report that, immediately after his baptism, Črtomir went to L'Áquila (a city in what is now northern Italy); that he was trained as a missionary; and that he devoted his remaining days to the conversion of pagans to Christianity. He and Bogomila never again saw each other in this world.

In Slovene literary theory and criticism, this poem has given rise to two opposed series of interpretations. 'Leftist' readings focus on the Prologue and assert the heroic resistance to the violent imposition of a foreign religion – Črtomir as a forerunner of contemporary struggles for national independence. 'Rightist' readings take Christianization at its face value and claim that the ultimate message of the poem is hope, not despair – at the end, Črtomir finds inner peace in Christ. Both series miss the subjective position of Črtomir at the poem's end, which, of course, is precisely that of *Versagung*: after renouncing everything that matters to him, his ethnic roots, the very substance of his social being, for the sake of his love, Črtomir is led to renounce the fulfilment of this love itself, so that he finds himself 'beyond the second death', reduced to a shell of his former self and forced to propagate a faith he himself doesn't believe in. One of the pop-psychological clichés about the so-called 'Slovene national character' is that this subjective position of Črtomir epitomizes the proverbial compromising, irresolute, self-hindered character-structure of a typical Slovene. Instead of making a clear choice and assuming all its consequences (which means, in this case, either sticking to our particular ethnic roots whatever it may cost or wholeheartedly embracing the new universal Christian order), a typical Slovene prefers the undecided intermediate state – Christianity, yes, but not quite; let us keep our fingers crossed and maintain an inner distance; better a finger crossed than a finger burnt ... The problem, however, is that the intersection of the two sets, the particular (one's ethnic roots) and the universal (Christianity), is empty, so that if one chooses the intersection, one loses all – and the name of this radical loss, of course, is 'subject'. In other words, the modern subject is strictly correlative with the dimension 'beyond the second death'. The first death is the sacrifice of our particular, 'pathological' substance for the universal Cause; the second death is the sacrifice, the 'betrayal', of this Cause itself, so that all that remains is the void which is $, the 'barred' subject. The subject only emerges via this double, self-relating sacrifice of the very Cause for which he was ready to sacrifice everything. Perhaps the fundamental fantasy of Modernity concerns the possibility of a 'synthesis' of the Particular and the Universal – the dream of a (universal) language permeated by (particular) passions; of universal-formal Reason permeated by the substance of a concrete life-world, etc. In short, fantasy *fills out the empty set of the intersection*: its wager is that this set is *not* empty. One of the ironies of our intellectual life is that, in the eyes of philosophical *doxa*, Hegel – the very philosopher who articulated the logic of the 'sacrifice of the sacrifice' – is considered the paradigmatic representative of this fantasy. Kierkegaard, Preeren's contemporary and Hegel's great opponent, is in this respect uncannily close to Hegel. Does not the Kierkegaardian notion of the Religious involve a strictly homologous gesture of double, self-relating sacrifice? First, one has to renounce the particular 'aesthetic' content for the sake of the universal ethical Law; then, Faith compels us to suspend this Law itself.

This is the trap into which Claudel's Sygne and Preeren's Črtomir get caught: they both abstractly oppose the Thing itself (for Sygne, the Christian religion; for Črtomir, his love for Bogomila) to the particular life-context within which only this Thing can thrive (Sygne's attachment to the family estate and feudal tradition; Črtomir's roots in the old pagan life-world). That is, they both fail to note how their renunciation of the particular content on behalf of the Thing itself effectively amounts to a renunciation of this Thing itself.

(Against this background, one can also elucidate the strategy of a ruthless and perspicacious interrogator's effort to break down the resistance of his victim and to wrest from him a confession that compromises his principles. He begins with inducing his victim to give way with regard to some particular point which seems in no way to jeopardize his principles. Then, after extracting from the victim a sufficient number of these 'inessential' concessions, the interrogator has only to remind him that the game is already over and that it's time to drop the false pretences. The victim's high principles have long ago been compromised, so why shouldn't we call things by their proper name? The trap in which the victim gets caught consisted in his illusory belief that the universal Essence, the Thing he really cares about, can persist outside the network of 'inessential' concrete circumstances.)

In Hegelian terms, Sygne and Črtomir both cling to the illusory belief that the Thing (the true Universal) can somehow persist, retain its consistency, outside its concrete conditions of existence. (That Christian religion can retain its meaning outside the *ancien régime*, in new, post-revolutionary conditions . . .) Therein resides the 'existential' kernel of the Hegelian 'negation of negation'. The subject has to experience how the negation (sacrifice) of particular content on behalf of the Thing is already the negation-sacrifice of the Thing, i.e., of that on behalf of which the particular content is sacrificed. In Claudel, the Thing – Christianity – survives, but as a mere lifeless shell of itself, bereft of its life-substance. In Preeren, Črtomir survives as a shell of his former self, bereft of his substantial content – in short, as a *subject*.

(At a somewhat different level, the same goes for every attempt to 'accommodate' psychoanalysis to particular circumstances. Suffice it to recall Jung's infamous advice to Freud, on the ocean-liner approaching New York, to avoid excessive emphasizing of sexuality in order to render psychoanalysis more acceptable to puritan Americans, and Freud's bitter reply that if they leave out even more of its content, psychoanalysis will become all the more acceptable. The fate of psychoanalysis in America, where it has survived as the lifeless shell of its true content, of course, fully justified Freud's rejection of such 'tactical concessions'.)

It is only through such a double movement of the 'sacrifice of the sacrifice', which bereaves the subject of its entire substantial content, that the pure subject *qua* $ emerges, i.e., that we pass from Substance to Subject.

NOTES

Originally published as 'Prolegomena to a Future Answer to Dr. Butler', *Agenda: Australian Contemporary Art* 44, 1995, pp. 45–67. This article was written in response to a series of questions that Rex Butler posed to Žižek following a series of public lectures delivered at

the Eighth Annual Conference of the Australian Centre for Psychoanalysis in the Freudian Field, Melbourne, 13 August 1994 (Žižek's
second lecture is reprinted in Chapter 4 of this volume, 'Connections
of the Freudian Field to Philosophy and Popular Culture'). These
questions appeared in *Agenda* 44, pp. 68–70 [eds].

1   Jacques Derrida, 'Le facteur de la vérité', in *The Post Card: From
    Socrates to Freud and Beyond*, trans. Alan Bass, Chicago,
    University of Chicago Press, 1987, pp. 413–96 [eds].
2   Žižek is referring here to Bernard Baas, 'Das öffentliche Ding', in
    Ethik und psychoanalyse, ed. Hans-Dieter Gondek and Peter
    Widmer, Frankfurt, Fisher, 1994 [eds].
3   Jacques Derrida, *Of Grammatology*, trans. Gayatri Chakravorty
    Spivak, Baltimore, Johns Hopkins University Press, 1974, pp. 68–9
    [eds].
4   Jacques Lacan, *Le séminaire de Jacques Lacan VIII: Le transfert,
    1960–61* 2nd edn, ed. Jacques-Alain Miller, Paris, Éditions du
    Seuil, 2001, pp. 315–86 [eds].
5   *Ibid.*, pp. 329–30 [eds].
6   *Ibid.*, p. 359 [eds].
7   *Ibid.*, p. 359 [eds].
8   *Ibid.*, pp. 359–60 [eds].
9   Jacques Lacan, *The Seminar of Jacques Lacan II: The Ego in
    Freud's Theory and in the Technique of Psychoanalysis, 1954–55*,
    ed. Jacques-Alain Miller, trans. Sylvana Tomaselli, Cambridge,
    Cambridge University Press, 1988, p. 128 [eds].

10 The Parallax View

When Jean Laplanche elaborates the impasses of the Freudian topic of seduction, does he not effectively reproduce the precise structure of a Kantian antinomy? On the one hand, there is the brutal empirical realism of the parental seduction: the ultimate cause of later traumas and pathologies is that children effectively were seduced and molested by adults; on the other hand, there is the (in)famous reduction of the seduction scene to the patient's fantasy. As Laplanche points out, the ultimate irony is that the dismissal of seduction as fantasy passes today for the 'realistic' stance, while those who insist on the reality of seduction end up advocating all kind of molestations, up to satanic rites and extra-terrestrial harassments ... Laplanche's solution is precisely the transcendental one: while 'seduction' *cannot* be reduced merely to the subject's fantasy, while it *does* refer to a traumatic encounter of the other's 'enigmatic message' bearing witness to the other's unconscious, it *also* cannot be reduced to an event in the reality of the actual interaction between a child and his/her adults. Seduction is rather a kind of transcendental structure, the minimal a priori formal constellation of the child confronted with the impenetrable acts of the Other which bear witness to the Other's unconscious. Neither are we dealing here with simple 'facts', but always with facts located in the indeterminate space between 'too soon' and 'too late': the child is originally helpless, thrown into the world while unable to take care of itself, i.e., his/her survival skills develop too late; at the same time, the encounter of the sexualized Other always, by a structural necessity, comes 'too soon', as an unexpected shock which cannot ever be properly symbolized, translated into the universe of meaning.[1] The fact of seduction is thus that of the Kantian transcendental X – a structurally necessary transcendental illusion.

In his formidable *Transcritique: On Kant and Marx*,[2] Kojin Karatani endeavours to assert the critical potential of such an in-between stance that he calls the 'parallax view': when confronted with an antinomy in the precise Kantian sense of the term, one should renounce all attempts to reduce one aspect to the other (or, for that matter, to enact a kind of 'dialectical synthesis' of the opposites). One should, on the contrary, assert the antinomy as irreducible, and conceive the point of radical critique not as a certain determinate position as opposed to another position, but as the irreducible gap between the positions themselves, the purely structural interstice between them.[3] Kant's stance is thus 'to see things neither from his own viewpoint, nor from the viewpoint of others, but to face the reality that is exposed through difference (parallax)'.[4] (Is this not Karatani's way of asserting the Lacanian Real as a pure antagonism, as an impossible difference which precedes its terms?) Karatani reads in this way the Kantian notion of the *Ding an sich* (the Thing-in-itself, beyond phenomena): this Thing is not simply a transcendental entity beyond our grasp, but something discernible only via the irreducibly antinomic character of our experience of reality. (And, as René Girard pointed out, the first full assertion of the ethical parallax is the Book of Job,[5] in which the two perspectives – the divine order of the world and Job's complaint – are contrasted, and neither is the 'truthful' one; the truth resides in their very gap, in the shift of perspective.)

Let us take Kant's confrontation with the epistemological antinomy which characterized his epoch: empiricism versus rationalism. Kant's solution is neither to chose one of the terms, nor to enact a kind of higher 'synthesis' which would 'sublate' the two as unilateral, as partial moments of a global truth (nor, of course, does he withdraw to pure scepticism); the stake of his 'transcendental turn' is precisely to avoid the need to formulate one's own 'positive' solution. What Kant does is to change the very terms of the debate. His solution – the transcendental turn – is unique in that it rejects any ontological closure: it recognizes the fundamental and irreducible limitation ('finitude') of the human condition, which is why the two poles – rational and sensual, active and passive – can never be fully mediated/ reconciled; the 'synthesis' of the two dimensions (i.e., the fact that our Reason seems to fit the structure of external reality that affects us) always relies on a certain *salto mortale* or 'leap of faith'. Far from designating a 'synthesis' of the two dimensions, the Kantian 'transcendental' rather stands for their irreducible gap 'as such': the 'transcendental' points at something in this gap, a new dimension which cannot be reduced to either of the two positive terms. Kant does the same with regard to the antinomy between the Cartesian *cogito* as *res cogitans* [the 'thinking substance'], a self-identical positive entity, and Hume's dissolution of the subject in the multitude of fleeting impressions: against both positions, he asserts the subject of transcendental apperception which, while displaying a self-reflective unity irreducible to the empirical multitude, nonetheless lacks any substantial positive being, i.e., it is in no way a *res cogitans*. Here, however, one should be more precise than Karatani, who directly identifies the transcendental subject with transcendental illusion:

> Yes, an ego is just an illusion, but functioning there is the transcendental apperception X. But what one knows as metaphysics is that which considers the X as something substantial. Nevertheless, one cannot really escape from the drive [*Trieb*] to take it as an empirical substance in various contexts. If so, it is possible to say that an ego is just an illusion, but a transcendental illusion.[6]

However, the precise status of the transcendental subject is not that of what Kant calls a transcendental illusion or what Marx calls the objectively necessary form of thought.[7] The transcendental I of pure apperception is a purely formal function which is neither noumenal nor phenomenal – it is empty, no phenomenal intuition corresponds to it since, if it were to appear to itself, its self-appearance would be the 'thing itself', i.e., the direct self-transparency of a noumenon.[8] The parallel between the void of the transcendental subject ($) and the void of the transcendental object – the inaccessible X that causes our perceptions – is misleading here: the transcendental object is the void *beyond* phenomenal appearances, while the transcendental subject *already appears as a void*.[9] Perhaps the best way to demonstrate the Kantian break with respect to this new dimension is by means of the changed status of the notion of the 'inhuman'. Kant introduced a key distinction between negative and indefinite judgement: the positive judgement 'the soul is mortal' can be negated when a predicate is denied to the subject ('the soul is not mortal') and when a non-predicate is affirmed ('the soul is non-mortal') – the difference is exactly the same as the one, known to every reader of Stephen King, between 'he is not dead' and 'he is un-dead'. The indefinite judgement, on the contrary, opens up a third domain which undermines the underlying distinction: the 'undead' are neither alive nor dead, they are precisely the monstrous 'living dead'.[10] And the same goes for 'inhuman': 'he is not human' is not the same as 'he is inhuman' – 'he is not human' means simply that he is external to humanity, animal or divine, while 'he is inhuman' means something thoroughly different, namely the fact that he is neither human nor inhuman, but marked by a terrifying excess which, although it negates what we understand as 'humanity', is inherent to being-human. And, perhaps, one should risk the hypothesis that *this* is the break signalled by the Kantian revolution: in the pre-Kantian universe, humans were simply humans, beings of reason, fighting the excesses of animal lusts and divine madness; with Kant and German Idealism, the excess to be fought is absolutely immanent, the very core of subjectivity itself (which is why, in German Idealism, the metaphor for the core of subjectivity is Night – 'Night of the World' – in contrast to the Enlightenment notion of the Light of Reason fighting the surrounding darkness). So when, in the pre-Kantian universe, a hero goes mad, it means he is deprived of his humanity – i.e., the animal passions or divine madness took over – while after Kant, madness signals the unconstrained explosion of the very core of a human being.

What, then, is this new dimension that emerges in the gap itself? It is that of the transcendental I itself, its irreducible 'spontaneity': the ultimate parallax, the third space between the phenomenal and the noumenal, is the subject's freedom/spontaneity, which – though not the property of a phenomenal entity, so that it cannot be dismissed as a false appearance which conceals the noumenal fact that we are totally caught in an inaccessible necessity – is also not simply noumenal. In a mysterious subchapter of his *Critique of Practical Reason*, entitled 'Of the Wise Adaptation of the Human Being's Cognitive Faculties to His Practical Vocation', Kant endeavours to answer the question of what would happen to us if we were to gain access to the noumenal domain, to the *Ding an sich*:

[I]nstead of the conflict that the moral disposition now has to carry on with the inclinations, in which, though after some defeats, moral strength of soul is to be gradually acquired, *God and eternity with their awful majesty* would stand unceasingly *before our eyes ...* [H]ence most actions conforming to the law would be done from fear, only a few from hope, and none at all from duty, and the moral worth of actions, on which alone in the eyes of supreme wisdom the worth of the person and even that of the world depends, would not exist at all. As long as human nature remains as it is, human conduct would thus be changed into mere mechanism in which, as in a puppet show, everything would *gesticulate* well but there would be *no life* in the figures.[11]

In short, the direct access to the noumenal domain would deprive us of the very 'spontaneity' which forms the kernel of transcendental freedom: it would turn us into lifeless automata, or, to put it in today's terms, into 'thinking machines'. The implication of this passage is much more radical and paradoxical than it may appear. If we discard its inconsistency (how could fear and lifeless gesticulation co-exist?), the conclusion it imposes is that, at both the phenomenal and nou-menal level, we – humans – are 'mere mechanisms' with no autonomy and freedom: as phenomena, we are not free, we are a part of nature, totally submitted to causal links, a part of the nexus of causes and effects; as noumena, we are again not free, but reduced to a 'mere mechanism'. (Isn't what Kant describes as a person who directly knows the noumenal domain strictly homologous to the utilitarian subject whose acts are fully determined by the calculus of pleasures and pains?) *Our freedom persists only in a space in between the phenomenal and the noumenal.* Clearly, then, Kant did not simply limit causality to the phenomenal domain in order to be able to assert that, at the noumenal level, we are free autonomous agents; instead, we are only free insofar as our horizon is that of the phenomenal, insofar as the noumenal domain remains inaccessible to us. Can we escape this predicament merely by asserting that we are free insofar as we *are* noumenally autonomous, *but* nonetheless our cognitive perspective remains constrained by the phenomenal? In this case, our noumenal freedom would be rendered meaningless if we were also to have cognitive insight into the noumenal domain, since that very insight would always determine our choices – who *would* choose evil when confronted with the fact that the price of doing so is divine punishment? But doesn't this case consequently provide us with the only legitimate answer to the question 'What would be a truly free act?', an act of true *noumenal* freedom? It would be to *know* all the inexorable consequences of choosing evil, *and nonetheless to choose it*. This would have been a truly 'nonpathological' act. Kant's own formulations are here misleading, since he often identifies the transcendental subject with the noumenal I whose phenomenal appearance is the empirical 'person', thus shirking away from his radical insight that the transcendental subject is a pure formal-structural function beyond the opposition of the noumenal and the phenomenal.

This displacement of freedom from the noumenal to the very gap between phenomenal and noumenal brings us back to the complex relationship between Kant and Hegel: is this not also the very shift from Kant to Hegel, from the tension between immanence and transcendence to the minimal difference/gap in immanence itself? Hegel is thus not external to Kant: the problem with Kant was that he effected the shift but was not able, for structural reasons, to formulate it explicitly; he 'knew' that the place of freedom is effectively not noumenal, but could not formulate it explicitly since, if he were to do so, his transcendental edifice would have collapsed. However, *without* this implicit 'knowledge', there would also have been no transcendental dimension, so that one is forced to conclude that, far from being a stable consistent position, the Kantian 'transcendental' can only sustain itself in a fragile balance between the said and the unsaid, by producing something the full consequences of which we refuse to articulate, to 'posit as such'. (The same goes for the Kantian dialectic of the Sublime: there is no positive 'Beyond' whose phenomenal representation fails; there is nothing 'beyond'; the 'Beyond' is only the void of the impossibility/failure of its own representation – or, as Hegel put it at the end of the chapter on consciousness in his *Phenomenology of Spirit*, beyond the veil of the phenomena, consciousness only finds what it itself has placed there.[12] Again, Kant 'knew it' without being able consistently to formulate it.)

According to Karatani, Marx, in his 'critique of political economy', when faced with the opposition of the 'classical' political economy (Ricardo and his labour-theory of value – the counterpart to philosophical rationalism) and the neo-classical reduction of value to a purely relational entity without substance (Bailey – the counterpart to philosophical empiricism), accomplished exactly the same breakthrough towards the 'parallax' view: he treated this opposition as a Kantian antinomy, i.e., value has to originate outside circulation, in production, *and* in circulation. The post-Marx 'Marxism' – in both its versions, Social Democratic and Communist – lost this 'parallax' perspective and regressed into the unilateral elevation of production as the site of truth against the 'illusory' sphere of exchange and consumption. As he emphasizes, even the most sophisticated formulations of commodity fetishism – from the young Lukács through Adorno up to Fredric Jameson – fall into this trap: the way they account for the lack of revolutionary movement is that the consciousness of workers is obfuscated by the seductions of consumerist society and/or manipulation by the ideological forces of cultural hegemony, which is why the focus of the critical work should shift to 'cultural criticism' (the so-called 'cultural turn') – the disclosure of ideological (or libidinal[13]) mechanisms which keep the workers under the spell of bourgeois ideology. In a close reading of Marx's analysis of the commodity-form, Karatani grounds the insurmountable persistence of the parallax gap in the *salto mortale* that a product has to accomplish in order to assert itself as a commodity:

The price [of iron expressed in gold], while on the one hand indicating the amount of labour-time contained in the iron, namely its value, at the same time signifies the pious wish to convert the iron into gold, that is to give the labour-time contained in the iron the form of universal social labour-time. If this transformation fails to take place, then the ton of iron ceases to be not only a commodity but also a product; since it is a commodity only because it is not a use-value for its owner, that is to say his labour is only really labour if it is useful labour for others, and it is useful for him only if it is abstract general labour. It is therefore the task of the iron or of its owner to find that location in the world of commodities where iron attracts gold. But if the sale actually takes place, as we assume in this analysis of simple circulation, then this difficulty, the *salto mortale* of the commodity, is surmounted. As a result of this alienation – that is its transfer from the person for whom it is a non-use-value to the person for whom it is a use-value – the ton of iron proves to be in fact a use-value and its price is simultaneously realised, and merely imaginary gold is converted into real gold.[14]

This jump by means of which a commodity is sold and thus effectively constituted as commodity is not the result of an immanent self-development of (the concept of) Value, but a *salto mortale* comparable to the Kierkegaardian leap of faith, a temporary fragile 'synthesis' between use-value and exchange-value comparable to the Kantian synthesis between sensitivity and understanding: in both cases, the two irreducibly external levels are brought together. For this precise reason, Marx abandoned his original project (discernible in the *Grundrisse* manuscripts) of 'deducing' in a Hegelian way the split between exchange-value and use-value from the very concept of Value: in *Capital*, the split of these two dimensions, the 'dual character of a merchandise', is the starting point. The synthesis had to rely on an irreducibly external element, as in Kant where being is not a predicate (i.e., cannot be reduced to a conceptual predicate of an entity), or as in Saul Kripke's *Naming and Necessity*, in which the reference of a name to an object cannot be grounded in the content of this name, in the properties it designates.[15]

The very tension between the processes of production and circulation is thus that of a parallax: yes, value is created in the production process, but only, as it were, potentially, since it is *actualized* as value when the produced commodity is sold and the circle 'M–C–M' is completed. What is crucial is this temporal *gap* between the production of value and its actualization: even if value is produced in production, without the successful completion of the process of circulation there is *stricto sensu* no value. The temporality is here the *futur antérieur*, i.e., value 'is' not immediately, it only 'will have been', it is retroactively actualized, performatively enacted. Or, in Hegelian terms, value is generated 'in itself' in production, but it is only through the completed process of circulation that it becomes 'for itself'. This is how Karatani resolves the Kantian antinomy of value which is *and* is not generated in the process of production – it is generated there only

'in itself' – and it is because of this gap between the in- and for-itself
that capitalism needs formal democracy and equality:

> What precisely distinguishes capital from the master–slave relation
> is that the *worker* confronts him as consumer and possessor of
> exchange values, and that in the form of the *possessor of money*, in
> the form of money he becomes a simple centre of circulation – one
> of its infinitely many centres, in which his specificity as worker is
> extinguished.[16]

What this means is that, in order to complete the circle of its
reproduction, Capital has to pass through this critical point at which
the roles are inverted: 'surplus value is realized in principle only by
workers *in totality* buying back what they produce'.[17] This is crucial
for Karatani because it provides the key leverage point from which to
oppose the rule of Capital today: is it not natural that the proletarians
should focus their attack on that unique point at which they approach
Capital from the position of buyers, and, consequently, at which
it is Capital which is forced to court them? '[I]f workers can become
subjects at all, it is only as consumers.'[18] This is perhaps the ultimate
example of the parallax situation: the position of worker-producer
and that of consumer should be sustained as irreducible in their
divergence, without privileging one as the 'deeper truth' of the other.
(And, incidentally, did not the planned economy of State Socialism pay
a terrible price for privileging production at the expense of consumption precisely by its failure to provide consumers with unneeded
goods, by producing projects which nobody needed and wanted?)
This brings us to Karatani's key motif: one should thoroughly reject
the (proto-Fascist, if anything) opposition of the financial-speculative
profiteering capital to the 'substantial' economy of capitalists engaged
in productive activity: in capitalism, the process of production is only
a detour in the speculative process of money engendering more
money – i.e., the profiteering logic is ultimately also what sustains the
incessant drive to revolutionize and expand production:

> The majority of economists warn today that the speculation of
> global financial capital is detached from the 'substantial' economy.
> What they overlook, however, is that the substantial economy as

such is also driven by illusion, and that such is the nature of the capitalist economy.[19]

There are, consequently, four basic positions apropos of money: (1) the mercantilist one – a direct naïve fetishist belief in money as a 'special thing'; (2) the 'classical bourgeois political economy' embodied in Ricardo, which dismissed money-fetishism as a mere illusion and perceived money as a mere sign of the quantity of socially useful labour – value was here conceived as inherent to a commodity; (3) the 'neo-classical' school which rejected the labour-theory of value and also any 'substantial' notion of value – for it, the price of a commodity is simply the result of the interplay of offer and demand, i.e., of the commodities' usefulness with regard to other commodities. Finally, Karatani is right to emphasize how, paradoxically, Marx broke out of the confines of the 'classical' labour-theory of value – (2) above – through his reading of Bailey, the first 'vulgar' economist who emphasized the purely *relational* status of value: value is not inherent to a commodity, but rather expresses the way this commodity relates to all other commodities. Bailey in this way opened up the path towards (4) the structural approach of Marx, which insists on the gap between an object and the formal place it occupies: in the same way that a king is a king not because of his inherent properties, but because people treat him as one (Marx's own example), a commodity is money because it occupies the formal place of the general equivalent of all commodities, not because, say, gold is 'naturally' money. But it is crucial to take note of how both mercantilists and their Ricardoan critics remain 'substantialist': Ricardo was, of course, aware that the object which serves as money is not 'naturally' money, and he laughed at the naïve superstition of money and dismissed mercantilists as primitive believers in magic properties; however, by reducing money to a secondary external sign of the value inherent to a commodity, he nonetheless again naturalized value, conceiving of it is a direct 'substantial' property of a commodity. This illusion opened up the way for the naïve early-Socialist and Proudhonian practical proposal to overcome the money fetishism by way of introducing a direct 'labour money' which would simply designate the amount each individual contributed to social labour.

This is why, although Marx's *Darstellung* of the self-deployment of Capital is full of Hegelian references,[20] the self-movement of Capital is far from the circular self-movement of the Hegelian Notion (or Spirit): Marx's point is that this movement never catches up with itself, that it never recovers its credit, that its resolution is postponed forever, that the crisis is its innermost constituent (the sign that the Whole of Capital is the non-True, as Adorno would have put it), which is why the movement is one of the 'spurious infinity', forever reproducing itself:

> Notwithstanding the Hegelian descriptive style *Capital* distinguishes itself from Hegel's philosophy in its motivation. The end of *Capital* is never the 'absolute Spirit'. *Capital* reveals the fact that capital, though organizing the world, can never go beyond its own limit. It is a Kantian critique of the ill-contained drive of capital/ reason to self-realize beyond its limit.[21]

It is interesting to note that it was already Adorno who, in his *Three Studies on Hegel*, critically characterized Hegel's system in the same 'financial' terms as a system which lives on a credit that it can never pay off.[22] The same 'financial' metaphor is often used for language itself; among others, Brian Rotman determined meaning as something which is always 'borrowed from the future', relying on its forever-postponed fulfilment-to-come.[23] But, on this very question of language, how does shared meaning emerge? The answer is what Alfred Schütz called 'mutual idealization': the subject cuts the impasse of the endless probing into 'do we all mean the same thing by "bird"?' by simply taking for granted, presupposing, acting *as if* we *do* mean the same thing. There is no language without this 'leap of faith'. This presupposition, this 'leap of faith', should not be conceived, in the Habermasian vein, as the normativity built into the functioning of language, as the ideal speakers (should) strive for: far from being an ideal, this presupposition is the fiction, the *as if*, that sustains language – as such, it should be undermined again and again in the progress of knowledge. So, if anything, this presupposed *as if* is profoundly anti-normative. To this, a Habermasian may reply that the ideal, the norm inscribed into language, is nonetheless the state in which this fiction would no longer be a fiction, i.e., in which, in smooth communication, subjects would effectively mean the same thing. However, this reproach misses the point; it is not only that such a state is inaccessible (and also undesirable), but that the very 'leap of faith' by means of which the subjects take for granted that they mean the same thing not only has no normative content, but can even block further elaboration – why strive for something that we allegedly already have? In other words, what this understanding of the *as if* as normativity misses is that the 'leap of faith' is necessary and productive (enabling communication) precisely insofar as it is a counterfactual fiction: its 'truth effect', its positive role of enabling communication, hinges precisely on the fact that it is *not* true, that it jumps ahead into fiction – its status is not normative because it cuts the debilitating deadlock of language, because of its ultimate lack of guarantee, by *presenting what we should strive for as already accomplished.*

The same logic of living off the credit borrowed from the future also goes for Stalinism. The standard evolutionary version is that, while Stalinist socialism did play a certain role in enabling the rapid industrialization of Russia, starting with the mid-1960s, the system obviously exhausted its potentials; however, what this judgement fails to take into account is the fact that the entire epoch of Soviet Communism from 1917 (or, more precisely, from Stalin's proclamation of the goal to 'build socialism in one country' in 1924) lived on borrowed time, was 'indebted to its own future', so that the final failure retroactively disqualified the earlier epochs themselves.

Is, however, the ultimate Marxian parallax not the one between economy and politics, between the 'critique of political economy' with its logic of commodities and the political struggle with its logic of antagonism? Both logics are 'transcendental', not merely ontico-empirical, and they are both irreducible to each other. Of course they both point towards each other (class struggle is inscribed into the very heart of economy, yet has to remain absent, non-thematized – recall how the manuscript of *Capital III* abruptly ends with class struggle, and class struggle itself is ultimately 'about' economic power-relations[24]), but this very mutual implication is twisted so that it prevents any direct contact (any direct translation of political struggle into a mere mirroring of economic 'interests' is doomed to fail, as well as any reduction of the sphere of economic production to a secondary 'reified' sedimentation of an underlying founding political process).

Thus the 'pure politics' of Badiou, Rancière and Balibar – more Jacobin than Marxist – shares with its great opponent, Anglo-Saxon Cultural Studies and their focus on the struggles for recognition, the degradation of the sphere of economy. That is to say, what all the new French (or French-oriented) theories of the Political, from Balibar through Rancière and Badiou to Laclau and Mouffe, aim at is – to put it in the traditional philosophical terms – the reduction of the sphere of economy (of the material production) to an 'ontic' sphere deprived of 'ontological' dignity. Within this horizon, there is simply no place for the Marxian 'critique of political economy': the structure of the universe of commodities and capital in Marx's *Capital* is *not* just that of a limited empirical sphere, but a kind of socio-transcendental *a priori*, a matrix which generates the totality of social and political relations. The relationship between economy and politics is ultimately that of the well-known visual paradox of the 'two faces or a vase': one either sees the two faces or a vase, never both of them – one has to make a choice. In the same way, one either focuses on the political, and the domain of economy is reduced to an empirical 'servicing of goods', or one focuses on economy, and politics is reduced to a theatre of appearances, to a passing phenomenon which will disappear with the arrival of a developed Communist (or technocratic) society, in which, as Engels already put it, the 'administration of people' will vanish in the 'administration of things'.

The 'political' critique of Marxism (the claim that, when one reduces politics to a 'formal' expression of some underlying 'objective' socio-economic process, one loses the openness and contingency constitutive of the political field proper) should thus be supplemented by its obverse: the field of economy is *in its very form* irreducible to politics – this level of the *form* of economy (of economy as the determining *form* of the social) is what French 'political post-Marxists' miss when they reduce economy to one of the positive social spheres.

The basic idea of the parallax view is that the very act of bracketing off produces its object – 'democracy' as a form emerges only when one brackets off the texture of economic relations as well as the inherent logic of the political state apparatus; they both have to be abstracted from people who are effectively embedded in economic processes and subjected to state apparatuses. The same goes also for the 'logic of domination', the way people are controlled/manipulated by the apparatuses of subjection: in order to clearly discern these mechanisms of power, one has to be abstracted not only from the democratic imaginary (as Foucault does in his analyses of the micro-physics of power, but also as Lacan does in his analysis of power in *Seminar XVII* [25]), but also from the process of economic (re)production. And, finally, the specific sphere of economic (re)production only emerges if one methodologically brackets off the concrete existence of state and political ideology – no wonder critics of Marx complained that Marx's 'critique of political economy' lacks a theory of power and state. And, of course, the trap to be avoided here is precisely the naïve idea that one should keep in view the social totality (parts of which are democratic ideology, the exercise of power and the process of economic (re)production): if one tries to keep the whole in view, one ends up seeing nothing, the contours disappear. This bracketing off is not only epistemological, but it concerns what Marx called the 'real abstraction': the abstraction from power and economic relations that is inscribed into the very actuality of the democratic process.

NOTES

1 See Jean Laplanche, *Life and Death in Psychoanalysis*, trans. Jeffrey Mehlman, Baltimore, The Johns Hopkins University Press, 1976, pp. 38–47.

2 See Kojin Karatani, *Transcritique: On Kant and Marx* (Cambridge MA, MIT Press, 2003.

3 A nice linguistic example of parallax is the different uses of 'pork' and 'pig' in modern English: 'pig' refers to an animal with which farmers deal, while 'pork' is the meat we consume. The class dimension is clear here: 'pig' is the old Saxon word, since Saxons were the underprivileged farmers, while 'pork' comes from French 'porque', used by the privileged Norman conquerors who mostly consumed the pigs raised by farmers.

4   Karatani, *Transcritique*, p. 3.

5   René Girard, *Job – The Victim of his People*, trans. Yvonne Freccero, London, Athlone Press, 1987 [eds].

6   Karatani, *Transcritique*, p. 6.

7   See, e.g., Karl Marx, *Capital: A Critique of Political Economy, Volume I*, trans. Ben Fowkes, London, Penguin/New Left Books, 1976, pp. 128, 166–7 [eds].

8   See Slavoj Žižek, *Tarrying With the Negative: Kant, Hegel, and the Critique of Ideology*, Durham, Duke University Press, 1993, pp. 15–18.

9   Doesn't the paradox of Kant's *Ding an sich* run along the same lines? It is, at one and the same time, the excess of receptivity over intellect (the unknowable external source of our passive sensible perceptions) *and* the purely intelligible contentless construct of an X without any support in our senses.

10 For a closer elaboration of this distinction, see Žižek, *Tarrying With the Negative*, pp. 108–14.

11 Immanuel Kant, *Critique of Practical Reason*, trans. Mary Gregor, Cambridge, Cambridge University Press, 1997, p. 122.

12 G. W. F. Hegel, *Phenomenology of Spirit*, trans. A. V. Miller, Oxford, Oxford University Press, 1977, p. 103 [eds].

13 It is here, of course, that the key role of psychoanalysis in western Marxism originates.

14 Karl Marx, 'A Contribution to the Critique of Political Economy', in *Collected Works*, Vol. 29, New York, International Publishers, 1976, p. 390.

15 Žižek further develops this point in *The Sublime Object of Ideology*, London and New York, Verso, 1989, pp. 87–92 [eds].

16 Karl Marx, *Grundrisse: Foundations of the Critique of Political Economy*, trans. Martin Nicolaus, Harmondsworth, Penguin, 1973, pp. 420–1.

17 Karatani, *Transcritique*, p. 20.

18 *Ibid.*, p. 290.

19 *Ibid.*, p. 241.

20 See, among others, Helmut Reichelt, *Zur logischen Struktur des Kapitalbegriffs*, Frankfurt, Fischer Verlag, 1969.

21 Karatani, *Transcritique*, p. 9.
22 'As if in a gigantic credit system, every individual piece is to be indebted to the other – nonidentical – and yet the whole is to be free of debt, identical.' Theodor Adorno, 'Skoteinos, or How to Read Hegel', in *Hegel: Three Studies*, trans. Shierry Weber Nicholsen, Cambridge MA, MIT Press, 1993, p. 147 [eds].
23 See Brian Rotman, *Signifying Nothing*, London, MacMillan, 1975.
24 Karl Marx, *Capital: A Critique of Political Economy, Volume III*, trans. David Fernbach, London, Penguin/New Left Books, 1981, pp. 1025–6 [eds].
25 See Jacques Lacan, *Le Séminaire de Jacques Lacan XVII: L'envers de la psychanalyse, 1969–70*, ed. Jacques-Alain Miller, Paris, Éditions du Seuil, 1991, esp. pp. 167–223 [eds].

Section III
THE FANTASY OF IDEOLOGY

11 Between Symbolic Fiction and Fantasmatic Spectre: Toward a Lacanian Theory of Ideology

In his movie version of Kafka's *The Trial,* Orson Welles accomplished an exemplary anti-obscurantist operation by way of reinterpreting the place and the function of the famous parable on 'the door of the Law'. In the film, we hear it twice: at the very beginning, it serves as a kind of prologue, read and accompanied by (faked) ancient engravings projected from lantern-slides; then, shortly before the end, it is told to Josef K., not by the priest (as in the novel) but by K.'s lawyer (played by Welles himself), who unexpectedly joins the priest and K. in the Cathedral. The action now takes a strange turn and diverges from Kafka's novel – even before the lawyer warms to his narrative, K. cuts him short: 'I've heard it. We've heard it all. The door was meant only for him.' What ensues is a painful dialogue between K. and the lawyer in which the lawyer advises K. to 'plead insanity' by claiming that he is persecuted by the idea of being the victim of the diabolical plot of a mysterious State agency. K., however, rejects the role of the victim offered to him by the lawyer: 'I don't pretend to be a martyr.' 'Not even a victim of society?' 'No, I'm not a victim, I'm a member of society ...' In his final outburst, K. then asserts that the true conspiracy (of Power) consists in the very attempt to persuade the subjects that they are victims of irrational impenetrable forces, that everything is crazy, that the world is absurd and meaningless. When K. thereupon leaves the Cathedral, two plainclothes policemen are already waiting for him; they take him to an abandoned building site and dynamite him. In the Welles version, the reason K. is killed is therefore the exact opposite of the reason implied in the novel – *he presents a threat to power the moment he unmasks, 'sees through', the fiction upon which the social link of the existing power structure is founded.*

Welles' reading of *The Trial* thus differs from both predominant approaches to Kafka, the obscurantist-religious as well as the naïve, enlightened humanist. According to the former, K. is effectively guilty: what makes him guilty is his very naïve protestation of innocence, his arrogant reliance on naïve-rational argumentation. The conservative message of this reading that perceives K. as the representative of the enlightened questioning of authority is unmistakeable: K. himself is the true nihilist who acts like the proverbial bull in the china shop – his confidence in public reason renders him totally blind to the Mystery of Power, to the true nature of bureaucracy. The Court appears to K. as a mysterious and obscene agency bombarding him with 'irrational' demands and accusations exclusively on account of K.'s distorted subjectivist perspective: as the priest in the Cathedral points out to K., the Court is in fact indifferent, it wants nothing from him ... For the opposite reading, Kafka is a deeply ambiguous writer who staged the fantasmatic support of the totalitarian bureaucratic machinery, yet was himself unable to resist its fatal attraction. Therein resides the uneasiness felt by many an 'enlightened' reader of Kafka: in the end, did he not participate in the infernal machinery he was describing, thereby strengthening its hold instead of breaking its spell?

Although it may seem that Welles aligns himself with the second reading, things are by no means so unequivocal: he as it were adds another turn of the screw by raising 'conspiracy' to the power of two – as K. puts it in the Welles version of his final outburst, the true conspiracy of Power resides in the very notion of conspiracy, in the notion of some mysterious Agency that 'pulls the strings' and effectively runs the show, that is to say, in the notion that, behind the visible, public Power, there is another obscene, invisible, 'crazy' power structure. This other, hidden Law acts the part of the 'Other of the Other' in the Lacanian sense, the part of the meta-guarantee of the consistency of the big Other (the symbolic order that regulates social life). The 'conspiracy-theory' provides a guarantee that the field of the big Other is not an inconsistent bricolage: its basic premise is that, behind the public Master (who, of course, is an impostor), there is a hidden Master who effectively keeps everything under control.

'Totalitarian' regimes were especially skilled in cultivating the myth of a secret parallel power, invisible and for that very reason all-powerful, a kind of 'organization within the organization' – KGB, Freemasons, or whatever – that compensated for the blatant inefficiency of the public, legal Power and thus assured the smooth operation of the social machine: this myth is not only in no way subversive, it serves as the ultimate support of Power. The perfect American counterpart to it is (the myth of) J. Edgar Hoover, the personification of the obscene 'other power' behind the President, the shadowy double of legitimate Power. He held on to power by means of secret files that allowed him to keep in check the entire political and power elite, whereas he himself regularly indulged in homosexual orgies dressed up as a woman ...

K.'s lawyer offers him, as a desperate last resort, this role of the martyr-victim of a hidden conspiracy; K., however, turns it down, being well aware that by accepting it he would walk into the most perfidious trap of Power. This obscene mirage of the Other Power brings into play the same fantasmatic space as the famous publicity spot for Smirnoff vodka, which also deftly manipulates the gap between reality and the 'other surface' of the fantasy space: the camera wanders around on the deck of a luxurious ocean-liner, placed behind the bottle of vodka on a tray carried by a waiter; every time it passes an object, we first see this object as it is in its everyday reality, and then, when, for a brief moment, the transparent glass of the bottle comes between our gaze and the object, we perceive it distorted in its fantasy dimension – two gentlemen in black evening attire become two penguins, the necklace around a lady's neck a living snake, stairs a set of piano keys, etc. The Court in Kafka's *Trial* possesses the same purely fantasmagorical existence; its predecessor is Klingsor's Castle in Wagner's *Parsifal*. Since its hold upon the subject is entirely fantasmatic, it is sufficient to break its spell via a gesture of distanciation and the Court or Castle falls to dust. Therein resides the political lesson of *Parsifal* and of Welles' *The Trial*: if we are to overcome the 'effective' social power, we have first to break its fantasmatic hold upon us.

To avoid the reproach of committing a *petitio principii* by resorting to an example from literary fiction in order to prove that violence emerges when a fiction is threatened, let us evoke another exemplary case of Evil which, although it has passed into fiction, originated in 'real life': the unfortunate Captain Bligh of the *Bounty*. We are dealing here with a true enigma: why was this exemplary officer, obsessed with the safety and health of his sailors, elevated into one of the archetypal figures of Evil in our popular culture? The successive changes in the predominant image of Bligh serve as the perfect index to the shifts in hegemonic ideology – each epoch had its own Bligh. Suffice it to mention the three principal cinema portraits: the decadently aristo-cratic Charles Laughton in the 1930s, the coldly bureaucratic Trevor Howard in the 1960s, the mentally tortured Anthony Hopkins in the 1980s.

Even more interesting than these vicissitudes is, however, the enigma of the origins: what did 'truly happen' on HMS *Bounty*? What was the 'true cause' of the mutiny?[1] Our first temptation, of course, is to propose a counter-myth to the official myth: Bligh was a severe, over-zealous and pedantic, yet profoundly fair and caring, captain of an impeccable personal integrity. The mutiny against him resulted from the coalition of the spoiled young officers of aristocratic descent annoyed by the fact that Bligh, their superior, was not a true gentleman, 'one of them', but of lower descent and equitable in dealing with ordinary sailors, and the lumpenproletarian sailors-criminals who were also disturbed by Bligh's sense of justice which led him to restrain their terrorizing of decent common sailors. His 'progressive' attitude, unusual for his time, was attested again when, two decades after the *Bounty* mutiny, in the only case of a military coup in all of English history, he was forcefully deposed as the Governor of New South Wales. The corrupt officers of New South Wales overthrew him because of his politics: Bligh threatened to break their illegal monopoly on the rum trade; after the prisoners had served their term, he endeavoured to integrate them into normal social life and even gave them employment in government agencies, etc.

This counter-myth, however, provides a much too simplified picture of the affair. The element of truth in it is that Bligh was perceived as 'not a true gentleman', as somebody who did have power (as the ship's commander, he had the right to make decisions and give orders, a right he took full advantage of), yet did not irradiate true authority (the charisma, the *je ne sais quoi*, that would arouse respect and make him into a natural leader). All descriptions converge on this point: Bligh was somehow 'stiff', lacking the sensitivity that tells a good leader when and how to apply rules, how to take into account the 'organic', spontaneous network of relations between his subordinates, etc. However, even this analysis is not precise enough: Bligh's mistake was not simply that of being insensitive to the concrete network of 'organic' relations among the sailors; his crucial limitation consisted in the fact that he was completely 'blind' to the structural function of the ritualized power relations among the sailors (the right of the older, more experienced sailors to humiliate the younger and inexperienced, to exploit them sexually, to submit them to ordeals, etc.). These rituals provided an ambiguous supplement to the public-legal power relations: they acted as their shadowy double, apparently transgressing and subverting them, yet actually serving as their ultimate support. Suffice it to mention the so-called 'crossing the line', an extremely cruel and humiliating ordeal to which were submitted those who were crossing the equator for the first time (tied to a rope, they were thrown into the ocean and trailed for hours, made to drink sea water, etc.):

It was that Line that divided [the world] into hemispheres, the equator. That Line marked entry into a topsy-turvy world – into an antipodes, a place of mirror opposites, where seasons were reversed, where even the unchanging heavens were different ...

Across time and between nationalities, the ceremonies differed, but their expressions had a common character. Firstly, they played out a reversed world in which for a time the true authority of the ship belonged to those who had already Crossed the Line, and not to any by right of their commissions or warrants or appointments ... A second common quality was that the theatre of the ceremony was always a grotesque satire on institutions and roles of power. The satire could be about the sacraments of the state – the accolade of a knight – or the sacraments of the Church – baptism by the priest. On English ships in the late eighteenth century the satire was of kingship and the power over life and death ...

The trial was full of insults, humiliations, injustices, erotic oaths, and compromising choices.[2]

Again, one must be attentive to the deeply ambiguous character of these rituals: they are a satire on legal institutions, an inversion of public Power, yet they are a transgression that consolidates what it transgresses. In his blindness to the stabilizing role of these rituals, Bligh prohibited them, or at least modified them by changing them into a harmless folkloristic exercise. Caught in the Enlightenment trap, Bligh was able to perceive only the brutal-inhuman aspect of this ritual ('of all customs it is the most brutal and inhuman', he wrote), not the satisfaction it brought about. Henningsen[3] found observers using the following words to describe the ceremony of 'Crossing the Line': ridiculous, childish, foolish, stupid, silly, ludicrous, bizarre, grotesque, crazy, repulsive, burlesque, profane, superstitious, shameless, outrageous, revolting, tiresome, dangerous, barbarous, brutal, cruel, coarse, rapacious, vindictive, riotous, licentious, mad – are not all these words eventually so many synonyms for enjoyment? The mutiny, the violence, broke out when Bligh interfered with this murky world of obscene rituals that served as the fantasmatic background of Power.

Our third example comes from 'real life' at its most brutal: acts of violence (torture and murder) in today's gold-digger communities in the Amazon basin.[4] We are dealing here with isolated communities in which it is possible to observe the logic of power relations and the eruption of violence in laboratory conditions, as it were. These communities consist of a dispersed multitude of individual gold-diggers; although nominally free entrepreneurs, they are all effectively dependent on the local merchant who monopolizes the trade in the area. The merchant sells them food and digging instruments as well as other utensils, and buys their nuggets; they are all heavily in debt to the merchant who does *not* want this debt to be recovered, since his entire power is based upon the permanent debt of his customers. Social relations in such a community are regulated by a double fiction, or, rather, by a paradoxical, overdetermined co-existence of two incompatible fictions. On the one hand, there is the fiction of equal exchange, as if a gold-digger and his merchant are two free subjects that meet on the market on equal terms. The obverse of it is the image of the monopolistic merchant as a patriarchal Master who takes care of his customers, the latter repaying him for this paternal care with respect and love.[5] Beneath this contradictory fiction there is, of course, the reality of the merchant's monopoly, of his brutal exploitation. The violence which, from time to time, erupts in these communities is directed primarily against those who pose a threat to the fragile balance of this double fiction: the preferable targets of the merchant's mercenaries are not those who are unable to repay their debt but those who try to escape the area while still in debt, and especially those who have become too successful and are thus in a position to repay their debt in full – they pose the most serious threat to the merchant's power. (A typical scenario is for the merchant to summon a gold-digger who is heavily in debt and inform him that he is prepared to write off half of his debt if he sets on fire the house of another, exceedingly successful gold-digger.) What we have here is an exemplary case of how desire is inscribed in the ambiguity of the French *ne expletif*: the 'official' desire of the merchant is for his customers to repay their debt as soon as possible, he incessantly harasses them for being late with the last payment, yet what he truly fears is for them to get out of debt, i.e., his true desire is for them to remain in debt to him indefinitely. As was demonstrated by Bruce Fink, an approximate equivalent to this *ne expletif* in English would be the ambiguously superfluous use of 'but': the interpolation of 'but' often conveys an accent which runs counter to the 'official' intention of the statement.[6] So we can well imagine the merchant saying to an indebted gold-digger: 'I do not fear *but* that you will fail to honour your debt', or, 'I will not deny *but* that your ability to repay your debt pleases me immensely.'

Our argument can be briefly summarized as follows: the outbreak of 'real' violence is conditioned by a symbolic deadlock. *'Real' violence is a kind of acting out that emerges when the symbolic fiction that guarantees the life of a community is in danger.* There is, however, a feature with regard to which the example of the Amazon gold-diggers differs from the first two: in the first two examples, the disturbed fiction was a publicly unacknowledged, shadowy, obscene agency (Kafka's Court, the sailors' obscene initiation rituals), whereas in the Amazon gold-digger community the disturbance affected the symbolic fiction that determines the very structure of public authority. The best way to elaborate this crucial difference is to approach the problem from the other end: what is the *target* of the outbursts of violence? What are we aiming at, what do we endeavour to annihilate, when we exterminate Jews or beat up foreigners in our cities?

The first answer that offers itself again involves symbolic fiction: is not, beyond direct physical pain and personal humiliation, the ultimate aim of the rapes in the Bosnian war, for example, to undermine the fiction (the symbolic narrative) that guarantees the coherence of the Muslim community? Is it not a consequence of extreme violence also that 'the story the community has been telling itself about itself no longer makes sense' (to paraphrase Richard Rorty)? This destruction of the enemy's symbolic universe, this 'culturocide', however, is in itself not sufficient to explain an outburst of ethnic violence – its ultimate cause (in the sense of driving force) is to be sought at a somewhat deeper level. What does our 'intolerance' towards foreigners feed on? What is it that irritates us in them and disturbs our psychic balance? Already at the level of a simple phenomenological description, the crucial characteristic of this cause is that it cannot be pinpointed to some clearly defined observable property: although we usually can enumerate a series of features that annoy us about 'them' (the way they laugh too loudly, the bad smell of their food, etc.), these features function as indicators of a more radical strangeness. Foreigners may look and act like us, but there is some unfathomable *je ne sais quoi*, something 'in them more than themselves' that makes them 'not quite human' ('aliens' in the precise sense this term acquired in the science-fiction films of the 1950s). Our relationship to this unfathomable traumatic element that 'bothers us' in the other is structured in fantasies (about the other's political and/or sexual omnipotence, about 'their' strange sexual practices, about their secret hypnotic powers, etc.). Jacques Lacan baptized this paradoxical uncanny object that stands for what in the perceived positive, empirical object necessarily eludes my gaze and as such serves as the driving force of my desiring it, *objet petit a*, the object-cause of desire; another name for it is *plus-de jouir*, the 'surplus-enjoyment' that designates the excess over the satisfaction brought about by the positive, empirical properties of the object. At its most radical level, violence is precisely an endeavour to strike a blow at this unbearable surplus-enjoyment contained in the Other. Since hatred is thus not limited to the 'actual properties' of its object but targets its real kernel, *objet a*, what is 'in the object more than itself', the object of hatred is *stricto sensu indestructible*: the more we destroy the object in reality, the more powerful its sublime kernel rises in front of us. This paradox has already emerged apropos of the Jews in Nazi Germany: the more they were ruthlessly exterminated, the more horrifying were the dimensions acquired by the remainder.

The paradox of a fantasmatic element, which the more it is annihilated in reality the stronger it returns in its spectral presence, points towards the Freudian problematic of the castration complex. The notion of the castration complex has for years been the target of feminist criticism: only if we silently accept 'having the phallus' as the standard by which we measure both sexes does 'not having the phallus' appear as a lack, i.e., is the woman perceived as 'castrated'. In other words, the notion of feminine castration ultimately amounts to a variation on the notorious old Greek sophism, 'What you don't have, you have lost; you don't have horns, so you have lost them.' It is nonetheless too hasty to dismiss this sophism (and thereby the notion of castration) as inconsequential false reasoning. To get a presentiment of the existential anxiety that may pertain to its logic, suffice it to recall the Wolf-Man, Freud's Russian analysand, who was suffering from a hypochondriacal *idée fixe*: he complained that he was the victim of a nasal injury caused by electrolysis; however, when thorough dermatological examinations established that absolutely nothing was wrong with his nose, this triggered an unbearable anxiety in him: 'Having been told that nothing could be done for his nose because nothing was wrong with it, he felt unable to go on living in what he considered his irreparably mutilated state.'[7] This 'irreparable mutilation', of course, stands for castration, and the logic is here exactly the same as that of the above-quoted Greek sophism: if you do not have horns, you have lost them; if nothing can be done, then the loss is irreparable.

According to Freud, the attitude of the male subject towards castration involves a paradoxical splitting: I know that castration is not an actual threat, that it will not really occur, yet I am nonetheless haunted by its prospect. And the same goes for the figure of the 'conceptual Jew': he doesn't exist (as part of our experience of social reality), yet for that reason I fear him even more – in short, *the very non-existence of the Jew in reality functions as the main argument for anti-Semitism.* That is to say, the anti-Semitic discourse constructs the figure of the Jew as a phantom-like entity that is to be found nowhere in reality, and then uses this very gap between the 'conceptual Jew' and the reality of actually existing Jews as the ultimate argument against Jews. We are thus caught in a kind of vicious circle: the more things appear to be normal, the more suspicion they arouse and the more panic-stricken we become. In this respect the Jew is like the maternal phallus: there is no such thing in reality, yet for that very reason its phantom-like, spectral presence gives rise to an unbearable anxiety. Therein consists also the most succinct definition of the Lacanian Real: the more my (symbolic) reasoning tells me that X is not possible, the more its spectre haunts me – like the proverbial courageous Englishman who not only did not believe in ghosts but was not even afraid of them.

A homology imposes itself here between the 'conceptual Jew' and the Name-of-the-Father: in the latter case, we are also dealing with the splitting between knowledge and belief ('I know very well that my father is actually an imperfect, confused, impotent creature, yet I nonetheless believe in his symbolic authority'). The empirical person of the father never lives up to his Name, to his symbolic mandate – insofar as he *does* live up to it, we are dealing with a psychotic constellation (a clear case of a father who did live up to his Name was Schreber's father from the case analyzed by Freud). Is therefore the 'transubstantiation', the 'sublation', '*Aufhebung*' of the real father in the Name-of-the-Father not strictly homologous to the 'transubstantiation' of the empirical Jew into (the form of appearance of) the 'conceptual Jew'? Is the gap that separates effective Jews from the fantasmatic figure of 'conceptual Jew' not of the same nature as the gap that separates the empirical, always deficient person of the father from the Name-of-the-Father, from his symbolic mandate? Is it not that, in both cases, a real person acts as the personification of an irreal, fictitious agency – the actual father is a stand-in for the agency of symbolic authority and the actual Jew a stand-in for the fantasmatic figure of the 'conceptual Jew'?

Convincing as it may sound, this homology has to be rejected as deceptive: in the case of the Jew, the standard logic of symbolic castration is *reversed*. In what, precisely, does symbolic castration consist? A real father exerts authority only insofar as he posits himself as the embodiment of a transcendent symbolic agency, i.e., insofar as he accepts that it is not himself, but the big Other who speaks through him, in his words – like the millionaire from a film by Claude Chabrol who inverts the standard complaint about being loved only for his millions: 'If only I were to find a woman who would love me only for my millions, not for myself!' Therein resides the ultimate lesson of the Freudian myth of the parricide of the primordial father who, after his violent death, returns stronger than ever in the guise of his Name, as a symbolic authority: *if the real father is to exert paternal symbolic authority, he must in a way die alive* – it is his identification with the 'dead letter' of the symbolic mandate that bestows authority on his person.

The trouble with the critics of Lacan's 'phallocentrism' is that, as a rule, they refer to 'phallus' and/or 'castration' in a pre-conceptual, commonsense metaphoric way: in standard feminist film studies, for example, every time a man behaves aggressively towards a woman or asserts his authority over her, one can be sure that his act will be designated as 'phallic'; every time a woman is framed, rendered helpless, cornered, etc., one can be sure that her experience will be designated as 'castrating'. What gets lost here is precisely the paradox of phallus as the signifier of castration: if we are to assert our (symbolic) 'phallic' authority, the price to be paid for it is that we have to renounce the position of agent and consent to function as the medium through which the big Other acts and speaks. Insofar as phallus *qua* signifier designates the agency of symbolic authority, its crucial feature therefore resides in the fact that it is not 'mine', the organ of a living subject, but a place at which a foreign power intervenes and inscribes itself onto my body, a place at which the big Other acts through me – in short, the fact that phallus is a signifier means above all that it is structurally an organ without a body, somehow 'detached' from my body.[8] This crucial feature of the phallus, its detachability, is rendered visible in the use of the plastic artificial phallus, the 'dildo', in lesbian sado-masochistic practices where one can play with it, where it circulates – the phallus is far too serious a thing for its use to be left to stupid creatures like men.[9]

There is, however, a pivotal difference between this symbolic authority guaranteed by the phallus as the signifier of castration and the spectral presence of the 'conceptual Jew': although in both cases we are dealing with the split between knowledge and belief, the two splits are fundamentally different in nature. In the first case, the belief concerns the 'visible' symbolic authority (notwithstanding my awareness of the father's imperfection and debility, I still accept him as a figure of authority), whereas in the second case, what I believe in is the power of an invisible spectral apparition.[10] The fantasmatic 'conceptual Jew' is not a paternal figure of symbolic authority, a 'castrated' bearer-medium of public authority, but something decidedly different, a kind of uncanny double of the public authority that perverts its proper logic: he has to act in shadow, invisible to the public eye, irradiating a phantom-like, spectral omnipotence. On account of this unfathomable, elusive status of the kernel of his identity, the Jew is – in contrast to the 'castrated' father – perceived as *uncastratable*: the more his actual, social, public existence is cut short, the more threatening becomes his elusive fantasmatic ex-sistence.[11]

In short, the difference between the Name-of-the-Father and the 'conceptual Jew' is that between symbolic *fiction* and fantasmatic *spectre*: in Lacanian algebra, between S_1, the Master-Signifier (the empty signifier of symbolic authority), and *objet petit a*. When the subject is endowed with symbolic authority, he acts as an appendix of his symbolic title, i.e., it is the big Other who acts through him: suffice it to recall a judge who may be a miserable and corrupted person, yet the moment he puts on his robe and other insignia, his words are the words of Law itself. In the case of spectral presence, on the other hand, the power I exert relies on something 'in me more than myself' that is best exemplified by numerous science-fiction thrillers from *Alien* to *Hidden*: an indestructible foreign body that stands for the presymbolic life-substance, a nauseous mucous parasite that invades my interior and dominates me. So, back to Chabrol's joke about the millionaire, when somebody says that he loves me not because of myself but because of my symbolic place (power, wealth), my predicament is decidedly better than when I am told that I am loved because somebody feels the presence in me of 'something more than myself'. If a millionaire loses his millions, the partner who loved him for his wealth will simply lose his interest and abandon him, no deep traumas involved; if, however, I am loved because of 'something in me more than myself', the very intensity of this love can easily convert into a no less passionate hatred, into a violent attempt to annihilate the surplus-object in me that disturbs my partner. One can therefore sympathize with the poor millionaire's plight: it is far more comforting to know that a woman loves me because of my millions (or power or glory) – this awareness allows me to maintain a safe distance, to avoid being caught in the game too deeply, to expose to the other the very kernel of my being. The problem arises when the other sees *in me* 'something more than myself' – the path is then wide open for the paradoxical short-circuit between love and hate for which Lacan coined the neologism *l'hainamoration*.

This problematic enables us to approach in a new way Wagner's *Lohengrin*: what is ultimately at stake in this opera is precisely the impasse of Chabrol's unfortunate millionaire, namely the status of that something 'in him more than himself' that the woman perceives in the hero. The opera is centred on the theme of the forbidden question, i.e., on the paradox of self-destructive female curiosity. A nameless hero saves Elsa von Brabant and marries her, but enjoins her not to ask him who he is or what his name is – as soon as she does so, he will be obliged to leave her. Unable to resist temptation, Elsa asks him the fateful question; so Lohengrin tells her that he is a knight of the Grail, the son of Parsifal from the castle of Montsalvat, and then departs on a swan, while the unfortunate Elsa falls dead. In what, then, on closer examination, does the discord that corrupts the relationship between Elsa and Lohengrin consist? It may appear that *Lohengrin* is just another variation on the old theme of a prince who, in order to make sure that his future bride will love him for himself, not because of his symbolic title, first wants to arouse her love dressed up as a servant or a messenger. However, the enigma of *Lohengrin* resides elsewhere: why can he exert his *power* only insofar as his name remains *unknown*, i.e., only insofar as he is not inscribed in the 'big Other' of inter-subjective public space, so that he has to withdraw the moment his symbolic identity is publicly revealed? What we are dealing with is thus again the opposition between Master-Signifier and *a*, the 'uncastra-table' object that can exert its efficiency only *qua* concealed: the misunderstanding between Elsa and Lohengrin resides in the fact that Elsa perceives Lohengrin as the traditional figure of symbolic authority, whereas he functions as a spectral apparition that cannot sustain its disclosure in the public symbolic medium.

This difference between (symbolic) fiction and fantasy is of crucial importance for the psychoanalytical theory of ideology. In his recent book on Marx, Jacques Derrida brought into play the term 'spectre' in order to indicate the elusive pseudo-materiality that subverts the classic ontological oppositions of reality and illusion, etc.[12] And, perhaps, it is here that we should look for the last resort of ideology, for the pre-ideological kernel, the formal matrix, on which are grafted various ideological formations: in the fact that there is no reality without the spectre, that the circle of reality can be closed only by means of an uncanny spectral supplement. Why, then, is there no reality without the spectre? Lacan provides a precise answer to this question: (what we experience as) reality is not the 'thing itself', it is always-already symbolized, constituted, structured by way of symbolic mechanisms. The problem resides in the fact that symbolization ultimately always fails, that it never succeeds in fully 'covering' the Real, that it always involves some unsettled, unredeemed symbolic debt. *This Real (the part of reality that remains non-symbolized) returns in the guise of spectral apparitions.* Consequently, 'spectre' is not to be confused with 'symbolic fiction', with the fact that reality itself has the structure of a fiction in that it is symbolically (or, as some sociologists put it, 'socially') constructed; the notions of spectre and (symbolic) fiction are codependent in their very incompatibility (they are 'complementary' in the quantum-mechanical sense). To put it simply, reality is never directly 'itself', it presents itself only via its incomplete-failed symbolization, and spectral apparitions emerge in this very gap that forever separates reality from the real, and on account of which reality has the character of a (symbolic) fiction: the spectre gives body to that which escapes (the symbolically structured) reality.

The pre-ideological 'kernel' of ideology thus consists of the *spectral apparition that fills up the hole of the Real.* This is what all attempts to draw a clear line of separation between 'true' reality and illusion (or attempts to ground illusion in reality) fail to take into account:

if (what we experience as) 'reality' is to emerge, something has to be foreclosed from it; i.e., 'reality', like truth, is by definition never 'whole'. *What the spectre conceals is not reality but its 'primordially repressed', the unrepresentable X on whose 'repression' reality itself is founded.* It may seem that we have thereby lost our way in speculative murky waters that have nothing whatsoever to do with concrete social struggles. However, is the supreme example of such a 'Real' not provided by the Marxist concept of *class struggle?* The consequent thinking through of this concept compels us to admit that there is no class struggle 'in reality': 'class struggle' designates the very antagonism that prevents the objective (social) reality from constituting itself as a self-enclosed whole.[13]

This interpretation of social antagonism (class struggle) as Real, not as (part of) objective social reality, enables us to counter the worn-out line of argumentation, according to which one has to abandon the notion of ideology since the gesture of distinguishing 'mere ideology' from 'reality' implies the epistemologically untenable 'God's view', i.e., access to objective reality as it 'truly is'. The question of the suitability of the term 'class struggle' to designate today's dominant form of antagonism is here secondary, it concerns concrete social analysis; what matters is that the very constitution of social reality involves the 'primordial repression' of an antagonism, so that the ultimate support of the critique of ideology – the extra-ideological point of reference that authorizes us to denounce the content of our immediate experience as 'ideological' – is not 'reality' but the 'repressed' Real of antagonism.

In order to clarify this uncanny logic of antagonism *qua* Real, let us recall Claude Lévi-Strauss's exemplary analysis of the spatial disposition of buildings in an aboriginal South American village from his *Structural Anthropology*.[14] The inhabitants are divided into two subgroups; when we ask an individual to draw on a piece of paper or on sand the ground-plan of his/her village (the spatial disposition of cottages), we obtain two quite different answers, according to whether he or she belongs to one or the other sub-group: a member of the first sub-group (let us call it 'conservative-corporatist') perceives the ground-plan of the village as circular – a ring of houses more or less symmetrically disposed around the central temple, whereas a member of the second ('revolutionary-antagonistic') sub-group perceives his/her village as two distinct heaps of houses separated by an invisible frontier.

The central point of Lévi-Strauss is that this example should in no way entice us into cultural relativism according to which the perception of social space depends on the observer's group-belonging: the very splitting into the two 'relative' perceptions implies the hidden reference to a constant – not the objective, 'actual' disposition of buildings but a traumatic kernel, a fundamental antagonism the inhabitants of the village were not able to symbolize, to account for, to 'internalize', to come to terms with, an imbalance in social relations that prevented the community from stabilizing itself into a harmonious whole. The two perceptions of the ground-plan are simply the two mutually exclusive endeavours to cope with this traumatic antagonism, to heal its wound via the imposition of a balanced symbolic structure. (Is it necessary to add that things stand exactly the same with respect to sexual difference: 'masculine' and 'feminine' are like the two configurations of houses in the Lévi-Straussian village?) And in order to dispel the illusion that our 'developed' universe is not dominated by the same logic, suffice it to recall the splitting of our political space into Left and Right: a Leftist and a Rightist behave exactly like members of the opposite sub-groups of the Lévi-Straussian village. They not only occupy different places within the political space; each of them perceives differently the very disposition of the political space – a Leftist as the field that is inherently split by some fundamental antagonism, a Rightist as the organic unity of a community disturbed only by foreign intruders.

Common sense tells us that it is easy to rectify the bias of subjective perceptions and to ascertain the 'true state of things': we rent a helicopter and take a snapshot of the village directly from above. What we obtain this way is the undistorted view of reality, yet we miss completely the Real of social antagonism, the non-symbolizable traumatic kernel that finds expression in the very distortions of reality, in the fantasized displacements of the 'actual' disposition of houses. This is what Lacan has in mind when he claims that *the very distortion and/or dissimulation is revealing*: what emerges via the distortions of the accurate representation of reality is the real, i.e., the trauma around which social reality is structured. In other words, if all inhabitants of the village were to draw the same accurate ground-plan, we would be dealing with a non-antagonistic, harmonious community. However, if we are to arrive at the fundamental paradox implied by the Marxian notion of commodity fetishism, we have to accomplish a step further and imagine, say, two different 'actual' villages each of which realizes, in the disposition of its dwellings, one of the two fantasized ground-plans evoked by Lévi-Strauss. In this case the structure of social reality itself materializes an attempt to cope with the real of antagonism. That is to say, what one should never forget is that 'commodity fetishism' does not designate a (bourgeois) theory of political economy but a series of presuppositions that determine the structure of the very 'real' economic practice of market exchange – in theory, a capitalist clings to utilitarian nominalism, yet in his own practice (of exchange, etc.) he follows 'theological whimsies' and acts as a speculative idealist. 'Reality' itself, insofar as it is regulated by a symbolic fiction, conceals the Real of an antagonism, and it is this Real, foreclosed from the symbolic fiction, that returns in the guise of spectral apparitions – in exemplary fashion, of course, in the guise of the 'conceptual Jew'.

This duality of symbolic fiction and spectral apparition can be discerned also via the utter ambiguity that pertains to the notion of fantasy. That is to say, the notion of fantasy offers an exemplary case of the dialectical *coincidentia oppositorum*: on the one hand, fantasy in its beatific side, the dream of a state without disturbances, out of reach of human depravity; on the other hand, fantasy in its aspect whose elementary form is envy – all that 'irritates' me about the Other, images that haunt me of what he or she is doing when out of my sight, of how he or she deceives me and plots against me, of how he or she ignores me and indulges in an enjoyment that is intensive beyond my capacity of representation, etc. (This, for example, is what bothers Swann apropos of Odette in *Un amour de Swann*.) And does the fundamental lesson of so-called totalitarianism not concern the co-dependence of these two aspects of the notion of fantasy? Those who are alleged to realize fully fantasy$_1$ (the symbolic fiction) had to have recourse to fantasy$_2$ (spectral apparitions) in order to explain their failure – the foreclosed obverse of the Nazi harmonious *Volksge-meinschaft* returned in the guise of their paranoiac obsession with the Jewish plot. Similarly, the Stalinist's compulsive discovery of ever new enemies of Socialism was the unavoidable obverse of their pretending to realize the ideal of the 'new Socialist man'. Perhaps, the freedom from the infernal hold of fantasy$_2$ provides the most succinct definition of a saint.

Fantasy$_1$ and fantasy$_2$, symbolic fiction and spectral apparition, are thus like the front and the reverse of the same coin: insofar as a community experiences its reality as regulated, structured, by fantasy$_1$, it has to disavow its inherent impossibility, the antagonism in its very heart – and fantasy$_2$ (the figure of the 'conceptual Jew', for example) gives body to this disavowal. In short, the effectiveness of fantasy$_2$ is the condition for fantasy$_1$ to maintain its hold.[15] Lacan rewrote Descartes's 'I think, therefore I am' as 'I am the one who thinks "therefore I am"' – the point of it being, of course, the non-coincidence of the two 'ams', i.e., the fantasmatic nature of the second 'am'. One should submit to the same reformulation the pathetic assertion of ethnic identity: the moment 'I am French (German, Jew, American)' is rephrased as 'I am the one who thinks "therefore I am French"', the gap in the midst of my self-identity becomes visible – and the function of the 'conceptual Jew' is precisely to render this gap invisible.

NOTES

Published in *Analysis* 5, 1994, pp. 49–62 [eds].
1   I am relying here on the excellent book by Greg Dening, *Mr Bligh's Bad Language: Passion, Power and Theatre on the Bounty*, Cambridge, Cambridge University Press, 1994, esp. pp. 55–87.
2   *Ibid.*, pp. 77–9.
3   Henning Henningsen, *Crossing the Equator: Sailors' Baptisms and Other Initiation Rites*, Copenhagen Munkgaarde, 1961, quoted in Dening, *Mr Bligh's Bad Language*, p. 79.
4   See Christian Geffrey, intervention at the round-table, 'L'ordre et la loi', a symposium on *Violence et politique*, Cérisy-la-Salle (France), 23–30 June 1994.

5   This example also enables us to outline the precise formal conditions in which the relationship of subjects to their (political) Master is that of love. Love has nothing whatsoever to do with some primordial passions set in motion by the Leader's charisma; it emerges as it were automatically when the short-circuit occurs between the ruler and the frame of Law, that is to say, when the ruler is not able to ground his rule in a third, independent agency – in some set of formal legal Rules that regulate his relationship to his subjects – but when he himself has to vouch for the Rule that legitimizes his rule. In other words, love bears witness to the abyss of a self-relating gesture by means of which, due to the lack of an independent guarantee of the social pact, the ruler himself has to guarantee the Truth of his word.

6   See Bruce Fink, *The Lacanian Subject: Between Language and Jouissance*, Princeton, Princeton University Press, 1995, pp. 38–9 [eds].

7   Muriel Gardiner, *The Wolf-Man and Sigmund Freud*, Harmondsworth, Penguin, 1973, p. 287.

8   If we were to indulge in speculations as to why was phallus *qua* organ chosen to function as the phallic signifier, then the characteristic that 'predisposes' it for this role would be the feature evoked already by Saint Augustine: phallus is an organ of power-potency, yet an organ whose display of potency essentially eludes the subject's control – with the alleged exception of some Hindu priests, one cannot bring about erection at one's will, so that erection bears witness to some foreign power at work in the very heart of the subject.

9   The other (mis)reading, closely linked to the first one, concerns the opposition between the phallic economy and the polymorphous plurality of subject-positions: according to the standard view, the task of the phallic economy is to mould the pre-Oedipal dispersed plurality of subject-positions into the unified subject who is subordinated to the rule of the Name-of-the-Father (bearer and relay of social authority) and is as such the ideal subject of (social) Power. What one has to call into question here is the underlying assumption that social Power exerts itself via the

unified Oedipal subject entirely submitted to the phallic paternal Law, and, inversely, that the dispersion of the unified subject into a multitude of subject-positions as it were automatically undermines the authority and exercise of Power. Against this commonplace, one has to point out again and again that Power always interpellates us, addresses us, as *split* subjects; that, in order to reproduce itself, it relies upon our splitting: the message the power discourse bombards us with is by definition inconsistent; there is always a gap between public discourse and its fantasmatic support. Far from being a kind of secondary weakness, a sign of Power's imperfection, this splitting is constitutive for its exercise. As to this splitting, see Slavoj Žižek, *Metastases of Enjoyment: Six Essays on Woman and Causality*, London and New York, Verso, 1994, pp. 54–85. With regard to the so-called 'postmodern' form of subjectivity that befits late capitalism, one has to go even a step further: the 'postmodern' object is even directly, at the level of public discourse, constituted as an inconsistent bundle of multiple 'subject-positions' (economically conservative, yet sexually 'enlightened' yuppie, etc.).

10 For a classic statement of the different versions of 'I know very well, but still . . .', see Octave Mannoni, 'I Know Well, but All the Same . . .', in *Perversion and the Social Relation*, ed. Molly Anne Rothenberg, Dennis A. Foster and Slavoj Žižek, Durham, Duke University Press, 2003, pp. 68–92; for a political reading of it, see Slavoj Žižek, *For They Know Not What They Do: Enjoyment as a Political Factor*, London and New York, Verso, 1991, pp. 229–77. For a conflation of the 'normal' distance between belief in symbolic fiction and knowledge of reality with the fetishist disavowal of reality, see Mary Ann Doanne, *The Desire to Desire*, Bloomington, Indiana University Press, 1987: for example: 'In short, [women's films] assume that the woman can move into the position of fetishist, carefully balancing knowledge and belief' (p. 118). Incidentally, another critical point in this otherwise excellent book seems to be the notion that the feminine-hysteric 'desire to desire' is somehow defective with regard to the masculine desire *tout court*: 'Desire may be insatiable, it may entail the constantly renewed pursuit for a perpetually lost object, but at

least the male has desire. The woman's relation to desire, on the other hand, is at best a mediated one. Lacan defines the hysteric's desire as "the desire for an unsatisfied desire" ' (p. 12). For Lacan, however, desire as such is always, by definition, the 'desire to desire', never 'straight' desire – this is what he aims at with his classic formula, 'desire of man is the desire of the Other'. It is this very reflexivity of desire that accounts for its 'excessive' character, so that when Doanne says, 'Desire is always in excess – even if it is simply the desire to desire, the striving for an access to a desiring subjectivity' (p. 122), one should replace 'even if' with 'because': 'Desire is always in excess because it is always the desire to desire …' In other words, from the Lacanian perspective, the 'desiring subjectivity' par excellence is precisely that of a hysterical woman.

11 The same logic seems to be at work in the anti-Communist right-wing populism that is recently gaining strength in the ex-Socialist East European countries: its answer to the present economic and other hardships is that, although they lost legal, public power, Communists continue to pull the strings, to dominate the levers of effective economic power, to control media and state institutions … Communists are thus perceived as a fantasmatic entity à la Jew: the more they lose public power and become invisible, the stronger their phantom-like all-presence, their shadowy effective control. This idée fixe of the populists, according to which what is now emerging in post-Socialist countries is not 'true' capitalism but its false imitation in which actual power and control remain in the hands of ex-Communists dressed up as newly baked capitalists, also offers an exemplary case of the illusion whose mechanism was laid bare for the first time by Hegel: what they fail to recognize is that their opposition to this 'false' capitalism effectively is opposition to capitalism tout court, i.e., that they, not the ex-Communists, are the true ideological inheritors of Socialism – no wonder that the populists are compelled to resuscitate the old Communist opposition between 'formal' and 'true' democracy. In short, we are dealing with yet another example of the irony that pertains to the revolutionary process, the irony described already by Marx: all of a sudden, the amazed

revolutionaries perceive that they were mere vanishing mediators whose 'historical role' was to prepare the terrain for the old masters to take over in new guises.

12 Jacques Derrida, *Spectres of Marx: The State of Debt, the Work of Mourning and the New International*, trans. Peggy Kamuf, New York and London, Routledge, 1994.

13 This notion of antagonism is of course due to Ernesto Laclau and Chantal Mouffe, *Hegemony and Sociality Strategy*, London and New York, Verso, 1985.

14 Claude Lévi-Strauss, *Structural Anthropology, Volume 1*, trans. Claire Jacobson and Brooke Grundfest-Schoepf, Harmondsworth, Penguin, 1963, pp. 133–5 [eds].

15 For a more detailed elaboration of the logic of anti-Semitism with regard to its specific function in capitalism, see Slavoj Žižek, *The Sublime Object of Ideology*, London and New York, Verso, 1989, pp. 11–53; *Enjoy Your Symptom! Jacques Lacan In Hollywood and Out*, New York and London, Routledge, 1992, pp. 69–110; as well as *Tarrying with the Negative: Kant, Hegel, and the Critique of Ideology*, Durham, Duke University Press, 1993, pp. 125–61.

12 Beyond Discourse Analysis

Hegemony and Socialist Strategy[1] is usually read as an essay in 'post-structuralist' politics, an essay in translating into a political project the basic 'post-structuralist' ideas: there is no transcendental Signified; so-called 'reality' is a discursive construct; every given identity, including that of a subject, is an effect of contingent differential relations, etc. This reading also provokes the usual criticism: language serves primarily as a medium of extra-linguistic power-relations; we cannot dissolve all reality into a language-game, etc. It is our claim that such a reading misses the fundamental dimension of *Hegemony*, the dimension through which this book presents perhaps the most radical breakthrough in modern social theory.

It is no accident that the basic proposition of *Hegemony* – 'Society doesn't exist' – evokes the Lacanian proposition 'la Femme n'existe pas' ('Woman doesn't exist'). The real achievement of *Hegemony* is crystallized in the concept of 'social antagonism': far from reducing all reality to a kind of language-game, the socio-symbolic field is conceived as structured around a certain traumatic impossibility, around a certain fissure that *cannot* be symbolized. In short, Laclau and Mouffe have, so to speak, reinvented the Lacanian notion of the Real as impossible, they have made it useful as a tool for social and ideological analysis. Simple as it may sound, this breakthrough is of such a novelty that it was usually not even perceived in most responses to *Hegemony*.[2]

1. THE SUBJECT OF ANTAGONISM

Why this stress on the homology between the Laclau–Mouffe concept of antagonism and the Lacanian concept of the Real? Because it is our thesis that the reference to Lacan allows us to draw some further conclusions from the concept of social antagonism, above all those that concern the status of the subject corresponding to the social field structured around a central impossibility.

As to the question of the subject, *Hegemony* presents even a certain regression from Laclau's previous book *Politics and Ideology in Marxist Theory*:[3] in this book we find a finely elaborated Althusserian theory of interpellation, while in *Hegemony*, Laclau and Mouffe are basically still conceiving the subject in a way that characterizes 'post-structuralism', from the perspective of assuming different 'subject-positions'. Why this regression? My optimistic reading of it is that it is – to use the good old Stalinist expression – 'a dizziness from too much success', an effect of the fact that Laclau and Mouffe had progressed too quickly, i.e., that, with the elaboration of their concept of antagonism, they have accomplished such a radical breakthrough that it was not possible for them to follow it immediately with a cor-responding concept of subject – hence the uncertainty regarding the subject in *Hegemony*.

The main thrust of its argumentation is directed against the classical notion of the *subject* as a substantial, essential entity, given in advance, dominating the social process and not being produced by the contingency of the discursive process itself: against this notion, they affirm that what we have is a series of particular subject-positions (feminist, ecologist, democratic ...), the signification of which is not fixed in advance: it changes according to the way they are articulated in a series of equivalences through the metaphoric surplus which defines the identity of every one of them. Let us take, for example, the series feminism–democracy–peace movement–ecologism: insofar as the participant in the struggle for democracy 'finds out by experience' that there is no real democracy without the emancipation of women, insofar as the participant in the ecological struggle 'finds out by experience' that there is no real reconciliation with nature without abandoning the aggressive-masculine attitude towards nature, insofar as the participant in the peace movement 'finds out by experience' that there is no real peace without radical democratization, etc., that is to say, insofar as the identity of each of the four above-mentioned positions is marked with the metaphoric surplus of the other three positions, we can say that something like a unified subject-position is being constructed: to be a democrat means at the same time to be a feminist, etc. What we must not overlook is, of course, that such a unity is always radically contingent, the result of a symbolic condensation, and not an expression of some kind of internal necessity according to which the interests of all the above-mentioned positions would in the long run 'objectively convene'. It is quite possible, for example, to imagine an ecological position which sees the only solution in a strong anti-democratic, authoritarian state resuming control over the exploitation of natural resources, etc.

Now, it is clear that such a notion of subject-positions still enters the frame of Althusserian ideological interpellation as constitutive of the subject: the subject-position is a mode of how we recognize our position of an (interested) agent of the social process, of how we experience our commitment to a certain ideological cause. But, as soon as we constitute ourselves as ideological subjects, as soon as we respond to interpellation and assume a certain subject-position, we are *a priori*, *per definitionem* deluded, we are overlooking the radical dimension of social antagonism, that is to say, the traumatic kernel the symbolization of which always fails; and – this is our hypothesis – it is precisely the Lacanian notion of the subject as 'the empty place of the structure' which describes the subject in its confrontation with antagonism, the subject which isn't covering up the traumatic dimension of social antagonism.

To explain this distinction between subject and subject-positions, let us take again the case of class antagonism. The relationship between the classes is antagonistic in the Laclau–Mouffe sense of the term, i.e., it is neither contradiction nor opposition but the 'impossible' relationship between two terms: each of them preventing the other from achieving its identity with itself, becoming what it really is. As soon as I recognize myself, in an ideological interpellation, as a 'proletarian', I am engaged in social reality, fighting against the 'capitalist' who is preventing me from realizing fully my human potential, blocking my full development. Where here is the ideological illusion proper to the subject-position? It lies precisely in the fact that it is the 'capitalist', this external enemy, who is preventing me from achieving an identity with myself: the illusion is that after the eventual annihilation of the antagonistic enemy, I will finally abolish the antagonism and arrive at an identity with myself. And it is the same with sexual antagonism: the feminist struggle against patriarchal, male chauvinist oppression is necessarily filled out by the illusion that afterwards, when patriarchal oppression is abolished, women will finally achieve their full identity with themselves, realize their human potential, etc.

However, to grasp the notion of antagonism, in its most radical dimension, we should *invert* the relationship between the two terms: it is not the external enemy who is preventing me from achieving identity with myself, but every identity is already in itself blocked, marked by an impossibility, and the external enemy is simply the small piece, the rest of reality upon which we 'project' or 'externalize' this intrinsic, immanent impossibility. That would be the last lesson of the famous Hegelian dialectics of the Lord and the Bondsman,[4] the lesson usually overlooked by the Marxist reading: the Lord is ultimately an invention of the Bondsman, a way for the Bondsman to 'give way as to his desire', to evade the blockade of his own desire by projecting its reason into the external repression of the Lord. This is also the real ground for Freud's insistence that the *Verdrängung* cannot be reduced to an internalization of the *Unterdrückung* [the external repression]: there is a certain fundamental, radical, constitutive, self-inflicted impediment, a hindrance of the drive; and the role of the fascinating figure of external Authority, of its repressive force, is to make us blind to this self-impediment of the drive. That is why we could say that it is precisely in the moment when we achieve victory over the enemy in the antagonistic struggle in social reality that we experience antagonism in its most radical dimension, as a self-hindrance: far from enabling us finally to achieve full identity with ourselves, the moment of victory is the moment of greatest loss. The Bondsman frees himself from the Lord only when he experiences how the Lord was only embodying the auto-blockage of his own desire: what the Lord through his external repression was supposed to deprive him of, to prevent him from realizing, he – the Bondsman – never possessed. This is the moment called by Hegel 'the loss of the loss': the experience that we *never had* what we were supposed to have lost. We can also determine this experience of the 'loss of the loss' as the experience of the 'negation of the negation', i.e., of pure antagonism where the negation is brought to the point of self-reference.

This reference to Hegel might seem strange: isn't Hegel the 'absolute idealist' par excellence, the philosopher reducing all antagonism to a subordinate moment of self-mediating identity? But perhaps such a reading of Hegel is itself victim of the 'metaphysics of presence': perhaps another reading is possible where the reference to Hegel enables us to distinguish pure antagonism from the antagonistic fight in reality. What is at stake in pure antagonism is no longer the fact that – as in an antagonistic fight with an external adversary – all the positivity, all the consistency of our position lies in the negation of the adversary's position and *vice versa*; what is at stake is the fact that the negativity of the other which is preventing me from achieving my full identity with myself is just an externalization of my own auto-negativity, of my self-hindering. The point here is how exactly to read, which accent to give to, the crucial thesis of Laclau and Mouffe that in antagonism negativity as such assumes a positive existence. We can read this thesis as asserting that in an antagonistic relationship the positivity of 'our' position consists only in the positivization of our negative relation to the other, to the antagonist adversary: the whole consistency of our position is in the fact that we are negating the other, 'we' are nothing but this drive to abolish, to annihilate our adversary. In this case, the antagonistic relationship is in a way symmetrical: each position is only its negative relation to the other (the Lord prevents the Bondsman from achieving full identity with himself and vice versa). But if we radicalize the antagonistic fight in reality to the point of pure antagonism, the thesis that, in antagonism, negativity as such assumes a positive existence must be read in another way: the other itself (the Lord, let's say) is, in his positivity, in his fascinating presence, just the positivization of our own – the Bondsman's – negative relationship toward ourselves, the positive embodiment of our own self-blockage. The point is that, here, the relationship is no longer symmetrical: we cannot say that the Bondsman is also in the same way just the positivization of the negative relationship of the Lord. What we can perhaps say is that he is the Lord's symptom. When we radicalize the antagonistic fight to a point of pure antagonism, it is always one of the two moments which, through the positivity of the other, maintains a negative self-relationship: to use a Hegelian term, this other element functions as a 'reflexive determination ['*Reflexionsbestimmung*']' of the first – the Lord, for example, is just a reflexive determination of the Bondsman. Or, to take sexual difference/antagonism: man is a reflexive determination of woman's impossibility of achieving an identity with herself (which is why woman is a symptom of man).

We must then distinguish the experience of antagonism in its radical form, as a limit of the social, as the impossibility around which the social field is structured, from antagonism as the relation between antagonistic subject-positions: in Lacanian terms, we must distinguish antagonism as *Real* from the social *reality* of the antagonistic fight. And the Lacanian notion of the subject aims precisely at the experience of 'pure' antagonism as self-hindering, self-blockage, this internal limit preventing the symbolic field from realizing its full identity: the stake of the entire process of subjectivization, of assuming different subject-positions, is ultimately to enable us to avoid this traumatic experience. The limit of the social as it is defined by Laclau and Mouffe, this paradoxical limit which means that 'Society doesn't exist', isn't just something that subverts each subject-position, each defined identity of the subject; on the contrary, it is at the same time what sustains the subject in its most radical dimension: 'the subject' in the Lacanian sense is the name for this internal limit, this internal impossibility of the Other, of 'substance'. The subject is a paradoxical entity which is, so to speak, its own negative, i.e., which persists only insofar as its full realization is blocked – the fully realized subject would be no longer subject but substance. In this precise sense, subject is beyond or before subjectivization: subjectivization designates the movement through which the subject integrates what is given them into the universe of meaning – this integration always ultimately fails, there is a certain left-over which cannot be integrated into the symbolic universe, an object which resists subjectivization, and the subject is precisely correlative to this object. In other words, the subject is correlative to its own limit, to the element which cannot be subjectivized, it is the name of the void which cannot be filled out with subjectivization: the subject is the point of failure of subjectivization (that's why the Lacanian mark for it is $).

2. THE DIMENSION OF SOCIAL FANTASY

The 'impossible' relationship of the subject to this object the loss of which constitutes the subject is marked by the Lacanian formula of fantasy: $\$ \diamond a$. Fantasy is then to be conceived as an imaginary scenario the function of which is to provide a kind of positive support filling out the subject's constitutive void. And the same goes, *mutatis mutandis*, for social fantasy: it is a necessary counterpart to the concept of antagonism, a scenario filling out the voids of the social structure, masking its constitutive antagonism by the fullness of enjoyment (racist enjoyment, for example).[5] This is the dimension overlooked in the Althusserian account of interpellation: before being caught in identification, in symbolic (mis)recognition, the subject is trapped by the *Other* through a paradoxical object-cause of desire, in the midst of it, embodying enjoyment, through this secret supposed to be hidden in the Other, as exemplified by the position of the man from the country in the famous apologue about the door of the Law in Kafka's *The Trial*, this small history told to K. by the priest to explain to him his situation vis-à-vis the Law. The patent failure of all the main interpretations of this apologue seems only to confirm the priest's thesis that 'the comments often enough merely express the commentator's bewilderment'.[6] But there is another way to penetrate the mystery of this apologue: instead of seeking directly its meaning, it would be preferable to treat it the way that Claude Lévi-Strauss treats a given myth: to establish its relations to a series of other myths and to elaborate the rule of their transformation. Where can we find, then, in *The Trial* another 'myth' which functions as a variation, as an inversion of the apologue concerning the door of the Law?

We don't have to look far: at the beginning of the second chapter ('First Interrogation'), Josef K. finds himself in front of another door of the Law (the entrance to the interrogation chamber); here also, the door-keeper lets him know that this door is intended only for him – the washerwoman says to him: 'I must shut this door after you, nobody else must come in', which is clearly a variation of the last words of the door-keeper to the man from the country in the priest's apologue: 'No one but you could gain admittance through this door, since this door was intended only for you. I am now going to shut it.'

At the same time, the apologue concerning the door of the Law (let's call it, in the style of Lévi-Strauss, m^1) and the first interrogation (m^2) can be opposed through a whole series of distinctive features: in m^1, we are in front of the entrance to a magnificent court of justice, in m^2, we are in a block of workers' flats, full of filth and obscene crawling; in m^1, the door-keeper is an employee of the court, in m^2, it is an ordinary woman washing children's clothes; in m^1, it is a man, in m^2, a woman; in m^1, the door-keeper prevents the man from the country from passing the door and entering the court, in m^2, the washerwoman pushes him into the interrogation chamber half against his will, i.e., the frontier separating everyday life from the sacred place of the Law cannot be crossed in m^1, but in m^2, it is easy to cross.

The crucial feature of m^2 is already indicated with its localization: the court is situated in the middle of the vital promiscuity of workers' lodgings – Reiner Stach is quite justified in recognizing in this detail a distinctive trait of Kafka's universe, 'the trespass of the frontier which separates the vital domain from the judicial domain'.[7] The structure is here that of the Möbius strip: if we progress far enough in our descent to the social underground, we find ourselves suddenly on the other side, i.e., in the middle of the sublime and noble Law. The place of transition from one domain to the other is a door guarded by an ordinary washerwoman of a provocative sensuality. In m^1, the door-keeper doesn't know anything, whereas here, the woman possesses a kind of advance knowledge: she simply ignores the naïve cunning of K., his excuse that he is looking for a joiner called Lanz, and makes him understand that they have been waiting for him a long time, although K. chose to enter her room quite by chance, as a last desperate essay after a long and useless ramble:

> The first thing he saw in the little room was a great pendulum clock which already pointed to ten. 'Does a joiner called Lanz live here?' he asked. 'Please go through', said a young woman with sparkling black eyes, who was washing children's clothes in a tub, and she pointed her damp hand to the open door of the next room ... 'I asked for a joiner, a man called Lanz.' 'I know', said the woman, 'just go right in.' K. might not have obeyed if she had not come up

to him, grasped the handle of the door, and said: 'I must shut this door after you, nobody else must come in.'[8]

The situation here is the same as in the well-known accident from *The Arabian Nights*: the hero, lost in the desert, enters quite by chance a cave where he finds three old wise men awakened by his entry who say to him: 'Finally, you have arrived! We have waited for you for the last three hundred years!' This mystery of the necessity behind the contingent encounter is again that of transference: the knowledge that we seek to produce is presupposed to exist already in the other. The washerwoman's paradoxical advance knowledge has nothing whatsoever to do with a so-called 'feminine intuition': it is based on a simple fact that she is connected with the Law. Her position regarding the Law is far more crucial than that of a small functionary; K. discovers it soon afterwards when his passionate argumentation before the tribunal is interrupted by an obscene intrusion:

> Here K. was interrupted by a shriek from the end of the hall; he peered from beneath his hand to see what was happening, for the reek of the room and the dim light together made a whitish dazzle of fog. It was the washerwoman, whom K. had recognized as a potential cause of disturbance from the moment of her entrance. Whether she was at fault now or not, one could not tell. All K. could see was that a man had drawn her into a corner by the door and was clasping her in his arms. Yet it was not she who had uttered the shriek but the man; his mouth was wide open and he was gazing up at the ceiling.[9]

What is then the relation between the woman and the court of Law? In Kafka's work, the woman as a 'psychological type' is wholly consistent with the anti-feminist ideology of an Otto Weininger: a being without a proper self, incapable of assuming an ethical attitude (even when she appears to act on ethical grounds, there is a hidden calculation of enjoyments behind it), a being who hasn't got access to the dimension of truth (even when what she is saying is literally true, she is lying with her subjective position), a being about whom it is not sufficient to say that she is feigning her affections to seduce a man –

the problem is that there is nothing behind this mask of simulation, nothing but a certain gluttonous enjoyment which is her only substance. Confronted with such an image of woman, Kafka doesn't succumb to the usual critical-feminist temptation (of demonstrating how this figure is the product of certain social-discursive conditions, of opposing to it the outlines of another type of femininity, etc.). His gesture is much more subversive – he wholly accepts this Weiningerian portrait of woman as a 'psychological type', but he makes it occupy an unheard of, unprecedented place, the place of the Law. This is perhaps, as was already pointed out by Stach, the elementary operation of Kafka: this short-circuit between the feminine 'substance' ('psychological type') and the place of the Law. Smeared over by an obscene vitality, the Law itself – in the traditional perspective a pure, neutral universality – assumes the features of a heterogeneous, inconsistent bricolage penetrated with enjoyment.

In Kafka's universe, the court is above all *lawless* in a formal sense: as if the chain of 'normal' connections between causes and effects is suspended, put in parentheses. Every attempt to establish the mode of functioning of the court by means of logical reasoning is doomed in advance to fail: all the oppositions noted by K. (between the anger of the judges and the laughter of the public in the gallery; between the merry right side and the severe left side of the public) prove themselves false as soon as he tries to base his tactics on them; after an ordinary answer by K., the public bursts out in laughter.

The other, positive side of this inconsistency is of course enjoyment: it erupts openly when K.'s presentation of his case is interrupted by a public act of sexual intercourse. This act, difficult to perceive because of its over-exposure itself (K. had to 'peer beneath his hands to see what was happening'), marks the moment of the eruption of the traumatic Real, and the error of K. consists in overlooking the *solidarity* between this obscene perturbation and the court. He thinks that everybody would be anxious to have order restored and the offending couple at least ejected from the meeting, but when he tries to rush across the room, the crowd obstructs him, someone seizes him from behind by the collar ... at this point, the game is over: puzzled and confused, K. loses the thread of his argument; filled with impotent rage, he soon leaves the room.

The fatal error of K. was to address the court, the Other of the Law, as a homogeneous entity, attainable by means of consistent argument, whereas the court can only return him an obscene smile mixed with signs of perplexity – in short, K. expects from the court *acts* (legal deeds, decisions), but what he gets is an *act* (a public copulation). Kafka's sensitiveness to this 'trespass of the frontier which separates the vital domain from the judicial domain' depends upon his Judaism: the Jewish religion marks the moment of their most radical separation. In all previous religions, we always run into a place, a domain of sacred enjoyment (in the form of ritual orgies, for example), whereas Judaism evacuates from the sacred domain all traces of vitality and subordinates the living substance to the dead letter of the Father's Law. With Kafka, on the contrary, the judicial domain is again flooded with enjoyment, we have a short-circuit between the *Other* of the Law and the *Thing*, the substance of enjoyment.

That is why his universe is eminently one of *superego*: the Other as the Other of the symbolic Law is not only dead, it does not even know that it is dead (like the terrible figure from Freud's dream) – it could not know it insofar as it is totally insensible to the living substance of enjoyment. The superego embodies on the contrary the paradox of a Law which 'proceeds from the time when the Other wasn't yet dead. The superego is a surviving remainder' (Jacques-Alain Miller). The superego imperative 'Enjoy!', the turning round of the dead Law into the obscene figure of superego, implies a disquieting experience: suddenly, we become aware of the fact that what a minute ago appeared to us a dead letter is really alive, respiring, palpitating. Let us remind ourselves of a scene from the movie *Aliens 2*: the group of heroes is advancing along a long tunnel, the stone walls of which are twisted like interlaced plaits of hair; suddenly, the plaits start to move and to secrete a glutinous mucus, the petrified corpses come to life again.

We should then reverse the usual metaphorics of 'alienation' where the dead, formal letter sucks out, as a kind of parasite or vampire, the living present force, i.e., where the living subjects are prisoners of a dead cobweb. This dead, formal character of the Law is a *sine qua non* of our freedom: the real totalitarian danger arises when the Law no longer wants to stay dead. The result of m^1 is then that there isn't any truth about *truth*: every warrant of the Law has the status of a semblance, the Law doesn't have any support in the truth, it is necessary without being true; the meeting of K. with the washerwoman thus adds to the reverse side usually passed by in silence: insofar as the Law isn't grounded in truth, it is impregnated with enjoyment.

3. TOWARDS AN ETHICS OF THE REAL

Now, it should be clear how the two notions with which we tried to supplement the theoretical apparatus of *Hegemony* – the *subject* as an empty place correlative to antagonism; social *fantasy* as the elementary ideological mode to mask antagonism – proceed simply from taking into account the consequences of the breakthrough accomplished by this book.

The main achievement of *Hegemony*, the achievement because of which this book – far from being just one in the series of 'post'-works (post-Marxist, post-structuralist, etc.) – occupies in relation to this series a position of *extimité*, is that, perhaps for the first time, it articulates the contours of a political project based on an ethics of the real, of the 'going through the fantasy [*la traversée du fantasme*]', an ethics of confrontation with an impossible, traumatic kernel not covered by any *ideal* (of unbroken communication, of the invention of the self). That's why we can effectively say that *Hegemony* is the only real answer to Habermas, to his project based on the ethics of the ideal of communication without constraint. The way Habermas formulates the 'ideal speech situation' already betrays its status as fetish: 'ideal speech situation' is something which, as soon as we engage in communication, is 'simultaneously denied and laid claim to',[10] i.e., we must presuppose the ideal of an unbroken communication to be already realized, even though we know simultaneously that this cannot be the case. To the examples of the fetishist logic *je sais bien, mais quand même*, we must then add the formula of the 'ideal speech situation': 'I know very well that communication is broken and perverted, but still ... (I believe and act as if the ideal speech situation is already realized).'[11]

What this fetishist logic of the ideal is masking, of course, is the limitation proper to the symbolic field as such: the fact that the signifying field is always structured around a certain fundamental deadlock. Thus deadlock doesn't entail any kind of resignation – or, if there is a resignation, it is a paradox of *enthusiastic resignation*: we are using here the term 'enthusiasm' in its strict Kantian meaning, as indicating an experience of the object through the very failure of its adequate representation. Enthusiasm and resignation are not then two opposed moments: it is 'resignation' itself, i.e., the experience of a certain impossibility, which incites enthusiasm.

NOTES

This paper first appeared as the Afterword to Ernesto Laclau's *New Reflections on the Revolution of our Time*, London and New York, Verso, 1990, pp. 249–60 [eds].

1 Ernesto Laclau and Chantal Mouffe, *Hegemony and Socialist Strategy*, London and New York, Verso, 1985 [eds].

2 For an explication of the paradoxes of the Lacanian Real, see Slavoj Žižek, *The Sublime Object of Ideology*, London and New York, Verso, 1989, pp. 161–73.

3 Ernesto Laclau, *Politics and Ideology in Marxist Theory: Capitalism–Fascism–Populism*, London, New Left Books, 1977.

4 G. W. F. Hegel, *Phenomenology of Spirit*, trans. A. V. Miller, Oxford, Oxford University Press, 1977, pp. 111–19.

5 For an explication of the notion of social fantasy, see Žižek, *Sublime Object of Ideology*, pp. 124–8.

6 Franz Kafka, *The Trial*, trans. Willa and Edwin Muir, Harmondsworth, Penguin, 1953, p. 240.

7 Reiner Stach, *Kafkas erotischer Mythos*, Frankfurt, Fischer Verlag, 1987, p. 35.

8 Kafka, *The Trial*, pp. 45–6.

9 *Ibid.*, p. 55.

10 Jürgen Habermas, *Der philosophische Diskurs der Moderne*, Frankfurt, Fischer Verlag, 1985, p. 378.

11 Žižek is referring to the development of this 'fetishist denial' in Octave Mannoni's famous essay, 'I Know Well, but All the Same . . .', in *Perversion and the Social Relation*, ed. Molly Anne

Rothenberg, Dennis A. Foster and Slavoj Žižek, Durham, Duke University Press, 2003), pp. 68–92. See also Chapter 11 of this volume, 'Between Symbolic Fiction and Fantasmatic Spectre: Towards a Lacanian Theory of Ideology', pages 260 and 268 note 10 [eds].

13 Re-visioning 'Lacanian' Social Criticism: The Law and its Obscene Double

My thesis is that what passes in American cultural criticism for 'Lacanian theory' presents a very limited and distorted reception of Lacan's work. I want to challenge this established picture and render palpable another dimension of Lacan, far more productive for critical social theory.

The predominant feature of this established picture is the notion of Lacan as the phallogocentrist 'philosopher of language' who emphasizes the price the subject has to pay in order to gain access to the symbolic order – all the false poetry of 'castration', of some primordial act of sacrifice and renunciation, of *jouissance* as impossible. So let's begin with this unfortunate castration.

In what, precisely, does symbolic castration consist? The trouble with the critics of Lacan's 'phallocentrism' is that, as a rule, they refer to 'phallus' or 'castration' in a rather commonsense metaphoric way. In standard feminist film studies, for example, every time a man behaves aggressively toward a woman or asserts his authority over her, one can be sure that his act will be designated as 'phallic'. Likewise, every time a woman is framed, rendered helpless or cornered, one can be sure her experience will be designated as 'castrating'.

What gets lost here is the paradox of the phallus itself as the signifier of castration: if we are to assert our (symbolic) 'phallic' authority, the price to be paid is that we have to renounce the position of agent and consent to function as the medium through which the big Other – the symbolic institution – acts and speaks. When the subject is endowed with symbolic authority, they act as an appendix of their symbolic title: it is the big Other who acts through them. Suffice it to recall a judge who is a miserable and corrupted person, but the moment they put on their robe and other insignia, their words are the words of Law itself.

It's the same with paternal authority: a real father exerts authority only insofar as he posits himself as the embodiment of a transcendent symbolic agency, insofar as he accepts that it is not himself, but the big Other who speaks through him, in his words. Recall the millionaire from a film by Claude Chabrol who inverts the standard complaint about being loved only for his millions: 'If only I could find a woman who would love me for my money and not for myself!'

Therein resides the lesson of the Freudian myth of the parricide, of the primordial father who, after his violent death, returns stronger than ever in the guise of his Name, as a symbolic authority. If a living, real father is to exert paternal symbolic authority, he must in a way die alive. It is his identification with the 'dead letter' of the symbolic mandate that bestows authority on his person; to paraphrase the old racist slogan: 'The only good father is a dead father!' Insofar as the phallus *qua* signifier designates the agency of symbolic authority, its crucial feature therefore resides in the fact that it is not 'mine', the organ of a living subject, but a place at which a foreign power intervenes and inscribes itself onto my body, a place at which the big Other acts through me. In short, the fact that phallus is a signifier means above all that it is structurally an organ without a body, somehow 'detached' from my body.

Another (mis)reading of Lacan, closely linked to this one, concerns the opposition between the phallic economy and the polymorphous plurality of subject-positions. According to the standard view, the task of the phallic economy is to mould the pre-Oedipal dispersed plurality of subject-positions into a unified subject who is subordinated to the rule of the Name-of-the-Father (bearer and relay of social authority) and is as such the ideal subject of (social) Power. What one has to call into question here is the underlying assumption that social Power exerts itself via the unified Oedipal subject entirely submitted to the phallic paternal Law, and, inversely, that the dispersion of the unified subject into a multitude of subject-positions as it were automatically undermines the authority and exercise of Power. Against this commonplace, one has to point out again and again that Power always interpellates us, addresses us, as split subjects. In order to reproduce itself, it relies upon our splitting. The message the power discourse bombards us with is by definition inconsistent: there is always a gap between public discourse and its fantasmatic support. Far from being a kind of secondary weakness, a sign of Power's imperfection, this splitting is necessary for its exercise. Today's 'postmodern' subject is directly constituted as an inconsistent bundle of multiple 'subject-positions' (economically conservative but sexually 'enlightened', tolerant but racist, etc.).

* * *

If we return now to symbolic paternal authority: a homology seems to impose itself here between this authority, the Name-of-the-Father, and what in the literature on anti-Semitism is called the 'conceptual Jew', the mythical-invisible agent of Jewish conspiracy, who, hidden behind the curtain, pulls the strings of our lives. Is the gap that separates active Jews from the fantasmatic figure of the 'conceptual Jew' not of the same nature as the gap that separates the empirical, always deficient person of the father from the Name-of-the-Father, from his symbolic mandate? Isn't it the case that, in both instances, a real person acts as the personification of an unreal, fictitious agency, the actual father being a stand-in for the agency of symbolic authority and the actual Jew a stand-in for the fantasmatic figure of the 'conceptual Jew'?

Convincing as it may sound, this homology has to be rejected as deceptive. Although in both cases we are dealing with the split between knowledge and belief ('I know very well that my father is an ordinary person, but still I believe in his authority'; 'I know very well that Jews are people like others, but still there is something strange about them'), the two splits are of a fundamentally different nature. In the first case, the belief concerns the 'visible' public symbolic authority (notwithstanding my awareness of the father's imperfection and debility, I still accept him as a figure of authority), whereas, in the second case, what I believe in is the power of an invisible spectral apparition. The fantasmatic 'conceptual Jew' is not a paternal figure of symbolic authority, a 'castrated' bearer or medium of public authority, but something decidedly different, a kind of uncanny double of the public authority that perverts its proper logic. The 'conceptual Jew' has to act in the shadow, invisible to the public eye, irradiating a phantom-like, spectral omnipotence. On account of this unfathomable, elusive status of the kernel of their identity, the Jew – in contrast to the 'castrated' father – is perceived as uncastratable: the more their actual, social, public existence is cut short, the more threatening becomes their elusive fantasmatic ex-sistence.

The same logic seems to be at work in the anti-Communist right-wing populism that has recently been gaining strength in the ex-Socialist East European countries. Its answer to the present economic and other hardships is that, although the Communists lost legal, public power, they continue to pull the strings, to operate the levers of actual economic power, controlling the media and state institutions. Communists are thus perceived as a fantasmatic entity like the Jew: the more they lose public power and become invisible, the stronger their phantom-like omnipresence, their shadowy actual control.

This fantasmatic logic of an invisible and for that very reason all-powerful Master was clearly at work in the way the figure of Abimael Guzman, 'Presidente Gonzalo', the leader of Sendero Luminoso in Peru, functioned prior to his arrest. The fact that his very existence was doubted (people were not sure if he actually existed or was just a mythical point of reference) added to his power. The most recent example of such an invisible and for that reason all-powerful Master is provided by Bryan Singer's *The Usual Suspects*, a film centred on the mysterious 'Keyser Soeze', a master criminal who it is not clear exists at all. As one of the persons in the film puts it, 'I don't believe in God, but I'm nonetheless afraid of him.' People are afraid to see him or, once forced to confront him face to face, to mention this to others. His identity is a tightly kept secret. At the end of the film, it is disclosed that Keyser Soeze is the most miserable of the group of suspects, a limping, self-humiliating wimp. What is crucial is this very contrast between the omnipotence of the invisible agent of power and the way this same agent is reduced to a crippled weakling once his identity is rendered public.

The next feature to be noted is the vocal status of this invisible omnipotent master: his power relies on the uncanny autonomization of the voice baptized by French cinema theorist Michel Chion 'acousmatization': the emergence of a spectral voice that floats freely in a mysterious intermediate domain and thereby acquires the horrifying dimension of omnipresence and omnipotence – the voice of an invisible Master, from Fritz Lang's *The Testament of Dr Mabuse* to the 'mother's voice' in Hitchcock's *Psycho*. In *Psycho*, the 'mother's voice' literally cuts out a hole in the visual reality: the screen image becomes a delusive surface, a lure secretly dominated by the bodiless voice of an invisible/absent Master, a voice that cannot be attached to any object in the diegetic reality.

* * *

In addition to symbolic castration and the distinction between the two Masters, the castrated and the non-castrated one, what one should further oppose to the usual picture of Lacan as a theorist of the primordial loss of *jouissance* is its obverse, which is usually passed over in silence. The trouble with *jouissance* is not that it is unattainable, that it always eludes our grasp, but rather that one can never get rid of it, that its stain forever drags along. Therein resides the point of Lacan's concept of surplus-enjoyment: the very renunciation of *jouissance* brings about a remainder or surplus of *jouissance*. Suffice it to recall the deep satisfaction brought about in the subject who follows the totalitarian call 'Renounce! Sacrifice! Enough of pleasures!'

This surplus-enjoyment complicates the problem of responsibility. The subject can exonerate themselves of responsibility with regard to the symbolic network of tradition that overdetermines their speech. For example, the author of a racist injury can always evoke the network of historical sedimentations in which their speech act is embedded. However, the subject is responsible for the little bit of enjoyment they find in their aggressive racist outburst.

The same goes for the reverse case of a victim. My description of the circumstances whose victim I was can be entirely truthful and accurate, but this very enunciation of my predicament provides me with a surplus-enjoyment: the report on my victimization, by means of which I impute the guilt to others and present myself as an innocent, passive victim of circumstances, always provides a deep libidinal satisfaction. Founding one's symbolic identity on a specific injury can be a source of deep satisfaction, and for this satisfaction contained in my subjective position of enunciation, while I report on my victimization, I am responsible.

Consider the way the citizens of Sarajevo perceive themselves in these difficult times of the city under siege. Their suffering is, of course, very material, but it is impossible not to take note of the narcissistic satisfaction contained in the narrativization of their predicament. They are well aware that their city has become a symbol, that they are in a sense the 'centre of the world', that the eyes of the media are turned on them. Consequently, in their very direct self-experience of their painful everyday life, they are already playing a role for the gaze of the virtual Other. What they fear (at an unconscious level, at least) is the loss of this privileged 'sacred' role of the exemplary victim, that is to say, the moment when Sarajevo will become a city like others.

This excessive *jouissance* can be best grasped via the question: what is the target of the outbursts of violence? What are we aiming at, what do we endeavour to annihilate, when we exterminate Jews or beat up foreigners in our cities? The first answer that offers itself again involves symbolic fiction: is not, beyond direct physical pain and personal humiliation, the ultimate aim of the rapes in the Bosnian war, for example, to undermine the fiction (the symbolic narrative) that guarantees the coherence of the Muslim community? Is not a consequence of extreme violence also that 'the story the community has been telling itself about itself no longer makes sense' (to paraphrase Richard Rorty)?

This destruction of the enemy's symbolic universe, this 'culturocide', however, is in itself not sufficient to explain an outburst of ethnic violence. Its ultimate cause (in the sense of driving force) is to be sought at a somewhat different level. What does our 'intolerance' towards foreigners feed on? What is it that irritates us in them and disturbs our psychic balance? Even at the level of a simple phenomenological description, the crucial characteristic of this cause is that it cannot be pinpointed as some clearly defined observable property. Although we can usually enumerate a series of features about 'them' that annoy us (the way they laugh too loudly, the bad smell of their food, etc.), these features function as indicators of a more radical strangeness. Foreigners may look and act like us, but there is some unfathomable *je ne sais quoi*, something 'in them more than themselves', that makes them 'not quite human' ('aliens' in the precise sense this term acquired in the science-fiction films of the 1950s).

Let me recall a rather personal experience, that of my own mother. Her best friend, as the cliché goes, is Jewish. One day, after a financial transaction with this old Jewish woman, my mother said to me: 'What a nice lady, but did you notice the strange way she counted the money?' In my mother's eyes, this feature, the way the Jewish lady handled the money, functioned exactly like the mysterious feature from the science-fiction novels and films which enables us to identify aliens who are otherwise indistinguishable from ourselves: a thin layer of transparent skin between the third finger and the little finger, a strange gleam in the eye, and so on. Our relationship to this unfathomable traumatic element that 'bothers us' in the Other is structured in fantasies (about the Other's political and/or sexual omnipotence, about 'their' strange sexual practices, about their secret hypnotic powers). Lacan baptized this paradoxical uncanny object that stands for what in the perceived positive, empirical object necessarily eludes my gaze and as such serves as the driving force of my desiring it, *objet petit a*, the object-cause of desire. At its most radical level, violence is precisely an endeavour to strike a blow at this unbearable surplus-enjoyment contained in the Other.

* * *

This stain of enjoyment, moreover, is crucial for the 'normal' functioning of power. A personal experience revealed to me this inherent obscenity of Power in a most distastefully enjoyable way. In the 1970s, I did my (obligatory) army service in the old Yugoslav People's Army, in small barracks with no proper medical facilities. In a room which also served as sleeping quarters for a private trained as a medical assistant, once a week a doctor from the nearby military hospital held his consulting hours. On the frame of the large mirror above the wash-basin in this room, the soldiers had stuck a couple of postcards of half-naked women – a standard resource for masturbation in those pre-pornography times, to be sure. When the doctor was paying us his weekly visit, all of us who had reported for medical examination were seated on a long bench alongside the wall opposite the wash-basin and were then examined in turn.

One day while I was also waiting to be examined, it was the turn of a young, half-illiterate soldier who complained of pains in his penis (which, of course, was in itself sufficient to trigger obscene giggles from all of us, the doctor included): the skin on its head was too tight, so he was unable to draw it back normally. The doctor ordered him to pull down his trousers and demonstrate his trouble. The soldier did so and the skin slid down the head smoothly, though the soldier was quick to add that his trouble occurred only during erection. The doctor then said: 'OK, then masturbate, get an erection, so that we can check it!' Deeply embarrassed and red in the face, the soldier began to masturbate in front of all of us but, of course, failed to produce an erection.

The doctor then took one of the postcards of half-naked women from the mirror, held it close to the soldier's head, and started to shout at him: 'Look! What breasts! What a cunt! Masturbate! How is it that you don't get the erection? What kind of a man are you! Go on, masturbate!' All of us in the room, including the doctor himself, accompanied the spectacle with obscene laughter. The unfortunate soldier himself soon joined us with an embarrassed giggle, exchanging looks of solidarity with us while continuing to masturbate.

This scene brought about in me an experience of quasi-epiphany. *In nuce*, there was everything in it, the entire apparatus of Power: the uncanny mixture of imposed enjoyment and humiliating coercion; the agency of Power which shouts severe orders, but simultaneously shares with us, his subordinates, obscene laughter bearing witness to a deep solidarity; the grotesque excess by means of which, in a unique short-circuit, attitudes which are officially opposed and mutually exclusive reveal their uncanny complicity, where the solemn agent of Power suddenly starts to wink at us across the table in a gesture of obscene solidarity, letting us know that the thing (his orders) is not to be taken too seriously, and thereby consolidating his power. The aim of the 'critique of ideology', of the analysis of an ideological edifice, is to extract this symptomatic kernel which the official, public ideological text simultaneously disavows and needs for its undisturbed functioning.

Let me recall a further example, as far away as possible from the poor Yugoslav Army: life in English colleges as depicted in numerous memoirs and, among others, in Lindsay Anderson's film *If*. Beneath the civilized, open-minded, liberal surface of the daily life in these colleges, with its dull but charming atmosphere, there is another world of brutal power relations between younger and elder pupils. A detailed set of unwritten rules prescribes the ways elder pupils are allowed to exploit and to humiliate in different ways their younger peers, all of this pervaded with prohibited homosexuality. We do not have the public 'repressive' rule of law and order undermined by undercover forms of rebellion – mocking the public authority, and so on – but rather its opposite: the public authority maintains a civilized, gentle appearance, whereas beneath it there is a shadowy realm in which the brutal exercise of power is itself sexualized. And the crucial point, of course, is that this obscene shadowy realm, far from undermining the civilized semblance of the public power, serves as its inherent support. It is only by way of initiation into the unwritten rules of this realm that a pupil is able to participate in the benefits of the school life. The penalty for breaking these unwritten rules is much harsher than for breaking the public rules.

Did not the blindness for this same split seal the fate of the unfortunate Captain Bligh of the *Bounty*? We are dealing here with a true enigma: why was this exemplary officer, obsessed with the safety and health of his sailors, elevated into one of the archetypal figures of Evil in our popular culture? Successive changes in the predominant image of Bligh serve as a perfect index to shifts in hegemonic ideology – each epoch had its own Bligh. Suffice it to mention the three principal cinema portraits: the decadently aristocratic Charles Laughton in the 1930s, the coldly bureaucratic Trevor Howard in the 1960s, the mentally tortured Anthony Hopkins in the 1980s ... What 'really happened' on HMS *Bounty*? What was the 'true cause' of the mutiny? Bligh was perceived as 'not a proper gentleman', as somebody who did have power (as the ship's commander, he had the right to make decisions and give orders, a right he took full advantage of), yet was somehow 'stiff', lacking the sensitivity that tells a good leader when and how to apply rules, how to take into account the 'organic', spontaneous network of relations among his subordinates.

More precisely, Bligh's mistake was not simply that of being insensitive to the concrete network of 'organic' relations among the sailors; his crucial limitation was that he was completely blind to the

structural function of the ritualized power relations among the sailors
(the right of older, more experienced sailors to humiliate the younger
and inexperienced, to exploit them sexually, to submit them to ordeals,
etc.). These rituals provided an ambiguous supplement to the public-
legal power relations. They acted as their shadowy double, transgressing and subverting them, yet at the same time serving as their ultimate
support: a satire on the legal institutions, an inversion of public Power,
yet a transgression that consolidates what it transgresses.

In his blindness to the stabilizing role of these rituals, Bligh prohibited them, or at least took their edge off by changing them into a
harmless folkloric exercise. Caught in the Enlightenment trap, he was
able to perceive only the brutal, inhuman aspect of these rituals, not
the satisfaction they brought about, not the extent to which his own
public, legal power relied on this obscene underworld of unwritten
rules. The mutiny – the violence – broke out when Bligh interfered
with this murky world of obscene rituals that served as the fantasmatic
background of Power.

Here, however, one should be careful to avoid a confusion: this
set of obscene unwritten rules misrecognized by Bligh is not to be
identified too quickly with the so-called implicit, impenetrable background of our activity, i.e., with the fact that, as Heideggerians would
have put it, we finite human beings are always 'thrown' into a situation
and have to find ourselves in it in a way which can never be formalized
into a set of explicit rules.

Let us recall another film which stages the obscene ritual of Power:
Stanley Kubrick's *Full Metal Jacket*. What we get in its first part is the
military drill, the direct bodily discipline, saturated by a unique blend
of humiliating display of power, sexualization and obscene blasphemy
(at Christmas, the soldiers are ordered to sing 'Happy birthday, dear
Jesus') – in short, the superego machine of Power at its purest. As to
the status of this obscene machine with respect to our everyday life-
world, the lesson of the film is clear: the function of this obscene
underworld of rituals is not to enable the official 'public' ideology to
'catch on', to start to function as a constituent of our actual social life.
That is, this obscene underworld does not 'mediate' between the
abstract structure of symbolic law and the concrete experience of
the actual life-world. The situation is rather inverse: we need a 'human

face', a sense of distance, in order to be able to accommodate ourselves to the crazy demands of the superego machine.

The first part of the film ends with a soldier who, on account of his over-identification with the military superego machine, runs amok and shoots first the drill sergeant, then himself: the radical, unmediated identification with the superego machine necessarily leads to a murderous *passage à l'acte*. (*Full Metal Jacket* successfully resists the temptation to 'humanize' the drill sergeant, in opposition to *An Officer and a Gentleman*, for example, which performs the ideological gesture of letting us know that, beneath his cruel and demanding appearance, the drill sergeant is a warm, father-like figure.) The second, main part of the film ends with a scene in which a soldier (Matthew Modine) who, throughout the film, displayed a kind of ironic 'human distance' toward the military machine (on his helmet, the inscription 'born to kill' is accompanied by the peace sign, etc.), kills out of compassion the wounded Vietcong sniper girl. He is the one in whom the interpellation by the military big Other has fully succeeded; he is the fully constituted military subject.

Insofar as the obscene superego machine displays the structure of the unconscious and thus exemplifies in an outstanding way Lacan's thesis that the Master is unconscious, there is a more general conclusion to be drawn from it. The paradoxical achievement of Lacan which usually passes unnoticed even by his advocates is that, on behalf of psychoanalysis, he returns to the Modern Age 'decontextualized' rationalist notion of subject.

One of the commonplaces of today's American appropriation of Heidegger is to emphasize how he, alongside Wittgenstein, Merleau-Ponty and others, elaborated the conceptual framework that enables us to get rid of the rationalist notion of subject as an autonomous agent who, excluded from the world, in a computer-like way processes data provided by the senses. Heidegger's notion of 'being-in-the-world' points toward our irreducible and unsurpassable 'embeddedness' in a concrete and ultimately contingent life-world: we are always-already in the world, engaged in an existential project within a background that eludes our grasp and remains forever the opaque horizon into which we are 'thrown' as finite beings. It is customary to interpret the opposition between consciousness and the unconscious along the same lines: the disembodied Ego stands for rational consciousness, whereas the 'unconscious' is synonymous with the opaque background that we cannot ever fully master, since we are always-already part of it, caught in it.

Lacan, however, in an unheard-of gesture, claims the exact opposite: the Freudian 'unconscious' has nothing whatsoever do to with the structurally necessary and irreducible opaqueness of the background, of the life-context in which we, the always-already engaged agents, are embedded. The 'unconscious' is rather the disembodied rational machine which follows its path irrespectively of the demands of the subject's life-world. It stands for the rational subject insofar as it is originally 'out of joint', in discord with its contextualized situation. 'Unconscious' is the crack on account of which the subject's primordial stance is not that of 'being-in-the-world'.

With this formulation, one can also provide a new, unexpected solution to the old phenomenological problem of how it is possible for the subject to disengage itself from its concrete life-world and (mis)perceive itself as a disembodied rational agent. This disengagement can only occur because there is from the very outset something in the subject that resists its full inclusion into its life-world context, and this 'something', of course, is the unconscious as the psychic machine that disregards the requirements of the 'reality-principle'.

* * *

It is crucial that we recognize the inherently vocal status of these unwritten rules, of this shadowy paralegal domain, which can teach us a lot about the voice. True, the experience of *s'entendre-parler*, of hearing-oneself-speaking, grounds the illusion of the transparent self-presence of the speaking subject. Is, however, the voice not at the same time that which undermines most radically the subject's self-presence and self-transparency? I hear myself speaking, yet what I hear is never fully myself but a parasite, a foreign body in my very heart. This stranger in myself acquires positive existence in different guises, from the voice of conscience and the opaque voice of the hypnotist to the persecutor in paranoia. Voice is that which, in the signifier, resists meaning; it stands for the opaque inertia which cannot be recuperated by meaning.

It is only the dimension of writing that accounts for the stability of meaning, or, to quote the immortal words of Samuel Goldwyn: 'A verbal agreement isn't worth the paper it's written on.' As such, voice is neither dead nor alive: its primordial phenomenological status is rather that of a living dead, of a spectral apparition that somehow survives its own death, i.e., the eclipse of meaning. In other words, it is true that the life of a voice can be opposed to the dead letter of writing, but this life is the uncanny life of an undead monster, not a 'healthy' living self-presence of Meaning.

In order to render manifest this uncanny voice, it is sufficient to cast a cursory glance at the history of music, which reads as a kind of counter-history to the usual story of Western metaphysics as the domination of voice over writing. What we encounter in it again and again is a voice that threatens the established Order and that, for that reason, has to be brought under control, subordinated to the rational articulation of spoken and written word, fixed into writing. In order to designate the danger that lurks there, Lacan coined the neologism *jouis-sense*, enjoyment-in-meaning, which is present the moment the singing voice cuts loose from its anchoring in meaning and accelerates into a consuming self-enjoyment.

The effort to dominate and regulate this excess runs from ancient China, where the emperor himself legislated music, to the fear of Elvis Presley that brought together the conservative moral majority in the USA and the Communist hard-liners in the Soviet Union. In his *Republic*, Plato tolerates music only insofar as it is strictly subordinated to the order of the Word. Music is located at the very crossroads of Nature and Culture. It seizes us as it were 'in the real', far more directly than the meaning of words. For that reason, it can serve as the mightiest weapon of education and discipline, yet the moment it loses its footing and gets caught in the self-propelling vicious circle of enjoyment, it can undermine the very foundations not only of the State, but of the social order as such.

In medieval times, Church power confronted the same dilemma. It is amazing to observe how much energy and care the highest ecclesiastic authority (popes) put into the seemingly trifling question of the regulation of music (the problem of polyphony, the 'devil's fourth', etc.). The figure that personifies the ambiguous attitude of

Power towards the excess of the Voice is, of course, Hildegarde von Bingen, who put mystical enjoyment into music and was thus constantly on the verge of excommunication, although she was integrated into the highest level of the hierarchy of power, regularly counselling the emperor.

The same matrix is again at work in the French Revolution, whose ideologues endeavoured to assert 'normal' sexual difference under the domination of the male spoken word against decadent aristocratic indulgence in the pleasures of listening to castrati. One of the last episodes in this everlasting struggle is the notorious Soviet campaign, instigated by Stalin himself, against Shostakovich's *Katarina Izmajlova*. Rather curiously, one of the main reproaches was that the opera is a mass of unarticulated screams.

The problem is thus always the same: how are we to prevent the voice from sliding into a consuming self-enjoyment that 'effeminizes' the reliable masculine Word? The voice functions here as a 'supplement' in the Derridean sense: one endeavours to restrain it, to regulate it, to subordinate it to the articulated Word, yet one cannot dispense with it altogether, since a proper dosage is vital for the exercise of power (suffice it to recall the role of patriotic military songs in the building up of a totalitarian community).

However, this brief description of ours can give rise to the wrong impression that we are dealing with a simple opposition between the 'repressive' articulated Word and the 'transgressive' consuming voice: on the one hand, the articulated Word that disciplines and regulates the voice as a means of asserting social discipline and authority, and on the other hand, the self-enjoying Voice that acts as the medium of liberation, of tearing apart the disciplinary chains of law and order. But what about the US Marine Corps' mesmeric 'marching chants'? Are their debilitating rhythm and sadistically sexualized nonsensical content not an exemplary case of the consuming self-enjoyment in the service of Power? The excess of the voice is thus radically undecidable.

* * *

Where does the split between public, written law and its obscene paralegal supplement come from? What is behind it is the paradox of the forced choice that marks our most fundamental relationship to the society to which we belong: at a certain point, society impels us to choose freely what is already necessarily imposed upon us. This notion of freely choosing what is nonetheless inevitable is strictly co-dependent with the notion of an empty symbolic gesture, a gesture – an offer – that is meant to be rejected. The one is the obverse of the other. That is, what the empty gesture offers is the possibility to choose the impossible, that which inevitably will not happen.

An exemplary case of such an empty gesture is found in John Irving's *A Prayer for Owen Meany*. After the little boy Owen accidentally kills John's – his best friend's, the narrator's – mother, he is, of course, terribly upset. So, to show how sorry he is, he discreetly gives to John his complete collection of baseball cards, his most precious possession. However, Dan, John's delicate stepfather, tells him that the proper thing to do is to return the gift. What we have here is symbolic exchange at its purest: a gesture made to be rejected. The point, the 'magic' of symbolic exchange, is that, although at the end we are where we were at the beginning, the overall result of the operation is not zero but a distinct gain for both parties, the pact of solidarity.

Is not something similar part of our everyday mores? When, after being engaged in a fierce competition for a job promotion with my closest friend, I win, the proper thing to do is to offer to withdraw, so that he will get the promotion. And the proper thing for him to do is to reject my offer. This way, perhaps, our friendship can be saved. The problem, of course, is: what if the other to whom the offer is made actually accepts it? What if, upon being beaten in the competition, I accept my friend's offer to get the promotion instead of him? A situation like this is catastrophic: it causes the disintegration of the semblance (of freedom) that pertains to social order. However, since at this level things in a way are what they seem to be, this disintegration of the semblance equals the disintegration of the social substance, of the social link itself. Ex-Communist societies present an extreme case of such a forced free choice. In them, the subjects were incessantly bombarded with the request to express freely their attitude towards Power, yet everybody was well aware that this freedom was strictly limited to the freedom to say 'Yes' to the Communist regime itself. For that very reason, Communist societies were extremely sensitive to the status of semblance: the ruling Party wanted at any cost whatsoever to maintain undisturbed the appearance (of the broad popular support of the regime).

The ending of Michael Curtiz' *Casablanca* (Humphrey Bogart staying at Casablanca and letting Ingrid Bergman go with her heroic husband) is so deeply satisfactory to our male-chauvinist attitude because it also centres on such a gesture meant to be refused: Bogart correctly reads Ingrid Bergman's offer from the previous night to stay with him if he arranges for the visa for her husband as such a gesture.

This scene condenses, in one and the same gesture, three attitudes which correspond to the Kierkegaardian triad of Aesthetic, Ethical and Religious. The first, 'aesthetic' way to read Bogart's gesture is to discern in it an awareness that, although they are passionately in love, the fulfilment of their relationship (the two of them staying together) would necessarily turn sour, so it's better to maintain the dream of possible happiness. What we encounter here is the basic feature of the symbolic order, the fact that, in it, possibility already counts as actuality: often, satisfaction is provided by the mere awareness that we could have done something that we desired (slept with a passionately desired sexual partner, taken revenge on a long-time enemy), as if the realization of this possibility would somehow spoil the purity of our success.

The second reading is ethical: Bogart gives preference to the universal political Cause over the idiosyncrasy of private pleasure (and thereby proves worthy of Bergman's love). This motif of a man who proves he is worthy of woman's love by demonstrating to her that he is able to survive without her is a fundamental constituent of our male symbolic identity.

There is, however, a third possible reading which renders visible Bogart's final renunciation as a cruel narcissistic act of vengeance on Bergman, i.e., a punishment for her letting him down in Paris: after making her confess that she truly loves him, it's now his turn to reject her in a gesture whose cynical message is, 'You wanted your husband and now you're stuck with him, even if you prefer me!' This very logic of vengeful, humiliating and cruel 'settling of accounts' makes Bogart's final gesture 'religious', not merely 'aesthetic'. My point is that Bogart's gesture of renunciation is the symbolic gesture at its purest, which is why it is wrong to ask the question, 'Which of these three readings is true?' The impact of Bogart's final gesture relies precisely on the fact that it serves as a kind of neutral 'container' for all three libidinal attitudes, so that one and the same gesture satisfies a multitude of inconsistent, even contradictory, desires: to avoid the disappointment of realizing one's desire, to fascinate the woman by assuming a moral stance of self-sacrifice, and to take vengeance for a narcissistic wound. Therein resides the paradoxical achievement of symbolization: the vain quest for the 'true meaning' (the ultimate signified) is supplanted by a unique signifying gesture.

One can see, now, how this gesture meant to be rejected, this semblance of the free choice, is connected to the splitting of the law into the public-written law on the one hand and the superego (the obscene-unwritten-secret law) on the other. The unwritten obscene law articulates the paradoxical injunction of what the subject, its addressee, has to choose freely; as such, this injunction has to remain invisible to the public eye if Power is to remain operative. In short, what we, ordinary subjects of law, actually want is a command in the guise of freedom, of a free choice: we want to obey, but simultaneously to maintain the semblance of freedom and thus save face. If the command is delivered directly, bypassing the semblance of freedom, the public humiliation hurts us and can induce us to rebel; if there is no order discernible in the Master's discourse, this lack of a command is experienced as suffocating and gives rise to the demand for a new Master capable of providing a clear injunction.

* * *

This distance between the public written law and its obscene superego supplement also enables us to demonstrate clearly where cynicism, cynical distance, falls short. How does cynical distance function today? In one of his letters, Freud refers to the well-known joke about the newly married man who, when asked by his friend how his wife looks, how beautiful she is, answers: 'I personally don't like her, but that's a matter of taste.' The paradox of this answer is that the subject pretends to assume the standpoint of universality from which 'to be like-able' appears as an idiosyncrasy, as a contingent 'pathological' feature which, as such, is not to be taken into consideration.

One encounters the same 'impossible' position of enunciation in contemporary 'postmodern' racism. When asked about the reasons for their violence against foreigners, neo-Nazi skinheads in Germany usually gave three types of answers: utilitarian ones (foreigners are stealing our jobs, raping our women), ideological ones (foreigners are a threat to our Western way of life), and a kind of primitive reference to pleasure-principle (they simply get on my nerves, I cannot stand the sight of them, it makes me feel good when I beat them up). Now, however, more and more, they tend to invoke a fourth kind of answer: they suddenly start to talk like social workers, sociologists and social psychologists, citing diminished social mobility, rising insecurity, the disintegration of paternal authority, the lack of maternal love in their family, and so on.

We encounter a homologous falsity in the attitude of those traditional psychoanalysts who prefer their patients to be 'naïve' and ignorant of psychoanalytic theory, an ignorance that allegedly enables them to produce 'purer' symptoms, i.e., symptoms in which their unconscious is not too much distorted by their rational knowledge. For example, the incestuous dream of a patient who already knows all about the Oedipus complex will be far more distorted, resorting to more complex strategies to conceal its desire, than the dream of a 'naïve' patient. We all have a longing for the good old heroic times of psychoanalysis, in which a patient told his analyst, 'Last night, I had a dream about killing a dragon and then advancing through a thick forest to a castle', whereupon the analyst triumphantly answered, 'Elementary, my dear patient! The dragon is your father and the dream expresses your desire to kill him in order to return to the safe haven of the maternal castle.'

Lacan's wager is here exactly the opposite: the subject of psychoanalysis is the modern subject of science, which means, among other things, that its symptoms are by definition never 'innocent', they are always addressed to the analyst *qua* subject supposed to know (their meaning) and thus as it were imply, point towards, their own interpretation. For that reason, one is quite justified in saying that we have not only Jungian, Kleinian and Lacanian interpretations of a symptom, but also symptoms which are in themselves Jungian,

Kleinian and Lacanian, that is to say, whose reality involves implicit reference to some psychoanalytic theory.

So, at the political level, the problem today is how to counteract this 'reflected' cynical attitude: is there a specific kind of knowledge which renders impossible the act, a knowledge which can no longer be co-opted by cynical distance ('I know what I am doing, but I am nevertheless doing it')? Or must we leave behind the domain of knowledge and have recourse to a direct, extra-symbolic, bodily intervention, or to an intuitive 'Enlightenment', a change of subjective attitude, beyond knowledge?

The fundamental wager of psychoanalysis is that there exists such a knowledge which produces effects in the Real, that we can 'undo things (symptoms) with words'. The whole point of psychoanalytic treatment is that it operates exclusively at the level of 'knowledge' (words), yet has effects in the Real of bodily symptoms.

How, then, are we to specify this 'knowledge' which, even in our era of cynicism, brings about effects in the Real? What is it that the cynic does not put in question? The answer is clear: a cynic mocks the public Law from the position of its obscene underside, which consequently it leaves intact. Insofar as the enjoyment which permeates this obscene underside is structured in fantasies, one can also say that what the cynic leaves intact is the fantasy, the fantasmatic background of the public written ideological text.

* * *

However, the notion of fantasy is today so overused that it needs some explication. What is fantasy? The first thing to take note of is the utter ambiguity that pertains to the notion of fantasy. That is to say, the notion of fantasy offers an exemplary case of the dialectical *coincidentia oppositorium*. On the one hand there is fantasy in its beatific side, in its stabilizing dimension, the dream of a state without disturbances, out of reach of human depravity. On the other hand there is fantasy in its destabilizing dimension whose elementary form is envy – all that 'irritates' me about the Other, images that haunt me of what they are doing when out of my sight, of how they deceive me and plot against me, of how they ignore me and indulge in an enjoyment that is intense beyond my capacity of representation, and so on. (This, for example, is what bothers Swan apropos of Odette in *Un amour de Swan*.)

Does the fundamental lesson of so-called totalitarianism not concern the codependence of these two aspects of the notion of fantasy? The obverse of the Nazi harmonious 'people's community [*Volksgemeinschaft*]' was the paranoiac obsession with the Jewish plot. Similarly, the Stalinists' compulsive discovery of ever new enemies of Socialism was the inescapable obverse of their pretending to realize the ideal of the 'new Socialist man'. Perhaps freedom from the infernal hold of the destabilizing aspect of fantasy provides the most succinct definition of a saint.

So, again, what is fantasy? As everybody knows, fantasy is a hallucinatory realization of desire. In principle, this is true; however, the actual state of things rather resembles the good old Soviet joke on Rabinovitch: Did he really win a car in the lottery? In principle, yes, only it wasn't a car but a bicycle; besides, he didn't win it, it was stolen from him. It's the same with fantasy: yes, fantasy is the realization of desire, however, not 'realization' in the sense of fulfilling it, but rather 'realization' in the sense of bringing it forth, of providing its coordinates. It is not the case that the subject knows in advance what he wants and then, when he cannot get it in reality, proceeds to obtain a hallucinatory satisfaction in fantasy. Rather, the subject originally doesn't know what he wants, and it is the role of fantasy to tell him that, to 'teach' him to desire.

Besides, the desire realized in fantasy is not the subject's own but the Other's desire. That is to say, fantasy, fantasmatic formation, is an answer to the enigma of '*Che vuoi?*' – 'What do you want?' – which produces the subject's primordial, constitutive position. The original question of desire is not directly, 'What do I want?' but, 'What do others want from me? What do they see in me? What am I for the others?' A small child is embedded in a complex network of relations, serving as a kind of catalyst and battlefield for the desires of those around him. His father, mother, brothers and sisters fight their battles around him, the mother sending a message to the father through her care for the son, and so on. While being well aware of this role, the child cannot fathom, precisely, what kind of object they are for the others, what the exact nature is of the games they are playing with them. Fantasy provides an answer to this enigma. At its most fundamental, fantasy tells me what I am for my others. It is again anti-Semitism, the anti-Semitic paranoia, which renders visible in an exemplary way this radically intersubjective character of fantasy: fantasy (e.g., the social fantasy of the Jewish plot) is an attempt to provide an answer to the question 'What does society want from me?' – i.e., to unearth the meaning of the murky events in which I am forced to participate. For that reason, the standard theory of 'projection', according to which the anti-Semite 'projects' onto the figure of the Jew the disavowed part of himself, is not sufficient. The figure of the 'conceptual Jew' cannot be reduced to the externalization of the (anti-Semite's) 'inner conflict'; on the contrary, it bears witness to (and tries to cope with) the fact that the subject is originally decentred, part of an opaque network whose meaning and logic elude their control.

* * *

We can see, again, how cynical distance and full reliance on fantasy are strictly codependent: the typical subject today is the one who, while displaying cynical distrust of any public ideology, indulges without restraint in paranoiac fantasies about conspiracies, threats, and excessive forms of enjoyment of the Other. The best term to designate the awareness of the constraints of which the cynic himself is prisoner is, perhaps, irony. The fundamental gesture of cynicism is to denounce 'genuine authority' as a pose, whose sole effective content is raw coercion or submission for the sake of some material gain. An ironist, in contrast, doubts if a cold, calculating utilitarian is really what they pretend to be. The ironist suspects that this appearance of calculating distance conceals a much deeper commitment. The cynic is quick to denounce the ridiculous pretence of solemn authority; the ironist is able to discern true attachment in dismissive disdain or in feigned indifference.

A common notion of psychoanalysis makes it almost an epitome of cynicism as an interpretative attitude: does psychoanalytic interpretation not involve in its very essence the act of discerning 'lower' motivations (e.g. sexual lust, unacknowledged aggressivity) behind the apparently 'noble' gestures of spiritual elevation of the beloved, of heroic self-sacrifice, and so on? However, this notion is somewhat too slick. Perhaps the original enigma that psychoanalysis endeavours to explain is exactly the opposite: how can the actual behaviour of a person who professes their freedom from 'prejudices' and 'moralistic constraints' bear witness to innumerable inner impediments and unavowed prohibitions? Why does a person who is free to 'enjoy life' engage in the systematic 'pursuit of unhappiness', methodically organize their failures? What's in it for them – what perverse libidinal profit?

One should recall here Lacan's reversal of Dostoevsky's famous proposition from *The Brothers Karamazov*: 'If God doesn't exist, then nothing at all is permitted any longer.' Is not the ultimate proof of the pertinence of this reversal the shift from the Law as Prohibition to the rule of 'norms' or 'ideals' we are witnessing today, in our 'permissive' societies: in all domains of our everyday lives, from eating habits to sexual behaviour and professional success, there are fewer and fewer prohibitions, yet more and more guilt when the subject's performance is found lacking with respect to the norm or ideal. This enigma is the proper theme of psychoanalysis: how is it that the very lack of explicit prohibitions burdens the subject with an often unbearable guilt? How is it that the very injunction to be happy and just to enjoy yourself can turn into a ferocious superego monster?

NOTES

Published in *JPCS: Journal for the Psychoanalysis of Culture and Society* 1, 1996, pp. 15–25 [eds].

14 Why is Wagner Worth Saving?

With Romanticism, music changes its role: it no longer merely accompanies the message delivered in speech, but contains/renders a message of its own, 'deeper' than the one delivered in words. It was Rousseau who first clearly articulated the expressive potential of music as such when he claimed that, instead of just imitating the affective features of verbal speech, music should be given the right to 'speak for itself' – in contrast to deceiving verbal speech, in music, it is, to paraphrase Lacan, the truth itself which speaks. As Schopenhauer put it, music directly enacts/renders the noumenal Will, while speech remains limited to the level of phenomenal representation. Music is the substance which renders the true heart of the subject, what Hegel called the 'Night of the World', the abyss of radical negativity: music becomes the bearer of the true message beyond words during the shift from the Enlightenment subject of rational *logos* to the Romantic subject of the 'night of the world', i.e., with the change of metaphor for the kernel of the subject from Day to Night. Here we encounter the Uncanny: no longer external transcendence, but, following Kant's transcendental turn, the excess of the Night in the very heart of the subject (the dimension of the Undead), what Tomlison called the 'internal otherworldliness that marks the Kantian subject'.[1] What music renders is thus no longer the 'semantics of the soul', but the underlying 'noumenal' flux of *jouissance* beyond linguistic meaningfulness. This noumenal is radically different from the pre-Kantian transcendent divine Truth: it is the inaccessible excess which forms the very core of the subject.

In the history of opera, this sublime excess of life is discernible in two main versions, Italian and German, Rossini and Wagner – so, maybe, although they are the great opposites, Wagner's surprising private sympathy for Rossini, as well as their friendly meeting in Paris, do bear witness to a deeper affinity. Rossini's great male portraits, the three from *Barbiere di Siviglia* (Figaro's 'Largo il factotum', Basilio's

'Calumnia' and Bartolo's 'Un dottor della mia sorte'), along with the father's wishful self-portrait of corruption in *Cinderella*, enact a mock self-complaint, where one imagines oneself in a desired position, being bombarded by demands for a favour or service. The subject twice shifts his position: first, he assumes the roles of those who address him, enacting the overwhelming multitude of demands which bombard him; then, he feigns a reaction to it, the state of deep satisfaction in being overwhelmed by demands one cannot fulfil. Let us take the father in *Cinderella*: he imagines how, when one of his daughters will be married to the Prince, people will turn to him, offering him bribes for a service at the court, and he will react to it first with cunning deliberation, then with fake despair at being bombarded with too many requests ... The culminating moment of the archetypal Rossinian aria is this unique moment of happiness, of the full assertion of the excess of Life which occurs when the subject is overwhelmed by demands, no longer being able to deal with them. At the highpoint of his 'factotum' aria, Figaro exclaims: 'What a crowd [of the people bombarding me with their demands] – have mercy, one after the other [*uno per volta, per carita*]!', referring thereby to the Kantian experience of the Sublime, in which the subject is bombarded with an excess of data that he is unable to comprehend. The basic economy is here obsessional: the object of the hero's desire is the other's demand.

This excess is the proper counterpoint to the Wagnerian Sublime, to the *höchste Lust* of the immersion into the Void that concludes *Tristan und Isolde*. This opposition of the Rossinian and the Wagnerian Sublime perfectly fits the Kantian opposition between the mathematical and the dynamic Sublime: as we have just seen, the Rossinian Sublime is mathematical, it enacts the inability of the subject to comprehend the pure quantity of the demands that overflow him, while the Wagnerian Sublime is dynamic, it enacts the concentrated overpowering force of the *one* demand, the unconditional demand of love. One can also say that the Wagnerian Sublime is absolute Emotion – this is how one should read the famous first sentence of Wagner's 'Religion and Art', where he claims that, when religion becomes artificial, art can save the true spirit of religion, its hidden truth – how? Precisely by abandoning dogma and rendering only authentic religious emotion, i.e., by transforming religion into the ultimate aesthetic experience.

Tristan should thus be read as the resolution of the tension between sublime passion and religion still operative in *Tannhäuser*. The beginning of *Tannhäuser* enacts a strange reversal of the standard entreaty: not to escape the constraints of mortality and rejoin the beloved, but the entreaty addressed to the beloved to let the hero go and return to the mortal life of pain, struggle and freedom. Tannhäuser complains that, as a mortal, he cannot sustain the continuous enjoyment ('Though a god can savour joy [Geniessen] forever,/I am subject to change;/I have at heart not pleasure alone;/and in my joy long for suffering'). A little later, Tannhäuser makes it clear that what he is longing for is the peace of death itself: 'My longing urges me to combat/I do not seek pleasure and rapture!/Oh, if you could understand it, goddess!/Hence to death I seek! I am drawn to death!' If there is a conflict between eternity and temporal existence, between transcendence and this terrestrial reality, then Venus is on the side of a terrifying *eternity* of unbearable excessive enjoyment [*Geniessen*].

This provides the key to the opera's central conflict: it is *not*, as it is usually claimed, the conflict between the spiritual and the bodily, the sublime and the ordinary pleasures of flesh, but a conflict inherent to the Sublime itself, dividing it. Venus and Elisabeth are *both* metaphysical figures of the sublime: neither of the two is a woman destined to become a common wife. While Elisabeth is, obviously, the sacred virgin, the purely spiritual entity, the *untouchable* idealized Lady of courtly love, Venus also stands for a metaphysical excess, that of excessively intensified sexual enjoyment; if anything, it is Elisabeth who is closer to ordinary terrestrial life. In Kierkegaard's terms, one can say that Venus stands for the Aesthetic and Elisabeth for the Religious – on condition that one conceives here of the Aesthetic as included in the Religious, elevated to the level of the unconditional Absolute. And therein resides the unpardonable sin of Tannhäuser: not in the fact that he engaged in a little bit of free sexuality (in this case, the severe punishment would have been ridiculously exaggerated), but that he elevated sexuality, sexual lust, to the level of the Absolute, asserting it as the inherent obverse of the Sacred. This is the reason why the roles of Venus and Elisabeth definitely should be played by the same singer: the two *are* one and the same person, the only difference resides in the male hero's attitude towards her. Is this not clear from the final choice Tannhäuser has to make between the two? When he is in his mortal agony, Venus is calling him to join her again ('Komm, O komm! Zu mir! Zu mir!'); when he gets close to her, Wolfram cries from the background 'Elisabeth!', to which Tannhäuser replies: 'Elisabeth!' In the standard staging, the mention of the dead sacred Elisabeth gives Tannhäuser the strength to avoid Venus' embrace, and Venus then leaves in fury; however, would it not be much more logical to stage it so that Tannhäuser continues to approach the *same* woman, discovering, when he is close to her, that Venus really is Elisabeth? The subversive power of this shift is that it turns around the old courtly love poetry motif of the dazzlingly beautiful lady who, when one approaches her too closely, is revealed to be a disgusting entity of rotten flesh full of crawling worms – here, the sacred virgin is discovered in the very heart of the dissolute seductress. So the message is not the usual desublimation ('Beware of the beautiful woman! It is a deceptive lure which hides the disgusting rotten flesh!'), but unexpected sublimation, elevation of the erotic woman to the mode of appearance of the sacred Thing. The tension of *Tannhäuser* is thus the one between the two aspects of the Absolute, Ideal-Symbolic and Real, Law and Superego. The true topic of *Tannhäuser* is that of a *disturbance in the order of sublimation*: sublimation starts to oscillate between these two poles.

We can see, now, in what precise sense *Tristan* embodies the 'aesthetic' attitude (in the Kierkegaardian sense of the term): refusing to compromise one's desire, one goes to the end and willingly embraces death. *Meistersinger von Nuremberg* counters it with the ethical solution: the true redemption resides not in following immortal passion to its self-destructive conclusion; one should rather learn to overcome it via creative sublimation and to return, in a mood of wise resignation, to the 'daily' life of symbolic obligations. In *Parsifal*, finally, passion can no longer be overcome via its reintegration into a society in which it survives in a gentrified form: one has to deny it thoroughly in the ecstatic assertion of religious *jouissance*. The triad *Tristan–Meistersinger–Parsifal* thus follows a precise logic: *Meistersinger* and *Tristan* render the two opposite versions of the Oedipal matrix, within which *Meistersinger* inverts *Tristan* (the son steals the woman from the paternal figure; passion breaks out between the paternal figure and the young woman destined to become the partner of the young man), while *Parsifal* gives the coordinates themselves an anti-Oedipal twist – the lamenting wounded subject is here the paternal figure (Amfortas), not the young transgressor (Tristan). (The closest one comes to lament in *Meistersinger* is Sachs' 'Wahn, wahn!' song from Act III.) Wagner planned to have, in the first half of Act III of *Tristan*, Parsifal visit the wounded Tristan, but he wisely renounced it: not only would the scene ruin the perfect overall structure of Act III, it would also stage the *impossible* encounter of a character with (the different, alternate reality, version of) *itself*, as in the time-travel science-fiction narratives where I encounter *myself*. One can even bring things to the ridiculous here by imagining a *third* hero joining the first two – Hans Sachs (in his earlier embodiment, as King Marke who arrives with a ship prior to Isolde) – so that the three of them (Tristan, Marke, Parsifal), standing for the three attitudes, debate their differences in a Habermasian undistorted communicational exchange ...

And one is tempted to claim that the triad of *Tristan–Meistersinger–Parsifal* is reproduced in three exemplary post-Wagnerian operas: Richard Strauss's *Salome*, Puccini's *Turandot* and Schoenberg's *Moses und Aron*. Is not *Salome* yet another version of the possible outcome of *Tristan*? What if, at the end of Act II, when King Marke surprises the lovers, he were to explode in fury and order Tristan's head to be cut off; the desperate Isolde would then take her lover's head in her hands and start to kiss his lips in a Salomean *Liebestod* ... (And, to add yet another variation on the virtual link between *Salome* and *Tristan*: what if, at the end of *Tristan*, Isolde would not simply die after finishing her 'Mild und leise' – what if she were to remain entranced by her immersion in ecstatic *jouissance*, and, disgusted by it, King Mark would give the order: 'This woman is to be killed!'?) It is often noted that the closing scene of *Salome* is modelled on Isolde's *Liebestod*; however, what makes it a perverted version of the Wagnerian *Liebestod* is that what Salome demands, in an unconditional act of caprice, is to kiss the lips of John the Baptist ('I want to kiss your lips!') – not contact with a person, but with a partial object.

If *Salome* is a counterpart to *Tristan*, then *Turandot* is the counterpart to *Meistersinger* – let us not forget that they are both operas about a public contest with a woman as the prize won by the hero.

Salome insists to the end on her demand: first, she insists that the soldiers bring to her Jokanaan; then, after the dance of seven veils, she insists that King Herod bring her on a silver platter the head of Jokanaan – when the king, believing that Jokanaan effectively is a sacred man and that it is therefore better not to touch him, offers Salome in exchange for her dance anything she wants, up to half of his kingdom and the most sacred objects in his custody, just not the head (and thus the death) of Jokanaan, she ignores this explosive outburst of higher and higher bidding and simply repeats her inexorable demand: 'Bring me the head of Jokanaan.' Is there not something properly Antigonean in this request of hers? Like Antigone, she insists without regard to consequences. Is therefore Salome not in a way, no less than Antigone, the embodiment of a certain ethical stance? No wonder she is so attracted to Jokanaan – it is the matter of one saint recognizing another. And how can one overlook that, at the end of Oscar Wilde's play on which Strauss's opera is based, after kissing his head, she utters a properly Christian comment on how this proves that love is stronger than death, that love can overcome death?

Which, then, would be the counterpart to *Parsifal*? *Parsifal* was from the very beginning perceived as a thoroughly ambiguous work: the attempt to reassert art at its highest, the proto-religious spectacle bringing together Community (art as the mediator between religion and politics) against the utilitarian corruption of modern life with its commercialized kitsch culture – yet at the same time drifting towards a commercialized aesthetic kitsch of an *ersatz* religion, a fake, if there ever was one. In other words, the problem of *Parsifal* is not the unmediated dualism of its universe (Klingsor's kingdom of false pleasures versus the sacred domain of the Grail), but, rather, the lack of distance, the ultimate identity, of its opposites: is not the Grail ritual (which provides the most satisfying aesthetic spectacle of the work, its two 'biggest hits') the ultimate 'Klingsorian' fake? (The taint of bad faith in our enjoyment of *Parsifal* as similar to the bad faith in our enjoyment of Puccini.) For this reason, *Parsifal* was the traumatic starting point that allows us to conceive of the multitude of later operas as reactions to it, as attempts to resolve its deadlock. The key among these attempts is, of course, Schoenberg's *Moses und Aron*, the ultimate contender for the title 'the last opera', the meta-opera about the conditions of (im)possibility of opera itself: the sudden rupture at the end of Act II, after Moses' desperate 'O Wort, das mir fehlt!', the failure to compose the work to the end. *Moses und Aron* is effectively anti-*Parsifal*: while *Parsifal* retains a full naïve trust in the (redemptive) power of music, and finds no problem in rendering the noumenal divine dimension in the aesthetic spectacle of the ritual, *Moses und Aron* attempts the impossible: to be an opera directed against the very principle of opera, that of the stage-musical spectacle – it is an operatic representation of the Jewish prohibition of aesthetic representation ...

Is the buoyant music of the Golden Calf not the ultimate version of the bacchanalia music in Wagner, from *Tannhäuser* to the Flower Maidens' music in *Parsifal*? And is there not another key parallel between *Parsifal* and *Moses und Aron*? As was noted by Adorno, the ultimate tension of *Moses und Aron* is not simply between divine transcendence and its representation in music, but, inherent to music itself, between the 'choral' spirit of the religious community and the two individuals (Moses and Aron) who stick out as subjects; in the same way, in *Parsifal*, Amfortas and Parsifal himself stick out as forceful individuals – are the two 'complaints' by Amfortas not the strongest passages of *Parsifal*, implicitly undermining the message of the renunciation of subjectivity? The musical opposition between the clear choral style of the Grail community and the chromaticism of the Klingsor universe in *Parsifal* is radicalized in *Moses und Aron* in the guise of the opposition between Moses' *Sprechstimme* and Aron's full song – in both cases, the tension is unresolved.

What, then, can follow this breakdown? It is here that one is tempted to return to our starting point, to Rossinian comedy. After the complete breakdown of expressive subjectivity, comedy re-emerges – but a weird, uncanny one. What comes after *Moses und Aron* is the imbecilic, 'comic' *Sprechgesang* of *Pierrot Lunaire*, the smile of a madman who is so devastated by pain that he cannot even perceive his tragedy – like the smile of a cat in cartoons with birds flying around his head after he gets hit on the head with a hammer.

Comedy enters when the situation is too horrifying to be rendered as tragedy – which is why the only proper way to do a film about concentration camps is a comedy: there is something fake about doing a concentration camp tragedy ...[2]

Is this, however, the only way out? What if *Parsifal* also points in another direction, that of the emergence of a new collective? If *Tristan* enacts redemption as the ecstatic suicidal escape *from* the social order and *Meistersinger* the resigned integration *into* the existing social order, then *Parsifal* concludes with the invention of a new form of the Social. With Parsifal's 'Disclose the Grail!' ['Enthüllt den Graal!'], we pass from the Grail community as a closed order where the Grail is only revealed, in the prescribed time, to the circle of the initiated, to a new order in which the Grail has to remain revealed all the time: 'No more shall the shrine be sealed!' ['Nicht soll der mehr verschlossen sein!']. As to the revolutionary consequences of this change, recall the fate of the Master figure in the triad *Tristan–Meistersinger–Parsifal* (King Marke, Hans Sachs, Amfortas): in the first two works, the Master survives as a saddened, melancholic figure; in the third he is deposed and dies.

Why, then, should we not read *Parsifal* from today's perspective: the kingdom of Klingsor in Act II is a domain of digital phantasmagoria, of virtual amusement – Harry Kupfer was right to stage Klingsor's magic garden as a video parlour, with Flower Girls reduced to fragments of female bodies (faces, legs) appearing on dispersed TV screens. Is Klingsor not a kind of Master of the Matrix, manipulating virtual reality, a combination of Murdoch and Bill Gates? And when we pass from Act II to Act III, do we not effectively pass from the fake virtual reality to the 'desert of the real', the 'waste land' in the aftermath of ecological catastrophe that derailed the 'normal' functioning of nature? Is Parsifal not a model for Keanu Reeves in *The Matrix*, with Laurence Fishburne in the role of Gurnemanz?

One is thus tempted to offer a direct 'vulgar' answer to the question: what the hell was Parsifal doing on his journey during the long time which passes between Acts II and III? The true 'Grail' is the people, its very suffering. What if he simply got acquainted with human misery, suffering and exploitation? So what if the *new* collective is something like a revolutionary party? What if one takes the risk of reading *Parsifal* as the precursor of Brecht's *Lehrstücke*? What if its topic of sacrifice points towards Brecht's *Die Massnahme*, which was put to music by Hans Eisler, the third great pupil of Schoenberg, after Bert and Webern? Is the topic of both *Parsifal* and *Die Massnahme* not that of learning: the hero has to learn how to help people in their suffering. The outcome, however, is the opposite: in Wagner compassion, in Brecht/Eisler the strength not to give way to one's compassion and directly act on it. However, this opposition itself is relative: the shared motif is that of *cold/distanced compassion*. The lesson of Brecht is the art of cold compassion, compassion for suffering which learns to resist the immediate urge to help others; the lesson of Wagner is cold *compassion*, the distanced saintly attitude (recall the cold girl into which Parsifal turns in Syberberg's version) which nonetheless retains compassion. Wagner's lesson (and Wotan's insight) about how the greatest act of freedom is to accept and freely enact what necessarily has to occur, is strangely echoed in the basic lesson of Brecht's 'learning plays': what the young boy to be killed by his colleagues has to learn is the art of *Einverständnis*, of accepting his own killing, which will occur regardless.

And what about the misogyny that obviously sustains this option? Is it not that *Parsifal* negated the shared presupposition of the first two works, their assertion of love (ecstatic courtly love, marital love), opting for the exclusive male community? However, what if, here also, Syberberg was right: after Kundry's kiss, in the very rejection of (hysterical-seductive) femininity, Parsifal turns into a woman, adopts a feminine subjective position? What if what we effectively get is a dedicated 'radical' community led by a cold ruthless woman, a new Joan of Arc?

And what about the notion that the Grail community is an elitist, closed, initiatic circle? Parsifal's final injunction to disclose the Grail undermines this false alternative of elitism/populism: every true elitism is universal, addressed to everyone and all, and there is something inherently vulgar about initiatic, secret, gnostic wisdoms. There is a standard complaint by many *Parsifal* lovers: a great opera with numerous passages of breathtaking beauty – but, nonetheless, the two long narratives of Gurnemanz (taking most of the first half of Acts I and III) are Wagner at his worst: a boring recapitulation of past deeds already known to us, lacking any dramatic tension. Our proposed 'Communist' reading of *Parsifal* entails a full rehabilitation of these two narratives as crucial moments of the opera – the fact that they may appear 'boring' is to be understood along the lines of a short poem by Brecht from the early 1950s, addressed to a nameless worker in the GDR who, after long hours of work, is obliged to listen to a boring political speech by a local party functionary:

> You are exhausted from long work
> The speaker is repeating himself
> His speech is long-winded, he speaks with strain
> Do not forget, the tired one:
> He speaks the truth.[3]

This is the role of Gurnemanz – no more and no less than the agent – the mouth-piece, why not, of truth. In this precise case, the very predicate of 'boring' is an indicator (a vector even) of truth, as opposed to the dazzling perplexity of jokes and superficial amusements. (There is, of course, another sense in which, as Brecht knew very well, dialectics itself is inherently comical.)

And what about the final call of the Chorus, 'Redeem the Redeemer!', which some read as the anti-Semitic statement to 'redeem/save Christ from the clutches of the Jewish tradition, de-Semitize him'? However, what if we read this line more literally, as echoing the other 'tautological' statement from the finale, 'the wound can be healed only by the spear which smote it' ('die Wunde schliesst der Speer nur, der sie schlug')? Is this not the key paradox of every revolutionary process, in the course of which not only is violence needed to overcome the existing violence, but the revolution, in order to stabilize itself into a New Order, has to eat its own children?

So is Wagner a proto-Fascist? Why not leave behind this search for the 'proto-Fascist' elements in Wagner and, rather, in a violent gesture of appropriation, reinscribe *Parsifal* in the tradition of radical revolutionary parties? Perhaps such a reading enables us also to cast a new light on the link between *Parsifal* and *The Ring*. *The Ring* depicts a pagan world, which, following its inherent logic, *must* end in a global catastrophe; however, there are survivors of this catastrophe, the nameless crowd of humanity who silently witnesses God's self-destruction. In the unique figure of Hagen, *The Ring* also provides the first portrait of what will later emerge as the Fascist leader; however, since the world of *The Ring* is pagan, caught in the Oedipal family conflict of passions, it cannot even address the true problem of how this humanity, the force of the New, is to organize itself, of how it should learn the truth about its place; *this* is the task of *Parsifal*, which therefore logically follows *The Ring*. The conflict between Oedipal dynamics and the post-Oedipal universe is inscribed into *Parsifal* itself: Klingsor's and Amfortas' adventures are Oedipal, and what happens with Parsifal's big turn (rejection of Kundry) is precisely that he leaves behind the Oedipal incestuous eroticism, opening himself up to a new community.

The dark figure of Hagen is profoundly ambiguous: although initially depicted as a dark plotter, both in the *Nibelungenlied* and in Fritz Lang's film, he emerges as the ultimate hero of the entire work and is redeemed at the end as the supreme case of the *Nibelungentreue*, fidelity to death to one's cause (or, rather, to the Master who stands for this cause), asserted in the final slaughter at the Attila's court. The conflict is here between fidelity to the Master and our everyday moral obligations: Hagen stands for a kind of teleological suspension of morality on behalf of fidelity, he is the ultimate '*Gefolgsmann*'.

Significantly, it is *only* Wagner who depicts Hagen as a figure of Evil – is this not an indication of how Wagner nonetheless belongs to the modern space of freedom? And is Lang's return to the positive Hagen not an indication of how the twentieth century marked the re-emergence of a new barbarism? It was Wagner's genius to intuit ahead of his time the rising figure of the Fascist ruthless executive who is at the same time a rabble-rousing demagogue (recall Hagen's terrifying *Männerruf*) – a worthy supplement to his other great intuition, that of a hysterical woman (Kundry) well before this figure overwhelmed European consciousness (in Charcot's clinic, in art from Ibsen to Schoenberg).

What makes Hagen a 'proto-Fascist' is his role of the unconditional support for the weak ruler (King Gunther): he does the 'dirty jobs' for Gunther which, although necessary, have to remain concealed from the public gaze – 'Unsere Ehre heisst Treue'. We find this stance, a kind of mirror-reversal of the Beautiful Soul who refuses to dirty their hands, at its purest in the Rightist admiration for the heroes who are ready to do the necessary dirty job: it is easy to do a noble thing for one's country, up to sacrificing one's life for it – it is much more difficult to commit a *crime* for one's country when it is needed ... Hitler knew very well how to play this double game apropos of the Holocaust, using Himmler as his Hagen. In the speech to the SS leaders in Posen on 4 October 1943, Himmler spoke quite openly about the mass killing of the Jews as 'a glorious page in our history, and one that has never been written and never can be written', explicitly including the killing of women and children:

> I did not regard myself as justified in exterminating the men – that is to say, to kill them or have them killed – and to allow the avengers in the shape of children to grow up for our sons and grandchildren. The difficult decision had to be taken to have this people disappear from the earth.

This is Hagen's *Treue* brought to the extreme – however, was the paradoxical price for Wagner's negative portrayal of Hagen not his *Judifizierung*? A lot of historicist work has been done recently trying to bring out the contextual 'true meaning' of the Wagnerian figures and topics: the pale Hagen is really a masturbating Jew; Amfortas' wound is really syphilis, etc. The idea is that Wagner is mobilizing historical codes known to everyone in his epoch: when a person stumbles, sings in cracking high tones, makes nervous gestures, etc., 'everyone knew' this is a Jew, so Mime from *Siegfried* is a caricature of a Jew; the fear of syphilis as the illness in the groin one gets from having intercourse with an 'impure' woman was an obsession in the second half of the nineteenth century, so it was 'clear to everyone' that Amfortas really contracted syphilis from Kundry ... Marc Weiner developed the most perspicacious version of this decoding by focusing on the micro-texture of Wagner's musical dramas – the manner of singing, gestures, smells; it is at this level of what Deleuze would have called pre-subjective affects that anti-Semitism is operative in Wagner's operas, even if Jews are not explicitly mentioned: in the way Beckmesser sings, in the way Mime complains ...

However, the first problem here is that, even if accurate, such insights do not contribute much to a pertinent understanding of the work in question. One often hears that, in order to understand a work of art, one needs to know its historical context. Against this historicist commonplace, one should affirm that too much of a historical context can blur the proper contact with a work of art – in order to properly grasp, say, *Parsifal*, one should *abstract* from such historical trivia, one should *decontextualize* the work, tear it out from the context in which it was originally embedded. Even more, it is, rather, the work of art itself that provides a context enabling us properly to understand a given historical situation. If, today, someone were to visit Serbia, the direct contact with raw data there would leave them confused. If, however, they were to read a couple of literary works and see a couple of representative movies, they would definitely provide the context that would enable them to locate the raw data of their experience. There is thus an unexpected truth in the old cynical wisdom from the Stalinist Soviet Union: 'he lies as an eye-witness!'

There is another, more fundamental, problem with such historicist decoding: it is not enough to 'decode' Alberich, Mime, Hagen, etc., as Jews, making the point that *The Ring* is one big anti-Semitic tract, a story about how Jews, by renouncing love and opting for power, brought corruption to the universe; the more basic fact is that *the anti-Semitic figure of the Jew itself is not a direct ultimate referent, but already encoded, a cipher of ideological and social antagonisms*. (And the same goes for syphilis: in the second half of the nineteenth century, it was, together with tuberculosis, the other big case of 'illness as a metaphor' (Susan Sontag), serving as an encoded message about socio-sexual antagonisms, and this is the reason why people were so obsessed by it – not because of its direct real threat, but because of the ideological surplus-investment in it.) An appropriate reading of Wagner should take this fact into account and not merely 'decode' Alberich as a Jew, but also ask the question: *how does Wagner's encoding refer to the 'original' social antagonism of which the (anti-Semitic figure of the) 'Jew' itself is already a cipher*?

A further counter-argument is that Siegfried, Mime's opponent, is in no way simply the beautiful Aryan blond hero – his portrait is much more ambiguous. The short last scene of Act I of *Götterdämmerung* (Siegfried's violent abduction of Brünnhilde; under the cover of *Tarnhelm*, Siegfried poses as Gunther) is a shocking interlude of extreme brutality and ghost-like nightmarish quality. What makes it additionally interesting is one of the big inconsistencies of *The Ring*: why does Siegfried, after brutally subduing Brünnhilde, put his sword between the two when they lie down, to prove that they will not have sex, since he is just doing a service to his friend, the weak king Gunther? *To whom* does he have to prove this? Is Brünnhilde not supposed to think that he *is* Gunther? Before she is subdued, Brünnhilde displays to the masked Siegfried her hand with the ring on it, trusting that the ring will serve as protection; when Siegfried brutally tears the ring off her hand, this gesture has to be read as the repetition of the first extremely violent robbery of the ring in Scene IV of *Rhinegold*, when Wotan tears the ring off Alberich's hand. The horror of this scene is that it shows Siegfried's brutality naked, in its raw state: it somehow 'de-psychologizes' Siegfried, making him visible as an inhuman monster, i.e., the way he 'really is', deprived of his deceiving mask – *this* is the effect of the potion on him.

There is effectively in Wagner's Siegfried an unconstrained 'innocent' aggressivity, an urge directly to pass to the act and just squash what gets on your nerves – as in Siegfrid's words to Mime in Act I of *Siegfried*:

> When I watch you standing,
> shuffling and shambling,
> servilely stooping, squinting and blinking,
> I long to seize you by your nodding neck
> and make an end of your obscene blinking!

The sound of the original German is here even more impressive:

> *Seh'ich dich stehn, gangeln und gehn,*
> *knicken und nicken,*
> *mit den Augen zwicken,*
> *beim Genick möcht'ich den Nicker packen,*
> *den Garaus geben dem garst'gen Zwicker!*

The same outburst is repeated twice in Act II:

> *Das eklige Nicken*
> *und Augenzwicken,*
> *wann endlich soll ich's*
> *nicht mehr sehn,*
> *wann werd ich den Albernen los?*

> That shuffling and slinking,
> those eyelids blinking –
> how long must I
> endure the sight?
> When shall I be rid of this fool?

And, just a little later:

> *Grade so garstig,*
> *griesig und grau,*
> *klein und krumm,*
> *höckrig und hinkend,*
> *mit hängenden Ohren,*
> *triefigen Augen – Fort mit dem Alb!*
> *Ich mag ihn nicht mehr sehn.*

> Shuffling and slinking,
> grizzled and gray,
> small and crooked,
> limping and hunchbacked,
> with ears that are drooping, eyes that are bleary –
> Off with the imp! I hope he's gone for good!

Is this not the most elementary disgust/repulsion felt by the ego when confronted with the intruding foreign body? One can easily imagine a neo-Nazi skinhead uttering just the same words in the face of a worn-out Turkish *Gastarbeiter* . . .[4]

And, finally, one should not forget that, in *The Ring*, the source of all evil is not Alberich's fatal choice in the first scene of *Rhinegold*: long before this event took place, Wotan broke the natural balance, succumbing to the lure of power, giving preference to power over love – he tore out and destroyed the World-Tree, making out of it his spear upon which he inscribed the runes fixing the laws of his rule, plus he plucked out one of his eyes in order to gain insight into inner truth. Evil thus does not come from the Outside – the insight of Wotan's tragic 'monologue with Brünnhilde' in Act II of *Walküre* is that the power of Alberich and the prospect of the 'end of the world' is ultimately Wotan's own guilt, the result of his ethical fiasco – in Hegelese, external opposition is the effect of inner contradiction. No wonder, then, that Wotan is called the 'White Alb' in contrast to the 'Black Alb' Alberich – if anything, Wotan's choice was ethically worse than Alberich's: Alberich longed for love and only turned towards power after being brutally mocked and turned down by the Rhinemaidens, while Wotan turned to power after fully enjoying the fruits of love and getting tired of them. One should also bear in mind that, after his moral fiasco in *Walküre*, Wotan turns into 'Wanderer' – a figure of the Wandering Jew already like the first great Wagnerian hero, the Flying Dutchman, this 'Ahasver des Ozeans'.

And the same goes for *Parsifal*, which is not about an elitist circle of the pure-blooded threatened by external contamination (copulation by the Jewess Kundry). There are two complications to this image: first, Klingsor, the evil magician and Kundry's Master, is himself an ex-Grail knight, he comes from within; second, if one reads the text closely, one cannot avoid the conclusion that the true source of evil, the primordial imbalance which derailed the Grail community, resides at its very centre – it is Titurel's excessive fixation of enjoying the Grail which is at the origins of the misfortune. The true figure of Evil is Titurel, this obscene *père-jouisseur* (perhaps comparable to the giant worm-like members of the Space Guild from Frank Herbert's *Dune*, whose bodies are disgustingly distorted because of their excessive consumption of the 'spice').

This, then, undermines the anti-Semitic perspective according to which the disturbance always ultimately comes from outside, in the guise of a foreign body which throws out of joint the balance of the social organism: for Wagner, the external intruder (Alberich) is just a secondary repetition, an externalization, of an absolutely immanent inconsistency/antagonism (that of Wotan). With reference to Brecht's famous 'What is the robbery of a bank compared to the founding of a new bank?', one is tempted to say: 'What is a poor Jew's stealing of the gold compared to the violence of the Aryan's (Wotan's) grounding of the rule of Law?'

One of the signs of this inherent status of the disturbance is the failure of the big finales of Wagner's operas: the formal failure here signals the persistence of the social antagonism. Let us take the biggest of them all, the mother of all finales, that of *Götterdämmerung*. It is a well-known fact that, in the last minutes of the opera, the orchestra performs an excessively intricate cobweb of motifs, basically nothing less than the recapitulation of the motivic wealth of the entire *Ring* – is this fact not the ultimate proof that Wagner himself was not sure about what the final apotheosis of *Der Ring* 'means'? Not being sure of it, he took a kind of 'flight forward' and threw together *all* of the motifs ... So the culminating motif of 'Redemption through Love' (a beautiful and passionate melodic line which previously appears only in Act III of *Walküre*) cannot but make us think of Joseph Kerman's acerbic comment about the last notes of Puccini's *Tosca*, in which the orchestra bombastically recapitulates the 'beautiful' pathetic melodic line of the Cavaradossi's 'E lucevan le stelle', as if, unsure of what to do, Puccini simply desperately repeated the most 'effective' melody from the previous score, ignoring all narrative or emotional logic.[5] And what if Wagner did *exactly the same* at the end of *Götterdämmerung*? Not sure about the final twist that should stabilize and guarantee the meaning of it all, he took recourse to a beautiful melody whose effect is something like 'whatever all this may mean, let us make sure that the concluding impression will be that of something triumphant and upbeat in its redemptive beauty ...' In short, what if this final motif enacts an *empty gesture*?

It is a commonplace of Wagner studies that the triumphant finale of *Rhinegold* is a fake, an empty triumph indicating the fragility of the gods' power and their forthcoming downfall – however, does the same not go also for the finale of *Siegfried*? The sublime duet of Brünnhilde and Siegfried which concludes the opera fails a couple of minutes before the ending, with the entry of the motif announcing the couple's triumphant reunion (usually designated as the motif of 'happy love' or 'love's bond') – this motif is obviously a fake (not to mention the miserable failure of the concluding noisy-bombastic orchestral *tutti*, which lacks the efficiency of the gods' entry to Valhalla in *Rhinegold*). Does this failure encode Wagner's (unconscious?) critique of Siegfried? Recall the additional curious fact that this motif is almost the same as – or at least closely related to – the Beckmesser motif in *Meistersinger* (I owe this insight to Gerhard Koch: Act III of *Siegfried* was written just after *Meistersinger*)! Furthermore, does this empty bombastic failure of the final notes not also signal the catastrophe-to-come of Brünnhilde and Siegfried's love? As such, this 'failure' of the duet is a structural necessity.[6] (One should nonetheless follow closely the inner triadic structure of this duet: its entire dynamic is on the side of Brünnhilde who twice shifts her subjective stance, while Siegfried remains the same. First, from her elevated divine position, Brünnhilde joyously asserts her love for Siegfried; then, once she becomes aware of what Siegfried's passionate advances mean – the loss of her safe distanced position – she displays fear of losing her identity, of descending to the level of a vulnerable mortal woman, man's prey and passive victim. In a wonderful metaphor, she compares herself to a beautiful image in the water that gets blurred once man's hand directly touches and disturbs the water. Finally, she surrenders to Siegfried's passionate love advances and throws herself into the vortex.) However, excepting the last notes, Act III of *Siegfried*, at least from the moment when Siegfried breaks Wotan's spear to Brünnhilde's awakening, is not only unbearably beautiful, but also the most concise statement of the Oedipal problematic in its specific Wagnerian twist.

On his way to the magic mountain where Brünnhilde lies, surrounded by a wall of fire which can be tresspassed only by a hero who does not know fear, Siegfried first encounters Wotan, the deposed (or, rather, abdicated) supreme god, disguised as a Wanderer; Wotan tries to stop him, but in an ambiguous way – basically, he *wants* Siegfried to break his spear. After Siegfried disrespectfully does this, full of contempt, in his ignorance, for the embittered and wise old man, he progresses through the flames and perceives a wonderful creature lying there in deep sleep. Thinking that the armoured plate on the creature's chest is making its breathing difficult, he proceeds to cut off its straps by his sword; after he raises the plate and sees

Brünnhilde's breasts, he utters a desperate cry of surprise: 'Das ist kein Mann'. This reaction, of course, cannot but strike us as comic, exaggerated beyond credulity. However, one should bear in mind a couple of things here. First, the whole point of the story of *Siegfried* up to this moment is that, while Siegfried spent his entire youth in the forest in the sole company of the evil dwarf Mime who claimed to be his only parent, mother-father, he nonetheless observed that, in the case of animals, parents are always a couple, and thus longs to see his mother, the feminine counterpart of Mime. Siegfried's quest for a woman is thus a quest for sexual difference, and the fact that this quest is at the same time the quest of fear, of an experience that would teach him what fear is, clearly points in the direction of castration – with a specific twist. In the paradigmatic Freudian description of the scene of castration, the gaze discovers an absence where a presence (of penis) is expected,[7] while here, Siegfried's gaze discovers an excessive presence (of breasts – and should one add that the typical Wagnerian soprano is an opulent soprano with large breasts, so that Siegfried's 'Das ist kein Mann!' usually gives rise to hearty laughter in the public).[8]

Second, one should bear in mind here an apparent inconsistency in the libretto which points the way to a proper understanding of this scene: why is Siegfried so surprised at not encountering a man, when, prior to it, he emphasizes that he wants to penetrate the fire precisely in order to find there a woman? To the Wanderer, he says: 'Give ground then, for that way, I know, leads to the sleeping woman.' And, a couple of minutes later: 'Go back yourself, braggart! I must go there, to the burning heart of the blaze, to Brünnhilde!' From this, one should draw the only possible conclusion: *while Siegfried was effectively looking for a woman, he did not expect her not to be a man.* In short, he was looking for a woman who would be – not the same as man, but – a symmetrical supplement to man, with whom she would form a balanced signifying dyad, and what he found was an unbearable lack/excess ... What he discovered is the excess/lack not covered by the binary signifier, i.e., the fact that Woman and Man are not complementary but asymmetrical, that there is no yin-yang balance – in short, that there is no sexual relationship.

No wonder, then, that Siegfried's discovery that Brünnhilde 'is no man' gives rise to an outburst of true panic accompanied by a loss of reality, in which Siegfried takes refuge with his (unknown) mother: 'That's no man! A searing spell pierces my heart; a fiery anxiety fills my eyes; my senses swim and swoon! Whom can I call on to help me? Mother, mother! Think of me!' He then gathers all his courage and decides to kiss the sleeping woman on her lips, even if this will mean his own death: 'Then I will suck life from those sweetest lips, *though I die in doing so.*' What follows is the majestic awakening of Brünnhilde and then the love duet which concludes the opera. It is crucial to note that this acceptance of death as the price for contact with the feminine Other is accompanied musically by the echo of the so-called motif of 'renunciation', arguably the most important leitmotif in the entire tetralogy. This motif is first heard in Scene I of *Rhinegold*, when, answering Alberich's query, Woglinde discloses that 'only the one who renounces the power of love (*nur wer der Minne Macht versagt*)' can take possession of the gold; its next most noticeable appearance occurs towards the end of Act I of *Walküre*, at the moment of the most triumphant assertion of love between Sieglinde and Siegmund – just prior to his pulling out of the sword from the tree trunk, Siegmund sings it to the words: 'holiest love's highest need' ['Heiligster Minne höchste Not']. How are we to read these two occurrences together? What if one treats them as two fragments of the complete sentence that was distorted by 'dreamwork', that is, rendered unreadable by being split into two – the solution is thus to reconstitute the complete proposition: 'Love's highest need is to renounce its own power.' This is what Lacan calls 'symbolic castration': if one is to remain faithful to one's love, one should not elevate it into the direct focus of one's love, one should renounce its centrality. Perhaps a detour through the best (or worst) of Hollywood melodrama can help us to clarify this point. The basic lesson of King Vidor's *Rhapsody* is that, in order to gain the beloved woman's love, the man has to prove that he is able to survive without her, that he prefers his mission or profession to her. There are two immediate choices: (1) my professional career is what matters most to me, the woman is just an amusement, a distracting affair; (2) the woman is everything to me, I am ready to humiliate myself, to forsake all my public and professional dignity for her. They are both false, they lead to the man being rejected by the woman. The message of true love is thus: even if you are everything to me, I can survive without you, I am ready to forsake you for my mission or profession. The proper way for the woman to test the man's love is thus to 'betray' him at the crucial moment of his career (the first public concert in the film, the key exam, the business negotiation which will decide his career) – only if he can survive the ordeal and accomplish successfully his task although deeply traumatized by her desertion will he deserve her and will she return to him. The underlying paradox is that love, precisely as the Absolute, should not be posited as a direct goal – it should retain the status of a by-product, of something we get as an undeserved grace. Perhaps there is no greater love than that of a revolutionary couple, where each of the two lovers is ready to abandon the other at any moment if revolution demands it.

What, then, happens when Siegfried kisses the sleeping Brünnhilde, such that this act deserves to be accompanied by the 'renunciation' motif? What Siegfried says is that he will kiss Brünnhilde '*though I die in doing so*' – reaching out to the Other Sex involves accepting one's mortality. Recall here another sublime moment from *The Ring*: in Act II of *Die Walküre*, Siegmund literally renounces immortality. He prefers to stay a common mortal if his beloved Sieglinde cannot follow him to Valhalla, the eternal dwelling of the dead heroes – is this not the highest ethical act of them all? The shattered Brünnhilde comments on this refusal: 'So little do you value everlasting bliss? Is she everything to you, this poor woman who, tired and sorrowful, lies limp in your lap? Do you think nothing less glorious?' Ernst Bloch was right to remark that what is lacking in German history are more gestures like Siegmund's.

But which *love* is here renounced? To put it bluntly: the incestuous maternal love. The 'fearless hero' is fearless insofar as he experiences himself as protected by his mother, by the maternal envelope – what 'learning to fear' effectively amounts to is learning that one is exposed to the world without any maternal shield. It is essential to read this scene in conjunction with the scene, from *Parsifal*, of Kundry giving a kiss to Parsifal: in both cases, an innocent hero discovers fear and/or suffering through a kiss located somewhere between the maternal and the properly feminine. Up to the late nineteenth century, they practised in Montenegro a weird wedding night ritual: the evening after the marriage ceremony, the son gets into bed with his mother and, after he falls asleep, the mother silently withdraws and lets the bride take her place: after spending the rest of the night with the bride, the son has to escape from the village into a mountain and spend a couple of days there alone, in order to get accustomed to the shame of being married ... Does not something homologous happen to Siegfried?

However, the difference between *Siegfried* and *Parsifal* is that, in the first case, the woman is accepted; in the second case, she is rejected. This does not mean that the feminine dimension disappears in *Parsifal*, and that we remain within the homoerotic male community of the Grail. Syberberg was right when, after Parsifal's rejection of Kundry which follows her kiss, 'the last kiss of the mother and the first kiss of a woman', he replaced Parsifal-the-boy with another actor, a young cold woman – did he thereby not enact the Freudian insight according to which identification is, at its most radical, identification with the lost (or rejected) libidinal object? We *become* (identify with) the *object* that we were deprived of, so that our subjective identity is a repository of the traces of our lost objects.

NOTES

1 Gary Tomlison, *Metaphysical Song*, Princeton, Princeton University Press, 1999, p. 94.

2 Žižek develops this point further in *The Art of the Ridiculous Sublime: On David Lynch's Lost Highway*, Seattle, University of Washington Press, 2000, pp. 28–9 [eds].

3 Bertolt Brecht, *Die Gedichte in einem Band*, Frankfurt, Suhrkamp Verlag, 1999, p. 1005.

4 When, in his *The Case of Wagner*, Nietzsche mockingly rejects Wagner's universe, does his style not refer to these lines? Wagner himself was such a repulsive figure to him – and there is a kind of poetic justice in it, since Mime effectively is Wagner's ironic self-portrait.

5 Joseph Kerman, *Opera as Drama*, Berkeley, University of California Press, 1988.

6 This love duet is also one of the Verdi-relapses in Wagner (the best known being the revenge trio that concludes Act III of

Götterdämmerung, apropos of which Bernard Shaw remarked that it sounds like the trio of conspirators from *Un ballo in maschera*) – Gutman designated it as a farewell to music drama towards the 'rediscovered goal of the ultimate grand opera'. Robert Gutman, *Richard Wagner: The Man, his Mind and his Music*, London, Harcourt Brace Jovanovich, 1968, p. 299.

7   Sigmund Freud, 'Fetishism', in *The Penguin Freud Library, 7: On Sexuality*, ed. and trans. James Strachey, Harmondsworth, Penguin, 1977, pp. 351–7.

8   As if referring to this scene, Jacques-Alain Miller once engaged in a mental experiment, enumerating other possible operators of sexual difference that could replace the absence/presence of penis, and mentions the absence/presence of breasts.

15 The Real of Sexual Difference

1. THE 'FORMULAE OF SEXUATION'

Roger Ebert's *The Little Book of Hollywood Clichés*[1] contains hundreds of stereotypes and obligatory scenes – from the famous 'Fruit Cart' rule (during any chase scene involving a foreign or an ethnic locale, a fruit cart will be overturned and an angry peddler will run into the middle of the street to shake his fist at the hero's departing vehicle) and the more refined 'Thanks, but No Thanks' rule (when two people have just had a heart-to-heart conversation, as Person A starts to leave room, Person B tentatively says 'Bob [or whatever A's name is]?' and Person A pauses, turns, and says 'Yes?' and then Person B says, 'Thanks') to the 'Grocery Bag' rule (whenever a scared, cynical woman who does not want to fall in love again is pursued by a suitor who wants to tear down her wall of loneliness, she goes grocery shopping; her grocery bags then break, and the fruits and vegetables fall, either to symbolize the mess her life is in or so the suitor can help her pick up the pieces of her life, or both). This is what the 'big Other', the symbolic substance of our lives, is: a set of unwritten rules that effectively regulate our speech and acts, the ultimate guarantee of Truth to which we have to refer even when lying or trying to deceive our partners in communication, precisely in order to be successful in our deceit.

We should bear in mind, however, that in the last decades of his teaching, Lacan twice severely qualified the status of the big Other:

- first in the late 1950s, when he emphasized the fact that the 'quilting point' (or 'button tie') – the quasi-transcendental master-signifier that guarantees the consistency of the big Other – is ultimately a fake, an empty signifier without a signified. Suffice it to recall how a community functions: the master-signifier that guarantees the community's consistency is a signifier whose signified is an enigma for the members themselves – nobody really knows what it means, but each of them somehow presupposes that others know it, that it has to mean 'the real thing', and so they use it all the time. This logic is at work not only in politico-ideological links (with different terms for the *Cosa Nostra*: our nation, revolution, and so on), but even in some Lacanian communities, where the group recognizes itself through the common use of some jargon-laden expressions whose meaning is not clear to anyone, be it 'symbolic castration' or 'divided subject' – everyone refers to them, and what binds the group together is ultimately their shared *ignorance*. Lacan's point, of course, is that psychoanalysis should enable the subject to *break* with this safe reliance on the enigmatic master-signifier.

• and second, and even more radically, in *Seminar XX*, when Lacan developed the logic of the 'not-all' (or 'not-whole') and of the exception constitutive of the universal. The paradox of the relationship between the series (of elements belonging to the universal) and its exception does not reside merely in the fact that 'the exception grounds the [universal] rule', that is, that every universal series involves the exclusion of an exception (all men have inalienable rights, with the exception of madmen, criminals, primitives, the uneducated, children, etc.). The properly dialectical point resides, rather, in the way a series and exceptions directly coincide: the series is always the series of 'exceptions', that is, of entities that display a certain exceptional quality that qualifies them to belong to the series (of heroes, members of our community, true citizens, and so on). Recall the standard male seducer's list of female conquests: each is 'an exception', each was seduced for a particular *je ne sais quoi*, and the series is precisely the series of these exceptional figures.[2]

The same matrix is at work in the shifts in the Lacanian notion of the symptom. What distinguishes the last stage of Lacan's teaching from the previous ones is best approached through the changed status of this notion. Previously a symptom was a pathological formation to be (ideally, at least) dissolved in and through analytic interpretation, an index that the subject had somehow and somewhere compromised his desire, or an index of the deficiency or malfunctioning of the symbolic Law that guarantees the subject's capacity to desire. In short, symptoms were the series of exceptions, disturbances and malfunctionings, measured by the ideal of full integration into the symbolic Law (the Other). Later, however, with his notion of the universalized symptom, Lacan accomplished a paradoxical shift from the 'masculine' logic of Law and its constitutive exception to a 'feminine' logic, in which there is *no* exception to the series of symptoms – that is, in which there are *only* symptoms, and the symbolic Law (the paternal Name) is ultimately just one (the most efficient or established) in the series of symptoms.

This is, according to Jacques-Alain Miller, Lacan's universe in *Seminar XX*: a universe of the radical split (between signifier and signified, between *jouissance* of the drives and *jouissance* of the Other, between masculine and feminine), in which no *a priori* Law guarantees the connection or overlapping between the two sides, so that only partial and contingent knots-symptoms (quilting points, points of gravitation) can generate a limited and fragile coordination between the two domains. From this perspective, the 'dissolution of a symptom', far from bringing about a nonpathological state of full desiring capacity, leads instead to a total psychotic catastrophe, to the dissolution of the subject's entire universe. There is no 'big Other' guaranteeing the consistency of the symbolic space within which we dwell: there are just contingent, punctual and fragile points of stability.[3]

One is tempted to claim that the very passage from Judaism to Christianity ultimately obeys the matrix of the passage from the 'masculine' to the 'feminine' formulae of sexuation. Let us clarify this passage apropos of the opposition between the *jouissance* of the drives and the *jouissance* of the Other, elaborated by Lacan in *Seminar XX*, which also is sexualized according to the same matrix. On the one hand, we have the closed, ultimately solipsistic circuit of drives that find their satisfaction in idiotic masturbatory (auto-erotic) activity, in the perverse circulating around *objet a* as the object of a drive. On the other hand, there are subjects for whom access to *jouissance* is much more closely linked to the domain of the Other's discourse, to how they not so much talk as are talked about: erotic pleasure hinges, for example, on the seductive talk of the lover, on the satisfaction provided by speech itself, not just on the act in its stupidity. Does this contrast not explain the long-observed difference as to how the two sexes relate to cybersex? Men are much more prone to use cyberspace as a masturbatory device for their lone playing, immersed in stupid, repetitive pleasure, while women are more prone to participate in chat rooms, using cyberspace for seductive exchanges of speech.

Do we not encounter a clear case of this opposition between the masculine phallic-masturbatory *jouissance* of the drive and the feminine *jouissance* of the Other in Lars von Trier's *Breaking the Waves*? Confined to his hospital bed, Jan tells Bess that she must make love to other men and describe her experiences to him in detail – this way, she will keep awake his will to live. Although she will be physically involved with other men, the true sex will occur in their conversation. Jan's *jouissance* is clearly phallic-masturbatory: he uses Bess to provide him with the fantasmatic screen that he needs in order to be able to indulge in solipsistic, masturbatory *jouissance*, while Bess finds *jouissance* at the level of the Other (symbolic order), that is, in her words. The ultimate source of satisfaction for her is not the sexual act itself (she engages in such acts in a purely mechanical way, as a necessary sacrifice) but the way she *reports* on it to the crippled Jan.

Bess's *jouissance* is a *jouissance* 'of the Other' in more than one way: it is not only enjoyment in words but also (and this is ultimately just another aspect of the same thing) in the sense of utter alienation – her enjoyment is totally alienated/externalized in Jan as her Other. That is, it resides entirely in her awareness that she is enabling the Other to enjoy. (This example is crucial insofar as it enables us to dispense with the standard misreading of Lacan, according to which feminine *jouissance* is a mystical beatitude beyond speech, exempted from the symbolic order – on the contrary, it is women who are immersed in the order of speech *without exception*.)[4]

How does this allow us to shed new light on the tension between Judaism and Christianity? The first paradox to take note of is that the vicious dialectic between Law and its transgression elaborated by St Paul is the invisible third term, the 'vanishing mediator' between Judaism and Christianity. Its spectre haunts both of them, although neither of the two religious positions effectively occupies its place: on the one hand, Jews are *not yet* there, that is, they treat the Law as the written Real, which does not engage them in the vicious, superego cycle of guilt; on the other hand, as St Paul makes clear, the basic point of Christianity proper is to *break out* of the vicious superego cycle of the Law and its transgression via Love. In *Seminar VII*, Lacan discusses the Paulinian dialectic of the Law and its transgression at length. Perhaps we should thus read this Paulinian dialectic along with its corollary, the *other* paradigmatic passage by St Paul, the one on love from I Corinthians 13:

> If I speak in the tongues of mortals and of angels, but do not have love, I am a noisy gong or a clanging cymbal. And if I have prophetic powers, and understand all mysteries and all knowledge, and if I have all faith, so as to remove mountains, but do not have love, I am nothing. If I give away all my possessions, and if I hand over my body so that I may boast [alternative translation: 'may be burned'], but do not have love, I gain nothing ...
>
> Love never ends. But as for prophecies, they will come to an end; as for tongues, they will cease; as for knowledge, it will come to an end. For we know only in part, and we prophesy only in part; but when the complete comes, the partial will come to an end ... For now we see in a mirror, dimly, but then we will see face to face. Now I know only in part; then I will know fully, even as I have been fully known. And now faith, hope and love abide, these three; and the greatest of these is love.

Crucial here is the clearly paradoxical place of Love with regard to the All (to the completed series of knowledge or prophesies). First, St Paul claims that there is love, even if we possess *all* knowledge – then, in the second paragraph, he claims that there is love only for *incomplete* beings, that is, beings possessing incomplete knowledge. When I will 'know fully as I have been fully ... known', will there still be love? Although, unlike knowledge, 'love never ends', it is clearly only 'now' (while I am still incomplete) that 'faith, hope and love abide'.

The only way out of this deadlock is to read the two inconsistent claims according to Lacan's feminine formulas of sexuation: even when it is 'all' (complete, with no exception), the field of knowledge remains in a way not-all, incomplete. Love is not an exception to the All of knowledge but rather a 'nothing' that renders incomplete even the complete series or field of knowledge. In other words, the point of the claim that, even if I were to possess all knowledge, without love, I would be nothing, is not simply that *with* love I am 'something'. For in love, *I also am nothing*, but as it were a Nothing humbly aware of itself, a Nothing paradoxically made rich through the very awareness of its lack. Only a lacking, vulnerable being is capable of love: the ultimate mystery of love is therefore that incompleteness is in a way higher than completion.

On the one hand, only an imperfect, lacking being loves: we love because we do not know everything. On the other hand, even if we were to know everything, love would inexplicably still be higher than complete knowledge. Perhaps the true achievement of Christianity is to elevate a loving (imperfect) Being to the place of God, that is, the place of ultimate perfection. Lacan's extensive discussion of love in *Seminar XX* is thus to be read in the Paulinian sense, as opposed to the dialectic of the Law and its transgression. This latter dialectic is clearly 'masculine' or phallic: it involves the tension between the All (the universal Law) and its constitutive exception. Love, on the other hand, is 'feminine': it involves the paradoxes of the not-All.

2. SEXUAL DIFFERENCE AS A ZERO-INSTITUTION

The notion of sexual difference that underlies the formulae of sexuation in *Seminar XX* is strictly synonymous with Lacan's proposition that 'there's no such thing as a sexual relationship'. Sexual difference is not a firm set of 'static' symbolic oppositions and inclusions/exclusions (heterosexual normativity that relegates homosexuality and other 'perversions' to some secondary role) but the name of a deadlock, a trauma, an open question – something that *resists* every attempt at its symbolization. Every translation of sexual difference into a set of symbolic opposition(s) is doomed to fail, and it is this very 'impossibility' that opens up the terrain of the hegemonic struggle for what 'sexual difference' will mean. What is barred is *not* what is excluded under the present hegemonic regime.[5]

How, then, are we to understand the 'ahistorical' status of sexual difference? Perhaps an analogy to Claude Lévi-Strauss's notion of the 'zero-institution' might be of some help here. I am referring to Lévi-Strauss's exemplary analysis, in *Structural Anthropology*, of the spatial disposition of buildings among the Winnebago, one of the Great Lakes tribes. The tribe is divided into two sub-groups ('moieties'), 'those who are from above' and 'those who are from below'. When we ask an individual to draw the ground-plan of their village (the spatial disposition of cottages), we obtain two quite different answers, depending on which sub-group they belong to. Both groups perceive the village as a circle. For one sub-group, however, there is within this circle another circle of central houses, so that we have two concentric circles, while for the other sub-group, the circle is split into two by a clear dividing line. In other words, a member of the first sub-group (let us call it 'conservative-corporatist') perceives the ground-plan of the village as a ring of houses more or less symmetrically disposed around the central temple, whereas a member of the second ('revolutionary-antagonistic') sub-group perceives his or her village as two distinct heaps of houses, separated by an invisible frontier.[6]

Lévi-Strauss's central point here is that this example should in no way entice us into cultural relativism, according to which the perception of social space depends on which group the observer belongs to: the very splitting into the two 'relative' perceptions implies a hidden reference to a constant. This constant is not the objective, 'actual' disposition of buildings but rather a traumatic kernel, a fundamental antagonism the inhabitants of the village were unable to symbolize, account for, 'internalize' or come to terms with: an imbalance in social relations that prevented the community from stabilizing into a harmonious whole. The two perceptions of the ground-plan are simply two mutually exclusive endeavours to cope with this traumatic antagonism, to heal its wound via the imposition of a balanced symbolic structure.

Is it necessary to add that things are exactly the same with respect to sexual difference? 'Masculine' and 'feminine' are like the two configurations of houses in the Lévi-Straussian village. In order to dispel the illusion that our 'developed' universe is not dominated by the same logic, suffice it to recall the splitting of our political space into Left and Right: a leftist and a rightist behave exactly like members of the opposite sub-groups of the Lévi-Straussian village. They not only occupy different places within the political space, each of them perceives differently the very disposition of the political space – a leftist as a field that is inherently split by some fundamental antagonism, a rightist as the organic unity of a Community disturbed only by foreign intruders.

However, Lévi-Strauss makes a further crucial point here: since the two sub-groups nonetheless form one and the same tribe, living in the same village, this identity has to be symbolically inscribed somehow. Now how is that possible, if none of the tribe's symbolic articulations – none of its social institutions – are neutral, but are instead overdetermined by the fundamental and constitutive antagonistic split? It is possible through what Lévi-Strauss ingeniously calls the 'zero-institution' – a kind of institutional counterpart to 'mana', the empty signifier with no determinate meaning, since it signifies only the presence of meaning as such, in opposition to its absence. This zero-institution has no positive, determinate function – its only function is the purely negative one of signalling the presence and actuality of social institution as such in opposition to its absence, that is, in opposition to presocial chaos. It is the reference to such a zero-institution that enables all members of the tribe to experience themselves as members of the same tribe.

Is not this zero-institution ideology at its purest, that is, the direct embodiment of the ideological function of providing a neutral, all-encompassing space in which social antagonism is obliterated and all members of society can recognize themselves? And is not the struggle for hegemony precisely the struggle over how this zero-institution will be overdetermined, coloured by some particular signification? To provide a concrete example: is not the modern notion of the nation a zero-institution that emerged with the dissolution of social links grounded in direct family or traditional symbolic matrixes – that is, when, with the onslaught of modernization, social institutions were less and less grounded in naturalized tradition and more and more experienced as a matter of 'contract'?[7] Of special importance here is the fact that national identity is experienced as at least minimally 'natural', as a belonging grounded in 'blood and soil' and, as such, opposed to the 'artificial' belonging to social institutions proper (state, profession, and so on). Premodern institutions functioned as

'naturalized' symbolic entities (as institutions grounded in unques-
tionable traditions), and the moment institutions were conceived of as
social artifacts, the need arose for a 'naturalized' zero-institution that
would serve as their neutral common ground.

Returning to sexual difference, I am tempted to risk the hypothesis
that the same zero-institution logic should perhaps be applied not only
to the unity of a society, but also to its antagonistic split. What if
sexual difference is ultimately a kind of zero-institution of the social
split of humankind, the naturalized, minimal zero-difference, a split
that, prior to signalling any determinate social difference, signals this
difference as such? The struggle for hegemony would then, once again,
be the struggle for how this zero-difference is overdetermined by other
particular social differences.

It is against this background that one should read an important,
although usually overlooked, feature of Lacan's schema of the signifier. Lacan replaces the standard Saussurian scheme (above the bar
the word 'arbre', and beneath it the drawing of a tree) with the two
words 'gentlemen' and 'ladies' next to each other above the bar
and two identical drawings of a door below the bar. In order to
emphasize the differential character of the signifier, Lacan first
replaces Saussure's single signifier schema with a pair of signifiers:
the opposition gentlemen/ladies – that is, sexual difference. But the
true surprise resides in the fact that, at the level of the imaginary
referent, *there is no difference*: Lacan does not provide some graphic
index of sexual difference, such as the simplified drawings of a man
and a woman, as are usually found on the doors of most contemporary
restrooms, but rather *the same* door reproduced twice. Is it possible
to state in clearer terms that sexual difference does not designate
any biological opposition grounded in 'real' properties but a purely
symbolic opposition to which nothing corresponds in the designated
objects – nothing but the Real of some undefined X that cannot ever
be captured by the image of the signified?

Returning to Lévi-Strauss's example of the two drawings of the
village, let us note that it is here that we can see in what precise sense
the Real intervenes through anamorphosis. We have first the 'actual',
'objective' arrangement of the houses and then the two different sym-
bolizations that both distort the actual arrangement anamorphically.

However, the 'real' here is not the actual arrangement but the traumatic core of the social antagonism that distorts the tribe members' view of the actual antagonism. The Real is thus the disavowed X on account of which our vision of reality is anamorphically distorted. (Incidentally, this three-level apparatus is strictly homologous to Freud's three-level apparatus for the interpretation of dreams: the real kernel of the dream is not the dream's latent thought, which is displaced onto or translated into the explicit texture of the dream, but the unconscious desire which inscribes itself through the very distortion of the latent thought into the explicit texture.)

The same is true of today's art scene: in it, the Real does *not* return primarily in the guise of the shocking brutal intrusion of excremental objects, mutilated corpses, shit, and so on. These objects are, for sure, out of place – but in order for them to be out of place, the (empty) place must already be there, and this place is rendered by 'minimalist' art, starting with Kazimir Malevich. Therein resides the complicity between the two opposed icons of high modernism, Malevich's *The Black Square on the White Surface* and Marcel Duchamp's display of readymade objects as works of art. The underlying notion of Duchamp's elevation of an everyday common object into a work of art is that being a work of art is not an inherent property of the object. It is the artist himself who, by pre-empting the (or, rather, *any*) object and locating it at a certain place, makes it a work of art – being a work of art is not a question of 'why' but 'where'. What Malevich's minimalist disposition does is simply render – or isolate – this place as such, an empty place (or frame) with the proto-magic property of transforming any object that finds itself within its scope into a work of art. In short, there is no Duchamp without Malevich: only after art practice isolates the frame/place as such, emptied of all of its content, can one indulge in the readymade procedure. Before Malevich, a urinal would have remained just a urinal, even if it was displayed in the most distinguished gallery.

The emergence of excremental objects that are out of place is thus strictly correlative to the emergence of the place without any object in it, of the empty frame as such. Consequently, the Real in contemporary art has three dimensions, which somehow repeat the Imaginary–Symbolic–Real triad within the Real. The Real is first there as the anamorphic stain, the anamorphic distortion of the direct image of reality – as a distorted image, a pure semblance that 'subjectivizes' objective reality. Then the Real is there as the empty place, as a structure, a construction that is never actual or experienced as such but can only be retroactively constructed and has to be presupposed as such – the Real as symbolic construction. Finally, the Real is the obscene, excremental Object out of place, the Real 'itself'. This last Real, if isolated, is a mere fetish whose fascinating/captivating presence masks the structural Real, in the same way that, in Nazi anti-Semitism, the Jew as an excremental Object is the Real that masks the unbearable 'structural' Real of social antagonism. These three dimensions of the Real result from the three modes by which one can distance oneself from 'ordinary' reality: one submits this reality to anamorphic distortion; one introduces an object that has no place in it; and one subtracts or erases all content (objects) of reality, so that all that remains is the very empty place that these objects were filling.

3. 'POST-SECULAR THOUGHT'? NO, THANKS!

In *Seminar XX*, Lacan massively rehabilitates the religious problematic (Woman as one of the names of God, etc.). However, against the background of the properly Lacanian notion of the Real, it is easy to see why the so-called 'post-secular' turn of deconstruction, which finds its ultimate expression in a certain kind of Derridean appropriation of Lévinas, is totally incompatible with Lacan, although some of its proponents try to link the Lévinasian Other to the Lacanian Thing. This post-secular thought fully concedes that modernist critique undermined the foundations of onto-theology, the notion of God as the supreme Entity, and so on. Its point is that the ultimate outcome of this deconstructive gesture is to clear the slate for a new, undeconstructable form of spirituality, for the relationship to an unconditional Otherness that precedes ontology. What if the fundamental experience of the human subject is not that of self-presence, of the force of dialectical mediation-appropriation of all Otherness, but of a primordial passivity, sentiency, of responding, of being infinitely indebted to and responsible for the call of an Otherness that never acquires positive features but always remains withdrawn, the trace of its own absence? One is tempted to evoke here Marx's famous quip about Proudhon's *Poverty of Philosophy* (instead of actual people in their actual circumstances, Proudhon's pseudo-Hegelian social theory gives these circumstances themselves, deprived of the people who bring them to life):[8] instead of the religious matrix with God at its heart, post-secular deconstruction gives us this matrix itself, deprived of the positive figure of God that sustains it.

The same configuration is repeated in Derrida's 'fidelity' to the spirit of Marxism: 'Deconstruction has never had any sense or interest, in my view at least, except as a radicalization, which is also to say in the tradition of, a certain Marxism, in a certain spirit of Marxism.'[9] The first thing to note here (and of which Derrida is undoubtedly aware) is how this 'radicalization' relies on the traditional opposition between Letter and Spirit: reasserting the authentic spirit of the Marxist tradition means to leave behind its letter (Marx's particular analyses and proposed revolutionary measures, which are irreducibly tainted by the tradition of ontology) in order to save from the ashes the authentic messianic promise of emancipatory liberation. What cannot but strike the eye is the uncanny proximity of such 'radicalization' to (a certain common understanding of) Hegelian sublation (*Aufhebung*): in the messianic promise, the Marxian heritage is 'sublated', that is, its essential core is redeemed through the very gesture of overcoming/renouncing its particular historical shape. And – herein resides the crux of the matter, that is, of Derrida's operation – the point is not simply that Marx's particular formulation and proposed measures are to be left behind and replaced by other, more adequate formulations and measures but rather that the messianic promise that constitutes the 'spirit' of Marxism is betrayed by *any* particular formulation, by *any* translation into determinate economico-political measures. The underlying premise of Derrida's 'radicalization' of Marx is that the more 'radical' these determinate economico-political measures are (up to the Khmer Rouge or Sendero Luminoso killing fields), the less they are effectively radical and the more they remain caught in the metaphysical ethico-political horizon. In other words, what Derrida's 'radicalization' means is in a way (more precisely, practically speaking) its exact opposite: the renunciation of any actual radical political measures.

The 'radicality' of Derridean politics involves the irreducible gap between the messianic promise of the 'democracy to come' and all of its positive incarnations: on account of its very radicality, the messianic promise forever remains a promise – it cannot ever be translated into a set of determinate, economico-political measures. The inadequacy between the abyss of the undecidable Thing and any particular decision is irreducible: our debt to the Other can never be reimbursed, our response to the Other's call never fully adequate. This position should be opposed to the twin temptations of unprincipled pragmatism and totalitarianism, which both suspend the gap: while pragmatism simply reduces political activity to opportunistic manoeuvring, to limited strategic interventions in contextualized situations, dispensing with any reference to transcendent Otherness, totalitarianism identifies the unconditional Otherness with a particular historical figure (the Party *is* historical Reason embodied directly).

In short, we see here the problematic of totalitarianism in its specific deconstructionist twist: at its most elementary – one is almost tempted to say ontological – level, 'totalitarianism' is not simply a political force that aims at total control over social life, at rendering society totally transparent, but a short-circuit between messianic Otherness and a determinate political agent. The 'to come [*à venir*]' is thus not simply an additional qualification of democracy but its innermost kernel, what makes democracy a democracy: the moment democracy is no longer 'to come' but pretends to be actual – fully actualized – we enter totalitarianism.

To avoid a misunderstanding: this 'democracy to come' is, of course, not simply a democracy that promises to arrive in the future, but all arrival is forever postponed. Derrida is well aware of the 'urgency', of the 'now-ness', of the need for justice. If anything is foreign to him, it is the complacent postponement of democracy to a later stage in evolution, as in the proverbial Stalinist distinction between the present 'dictatorship of the proletariat' and the future 'full' democracy, legitimizing the present terror as creating the necessary conditions for the later freedom. Such a 'two stage' strategy is for him the very worst form of ontology; in contrast to such a strategic economy of the proper dose of (un)freedom, 'democracy to come' refers to the unforeseeable emergencies/outbursts of ethical responsibility, when I am suddenly confronted with an urgency to answer the call, to intervene in a situation that I experience as intolerably unjust. However, it is symptomatic that Derrida nonetheless retains the irreducible opposition between such a spectral experience of the messianic call of justice and its 'ontologization', its transposition into a set of positive legal and political measures. Or, to put it in terms of the opposition between ethics and politics, what Derrida mobilizes here is the gap between ethics and politics:

> On the one hand, ethics is left defined as the infinite responsibility of unconditional hospitality. Whilst, on the other hand, the political can be defined as the taking of a decision without any determinate transcendental guarantees. Thus, the hiatus in Levinas allows Derrida both to affirm the primacy of an ethics of hospitality, whilst leaving open the sphere of the political as a realm of risk and danger.[10]

The ethical is thus the (back)ground of undecidability, while the political is the domain of decision(s), of taking the full risk of crossing the hiatus and translating this impossible ethical request of messianic justice into a particular intervention that never lives up to this request, that is always unjust toward (some) others. The ethical domain proper, the unconditional spectral request that makes us absolutely responsible and cannot ever be translated into a positive measure/intervention, is thus perhaps not so much a formal a priori background/frame of political decisions but rather their inherent, indefinite *différance*, signalling that no determinate decision can fully 'hit its mark'.

This fragile, temporary unity of unconditional, ethical injunction and pragmatic, political interventions can best be rendered by paraphrasing Kant's famous formulation of the relationship between reason and experience: 'If ethics without politics is empty, then politics without ethics is blind.'[11] Elegant as this solution is (ethics is here the condition of possibility *and* the condition of impossibility of the political, for it simultaneously opens up the space for political decision as an act without a guarantee in the big Other and condemns it to ultimate failure), it is to be opposed to the act in the Lacanian sense, in which the distance between the ethical and the political collapses.

Consider the case of Antigone. She can be said to exemplify the unconditional fidelity to the Otherness of the Thing that disrupts the entire social edifice. From the standpoint of the ethics of *Sittlichkeit*, of the mores that regulate the intersubjective collective of the polis, her insistence is effectively 'mad', disruptive, evil. In other words, is not Antigone – in the terms of the deconstructionist notion of the messianic promise that is forever 'to come' – a proto-totalitarian figure? With regard to the tension (which provides the ultimate coordinates of ethical space) between the Other *qua* Thing, the abyssal Otherness that addresses us with an unconditional injunction, and the Other *qua* Third, the agency that mediates my encounter with others (other 'normal' humans) – where this Third can be the figure of symbolic authority but also the 'impersonal' set of rules that regulate my exchanges with others – does not Antigone stand for the exclusive and uncompromising attachment to the Other *qua* Thing, eclipsing the Other *qua* Third, the agency of symbolic mediation/reconciliation? Or, to put it in slightly ironic terms, is not Antigone the anti-Habermas par excellence? No dialogue, no attempt to convince Creon of the good reasons for her acts through rational argumentation, but just the blind insistence on her right. If anything, the so-called 'arguments' are on Creon's side (the burial of Polynices would stir up public unrest, etc.), while Antigone's counterpoint is ultimately the tautological insistence: 'Okay, you can say whatever you like, it will not change anything – I stick to my decision!'

This is no fancy hypothesis: some of those who read Lacan as a proto-Kantian effectively (mis)read Lacan's interpretation of Antigone, claiming that he condemns her unconditional insistence, rejecting it as the tragic, suicidal example of losing the proper distance from the lethal Thing, of directly immersing oneself in the Thing.[12] From this perspective, the opposition between Creon and Antigone is one between unprincipled pragmatism and totalitarianism: far from being a totalitarian, Creon acts like a pragmatic state politician, mercilessly crushing any activity that would destabilize the smooth functioning of the state and civil peace. Moreover, is not the very elementary gesture of sublimation 'totalitarian', insofar as it consists in elevating an object into the Thing (in sublimation, something – an object that is part of our ordinary reality – is elevated into the unconditional object that the subject values more than life itself)? And is not this short-circuit between a determinate object and the Thing the minimal condition of 'ontological totalitarianism'? Is not, as against this short-circuit, the ultimate ethical lesson of deconstruction the notion that the gap that separates the Thing from any determinate object is irreducible?

4. THE OTHER: IMAGINARY, SYMBOLIC AND REAL

The question here is whether Lacan's 'ethics of the Real' – the ethics that focuses neither on some imaginary Good nor on the pure symbolic form of a universal Duty – is ultimately just another version of this deconstructive-Levinasian ethics of the traumatic encounter with a radical Otherness to which the subject is infinitely indebted. Is not the ultimate reference point of what Lacan himself calls the ethical Thing the neighbour, *der Nebenmensch*, in his abyssal dimension of irreducible Otherness that can never be reduced to the symmetry of the mutual recognition of the Subject and his Other, in which the Hegelian-Christian dialectic of intersubjective struggle finds its resolution, that is, in which the two poles are successfully mediated?

Although the temptation to concede this point is great, it is *here* that one should insist on how Lacan accomplishes the passage from Law to Love, in short, from Judaism to Christianity. For Lacan, the ultimate horizon of ethics is *not* the infinite debt toward an abyssal Otherness. The act is for him strictly correlative to the suspension of the 'big Other', not only in the sense of the symbolic network that forms the 'substance' of the subject's existence but also in the sense of the absent originator of the ethical Call, of the one who addresses us and to whom we are irreducibly indebted and/or responsible, since (to put it in Levinasian terms) our very existence is 'responsive' – that is, we emerge as subjects in response to the Other's Call. The (ethical) act proper is *neither* a response to the compassionate plea of my neighbourly *semblable* (the stuff of sentimental humanism) *nor* a response to the unfathomable Other's call.

Here, perhaps, we should risk reading Derrida against Derrida himself. In *Adieu to Emmanuel Lévinas*, Derrida tries to dissociate decision from its usual metaphysical predicates (autonomy, consciousness, activity, sovereignty, and so on) and think of it as the 'other's decision in me': 'Could it not be argued that, without exonerating myself in the least, decision and responsibility are always *of the other*? They always come back or come down to the other, from the other, even if it is the other in me?'[13] When Simon Critchley tries to explicate this Derridean notion of 'the other's decision in me' with regard to its political consequences, his formulation displays a radical ambiguity:

> Political decision is made *ex nihilo*, and is not deduced or read off from a pre-given conception of justice or the moral law, as in Habermas, say, and yet it is not arbitrary. It is the demand provoked by the other's decision in me that calls forth political invention, that provokes me into inventing a norm and taking a decision.[14]

If we read these lines closely, we notice that we suddenly have *two* levels of decision: the gap is not only between the abyssal ethical Call of the Other and my (ultimately always inadequate, pragmatic, calculated, contingent, unfounded) decision how to translate this Call into a concrete intervention. Decision itself is split into the 'other's decision in me', and my decision to accomplish some pragmatic political intervention as my answer to this other's decision in me. In short, the first decision is identified with/as the injunction of the Thing in me to decide; it is a *decision to decide*, and it still remains my (the subject's) responsibility to translate this decision to decide into a concrete actual intervention – that is, to 'invent a new rule' out of a singular situation where this intervention has to obey pragmatic/strategic considerations and is never at the level of decision itself.

Does this distinction of the two levels apply to Antigone's act? Is it not rather that her decision (to insist unconditionally that her brother have a proper funeral) is precisely an *absolute* one in which the two dimensions of decision *overlap*? This is the Lacanian act in which the abyss of absolute freedom, autonomy and responsibility coincides with an unconditional necessity: I feel obliged to perform the act as an automaton, without reflection (I simply *have* to do it, it is not a matter of strategic deliberation). To put it in more 'Lacanian' terms, the 'other's decision in me' does *not* refer to the old structuralist jargon-laden phrases on how 'it is not I, the subject, who is speaking, it is the Other, the symbolic order itself, which speaks through me, so that I am spoken by it', and other similar babble. It refers to something much more radical and unheard of: what gives Antigone such unshakeable, uncompromising fortitude to persist in her decision is precisely the *direct* identification of her particular/determinate desire with the Other's (Thing's) injunction/call. Therein lies Antigone's monstrosity, the Kierkegaardian 'madness' of decision evoked by Derrida: Antigone does not merely relate to the Other-Thing; for a brief, passing moment of decision, she *is* the Thing directly, thus excluding herself from the community regulated by the intermediate agency of symbolic regulations.

The topic of the 'other' must be submitted to a kind of spectral analysis that renders visible its imaginary, symbolic and real aspects. It perhaps provides the ultimate case of the Lacanian notion of the 'Borromean knot' that unites these three dimensions. First there is the imaginary other – other people 'like me', my fellow human beings with whom I am engaged in mirror-like relationships of competition, mutual recognition, and so on. Then there is the symbolic 'big Other' – the 'substance' of our social existence, the impersonal set of rules that coordinate our existence. Finally there is the Other *qua* Real, the impossible Thing, the 'inhuman partner', the Other with whom no symmetrical dialogue, mediated by the symbolic Order, is possible. It is crucial to perceive how these three dimensions are linked. The neighbour [*Nebenmensch*] as the Thing means that, beneath the neighbour as my *semblable*, my mirror image, there always lurks the unfathomable abyss of radical Otherness, a monstrous Thing that cannot be 'gentrified'. Lacan indicates this dimension already in *Seminar III*:

And why [the Other] with a capital O? No doubt for a delusional reason, as is the case whenever one is obliged to provide signs that are supplementary to what language offers. That delusional reason is the following. 'You are my wife' – after all, what do you know about it? 'You are my master' – in point of fact, are you so sure?

Precisely what constitutes the foundational value of this speech is that what is aimed at in the message, as well as what is apparent in the feint, is that the other is there as absolute Other. Absolute, that is to say that he is recognized but that he isn't known. Similarly, what constitutes the feint is that ultimately you do not know whether it's a feint or not. It's essentially this unknown in the otherness of the Other that characterizes the speech relation at the level at which speech is spoken to the other.[15]

Lacan's early 1950s notion of 'founding speech', of the statement that confers on you a symbolic title and thus makes you what you are (wife or master), usually is perceived as an echo of the theory of performatives (the link between Lacan and Austin was Émile Benveniste, the author of the notion of performatives). However, it is clear from the above quote that Lacan is aiming at something more: we need to resort to performativity, to symbolic engagement, precisely and only insofar as the other whom we encounter is not only the imaginary *semblable* but also the elusive absolute Other of the Real Thing with whom no reciprocal exchange is possible. In order to render our co-existence with the Thing minimally bearable, the symbolic order *qua* Third, the pacifying mediator, has to intervene: the 'gentrification' of the homely Other-Thing into a 'normal fellow human' cannot occur through our direct interaction but presupposes a third agency to which we both submit – there is no intersubjectivity (no symmetrical, shared relation between humans) without the impersonal symbolic Order. So no axis between the two terms can subsist without the third one: if the functioning of the big Other is suspended, the friendly neighbour coincides with the monstrous Thing (Antigone); if there is no neighbour to whom I can relate as a human partner, the symbolic Order itself turns into the monstrous Thing that directly parasitizes upon me (like Daniel Paul Schreber's God, who directly controls me, penetrating me with the rays of *jouissance*); if there is no Thing to underpin our everyday, symbolically regulated exchange with others, we find ourselves in a 'flat', aseptic Habermasian universe in which subjects are deprived of their hubris of excessive passion, reduced to lifeless pawns in the regulated game of communication. Antigone–Schreber–Habermas: a truly uncanny ménage à trois.

5. HISTORICISM AND THE REAL

How, then, can we answer Judith Butler's well-known objection that the Lacanian Real involves the opposition between the (hypostasized, proto-transcendental, prehistorical and presocial) 'symbolic order', that is, the 'big Other', and 'society' as the field of contingent socio-symbolic struggles? Her main arguments against Lacan can be reduced to the basic reproach that Lacan hypostasizes some historically contingent formation (even if it is Lack itself) into a proto-transcendental presocial formal *a priori*. However, this critical line of reasoning only works if the (Lacanian) Real is silently reduced to a prehistorical a priori symbolic norm: only in this case can Lacanian sexual difference be conceived of as an ideal prescriptive norm, and all concrete variations of sexual life be conceived of as constrained by this non-thematizable, normative condition. Butler is, of course, aware that Lacan's 'il n'y a pas de rapport sexuel' means that any 'actual' sexual relationship is always tainted by failure. However, she interprets this failure as the failure of the contingent historical reality of sexual life fully to actualize the symbolic norm: the ideal is still there, even when the bodies in question – contingent and historically formed – do not conform to the ideal.

I am tempted to say that, in order to get at what Lacan is aiming at with his 'il n'y a pas de rapport sexuel', one should begin by emphasizing that, far from serving as an implicit symbolic norm that reality can never reach, sexual difference as real/impossible means precisely that there is no such norm: sexual difference is that 'bedrock of impossibility' on account of which every 'formalization' of sexual difference fails. In the sense in which Butler speaks of 'competing universalities', one can thus speak of competing symbolizations/normativizations of sexual difference: if sexual difference may be said to be 'formal', it is certainly a strange form – a form whose main result is precisely that it undermines every universal form that aims at capturing it.

If one insists on referring to the opposition between the universal and the particular, between the transcendental and the contingent/pathological, then one could say that sexual difference is the paradox of a particular that is more universal than universality itself – a contingent difference, an indivisible remainder of the 'pathological' sphere (in the Kantian sense of the term), that always somehow derails or destabilizes normative ideality itself. Far from being normative, sexual difference is thus pathological in the most radical sense of the term: a contingent stain that all symbolic fictions of symmetrical kinship positions try in vain to obliterate. Far from constraining in advance the variety of sexual arrangements, the Real of sexual difference is the traumatic cause that sets in motion their contingent proliferation.[16]

This notion of the Real also enables me to answer Butler's reproach that Lacan hypostasizes the 'big Other' into a kind of prehistorical transcendental *a priori*. For as we have already seen, when Lacan emphatically asserts that 'there is no big Other', his point is precisely that there is no *a priori* formal structural scheme exempted from historical contingencies: there are only contingent, fragile, inconsistent configurations. (Furthermore, far from clinging to paternal symbolic authority, the 'Name-of-the-Father' is for Lacan a fake, a semblance that conceals this structural inconsistency.) In other words, the claim that the Real is inherent to the Symbolic is strictly equivalent to the claim that 'there is no big Other': the Lacanian Real is that traumatic 'bone in the throat' that contaminates every ideality of the symbolic, rendering it contingent and inconsistent.

For this reason, far from being opposed to historicity, the Real is its very 'ahistorical' ground, the a priori of historicity itself. We can thus see how the entire topology changes from Butler's description of the Real and the 'big Other' as the prehistorical a priori to their actual functioning in Lacan's edifice. In her critical portrait, Butler describes an ideal 'big Other' that persists as a norm, although it is never fully actualized, the contingencies of history thwarting its full imposition, while Lacan's edifice is instead centred on the tension between some traumatic 'particular absolute', some kernel resisting symbolization, and the 'competing universalities' (to use Butler's appropriate term) that endeavour in vain to symbolize/normalize it. The gap between the symbolic a priori Form and history/sociality is utterly foreign to Lacan. The 'duality' with which Lacan operates is not the duality of the a priori form/norm, the symbolic Order and its imperfect historical realization: for Lacan, as well as for Butler, there is *nothing* outside of contingent, partial, inconsistent symbolic practices, no 'big Other' that guarantees their ultimate consistency. However, in contrast to Butler and historicism, Lacan grounds historicity in a different way: not in the simple empirical excess of 'society' over symbolic schemas but in the resisting kernel *within* the symbolic process itself.

The Lacanian Real is thus not simply a technical term for the neutral limit of conceptualization. We should be as precise as possible here with regard to the relationship between trauma as real and the domain of socio-symbolic historical practices: the Real is neither presocial nor a social effect. Rather, the point is that the Social itself is *constituted* by the exclusion of some traumatic Real. What is 'outside the Social' is not some positive a priori symbolic form/norm but merely its negative founding gesture itself.

In conclusion, how are we to counter the standard postmodern rejection of sexual difference as a 'binary' opposition? One is tempted to draw a parallel to the postmodern rejection of the relevance of class antagonism: class antagonism should not, according to this view, be 'essentialized' into the ultimate, hermeneutic point of reference to whose 'expression' all other antagonisms can be reduced, for today we are witnessing the thriving of new, multiple political (class, ethnic, gay, ecological, feminist, religious) subjectivities, and the alliance between them is the outcome of the open, thoroughly contingent, hegemonic struggle. However, philosophers as different as Alain Badiou and Fredric Jameson have pointed out, regarding today's multiculturalist celebration of the diversity of lifestyles, how this thriving of differences relies on an underlying One, that is, on the radical obliteration of Difference, of the antagonistic gap.[17] The same goes for the standard postmodern critique of sexual difference as a 'binary opposition' to be deconstructed: 'there are not only two sexes, but a multitude of sexes and sexual identities'. In all of these cases, the moment we introduce 'thriving multitude', what we effectively assert is the exact opposite: underlying all-pervasive Sameness. In other words, the notion of a radical, antagonistic gap that affects the entire social body is obliterated. The non-antagonistic Society is here the very global 'container' in which there is enough room for all of the multitudes of cultural communities, lifestyles, religions and sexual orientations.[18]

NOTES

Published in *Reading Seminar XX: Lacan's Major Work on Love, Knowledge and Feminine Sexuality*, ed. Suzanne Barnard and Bruce Fink, Albany, SUNY Press, 2002, pp. 57–75 [eds].

1　See Roger Ebert, *The Little Book of Hollywood Clichés*, London, Virgin Books, 1995.

2　I owe this point to a conversation with Alenka Zupančič. To give another example: therein also resides the deadlock of the 'open marriage' relationship between Jean-Paul Sartre and Simone de Beauvoir: it is clear, from reading their letters, that their 'pact' was effectively asymmetrical and did not work, causing de Beauvoir many traumas. She expected that, although Sartre had a series of other lovers, she was nonetheless the Exception, the one true love connection, while to Sartre, it was not that she was just one in the series but that she was precisely one *of the exceptions* – his series was a series of women, each of whom was 'something exceptional' to him.

3　The difference between these two notions of the symptom, the particular distortion and the universalized symptom ('sinthome'), accounts for the two opposed readings of the last shot of Hitchock's *Vertigo* (Scottie standing at the precipice of the church tower, staring into the abyss in which Judy-Madeleine, his absolute love, vanished seconds ago): some interpreters see in it the indication of a happy ending (Scottie finally got rid of his agoraphobia and is able fully to confront life), while others see in it utter despair (if Scottie survives the second loss of Judy-Madeleine, he will stay alive as one of the living dead). It all hinges upon how we read Lacan's statement that 'woman is a symptom of man'. If we use the term *symptom* in its traditional sense (a pathological formation that bears witness to the fact that the subject betrayed his desire), then the final shot effectively points toward a happy ending: Scottie's obsession with Judy-Madeleine was his 'symptom', the sign of his ethical weakness, so his rectitude is restored when he gets rid of her. However, if we use the term *symptom* in its more radical sense, that is, if Judy-Madeleine is his *sinthome*, then the final shot points toward a catastrophic ending: when Scottie is deprived of his *sinthome*, his entire universe falls apart, losing its minimal consistency.

4 For a closer reading of *Breaking the Waves*, see Slavoj Žižek, 'Death and the Maiden', in *The Žižek Reader*, ed. Elizabeth Wright and Edmond Wright, Oxford, Blackwell, 1998, pp. 206–21.

5 The gap that forever separates the Real of an antagonism from (its translation into) a symbolic opposition becomes palpable in a surplus that emerges apropos of every such translation. Say the moment we translate class antagonism into the opposition of classes *qua* positive, existing social groups (bourgeoisie versus working class), there is always, for structural reasons, a surplus, a third element that does not 'fit' this opposition (e.g., lumpenproletariat). And, of course, it is the same with sexual difference *qua* real: this means that there is always, for structural reasons, a surplus of 'perverse' excess over 'masculine' and 'feminine' as two opposed symbolic identities. One is even tempted to say that the symbolic/structural articulation of the Real of an antagonism is always a triad; today, for example, class antagonism appears, within the edifice of social difference, as the triad of 'top class' (the managerial, political and intellectual elite), 'middle class' and the non-integrated 'lower class' (immigrant workers, the homeless, etc.).

6 Claude Lévi-Strauss, 'Do Dual Organizations Exist?', in *Structural Anthropology, Volume 1*, trans. Claire Jacobson and Brooke Grundfest-Schoepf, New York, Basic Books, 1963, pp. 131–63.

7 See Rastko Močnik, 'Das "Subjekt, dem unterstellt wird zu glauben" und die Nation als eine Null-Institution', in *Denk-Prozesse nach Althusser*, ed. H. Boke, Hamburg, ArgumentVerlag, 1994, pp. 87–99.

8 Karl Marx, *The Poverty of Philosophy*, New York, International Publishers, 1963, p. 105 [eds].

9 Jacques Derrida, *Spectres of Marx: The State of Debt, the Work of Mourning and the New International*, trans. Peggy Kamuf, New York and London, Routledge, 1994, p. 92.

10 Simon Critchley, *Ethics–Politics–Subjectivity: Essays on Derrida, Lévinas and Contemporary French Thought*, London and New York, Verso, 1999, p. 275.

11   *Ibid.*, p. 283.

12   See Rudolf Bernet, 'Subjekt and Gesetz in der Ethik von Kant und Lacan', in *Ethik und Psychoanalyse*, ed. Hans-Dieter Gondek and Peter Widmer, Frankfurt, Fischer Verlag, 1994, pp. 15–27.

13   Jacques Derrida, *Adieu to Emmanuel Levinas*, trans. Pascale-Anne Brault and Michael Naas, Stanford, Stanford University Press, 1999, p. 23. [*Editorial note*: Žižek's original text quotes Derrida as follows: 'The passive decision, condition of the event, is always in me, structurally, an other decision, a rending decision as the decision of the other. Of the absolutely other in me, of the other as the absolute who decides of me in me.' He attributes this passage to *Adieu à Emmanuel Lévinas*, Paris, Éditions Galilée, 1997, p. 87, but it does not correspond to any part of that book. The passage with which we have replaced the original misquotation expresses the same sense of the 'other's decision in me'.]

14   Critchley, *Ethics–Politics–Subjectivity*, p. 277.

15   Jacques Lacan, *The Seminar of Jacques Lacan III: The Psychoses, 1955–56*, ed. Jacques-Alain Miller, trans. Russell Grigg, New York, W. W. Norton, 1993, pp. 37–8.

16   I rely here, of course, on Joan Copjec's pathbreaking 'Sex and the Euthanasia of Reason', in *Read My Desire: Lacan among the Historicists*, Cambridge MA, MIT Press, 1995, pp. 201–36. It is symptomatic how this essay on the philosophical foundations and consequences of the Lacanian notion of sexual difference is silently passed over in numerous feminist attacks on Lacan.

17   Alain Badiou, in his *Deleuze: The Clamor of Being*, trans. Louise Burchill, Minneapolis, University of Minnesota Press, 2000, fully emphasizes how Deleuze, the philosopher of the thriving rhizomatic multitude, is at the same time the most radical monist in modern philosophy, the philosopher of Sameness, of the One that pervades all differences – not only at the level of the content of his writings but already at the level of his formal procedure. Is not Deleuze's style characterized by an obsessive compulsion to assert the same notional pattern or matrix in all the phenomena he is analysing, from philosophical systems to literature and cinema?

18   There is already a precise *philosophical* reason antagonism has to be a dyad, that is, why the 'multiplication' of differences amounts

to the reassertion of the underlying One. As Hegel emphasized, each genus has ultimately only two species, that is, the specific difference is ultimately the difference between the genus itself and its species 'as such'. Say in our universe sexual difference is not simply the difference between the two species of the human genus but the difference between one term (man) that stands for the genus as such and the other term (woman) that stands for the Difference within the genus as such, for its specifying, particular moment. So in a dialectical analysis, even when we have the appearance of multiple species, we always have to look for the exceptional species that directly gives body to the genus as such: the true Difference is the 'impossible' difference between this species and all others.

Glossary

As we argued in the 'Introduction', Žižek's work operates by a process of *capitonnage*, with certain terms and examples momentarily 'bound' within an otherwise free-ranging discourse. However, three points need to be made with regard to the specificity of his method, the material production of the texts themselves. First, as can be seen in the way that certain material is revised from essay to essay, the same terms do not always play the same role in Žižek's work: sometimes a particular term is primary or absolute, the concept to be explained or elaborated; at other times this term is secondary, used to clarify some other concept. Second, for this reason, the *points de capiton* of Žižek's discourse tend not to be the usual ones of psychoanalytically inspired theory (Imaginary, Symbolic, Real . . .). Rather, they are often unusual or eccentric, seemingly of little interest to anyone other than Žižek himself (Lévi-Strauss's discussion of the two different conceptions of the village in *Structural Anthropology*, the parable of the Door of the Law from Kafka's *The Trial* . . .). Finally, for both of these reasons, this Glossary can only be a certain *capitonnage* or quilting of Žižek's own discourse: momentary, partial, provisional. There are any number of other terms we could have used to provide a focus for the texts collected here: for example, the logic of fetishistic denial, which is to be seen in Mannoni's canonical 'I know well, but all the same . . .', our willed ignorance in the face of the 'knowledge in the Real' embodied in the human genome, and ordinary commodity fetishism. In compiling our Glossary, we have had perhaps two precedents or sources of inspiration: the so-called 'Lynch-kit' with which Michel Chion ends his book on David Lynch (a book that Žižek has described as one of his favourites); and Daniel Siboni's Web project, 'Les mathèmes de Lacan', which attempts to reduce Lacan's thought to a series of short statements that can be considered either memorable aphorisms or as absolutely transmissable formulae. The numbers in brackets refer to page numbers within this text.

ABSOLUTE KNOWLEDGE (*see also* DIALECTICS)
In Žižek's reading of Hegel, Absolute Knowledge is not to be understood as any principle of completion or totality: '"Absolute Knowledge" is undeniably not a position of "omniscience", in which, ultimately, the subject "knows everything"' (p. 50). In fact, para-doxically, Absolute Knowledge is the realization of the impossibility of any such neutral position outside of its position of enunciation; and, beyond that, the absence of any similar guarantee in the Other: 'Absolute Knowledge appears to be the Hegelian name for that which Lacan outlined in his description of the *passe*, the final moment of the analytic process, the experience of lack in the Other' (p. 27). It is ultimately this refusal to take into account the subjective position of enunciation that distinguishes Knowledge from Truth: 'Politically correct proponents of cultural studies often pay for their arrogance and lack of a serious approach by confusing truth (the engaged subjective position) and knowledge, that is, by disavowing the gap that separates them, by directly subordinating knowledge to truth' (p. 98).

ADORNO (*see also* LÉVI-STRAUSS)
Žižek's open-ended, non-teleological conception of dialectics is un-doubtedly indebted – while he rarely acknowledges it – to Adorno, although Žižek pushes much further than him the possibility that Hegel was already proposing such a conception. Along these lines, Žižek also adopts Adorno's notion of the 'truth' of the social lying in the conflict or difference between its various constructions. As he says with regard to the split between 'organicist' and 'individualist' conceptions of the social: 'The dialectical turn takes place when this very contradiction becomes the answer: the different definitions of society do not function as an obstacle, but are inherent to the "thing itself"' (p. 39). However, in a later essay on Karatani's notion of the 'parallax view' – the idea that the 'truth' lies in the shift of perspective on to something – we can see Žižek criticizing or at least subtlizing his own earlier view. That is, in

Žižek's distance from Karatani, can we not see a certain self-critique of his own earlier use of Adorno?

ANTAGONISM (see also ADORNO, LÉVI-STRAUSS)

Throughout his work, Žižek presents the social as inherently split, antagonistic, with no possibility of any final unity or harmony. It is for this reason that the various ideological terms that construct society's image of itself (ecology, feminism, racism, etc.) are always disputed. But beyond any particular definition of these terms – whether left, right or centrist – it is in this dispute itself that the 'truth' of society is to be found: 'In social life, for example, what the multitude of (ideological) symbolizations-narrativizations fails to render is not society's *self-identity* but the *antagonism*, the constitutive splitting of the "body politic"' (p. 211). One of the names for this antagonism is *class struggle*, the ongoing conflict between the workers and those who control the means of production: 'Is the supreme example of such a "Real" not provided by the Marxist concept of *class struggle*? The consequent thinking through of this concept compels us to admit that there is no class struggle "in reality": "class struggle" designates the very antagonism that prevents the objective (social) reality from constituting itself as a self-enclosed whole' (p. 263). In other words, we might say that class struggle is merely the name for that underlying split between positively constituted ideological entities and the void from which they are enunciated. It is not some external limit or shortcoming that could one day be made up – as even the classical notion of class struggle would seem to promise – but an internal limit that is structurally necessary to the realization of the social itself: 'to grasp the notion of antagonism, in its most radical dimension, we should *invert* the relationship between the two terms: it is not the external enemy who is preventing me from achieving identity with myself, but every identity is already in itself blocked, marked by an impossibility, and the external enemy is simply the small piece, the rest of reality upon which we "project" or "externalize" this intrinsic, immanent impossibility' (p. 274).

ANTIGONE/MEDEA (see also DRIVE/DEATH-DRIVE, EXCEPTION/NOT-ALL, MASCULINE/FEMININE)

These two figures from classical Greek drama are used to illustrate certain conceptions of ethics, and generally Žižek understands both as positive, as breaking with a deconstructive 'respect for the Other' that is ultimately only a way of deferring the (ethical and political) act. 'Such a (mis)reading of Lacan led some German philosophers to interpret Antigone's clinging to her desire as a *negative* attitude, i.e., as the exemplary case of the lethal obsession with the Thing which cannot achieve sublimation and therefore gets lost in a suicidal abyss' (p. 207). But, in fact, 'what gives Antigone such unshakeable, uncompromising fortitude to persist in her decision is precisely the *direct* identification of her particular/determinate desire with the Other's (Thing's) injunction/call' (p. 347). Beyond this, Žižek makes a distinction between Antigone and Medea (and Paul Claudel's Sygne de Coûfontaine), in that with Antigone there is a particular exception made for which all else is sacrificed (for Žižek a 'masculine' logic of an exception generating a universality), while for Medea even this exception or cause itself must be sacrificed (a feminine logic of a not-all with no exceptions). And for Žižek this is the modern, as opposed to traditional, form of subjectivity: 'The modern subject constitutes themselves by means of such a gesture of redoubled renunciation, i.e., of sacrificing the very kernel of their being, their particular substance for which they are otherwise ready to sacrifice everything' (p.222).

CONCRETE UNIVERSALITY (*see also* EXCEPTION/NOT-ALL, MASCULINE/FEMININE)
Žižek takes up this Hegelian notion, developed at length in his *Greater Logic*, to speak of that final moment of the dialectic, in which something (Being) coincides with its opposite (Nothing). 'Concrete universality' is thus achieved not when there is one universal for which all others stand in, but – hence the connection with the 'feminine' logic of the not-all – when this universal is only the space that allows the equivalence of all the others, when this universal itself is only one of these others: 'What we have here is thus not a simple reduction of the universal to the particular, but a kind of surplus of the universal. No single universal encompasses the entire particular content, since each particular has its own universal, each contains a specific perspective on the entire field' (p. 73). In this sense, there is no neutral, objective construction of social reality, because any supposed master-signifier or quilting point is itself only one of the elements to be

sutured. This relates to Žižek's more general argument, following Adorno and Lévi-Strauss, that the definition of society is to be found neither in any of its various descriptions nor in their combination, but in the very split they indicate: 'There is no neutral position, but precisely because there is only one science, and this science is split from within' (p. 82). It is in this sense that Žižek can say that each genus has only two species, the genus itself and that void for which it stands in (p. 335). This is to be seen in the question of sexual difference: there are not two sexes that can be put together, but only one sex (masculine) and that for which it stands in (the feminine), and it is for this reason that sexual difference is one of the ways of properly rendering the 'concrete universality' of the social.

DERRIDA (*see also* KANT)

One of Žižek's long-running, though submerged, interlocutors is Derrida. It is certainly against his deconstruction that Žižek asserts his reading of Lacan and Hegel, for example: 'the Derridean deconstructive reading of Lacan reduces the corpus of Lacan's texts to a *doxa* on Lacan which restricts his teaching to the framework of traditional philosophy ... Lacan supplements Derrida with the Hegelian identity as the coincidence of opposites' (pp. 206, 210). It is for these reasons too – Derrida's insistence on the incompletion or deferral of identity – that Žižek disputes the ethical and political consequences of deconstruction, whose 'respect for the Other' simply amounts to a hysterical refusal of action: 'It is easy to see why the so-called "post-secular" turn of deconstruction, which finds its ultimate expression in a certain kind of Derridean appropriation of Lévinas, is totally incompatible with Lacan ... it is symptomatic that Derrida nonetheless retains the irreducible opposition between such a spectral experience of the messianic call of justice and its "ontologization", its transposition into a set of positive legal and political measures' (pp. 340, 343). We might wonder, however, how different Žižek actually is from Derrida, whether there is not a systematic misreading by him of Derrida that allows a distinction between them to be drawn? For example, is Žižek's conception of the origins of Law (pp. 127–32) fundamentally any different from that of Derrida in his 'Force of Law: "The Mystical Foundation of Authority" '?

DIALECTICS (*see also* ADORNO, HEGEL)

For Žižek, Hegelian dialectics is not some process of final sublation, of doing away with all difference in a completed unity. 'We should thus abandon the standard notion that the dialectical process advances by moving from particular (limited and "unilateral") elements towards some final totality' (p. 38). Rather, just as the master-signifier works by a kind of doubling whereby, as with St Paul, defeat itself is perceived as victory, so in dialectics what was initially perceived as a problem is now seen as its own solution. It is not that anything actually changes, but that our very ability to recognize what is as a defeat indicates that victory has already been achieved. In this regard, dialectics might even be related to that notion of the sublime that Žižek sees Hegel as developing from Kant: 'The dialectical turn takes place when this very contradiction becomes the answer . . . whatever presents itself initially as an obstacle becomes, in the dialectical turn, the very proof that we have made contact with the truth . . . the dialectical reversal consists in the change of perspective whereby *failure as such* appears as victory' (pp. 39, 45). A complicated question thus emerges in Žižek's work: how is Hegel's dialectical method not simply the basis for a new master-signifier? What is the difference between the turning of defeat into victory within dialectics and the transformation of nothing into something produced by the master-signifier?

DRIVE/DEATH-DRIVE (*see also* EMPTY PLACE/VOID, ENUNCIATED/ENUNCIATION)

Žižek takes this term from Freud and uses it to speak of that 'void' which underlies symbolic reality: drive can be understood as the repeated folding back of a process onto itself in order to expose that void for which it stands in. In this regard, it can even be understood as speaking of what makes desire possible: 'The Real *qua* drive is . . . the *agens*, the "driving force," of desiring . . . [This] in no way implies that the Real of drive is, as to its ontological status, a kind of full substantiality . . . a drive is not a primordial, positive force but a purely geometrical, topological phenomenon, the name for the curvature of the space of desire' (pp. 208–9). Coming back to the question of the empty place or void that runs throughout Žižek's work, however, this drive as abstract principle is not to be seen outside of the actual objects

that stand in for it: 'This "pure life" beyond death, this longing that
reaches beyond the circuit of generation and corruption, is it not the
product of symbolization, so that symbolization itself engenders the
surplus that escapes it?' (p. 172). In this sense, drive is not strictly
speaking opposed to desire – as the feminine is not opposed to the
masculine – but rather its extension to infinity, so that it applies even
to itself. As Žižek says, it is a 'curvature of the space of desire'.
Another name for this drive is in fact the *subject* (\$) – and this takes us
to the relationship between enunciated and enunciation in Žižek's
work: 'The psychoanalytic name for this gap [between cause and
effect] of course, is the death drive, while its philosophical name
in German Idealism is "abstract negativity", the point of absolute
self-contradiction that constitutes the subject as the void of pure self-
relating' (p. 112).

EMPTY PLACE/VOID (*see also* DERRIDA, HEGEL, KANT)
Running throughout Žižek's work is the important distinction
between the object within the symbolic order and that empty place
for which it stands in: 'It is necessary to introduce the crucial distinction between "symbolic signification" and its own place, the empty
place filled by signification' (p. 47). Žižek generally argues that it is the
'empty place' that precedes and makes possible the object that fills it:
'As soon as the symbolic order emerges, we are dealing with the
minimal difference between a structural place and the element that
occupies, fills out, this place: an element is always logically preceded
by the place in the structure it fills out' (pp. 192–3). Or, as he will say
with regard to modern art: '[the] objects are, for sure, out of place –
but in order for them to be out of place, the (empty) place must
already be there, and this place is rendered by 'minimalist' art, starting
with Kazimir Malevich' (p. 339). However, Žižek can occasionally be
inconsistent on this, arguing that in fact the object precedes and
reveals that empty space for which it stands in: 'The two readings
[of Kafka], although opposed, miss the same point: the way that
this absence, this empty place, is found always already filled by an
inert, obscene, dirty, revolting presence' (p.148). This ambiguity
can also be seen in various forms in Žižek's discussions of Derrida
(in his objection to Derrida's attempts at religion without an actual

God), Deleuze (in the relation between 'pre-symbolic depth' and 'surface events') and the differing status of the 'transcendental' in Kant and Hegel.

ENUNCIATED/ENUNCIATION (*see also* DRIVE/ DEATH-DRIVE, SUBJECT)

Picking up on the Hegelian theme of substance as subject, one of the ways of exposing the artificiality and arbitrariness of the symbolic construction of reality is to locate that place from which it is enunciated. This, of course, has some relation to that traditional demystifying method of posing the question to some abstract conception of justice: Whose justice? Which particular group in society does this conception of justice favour? But it goes beyond this to speak of that necessarily empty place from which *all* symbolic constructions are spoken: 'It is precisely the password *qua* empty speech that reduces the subject to the punctuality of the "subject of the enunciation": in it, he is present *qua* a pure symbolic point freed of all enunciated content ... it is only empty speech that, by way of its very emptiness (of its distance from the enunciated content ...), creates the space for "full speech"' (p. 153). And it is in this sense that the attempt to think this empty place might be seen as the attempt to think the empty subject (hence the way that Descartes might be understood to mark the beginning of philosophy in its modern, critical sense): 'What if the self is ... the void that is nothing in itself, that has no substantial positive identity, but which nonetheless serves as the unrepresentable point of reference?' (p. 109). And just as philosophy might be defined as the search for this empty position, so it might itself come from this empty position, embody that which has no place within our current situation: '*Cogito* is not a substantial entity, but a pure structural function, an empty place ... as such, it can only emerge in the interstices of substantial communal systems' (p. 12).

EXCEPTION/NOT-ALL (*see also* ANTIGONE/MEDEA, CONCRETE UNIVERSALITY, HEGEL, KANT)

These two concepts are usually opposed as respectively the masculine and feminine sides of Lacan's formulae of sexuation: the masculine side consists of a universality made possible by an exception to it;

the feminine side does not form such a universality, but there is no exception to it. 'Woman is not-all ... but this means precisely that woman is not-all caught into the phallic function' (p. 71). This masculine logic in fact coincides with that of the master-signifier, in which a certain term (always itself undefined) outside of a series of phenomena explains them and allows them to be exchanged for one another: 'The Master-Signifier ... [is] no longer a simple abbreviation that designates a series of markers but the name of the hidden ground of this series of markers that act as so many expressions-effects of this ground' (p. 202). But as Žižek's work has progressed, he has more and more emphasized the feminine logic of the not-all over this masculine logic of the exception, ultimately understanding it as its real cause. The masculine logic of the exception is an 'exception' within a larger logic of the not-all. For example, of the 'symptom', Žižek writes: 'Symptoms were the series of exceptions, disturbances and malfunctionings ... Later, however, with his notion of the universalized symptom, Lacan accomplished a paradoxical shift ... in which there is *no* exception to the series of symptoms ... and the symbolic Law ... is ultimately just one [of them]' (p. 332). This leads Žižek to consider the Hegelian logic of 'concrete universality', in which it is not that 'the exception grounds the [universal] rule ... [but the] series and [its] exceptions directly coincide' (p. 331). It is a logic that is also to be seen in Žižek's notion of 'love', which renders what is not-all, without nevertheless being an exception to it: 'Even when it is "all" (complete, with no exception), the field of knowledge remains in a way not-all, incomplete. Love is not an exception to the All of knowledge, but rather a "nothing" that renders incomplete even the complete series or field of knowledge' (p. 334–5).

FANTASY (*see also* JEW)

One of Žižek's decisive innovations is to think the role of fantasy within ideology: it is arguably in this way that he moves beyond someone like Althusser. Fantasy is both that which covers up inconsistencies within the symbolic order and that by which ideological interpellation works today in our seemingly 'post-ideological' times: it is through our apparent distance from ideology (non-ideological enjoyment, fantasy, cynicism) that ideology captures us.

'The message the power discourse bombards us with is by definition inconsistent; there is always a gap between public discourse and its fantasmatic support. Far from being a kind of secondary weakness, a sign of Power's imperfection, this splitting is constitutive for its exercise' (pp. 367 n. 9, 286–7). Or again: 'And, perhaps, it is here that we should look for the last resort of ideology, for the pre-ideological kernel, the formal matrix, on which are grafted various ideological formations: in the fact that there is no reality without the spectre [we might say fantasy], that the circle of reality can be closed only by means of an uncanny spectral supplement ... *This Real (the part of reality that remains non-symbolized) returns in the guise of spectral apparitions* ... the notions of spectre and (symbolic) fiction are codependent in their very incompatibility' (p. 262). This is why, for Žižek, the first task of any ideological critique is to attack the fantasy that keeps us bound to ideology: 'if we are to overcome the "effective" social power, we have first to break its fantasmatic hold upon us' (p. 251). And the way to do this is to prove that there is no fantasy or that the Other does not possess what we lack: 'If the traversing of the fantasy overlaps with the experience of any lack, *it is the lack of the Other* and not that of the subject themselves' (p. 49).

HEGEL (*see also* EXCEPTION/NOT-ALL, KANT)

Hegel forms a constant reference for Žižek, from his earliest writings to his most recent (if anything, he is becoming *even more Hegelian* as his work progresses). Žižek's chief insight is that Hegel completes the Kantian revolution in philosophy in that he proposes a 'transcendental' explanation for reality but without some cause that simply stands outside of it. For Hegel, reality does not need some exception standing outside of it. Rather, it is already its own exception, its own re-mark: 'A Hegelian corollary to Kant ... is that limitation is to be conceived as prior to what lies "beyond" it, so that it is ultimately Kant himself whose notion of the Thing-in-itself remains too "reified" ... What [Hegel] claims by stating that the Suprasensible is "appearance *qua* appearance" is precisely that the Thing-in-itself is the *limitation of the phenomena as such*' (p. 168). Žižek calls this precisely the modernity of Hegel, but we would call it his postmodernity. And indeed in Žižek's surprising comparison of Deleuze with Hegel, it is just this aspect that is emphasized in both: that this 'cause' is not outside of what it explains, that, to paraphrase Deleuze, it belongs to 'pure events-effects devoid of any substantial support' (p. 185). And it is in this sense that we might say that, as against Kant's 'negation' of what is, in Hegel we have a 'negation of negation', the 'negation' even of that negation or exception that remains outside of the positive order. 'This is why the Hegelian "loss of the loss" is definitively not the return to a full identity, lacking nothing: the "loss of the loss" is the moment in which loss ceases to be the loss *of* "something" and becomes the opening of the empty place that the object ("something") can occupy' (p. 47). And this 'tarrying with the negative' has great consequences for ethics and the political, and marks what truly is at stake in that revolutionary act Žižek can be seen to be arguing for: 'The "negation of negation" is not a kind of existential sleight of hand by means of which the subject feigns to put everything at stake, but effectively sacrifices only the inessential. Rather, it stands for the horrifying experience which occurs when, after sacrificing everything considered "inessential," I suddenly perceive that the very essential dimension, for the sake of which I sacrificed the inessential, is already lost' (p. 216).

JEW (*see also* MASTER-SIGNIFIER, *OBJET a*)

The importance of the ideological figure of the 'Jew' in anti-Semitism is that it occupies the positions both of master-signifier and *objet a*. As Žižek writes, in speaking of the difference between the Jew as master-signifier and the Jew as *objet a*: 'There is, however, a pivotal difference between this symbolic authority guaranteed by the phallus as the signifier of castration and the spectral presence of the "conceptual Jew" ... The fantasmatic "conceptual Jew" is not a paternal figure of symbolic authority, a "castrated" bearer-medium of public authority ... In short, the difference between the Name-of-the-Father and the "conceptual Jew" is that between symbolic *fiction* and fantasmatic *spectre*: in Lacanian algebra, between S_1, the Master-Signifier (the empty signifier of symbolic authority) and *objet petit a*' (p. 260). And this mention of the 'non-castrated' aspect of the Jew as *objet a* reminds us that the Jew in this logic of racism is a figure of enjoyment: that what we ultimately resent is the way that the Other, the Jew, seems to be able to enjoy in a way we cannot. The Jew in this sense becomes a symptom insofar as they suggest a seemingly external reason for the internal impossibility of *jouissance*. Speaking of this logic of the Jew as both master-signifier and *objet a*, Žižek says: 'The notion of fantasy offers an exemplary case of the dialectical *coincidentia oppositorum*: on the one hand, fantasy in its beautific side ... on the other hand, fantasy in its aspect whose elemental form is envy ... Those who are alleged to realize fully fantasy₁ (the symbolic fiction) had to have recourse to fantasy₂ (spectral apparitions) in order to explain their failure ... Fantasy₁ and fantasy₂, symbolic fiction and spectral apparition, are like the front and reverse of the same coin' (pp. 265–6). In fact, Žižek's point is that Jews are *not* holders of this secret enjoyment, not merely because they do not know their own secret – to paraphrase Hegel, the secret of the Jews is a secret for the Jews themselves – but the Jewish religion is perhaps the first to break with pagan vitalist enjoyment: 'In all previous religions, we always run into a place, a domain of sacred enjoyment ... whereas Judaism evacuates from the sacred domain all traces of vitality and subordinates the living substance to the dead letter of the Father's Law' (p. 281).

JEW/CHRISTIAN (*see also* MASCULINE/FEMININE)

Žižek has increasingly come to make a distinction between Judaism and Christianity in his more recent work. Although following a distinction originally made by Hegel, it is a way for Žižek to speak of two different relations to the law: the exception that founds the law (Judaism) and the 'not-all' law of love (Christianity). That is, in Judaism there is a transgression that both leads to and can only be thought within the law (the only thing not able to be spoken of within Judaism is the founding of the law). In Christianity, there is no transgression of or getting around the law (because it is par excellence the religion of internal guilt and conscience in which one is already guilty) and yet it is not-all (there always exists the possibility of forgiveness and love). Intriguingly, however, taking us back to a certain ambiguity in his thinking of the relationship between the masculine and the feminine, Žižek can shift in his characterization of the relationship between the two. On the one hand, he can oppose them as the masculine to the feminine: 'One is tempted to claim that the very passage from Judaism to Christianity ultimately obeys the matrix of the passage from the "masculine" to the "feminine" formulae of sexuation' (p. 332). And, on the other hand, they are not to be opposed because Christianity (like the feminine) is only a certain passage towards the limit of Judaism (the masculine): 'The vicious dialectic between Law and its transgression elaborated by St Paul is the invisible third term, the "vanishing mediator" between Judaism and Christianity ... Jews are *not yet* there, that is, they treat the Law as the written Real, which does not engage them ... on the other hand ... the basic point of Christianity proper is to *break out* of the vicious superego cycle of the Law and its transgression' (pp. 333–4). But if this is so, what is this to say about the relationship between the masculine and the feminine? In the same way, is the feminine merely a taking to the limit of the masculine principle (perhaps not a simple doing away with of the exception but an exception to its exception)? This might also be thought in terms of Žižek's reconceptualization of ethics and the relationship of 'loss' to the 'loss of the loss'.

KAFKA

Žižek often turns to Kafka's *The Trial* to consider the notion of ideological interpellation: his point is that what Kafka exposes in his parable of the door of the Law is the way that ideological interpellation exists only after it has been taken up. Through a kind of distortion of perspective, what we do not realize is that the Law does not exist until after us – thus both Žižek's notion of love taken from St Paul and diabolical Evil taken from Kant are ways of speaking of that 'freedom' or 'guilt' before the law, before the necessity of following the law (even in refusing or transgressing it). It is this 'distance' from the law that at once enables it – 'before being caught in identification, in symbolic (mis)recognition, the subject is trapped by the *Other* through a paradoxical object-cause of desire, in the midst of it, embodying enjoyment ... as exemplified by the position of the man from the country in the famous apologue about the door of the Law in Kafka's *The Trial*' (p. 277) – and opens up a certain way of thinking what is 'outside' it in the sense of coming 'before' it – 'the true conspiracy of Power resides in the very notion of conspiracy, in the notion of some mysterious Agency that "pulls the strings" and effectively runs the show' (p. 250).

KANT (see also ANTIGONE/MEDEA, DERRIDA, HEGEL)

The Kantian 'transcendental' critique is absolutely crucial to Žižek, and he draws on it throughout his work. As Žižek writes, summarizing Kant's contribution to the history of philosophy: 'On the one hand, the notion of the transcendental constitution of reality involves the loss of a direct naïve empiricist approach to reality; on the other hand, it involves the prohibition of metaphysics, that is, of an all-encompassing world-view providing the noumenal structure of the universe' (p. 167). And yet at the same time Žižek entirely agrees with Hegel's argument that Kant himself misunderstood the nature of his breakthrough, that it is necessary to read Kant against or beyond himself. It is this that Hegel represents for Žižek: not an opposition to Kant or even a simple surpassing of him, but a certain drawing out of consequences that are only implicit in him. As against the distinction between the noumenal and phenomenal in Kant, we can say that the 'shift from Kant to Hegel ... [is] from the tension between immanence and transcendence to the minimal difference/gap in immanence itself ... Hegel is thus not external to Kant: the problem with Kant was that he effected the shift but was not able, for structural reasons, to formulate it explicitly' (p. 236). In this regard, Kant becomes increasingly identified for Žižek with a certain 'masculine' logic of universality and its exception (S_1), while Hegel represents a 'feminine' logic of the not-all, in which there is nothing outside of phenomenal appearances but appearance is not all there is, precisely because of its ability to be marked as such ($). Žižek even goes on to compare Kant's noumenal/phenomenal split to Derrida's ethics of 'Otherness' and with Antigone's sacrifice of all things for one thing, as opposed to Hegel's truly modern ethics, in which even this cause itself must be sacrificed.

LAW (see also LOVE)

Žižek is concerned to show the secret transgression that underpins and makes possible the symbolic law: ' "At the beginning" of law, there is a transgression, a certain reality of violence, which coincides with the very act of the establishment of law' (p. 129). Or, as he will say about the seemingly illicit rituals that appear to overturn the law: 'They are a satire on legal institutions, an inversion of public Power, yet they are a transgression that consolidates what it transgresses' (p. 264). But, beyond this, the law itself possesses a certain obscene, unappeasable, superegoic dimension: 'On the one hand, there is Law *qua* symbolic Ego-Ideal, that is, Law in its pacifying function ... *qua* the intermediary Third that dissolves the impasse of imaginary aggressivity. On the other hand, there is law in its superego dimension, that is, law *qua* "irrational" pressure, the force of culpability, totally incommensurable with our actual responsibility' (p. 157). In other words, law itself is its own transgression, and it is just this circularity that Žižek seeks to dissolve or overcome. As he says, repeating at once the problem and the solution: 'The most appropriate form to indicate this curve of the *point de capiton*, of the "negation of negation," in ordinary language is, paradoxically, that of the tautology: "law is law"' (p. 127).

LÉVI-STRAUSS (*see also* ADORNO)

The key example Žižek takes from Lévi-Strauss is his famous analysis in *Structural Anthropology* concerning two different groups from the same tribe, each conceiving of their village in a different way. Žižek's point is that the 'truth' of the village is to be found neither in some reconciliation of the two competing versions nor in some neutral, 'objective' overhead view, but in this very split itself: 'Returning to Lévi-Strauss's example of the two drawings of the village, let us note that it is here that we can see in what precise sense the Real intervenes through anamorphosis' (p.338). This will be related by Žižek to that fundamental 'split' of sexual difference, where again the 'truth' is not to be found in some reconciliation or putting together of a whole, but in the antagonism itself. As he asks: 'How ... are we to understand the "ahistorical" status of sexual difference? Perhaps an analogy to Claude Lévi-Strauss's notion of the "zero-institution" might be of some help here' (p. 335–6). Žižek will use Adorno's analysis of the social in exactly the same sense as that of Lévi-Strauss here.

LOVE (*see also* EXCEPTION/NOT-ALL, JEW/CHRISTIAN)

Love in the sense Žižek understands it was first developed by Lacan in his *Seminar XX*. It is thus from the beginning associated with a certain 'feminine' logic of the not-all and implies a way of thinking beyond the master-signifier and its universality guaranteed by exception:

'Lacan's extensive discussion of love in *Seminar XX* is thus to be read in the Paulinian sense, as opposed to the dialectic of the Law and its transgression. This latter dialectic is clearly "masculine" or phallic ... Love, on the other hand, is "feminine": it involves the paradoxes of the not-All' (p. 335). Žižek associates love with St Paul, and it is a way for him to think the difference between Judaism, whose libidinal economy is still fundamentally that of the law and its transgression, and Christianity, which through forgiveness and the possibility of being born again seeks to overcome this dialectic: 'It is *here* that one should insist on how Lacan accomplishes the passage from Law to Love, in short, from Judaism to Christianity' (p. 345). In other words, this love might be seen to testify – as we also find with drive and enunciation – to a moment that precedes and makes possible the symbolic order and its social mediation, the way in which things are never directly what they are but only stand in for something else: 'Love bears witness to the abyss of a self-relating gesture by means of which, due to the lack of an independent guarantee of the social pact, the ruler himself has to guarantee the Truth of his word' (p. 267 n. 5).

MASCULINE/FEMININE (*see also* EXCEPTION/NOT-ALL)
The Lacanian 'formulae of sexuation' make up a crucial part of Žižek's thinking: one way of characterizing the overall trajectory of his work is as a movement from a masculine logic of the universal and its exception towards a feminine logic of a 'not-all' without exception. However, Žižek does not simply oppose the masculine and the feminine, but rather argues that the masculine is a certain effect of the feminine: 'Man is a reflexive determination of woman's impossibility of achieving an identity with herself (which is why woman is a symptom of man)' (p. 276). That is, everything in Žižek can ultimately be understood in terms of these two formulae. As Žižek asks: 'What if sexual difference is ultimately a kind of zero-institution of the social split of humankind, the naturalized, minimal zero-difference, a split that, prior to signalling any determinate social difference, signals this difference as such? The struggle for hegemony would then, once again, be the struggle for how this zero-difference is overdetermined by other particular social differences.' (p. 338) But, in fact, are these two positions consistent? On the one hand, Žižek argues that man is

explained by woman; on the other, that the split between the two sexes is irreconcilable, like the two different conceptions of the same village in Lévi-Strauss.

MASTER-SIGNIFIER (*see also* IDEOLOGY, JEW)

One of Žižek's key terms and the centrepiece of his renewed analysis of ideology is the notion of the master-signifier. Žižek provides perhaps two accounts of how the master-signifier works in making appear natural or conventional what is in fact a forced and artificial construction of reality: 'The elementary operation of the *point de capiton* should be sought in this "miraculous" turn, in this quid pro quo by means of which what was previously the very source of disarray becomes proof and testimony of a triumph' (p. 124); and 'the Master-Signifier [is] no longer a simple abbreviation that designates a series of markers but the name of the hidden ground of this series of markers that act as so many expressions-effects of this ground' (p. 202). That is, the master-signifier is not a simple empirical quality that makes sense of previously existing circumstances, but rather a kind of radical hypothesis that proposes an always unrepresentable signifier through which these very circumstances become visible for the first time. 'Therein resides the paradoxical achievement of symbolization: the vain quest for the "true meaning" (the ultimate signified) is supplanted by a unique signifying gesture' (p. 301). But if this is the unique strength and power of the master-signifier – that it is not simply an empirical designation, that it already takes into account our own distance from it, its inability to be definitively stated – it is also this that opens up a certain way out of it, for we are always able to point to a deeper explanation of it, what it itself stands in for and what allows it to be stated. It is something like this that is to be seen in Hegel's notion of concrete universality and in Žižek's thinking of the empty space of enunciation. As Žižek writes of the way that the master-signifier is its own limit: Lacan, in contrast to Derrida, *directly offers a concept of this element* [of the supplement], namely the concept of the Master-Signifier, S_1 in relation to S_2 ... In Lacan, S_1 stands for the supplement ... and, simultaneously, for the totalizing Master-Signifier ... the Centre which Derrida endeavours to "deconstruct" is ultimately the very supplement which threatens to disrupt its totalizing power' (p. 210).

OBJET a (*see also* JEW, MASTER-SIGNIFIER)

Objet a, one of Lacan's most famous 'mathemes' or conceptual neologisms, is first of all that element standing in for the Real within any symbolic system. It is at once what cannot be accounted for within this system and yet what produces this system as the attempt to speak of it. It is in this abstract, nonpathological sense that Žižek describes *objet a* as the object-cause of desire: 'The fundamental thesis of Lacan is that this impossible object is nevertheless given to us in a specific experience, that of the *objet petit a*, object-cause of desire, which is not "pathological," which does not reduce itself to an object of need or demand' (p. 129–30). And, as Žižek goes on to say, the aim of the analysis of ideology is to bring out the double status of this *objet a*, as both what completes the symbolic circle of authority, acting as the guarantee or Other of its Other, and what cannot be accounted for within it, what always appears as excessive within its officially stated rationale: 'The aim of the "critique of ideology," of the analysis of an ideological edifice, is to extract this symptomatic kernel which the official, public ideological text simultaneously disavows and needs for its undisturbed functioning' (p. 292). This *objet a* can take many forms within ideology: seemingly transgressive enjoyment, racism, paranoia, the belief in an explanation hidden behind the public one. To this extent, it functions as the 'master-signifier' of the master-signifier – and Žižek's point, following Lacan, is to reveal that there is no Other of the Other, that the Other does not possess *objet a* or the cause of our desire, but that in a way we do: we are ultimately our own cause. That is, if on the one hand, 'Lacan defines *objet a* as the fantasmatic "stuff" of the I, as that which confers on $, on the fissure in the symbolic order, on the ontological void that we call "subject," the ontological consistency of a "person"', on the other it is 'what Lacan, in his last phase at least, referred to as the "subjective destitution" which is involved in the position of the analyst, of the analyst as occupying the position of *objet petit a*' (p. 59).

OTHER (*see also* LOVE)

Žižek's ultimate position is that there is no 'Other of the Other', that is, no final guarantee of the symbolic order: 'There is no "big Other" guaranteeing the consistency of the symbolic space within which we

dwell: there are just contingent, punctual and fragile points of stability'
(p. 332). More precisely, a certain 'lack' in the Other at once is
necessary for the symbolic order to function and offers a way of
thinking an 'outside' of or 'beyond' to the symbolic order. That is, on
the one hand, 'if the Other is not fractured ... the only possible
relationship of the subject to the structure is that of total alienation, of
a subjection without remainder; but the lack in the Other means that
there is a remainder, a non-integratable residuum in the Other, *objet a*,
and the subject is able to avoid alienation only insofar as it posits itself
as the correlative of this remainder: $\mathcal{S} \diamond a$' (p. 31). And, on the other,
'This other, hidden Law acts the part of the "Other of the Other" in
the Lacanian sense, the part of the meta-guarantee of the consistency
of the big Other (the symbolic order that regulates social life)' (p. 250).
This lack of the Other of the Other has immense consequences for the
thinking of ethics and the political: their basis would not be some
'respect for the Other' but the attempt, for a moment, to *become* the
Other or embody the symbolic order, with the symbolic order itself
arising only as the after-effect of such 'free' actions: 'For Lacan, the
ultimate horizon of ethics is *not* the infinite debt towards an abyssal
Otherness. The act is for him strictly correlative to the suspension of
the "big Other"' (p. 345). This will lead Žižek towards consideration
of the Pauline notion of love: love as the giving of that which one does
not have, that is, something not backed by any symbolic guarantee.

SUBJECT (*see also* EMPTY PLACE/VOID)
For Žižek, the subject is first of all a critical position from which to
analyse ideology: it stands for that empty point which precedes
ideology and from which ideology is articulated. In this sense, the
subject is to be opposed to subjectivization, which is precisely that
process of the internalizing and the making natural of ideology:
'As soon as we constitute ourselves as ideological subjects, as soon as
we respond to interpellation and assume a certain subject-position ...
we are overlooking the radical dimension of social antagonism, that is
to say, the traumatic kernel the symbolization of which always fails;
and ... it is precisely the Lacanian notion of the subject as the "empty
place of the structure" which describes the subject in its confrontation
with antagonism, the subject which isn't covering up the traumatic

dimension of social antagonism' (p. 273). To this extent, the subject can be thought as a certain excess of ideological interpellation, that which in a way remains 'beyond interpellation': 'that which defines the subject, let us not forget, is precisely the question' (p. 41). The experience of subjectivity is thus an experience of pure negativity, in which every aspect of identity must be lost or sacrificed: '[In] "tarrying with the negative," ... Hegel's whole point is that the subject does *not* survive the ordeal of negativity: he *effectively* loses his very essence and passes over into his Other' (p. 217). The correlative of the subject within the symbolic order can therefore be thought of as *objet a*, that which stands in for the Real: 'the matheme for the subject is $, an empty place in the structure, an elided signifier, while *objet a* is by definition an excessive objet, an object that lacks its place in the structure' (p. 193). This equivalence must nevertheless be clarified: 'The parallel between the void of the transcendental subject ($) and the void of the transcendental object – the inaccessible X that causes our perceptions – is misleading here: the transcendental object is the void *beyond* phenomenal appearances, while the transcendental subject *already appears as a void*' (p. 233).

Index